MIGRANTS AND THE COURTS

Law and Migration

Series Editor
Satvinder S. Juss, King's College London, UK

Migration and its subsets of refugee and asylum policy are rising up the policy agenda at national and international level. Current controversies underline the need for rational and informed debate of this widely misrepresented and little understood area.

Law and Migration contributes to this debate by establishing a monograph series to encourage discussion and help to inform policy in this area. The series provides a forum for leading new research principally from the Law and Legal Studies area but also from related social sciences. The series is broad in scope, covering a wide range of subjects and perspectives.

Other titles in this series:

Immigration, Integration and the Law
The Intersection of Domestic, EU and International Legal Regimes
Clíodhna Murphy
978-1-4094-6251-4

Regulating Marriage Migration into the UK
A Stranger in the Home
Helena Wray
978-1-4094-0338-8

Chinese Immigration Law
Guofu Liu
978-1-4094-0940-3

The Control of People Smuggling and Trafficking in the EU
Experiences from the UK and Italy
Matilde Ventrella
978-0-7546-7466-5

Gender and Migration in 21st Century Europe
Edited by Helen Stalford, Samantha Currie and Samantha Velluti
978-0-7546-7450-4

Migrants and the Courts

A Century of Trial and Error?

GEOFFREY CARE
Former Deputy Chief Adjudicator
Immigration Appellate Authority, UK

Routledge
Taylor & Francis Group
LONDON AND NEW YORK

First published 2013 by Ashgate Publishing

Published 2016 by Routledge
4 Park Square, Milton Park, Abingdon, Oxon OX14 4RN
605 Third Avenue, New York, NY 10017

First issued in paperback 2023

Routledge is an imprint of the Taylor & Francis Group, an informa business

British Library Cataloguing in Publication Data
Care, Geoffrey.
Migrants and the courts : a century of trial and error?. --
(Law and migration)
1. Emigration and immigration law. 2. Emigration and
immigration law--History. 3. Emigration and immigration
law--Trial practice--History. 4. Administrative courts--
History.
I. Title II. Series
342'.082026-dc23

The Library of Congress has cataloged the printed edition as follows:
Care, Geoffrey.
Migrants and the courts : a century of trial and error? / by Geoffrey Care.
pages cm. -- (Law and migration)
Includes bibliographical references and index.
ISBN 978-1-4094-5196-9 (hardback : alk. paper)
1. Emigration and immigration law--Great Britain--History.
2. Emigration and immigration law--History. 3. Legal assistance to immigrants--Great Britain.
I. Title.
KD4134.C37 2013
342.08'7--dc23

2013000858

ISBN 13: 978-1-03-265240-5 (pbk)
ISBN 13: 978-1-4094-5196-9 (hbk)
ISBN 13: 978-1-315-59526-9 (ebk)

DOI: 10.4324/9781315595269

Dedicated to the memories of Mark, Guy, Victor and Larry, all my colleagues and friends, and to all the world's displaced.

'O GOD, the just and merciful Judge of all mankind; Look favourably, we beseech Thee, on Thy servants, who art set by Thy appointment to minister justice between man and man, to clear the innocent, and to convict and punish the guilty: Grant unto them Thy Holy Spirit, the spirit of uprightness, the spirit of discernment and the spirit of love; that they may boldly, discreetly, and mercifully fulfil their sacred duties, to the good of Thy people and the glory of Thy name'

Assize Prayer for Judges

Contents

List of Figures and Tables

Figures

Tables

Foreword

The Right Honourable Sir Stephen Sedley

By 1905, when the UK's first statutory control on immigration was introduced, the United Kingdom was already a rich melting-pot of migrants from all over the world. The intervening century has contributed massively to the mix; but the combination of global economic and political hardship with the facility of air travel and the proliferation of surface carriage has led to the closure of doors both here and throughout the developed world.

Much of the selectivity of modern immigration control has been driven by short-term political impulses, themselves often tainted by press xenophobia. But it is the overlay of asylum claims which has caused the greatest controversy and embittered the debate. Immigration controls can generally be managed by prescriptive rules. Asylum depends on something quite alien to a prescriptive system: a well-founded fear of persecution. The opportunities for abuse in such a formula are manifest; but so too, alarmingly, are the opportunities for error. An immigration judge who mistakenly disbelieves an account of persecution may be sending an innocent person back to their death.

So a knowledgeable account of how the UK's asylum and immigration system functions is greatly to be welcomed. No High Court judge, since the abolition of capital punishment, bears such a burden. In some respects, the story is that of all administrative adjudication in the UK: a determination on the part of departments of state that adjudication should be simply an instrument of departmental policy and practice; matched by a steady climb, enforced by the higher courts, out of the slough of dependency and into the daylight of reasoned and independent adjudication. Geoffrey Care's chronicle of this process in the asylum and immigration system, culminating in its incorporation into the new statutory structure as a judicial tribunal under the presidency of a High Court judge, is a significant part of the history of modern administrative law.

The history, moreover, is not confined to the United Kingdom. The 1951 Geneva Convention, with its open-textured but robust formula for refugee protection, binds scores of states, each with its own jurisprudence, but all seeking the same end. It was Geoffrey Care, by then the UK's acting Chief Adjudicator, who became the first president of the International Association of Refugee Law Judges (IARLJ) when it was founded in London in 1995. The IARLJ has gone on to become an important forum for the exchange and development of refugee jurisprudence among the world's specialist judges.

Meanwhile immigration and asylum law has itself become an established and complex part of the law of the United Kingdom, forming a significant part of the Supreme Court's workload and producing, both there and in the UK's other appellate courts, a now substantial body of jurisprudence. All of it is built on the decisions of the immigration judges, Geoffrey Care pre-eminent among them, who carry the huge responsibility of deciding case by case where the truth lies.

The business of immigration and asylum adjudication is, and probably always will be, unfinished. But Geoffrey Care's book is an important stocktaking of an enterprise located at the very interface of global economics and politics and the laws of humanity. We owe him a debt of gratitude both for writing it and for the years of untiring work which he himself has devoted to making the system what it is.

Stephen Sedley
Berkshire, August 2011

Preface and Acknowledgements

'The beginning is the most important part of the work': as the advice given by Plato in his *Republic*, for any would-be author goes.[1]

Man has been on the move since he first appeared on earth, so that is not news. Some of the reasons for movement likewise seem not to have changed, except that flight to escape persecution has become commonplace. There are now more people in the world who know more and can move further afield and faster.

As some states became wealthier, their attraction became greater and the response has been to impose controls on entry into their countries. As time went by, fertile minds invented more and more methods of exerting this control: visas, bilateral agreements for the return of unwanted guests, extra-territorial interceptions or some other form of extra-territorial barrier. With the EU, those controls are extended beyond domestic boundaries.[2]

The controls may curtail the free flow of people, but experience shows that the tighter the controls the more inventive people are in finding ways to evade the restrictions. Today, a common method of evasion has been to claim asylum.

The real or the imputed reasons why someone moves from their ancestral home and family is beyond the scope of this book, but the reasons may be hidden behind all manner of cultural, historical or even just family circumstances. Those concerned to know – the judge in the case of this book – may only be able to make a guess at the reason. Available published information of the backgrounds to various countries is rarely comprehensive and it is as well to remember that any guess may be based on intuition – hopefully, informed intuition – but inevitably therefore a most fertile ground for not getting things quite right – if not totally wrong.

To give some idea of the magnitude of present-day and future migratory patterns, in 2010 there were 64 million more people on the move than there were in 2000. It is predicted that by 2050 the numbers of people who will be forced to move from their homes (even though most may remain in their own countries, at least to start with) will increase tenfold, to 250 million. Professor Steven Castles, among others, claims that the effect of migration will be to erode the sovereignty of states.[3] But whether that is the ultimate consequence or not, on the evidence

---

1 Plato, *Republic*, Book II <http://www.classicreader.com/book/1788/22/>.

2 These are discussed in Chapter 6.

3 Gilligan, C. (2012), 'Immigration Controls and the Erosion of Popular Sovereignty', *Gritim (Interdisciplinary Research Group on Immigration Department of Political and Social Sciences Universitat Pompeu Fabra) Working Papers* 10 (Winter) <http://upf.edu/gritim>. The whole concept of sovereignty has long been challenged by Professor Joe

of the UK and Europe, which have had to cope with larger numbers of migrants than they think they should have to or can cope with, increasingly strict and far-reaching immigration controls have proved of very limited success in stopping the flow.

These figures, like any statistics, in the field of migration at least, are cited in this book to illustrate trends (or possible trends) and the reader is warned against attaching too much importance to any actual figure.

Having introduced the reader to people on the move and countries trying to control them, brings me to observe that the exercise of any control involves a decision made by the executive.

For a long time – in fact, up until the twentieth century – any such decision in the UK, regarding immigration was final and could not be challenged, since all authority was considered to lie solely with the Royal Prerogative. The grant of a right of review of an adverse decision was first implemented in 1905 and was the origin of what has become the monolithic tribunal now known as the Asylum and Immigration Tribunal: the First-tier Tribunal (Immigration and Asylum Chamber) and the Upper Tribunal. This book is about how and where these tribunals began and their subsequent growth.

The greater ease for people to move quickly over long distances, often *en masse*, has heightened the pressure on states to guard their borders (and their wealth and culture perhaps) to the extent that many states, especially wealthier and industrialized ones, feel that 'floods' of immigrants are about to overwhelm them.

I do not think I can summarize the overall picture better than Anthony Richmond:

> Globalization is not a new process. It is an acceleration of changes induced by the post-industrial revolution in transport and communication. The rapid growth of population in less developed countries combines with a reduction in barriers to migration from formerly authoritarian regimes to induce mobility. Economic inequality combines with demographic pressures and environmental crises to generate ethnic conflict and terrorist threats. Wealthier countries are placing restrictions on the admission of those seeking to improve their economic prospects and/or to escape persecution. Despite the number of asylum seekers in Europe and North America, African and Asian countries bear the greatest burden of refugees. Temporary migration, business travel and tourism have added to the numbers crossing state boundaries, making effective control difficult … .'[4]

Carens and among other works his paper 'The Ethics of Refugee Policy: The Problem of Asylum in Western States'', given at 'The Growth of Forced Migration' conference, 25–27 March 1998, Refugee Studies Programme, Wadham College, University of Oxford, pp. 16–17.

4 Abstract of article by Richmond, A. (2002), 'Globalization: Implications for Immigrants and Refugees', *Ethnic and Racial Studies* 25.5 (September): 707–727 <http://hdl.handle.net/10315/8009>.

Returning to the right to challenge an adverse decision by the Home Office, there was the period from 1905 until 1969 during which, as Chapter 1 will briefly describe, there existed, at best times of a limited form of review. In 1969, the Immigration Appellate Authority (IAA) was created, which in turn gave way to the Asylum and Immigration Tribunal (AIT) in 2002, and then the Immigration and Asylum Chamber in 2008.

The form which the review takes in the UK therefore is first by means of a tribunal, not a regular court. Some, like Robert Thomas,[5] consider, therefore, that the tribunal plays a role in implementing government policy; others, namely the courts, that it is a totally new decision which, on appeal, is what the higher courts will look at and forms part of a continuum of an administrative procedure.

Although I do deal with some immigration policy aspects, I do so only when I think they impact on the appellate jurisdiction of the immigration judge.

As indicated, the present-day tribunal did not appear out of nowhere; it has historical roots. A brief look into earlier history helps to explain something of the bumpy ride the whole structure of a review, or an appeal, has had on its journey into the last century and from then until the twenty-first century. Without an understanding of how we have arrived at the present position, we are to some extent impoverished and it is here, as well as in history in general, that personalities from the inside and government and public opinion from outside have played important parts in that history – and continue to do so today.

This book takes a look at this growth from the inside to see how the AIT grew into the second largest tribunal in the land and the one most frequently in the public eye.

For an erudite and up-to-date study of the role of the tribunal and commentaries based on interviews with the judges, the reader is directed to Robert Thomas, whose book, *Administrative Justice and Asylum Appeals*,[6] is one of the most recent comprehensive works on the subject and is an enlightenment of how he views the decision-making process. But his view is, as he will readily acknowledge, a view taken from the standpoint of someone observing from outside the tribunal, whereas this book is looking at things from the inside, from the perspective of a judge.

As in any court, the judge in an immigration tribunal tries to be independent. The extent to which this is possible is part of the story told in the chapters which follow. The press and television often peddle loose, inaccurate, incomplete or inflammatory talk about immigration playing on the emotions and stirring up native against foreigner.

This is nothing new, and part of the history and the atmosphere in which the judge in an immigration case must work. Graphic examples are given by Robert Winder in his uncomfortably titled book, *Bloody Foreigners*,[7] which, along with

5 Thomas, R. (2011), *Administrative Justice and Asylum Appeals* (Oxford: Hart).

6 Ibid.

7 Winder, R. (2004), *Bloody Foreigners* (London: Abacus).

Professor Philip Bobbitt's books *Terror and Consent*[8] and the pre-9/11 *The Shield of Achilles*, should probably be required reading by more than just politicians.

There are lessons to be learned from the many influences which affect judges' decision-making in this area: citizenship, security, the movements of peoples and the manipulation of public opinion, and so forth. What has gone on before, but is in a constant state of flux, helps mould our reactions and our attitudes toward our decisions. From reading press sources alone, I think that it is difficult for those on the outside looking at the decisions the judges reach, to grasp the pressures which lie behind those decisions.[9]

Sir Stephen Sedley, in his Foreword to this volume writes, 'No High Court judge, since the abolition of capital punishment, bears such a burden', but in the UK, even the judge did not have to decide the facts on which the fate of the accused depended. Judges had a way out whatever their feelings about the death penalty, since it was the jury who considered the facts upon which the conviction was based. In immigration appeals, a decision to refuse a wife permission to join her husband, or a son to visit his ailing parent, will affect the lives of men, women and children, perhaps for the rest of their lives. In asylum cases, and asylum-related appeals, return to one's country of origin may lead to torture or death.

The appeal is but a part of the whole coercive nature of any immigration control, and the judge must try to make a decision which is as just as it can be, but still remains within the confines of the law. It is all too easy for others to criticize a decision they do not like. This is especially so when the country is threatened by a faceless gangster masquerading under some spurious religious banner. Unfortunately, the criticism sometimes comes from a quarter which the public think should know what they are talking about, such as a government minister, or the press.

This account is written not only for immigration judges, but for the general reader as well. For judges, I hope to give the more recent appointments some idea of their 'ancestry' and perhaps to offer an opportunity for them take a step back from all the daily stress to see just how their decisions affect people and feel satisfaction that their decisions are as fair and just as they can make them. For other readers, I hope this volume opens a window, if not a 'flood of light', on the subject.

I have chosen the year 1905 as the point of departure because the Aliens Act of that year created, for the first time, a formal means of challenging a ministerial decision relating to the country's borders. One hundred years later, we can ask ourselves the question 'What have we learned between 1905 and now?' Is the decision-making process better or worse? If worse, why, and what can be done to

8 Bobbitt, R. (2008), *Terror and Consent* (London: Allen Lane); idem (2002), *The Shield of Achilles* (London: Allen Lane).

9 Pressure for stricter immigration controls may seem strong in the UK and is of itself divisive, but on a closer look, the UK's attempts to shape policy is dominated by state actors – as is the opposite by NGOs, so maintains Gilligan in 'Immigration Controls and the Erosion of Popular Sovereignty'.

improve it? Or should it be scrapped and a return made to the drawing board, as the Countess of Mar told her fellow Lords in December 2006?[10]

The development of the tribunal threw up a number of problem areas which seemed to affect the decision-making process, which is very different from that of the regular courts. Richard Posner, in his book *How Judges Think*, attempted a critical analysis of the judges' approach to decision-making, mainly in the United States, but his observations also hold up well in this jurisdiction and the reader may draw on his acute observations from the pages which follow.[11] Posner's rejection of reliance on foreign decisions, or the 'cosmopolitan approach' as he calls it, is not, however, relevant for judges in a jurisdiction which concerns the migrant (especially the migrant seeking asylum), who must apply international treaties.

The immigrant, particularly the asylum-seeker, often does not have any choice as to where his or her application will be considered or by whom. Thus, failing some global symmetry in decision making, whether in Albania or Zambia, the applicant is locked into a lottery – in which they do not have the opportunity to buy, or not to buy, a ticket.

Though the conventions put in place for the protection of those who are fleeing from persecution, such as the Refugee Convention of 1951, have universal application, decisions vary widely, even the interpretation of the common phraseology of those conventions in the manner in which they are applied. It was in part to encourage judges to correct this apparent shortcoming that the International Association of Refugee Law Judges was created in 1996.

The first half of the twentieth century was characterized by war, beginning with the Second Boer War, followed by the First World War, and then the Second World War, with its wholesale abuse of the Jews. The beginning of the twenty-first century witnessed increasing rejection of the immigrant and demonization of the asylum-seeker. While no Third World War has arrived in the conventional sense, warfare none the less there is, even if there are few set-piece battles between states and only fluid hostilities without boundaries and against an often unseen enemy.

Hostilities, insecure regimes, disregard for human rights (despite all the efforts of Professor René Cassin and others),[12] and natural and climatic disasters all compel people to look for somewhere less dangerous or more promising to live, while nation states equally continue to guard their borders jealously. Decisions regarding whether to admit or exclude individuals must be made, and democracy calls for some regulation of this and an opportunity to review those decisions. The UK therefore devised one manner of doing so, which was thought to be effective,

---

10 Hansard, House of Lords, 14 December 2006, col. 1688–90 et seq. <http://www.publications.parliament.uk/>.

11 Posner, R.A. (2008), *How Judges Think* (Cambridge, MA: Harvard University Press).

12 Winter, J. (Chapter 3) in C. Brants et al. (eds) (2013), *Transitional Justice: Images and Memories* (Ashgate).

and which has been modified at regular intervals over the years as the chapters which follow will explain. By way of comparison, five other countries' systems for dealing with migrants are also addressed in Chapters 6 and 7.

I have mentioned the reactions of nation states to migration. The inevitable consequential territorial imperative to protect themselves leads to all kind of security measures. Edward de Bono wrote many books on problem solving, but in his book *Children Solve Problems*, he records the answers to nine problem situations presented to a collection of children; one girl aged 13 answers the question 'How would you stop a cat and a dog fighting?' with an illustrative drawing thus: 'A variation on the ghetto concept. The cages here are the balls and chains which restrict free movement. For instance, the need for visas, special passports and so on which achieve the same effect as a cage-type or wall-type ghetto.'[13]

Professor James Carens opined:

> … because no one ever knows. There can be no useful definition of what is a 'correct' decision. The best that can be done is to devise a system which transparently, efficiently and swiftly, attempts to disentangle those with a right to remain from those who don't – and ensures that the latter leave and cannot secretly return.[14]

Perfection may be unobtainable but transparency should be possible if the legislator and the judge find a way to cooperate to achieve the right approach. Unfortunately, so far confrontation defeats all efforts towards cooperation.

The personalities of those involved in the earlier days, the 'family' differences – the growing pains of the tribunal – as well as the changing nature of the appeals with which the tribunal had to deal in those early days, are described in detail in Chapters 2 and 3. Where some people receive more mention than others, this is largely due to their roles in the development of the tribunal and because I came to know them all well.

Where possible, I have kept to some chronological order in relating events but the major issues are grouped without regard to the date on which they occurred because of their intrinsic importance.

Janice Cotton, my secretary and later Personal Secretary to Henry Hodge,[15] safely preserved all the archive materials from Mark Patey, Chief Adjudicator during an important period in the development of the tribunal, and I have drawn

13 de Bono, E. (1972), *Children Solve Problems* (London: Penguin Books), p. 15. De Bono's website describes him as the 'father of lateral thinking' <edwdebono.com/>.

14 Carens, J. (2000), *Culture, Citizenship and Community, A Contextual Exploration of Justice as Evenhandedness* (New York: Oxford University Press).

15 At the time, His Honour Henry Hodge, Chief Adjudicator, later Sir Henry Hodge, a High Court Judge and President of the Asylum and Immigration Appeal Tribunal; sadly, now deceased.

on them extensively to write this book.[16] I also have relied on my own memory and that of people with whom I've consulted. Among these are Professor David Jackson, other past and present tribunal judges, officials in the Lord Chancellor's Department and the Home Office. Many others have played important roles in other, and related, aspects of the system, such as John Ennals, the first Director of the United Kingdom Immigration and Advisory Service (UKIAS) (now the Immigrants Advisory Service and the Refugee Legal Centre), which represents appellants without fee, and Andrew Collins, who was the first High Court Judge to be appointed President of the Asylum and Immigration Appeals Tribunal (AIT).

No progress could have been made without the support staff (particularly those doing the day-to-day work as Executive and Administrative Officers) as well as the interpreters and such organizations as the Medical Foundation for the Care of Victims of Torture (now known as TortureCare), founded by Helen Bamber OBE.

The chapters are arranged to cover the tribunal's relationships with the Home Office and the Lord Chancellor's Department (LCD) now the Ministry of Justice, where they sit, the changes in types of appeal and numbers, the growth of the jurisprudence, training, representation and other discrete aspects of the judges' tasks, such as fact finding, security and terrorism.

The concept that some form of international recognition of an obligation shared by all nations to protect those forced, by persecution, to leave their own countries was manifested in the form of international and, later, regional conventions. The domestic and the EU aspects of these are covered, as their importance in the development of the tribunal increased.

Frances Webber wrote Chapter 5, 'What Price State Security?', and made valuable comments on earlier drafts of this book, for all of which I am profoundly grateful.

The description of how five other countries manage (or don't, as the case may be!) the same tasks but in different ways adds an opportunity for comparison – and sets the jurisdiction in an international scenario. The Belgian system is described by Katelijne Declerk, a judge of the Permanent Commission on Refugees; the Canadian system by Professor James Simeon of York University, Toronto and formerly a member of Canada's determination system (the Immigration and Refugee Board); Professor Amor Boubakri of Tunisia addresses the situation in respect of the North African countries; Ahmed Arbee, the Appeals Board's first chairman covers South Africa, and Göran Hakansson, a former director general of the Swedish Appeals Board and later Swedish Ambassador to Latvia, explains the Swedish system. The length of the Canadian contribution was such that it is described separately in Chapter 7.

To all of them I am singularly grateful.

16 In some cases, reference is made to correspondence or a statement is made which relies on this archive material. That material is preserved and available for inspection, but verbatim reproduction in this book would make it cumbersome.

Since this book is more concerned with drawing lessons from history and was written over a long period, it does not aspire to take account of all the more recent developments, particularly those which have taken place over the last three years (although some of these are mentioned). In order to try to give focus to the main factors which affect any immigration judge's decision, I have identified six issues which permeate the review process. Three of these issues, or threads as I call them, are government related: broadly speaking, government policies, the legislation and the administration (with the media thrown in for good measure, as it does not operate in a vacuum). The other three are the ones over which the judges can, and it is suggested, need, to do something more about: namely the judges' own approach and attitudes, the nature of the hearing process itself, and the manner in which the tribunal handles its own internal administration.[17].

The concluding chapter gathers these threads together to try to form some conclusions about the Tribunal, and determine whether Lady Margaret Mar was right in her remarks in the Lords, suggesting that it should be scrapped. I would add that it may only be practical for the judges themselves to achieve something in between these alternatives.[18]

Among others who have helped are Sebha Storey,[19] Barbara Mensah[20] and Mungo Deans,[21] Finn Jensen (of the Electric Information Network). I would also like to thank John Freeman[22] for his splendidly corrosive deconstruction of the *Surendran Guidelines* on how to handle a tribunal judge's interventions in a hearing, and Professor Elspeth Guild[23] for her encouragement; when all around seemed to propel this manuscript into 'Filing Basket 13', she would come up with something to stay my hand.

I also owe much to Professor Anthony Good – though I am sure he is unaware of my debt. In his book, *Anthropology and Expertise in the Asylum Courts*,[24] he grasps the nettle of fact finding unerringly and has crystallized my thinking on credibility, evidence, country information and even the form of the tribunal.

Licking the manuscript into the final form owes much to Jonathan Bridge. As he said to me, he felt he virtually owned part of the book; which he does, as he was my very close assistant during the crucial years when I was acting as Chief Adjudicator. I am also indebted to all those at Ashgate, particularly Alison Kirk,

17 See Chapter 8, p. 279.

18 Hansard, House of Lords, 14 December 2006, col. 1688–90 et seq. Online at www.publications.parliament.uk (accessed: 8 July 2013)

19 Chief Adjudicator, Immigration Support Adjudicators.

20 Formerly in charge of training, now a circuit judge.

21 Formerly in charge of training, now a regional immigration judge in Scotland

22 Senior Immigration Judge and Recorder.

23 Partner at Kingsley Napley and Professor of European Migration Law at Nijmegen University.

24 Good, A. (2007), *Anthropology and Expertise in the Asylum Courts* (London: Routledge-Cavendish).

whose astonishingly gentle hand has guided me away from my many bad habits in writing this story, and Laura Linder who patiently tried to achieve accuracy and greater clarity throughout.

Sir Stephen Sedley, until last year a Lord Justice of Appeal in England, has written the Foreword and for this I am indebted to him, as well as for his forthright suggestions in the course of preparation, given in such a kindly manner. There is a greater debt, however, which we all owe to him. If ever there were a need to find a judge who is the antithesis of a robed inhabitant of an ivory tower, it is Stephen – his robes never disguised either his brilliance or his humanity. May his change in direction (and attire) be as satisfying to him as has been his presence at the Bar and the Bench to us.

I cannot think that any government over the last hundred years has not at some time contemplated a total rehash of its immigration policy – usually when under pressure from the press or the voters. What no government has yet done so far is take Ted Heath's advice when in 1978 he said 'The 1971 Act and Rules had given the Government all the powers it needed to deal with immigration effectively'[25] and exhorted his colleagues to treat the issue as a cross-party one.

To explain coherently how any decision was reached is daunting and exhausting. I have been privileged to have been able to work among key decision makers, an experience characterized by struggle.

Finally, where there is criticism here, it is not of a personal nature but is critical of a policy or a questionable attitude or approach. I urge the reader – whether administrator, politician, immigration judge or an interested or curious member of the public – to reflect a little more on the modern-day migrant (who is more vulnerable than ever before). The way we think about the issues is reflected in how we talk to and even look at ourselves in a mirror and to others.

Geoffrey Care
Shetland
2013

25 Heath speaking at the Conservative Party Conference, 1978.

Table of Cases[1]

1 The Table of Cases comprises the main cases discussed in the book and is not a definitive list of all cases cited in the text.

Table of Legislation[1]

1 The Table of Legislation comprises the principal pieces of legislation discussed in the book and is not a definitive list of all examples cited in the text.

Abbreviations

ACPI Advisory Panel on Country Information
AIIER All England Law Reports
AIT Asylum and Immigration Appeal Tribunal
AMIAT Association of Members of the Immigration Tribunal
ATCSA Anti-Terrorism, Crime and Security Act
BJLS British Journal of Law and Society
CA Court of Appeal
CCR Canadian Council for Refugees
CGC Country Guidance Case
CGRS Office of the Commissioner General for Refugees and Stateless Persons
CIC Ministry of Citizenship and Immigration Canada
CIJ Council of Immigration Judges
CIPU Country Information and Policy Unit
CIREA The Centre for Information, Discussion and Exchange on Asylum
CJEU Court of Justice of the European Communities
CLP Current Legal Problems
Cmnd or Cmd Command Paper
COI Home Office Country of Origin Information Services
CPT European Committee for the Prevention of Torture and Inhuman or Degrading Treatment or Punishment
CRDD Convention Refugee Determination Division (Canada)
CSIH Court of Session Inner House (Scotland)
DCA Deputy Chief Adjudicator
DHA Department of Home Affairs (South Africa)
ECtHR European Court of Human Rights
ECHR European Convention on Human Rights
ECO Entry Clearance Officer
EHRR European Court of Human Rights Reports
EIN Electronic Information Network
EU and EC European Union
EXCOM Executive Committee of UNHCR
HLR House of Lords Reports
HOPO Home Office Presenting Officer
HX Hatton Cross
IAA Immigration Appellate Authority
IAD Immigration Appeal Division (Canada)
IARLJ International Association of Refugee Law Judges

IAS Immigration Advisory Service
IAT Immigration Appeal Tribunal
ICRC International Committee of the Red Cross
IDP Internally Displaced Person
IGC Intergovernmental Consultations on Asylum, Refugee and Migration Policies in Europe, North America and Australia
IGC Intergoverrmental Consultation on Asylum, Refugees and Migration Policies in Europe, North America and Australia
IJ Immigration Judge
ILPA Immigration Law Practitioners Association
Imm AR Immigration Appeal Reports
IPCC International Panel on Climate Change
IND Immigration and Nationality Department
INLR Immigration and Nationality Law Reports
IRB Immigration and Refugee Board of Canada
IRPA Immigration and Refugee Protection Act (Canada)
KLJ King's Law Journal
LCD Lord Chancellor's Department
MoJ Ministry of Justice
NGO non-governmental organization
NSA non-suspensive appeal
OAU Organization of African Unity
OISC Office of the Immigration Services Commissioner
RAB Refugee Appeal Board (South Africa)
RAD Refugee Appeal Division
RC 1951 Refugee Convention
RPD Refugee Protection Division
RRO Refugee Reception Officer (South Africa)
RSAC Refugee Status Advisory Committee
RSD refugee status determination
RSDO Refugee Status Determination Office (South Africa)
S. or s. Section
SIAC Special Immigration Appeal Commission
SI Statutory Instrument
SIJ Senior Immigration Judge
SR&O Statutory Rules and Orders
SSHD Secretary of State for the Home Department
TH Thanet House
TPIMs terrorism prevention and investigation measures
UKIAT United Kingdom Immigration Appeal Tribunal (report)
UNCAT UN Committee Against Torture
UNHCHR UN High Commission for Human Rights
UNHCR United Nations High Commission(er) for Refugees
*WLR Weekly Law Reports

Chapter 1
Laying the Foundations

> The Government recognises that the judges are the great enemies of every government, because they are always supporting people who allege that they're being downtrodden by government.
>
> Lord Donaldson, MR – 'The Guardian Interview', Channel 4, broadcast 10 February 1989

Early History

Hospitality toward the alien and those in need of protection dates back to biblical times[1] and the early nation states,[2] and is a tradition that is strongly embedded in Jewish and African cultures. In the second millennium BC, the Hittite king drew up treaties concerning refugees. Later, in the fourteenth century BC, Rameses II gave refuge to another Hittite king, Urhi-Teshup: even the Assyrian king, Ashurbanipal, in the seventh century was known to grant asylum. Let's not forget about the flight of Joseph and Mary with Jesus to Egypt, or Mohammed's *hijra* to Medina in AD622.[3] Joseph's story contains a message to today's decision makers when they have to address the plausibility of a story that they are told. Joseph seems to have left a good job as a carpenter and settled far away in Egypt with his family when at the time nothing materially significant had happened – except that he said he had had a dream – a scenario which would never have got past the Entry Clearance Officer nor the Home Office, and was very unlikely to have been accepted by even the most gullible immigration judge.

---

1 Numbers 35:9–15: God nominated that there be seven cities of refuge.

2 When there are no states and no borders, there may be refugees where there would seem to be no refugees. For example, the herdsman in what is now Afghanistan and the northwest frontiers of Pakistan, or the once-nomadic Rabari in India who can longer migrate because of political and landowning boundaries, have become deculturized and often distressed. See R. Davidson (1996), *Desert Places* (London: Viking).

3 See Q'uran, Surah 8:74.

Turning to later times in Europe, general compassion for the plight of refugees seems to have begun in the sixteenth century and led to modern ideas regarding asylum. The paragraphs that follow give a brief introduction for this.[4]

The Edict of Nantes in 1598 was aimed at protecting the Calvinist Protestants (or Huguenots) in France, and its revocation in 1685 reopened old wounds which followed the Thirty Years War (1618–48). The Edict of Potsdam (1685) provided for a territorial home for many Huguenots fleeing persecution in France, and helped to establish Potsdam as a centre of European immigration, as the city's reputation for tolerance attracted migrants from France and beyond. The schism between Roman Catholics and Protestants following the Reformation made Britain an attractive country for Protestant elsewhere in Europe and undoubtedly had a significant impact on migration within Europe.

England itself had no comprehensive policy of restriction on immigrants until as late as 1905 (discussed below), although even then some measure of immigration control was not new. For example, the Alien Act of 1705, but this was aimed solely at the Scots following the Act of Settlement in 1701.

The attitude in England toward the foreigner has fluctuated between laying out the welcome mat (at least to some), and attempts at mass removal. For example, in 1793 Parliament passed the Regulators to Aliens Act, the Preamble to which makes informative reading:

> Whereas a great and unusual number of persons, not being natural-born subjects of his Majesty … have lately resorted to this kingdom: and whereas, under the present circumstances, much danger may arise to the publick tranquillity from the resort and residence of aliens, unless due provisions be made in respect thereof.[5]

The 1793 Act immediately followed the French Revolution, and was a response to the earlier flows of Huguenots from France and Belgium. It was the panicked reaction of the eighteenth-century British government, equivalent to so many of those in the twentieth century. Intended to be of limited duration, the Act was extended, and amended in response to events in France in 1798.

The Revolutionary Period and the ensuing Napoleonic Wars (1803–15) were followed by relatively small incursions of Russian and French refugees. The response was, however, to curtail entry and it would seem that that was, at least

4 For more detail, see D. Stevens (1998), 'The Case of UK Asylum Law and Policy: Lessons from History?', in F. Nicholson and P. Twomey (eds), *Current Issues of UK Asylum Law and Policy* (Aldershot: Ashgate), and D. Stevens (2004), *UK Asylum Law and Policy* (London: Sweet and Maxwell).

5 Preamble to the Regulators of Aliens Act 1793 George III.

in part, due to fears surrounding national security, especially following the French Revolution.[6]

Despite relatively peaceful times for England in the nineteenth century, there were sporadic pieces of legislation, such as William IV's Registration of Aliens Act 1836. This required the registration of aliens along with their records, and the designation of specific ports for entry of immigrants; hefty fines (up to £10,000 in today's money) were imposed on captains and owners of vessels who brought in aliens illegally, though it is doubtful if those captains ever thought of themselves as unpaid border guards.[7]

The descent into the bloody wars in Europe, beginning with the Franco-Prussian War of 1870, again created a sense of insecurity, from which it is arguable that we have never completely recovered.

The legislative reaction in England to the Franco-Prussian War was the Extradition Act 1870, an 'Act to authorize the Removal of Aliens from the Realm'. There was no thought given to appeals from removal or exclusion, because at that time asylum and, indeed, immigration was considered the sole prerogative of the Crown. This notwithstanding, the Act recognized the need to protect political and religious refugees by exempting them from extradition, section 4(1) providing that there should be no extradition for political offences. The form of the Act was continued 100 years later, in the Fugitive Offenders Act 1967.[8]

This period covering the late sixteenth to the early twentieth centuries focuses attention on some eternal issues of immigration: the fear of 'floods' of refugees, threats to employment, political dissidents disturbing relations with 'friendly' nations, and, once again, security of our boundaries.[9]

From the time of the Huguenots to the twentieth century, no foreigner was allowed entry to the UK at least to stay or as a refugee without permission from the responsible minister, whose decision was final, because, as remarked in the Preface, it was considered to be solely within the Royal Prerogative.

---

6 Much more detailed history can be found in history books generally, but more specifically in Stevens, *UK Asylum Law and Policy*.

7 Immigration (Carriers Liability) Act 1987 c. 24 amended by s. 1 Immigration and Asylum Act 1999.

8 Whereas the Extradition Act applied to aliens, the Fugitive Offenders Act included Commonwealth citizens.

9 Conan Doyle's *The Refugees* concerned the flight of the Huguenots in and around 1690. Some 50,000 came to the UK alone and set up many industries. For a later account of both racist xenophobia and a backhanded justification for admitting Jewish refugees, see N. Angell and D.F. Buxton. (1939), *You and the Refugee* (Harmondsworth: Penguin).

The Twentieth Century

The right to question a decision by the executive (whether monarch or minister) only appeared in any recognizable form in 1905, and even then was very limited: the right of appeal did not last long. Before coming to 1905, a reminder[10] of what was happening at the time may put the present into a little more realistic perspective; when history does repeat itself, the form in which it does so comes as less of a surprise.

With regard to refugees, the events and the reactions of the public and in some of the methods of control in the eighteenth and nineteenth centuries have changed little in the twentieth or the present centuries. Public outcries, predominantly against Jews, became increasingly vicious from the latter part of the nineteenth century, both in Parliament and in the press.[11] After several false starts, this xenophobia led to the Aliens Act 1905.

By the beginning of the twentieth century, public reaction, encouraged by the press had again begun to 'sink its teeth into Refugees' on numerous occasions, lamenting that 'German Jews are pouring into the country', 'we're being swamped ... ' and '[the] Refugee tide [is] rising.'[12]

The *Daily Mail* for 3 January 1900 berated the 'ill behaved so-called refugee German Jews, who had been funded by the Lord Mayor's fund and were so abusing this generosity!'[13]

The rhetoric down the ages seems to portray not only a fear for national security and the integrity of one's national boundaries, but an inbuilt hostility by the indigenous population toward the alien. This hostility seems to arise more often than not out of ignorance, which is frequently fed by distorted facts. The result has always been increased restrictions upon the rights of appeal. This sort of reaction may be due to some unspoken and undefined fear, but is often revealed as some general expression of dislike of 'foreigners'[14]. This probably explains

10 Anyone interested in more detail can consult R. Winder (2004), *Bloody Foreigners* (London: Abacus).

11 For a very detailed account, see M.J. Landa (1911), *The Alien Problem and its Remedy* (PS King), digitized version to be found in Open Library <http://archive.org/details/alien problemitsr00landrich>, especially Chapter IX, detailing the way in which the tribunal carried out its work.

12 In 'History repeats itself', *The Times,* 19 February 1999, Dominic Kennedy depicts articles appearing in the newspapers of the day.

13 An article in *The Daily Mail* again said in 1938, 'German Jews pouring into this country', and on 14 September 2007, Comment (p. 14) remarked on a further deluge over the EU. A further comment in *The Clarion* in June 1906 stated that Jewish immigrants were 'a poison injected into the national veins', they were the 'unsavoury children of the ghetto', their numbers were 'appalling and their attitudes "unclean"'. See n 12 above

14 Chris Gilligan thinks it is actually 'engineered'; see Immigration Controls and the Erosion of Popular Sovereignty' http://upf.edu/gritim (accessed on: 30 June 2013).

Winder's title for his book *Bloody Foreigners*;[15] one fact which he reveals is that the Anglo-Saxons had a word for people (or things) from elsewhere: '*wealh*' (foreigner), which explains the etymology of some common names or words, such as 'walnut', which came from France. The same xenophobic attitudes remain, though the nature of the fears may change. They can arise out of social conditions, religion, employment and the economy, strangeness and racial purity, as well as sovereignty – indeed, the very conditions which contribute to the movement of peoples on the world stage.[16]

Rarely is mention made of the other side of the coin – that is, the benefits of immigration to this country and emigration from this country for business, settlement or simply a better life.

Attempts at a concerted policy toward immigration in the UK seem to have only started when the numbers of people arriving in Europe and the UK and claiming asylum escalated in the later years of the 1980s. If one were to attempt to put a definite date to it, perhaps the 1991 Immigration Bill is the most precise;[17] as extensive preparations for training and hearings were put in train in 1991 and in confidence since 1991 by the IAA.

The Aliens Act 1905[18]

The Aliens Act 1905 was the first immigration legislation in twentieth-century Britain; it defined some groups of migrants as 'undesirable', making their entry into the country discretionary, rather than automatic. It was passed, so it was claimed, due to fears of degenerating health and housing conditions in the East End of London. It is said that at the time this was seen to have been caused by the large number of Russian and Polish Jews fleeing persecution. However, there was considerable anti-Semitism at the time and in the view of some it was anti-Semitism primarily rather than anti-alienism which prompted the Act in 1905.[19]

---

15 See Stevens, *UK Asylum Law and Policy.*

16 Perhaps a somewhat extreme view was expressed in a lengthy article in 1999 by the League for the 5th International: 'Today's laws against asylum seekers descend directly from the Aliens Act 1905. While drawing inspiration from the struggles of Jewish immigrant workers and generations of African-Caribbean and Asian workers who have mounted resistance during the twentieth century, socialists must renew the tough ideological fight within the labour movement for the abolition of all immigration controls at the start of the twenty-first' <www.leagueforthefifthinternational.org Labours Racist Record 1999>.

17 Although the Bill fell in 1992 due to lack of time, there was considerable opposition to the Bill and the adjudicators themselves were of the opinion that where leave to appeal was involved, such leave would be granted in a high proportion of claims.

18 For a condensed history of the twentieth century, see 'Aliens Acts 1905–1919' in <www.20thcenturylondon.org.uk> at 'Time Line'.

19 c.13

The Act ensured that leave to land could be withheld if the immigrant was judged to be 'undesirable' by falling into one of four categories: 'a) if he cannot show that he has in his possession … the means of decently supporting himself and his dependents … '; 'b) if he is a lunatic or an idiot or owing to any disease of infirmity liable to become a charge upon the public rates … '; 'c) if he has been sentenced in a foreign country for a crime, not being an offence of a political character … ', or 'd) if an expulsion order under this act has [already] been made'.[20]

Campbell-Bannerman spoke at the second reading of the Bill and argued against provisions in the Bill which, he maintained, drew distinctions, between the poor and the rich.[21]

M.J. Landa, a correspondent with the *Jewish Chronicle* in the early years of the twentieth century, wrote of the Act:[22]

> After 5 years trial the Aliens Act [1905] stands before the bar of public opinion anathemised by almost all, understood by few. [It is] suggested that the powers of the Board be transferred to [a] court of summary jurisdiction – a Stipendiary Magistrate plus 2 assessors … A Memorial from the Jewish Board of Deputies states [inter alia] that there be an appeal to the Kings Bench Division … and better interpretation. Though Winston Churchill agreed with the former he said it would have little utility – and nothing was done.[23]

M.J. Landa's account of the period leading up to and following the Aliens Act 1905[24] opines that 'the history of alien immigration is marked throughout by exhibitions of intolerance, of fear and hatred', similar to those evinced in the present day. But, so he maintains, it was 'only with the coming of the alien that the uplifting of the Briton and the development of the land begins'.

To show the then concern with public attitudes towards the influx of aliens – particularly refugees (and one needs to bear in mind the links between the crowned heads of Russia and Britain at the time), Landa wrote further in 1906: 'Russians (refugees) were returned to possible execution and in the House of Commons on March 14 the whole work of the Home Office was being disorganised and seriously interfered with by the administration of the Act.'[25]

The fears and prejudices about the alien or foreigner have not gone away, only changed emphases. At the beginning of the twentieth century, the alien had few

20 'Aliens Act', <www.20thcenturylondon.org.uk> at 'Time Line'.

21 See the extract from the debates in The Aliens Act 1905. Available online at <http://hansard.millbanksystems.com/commons/1905/jul/19/aliens-bill#S4V0149P0_19050719_HOC_311>.

22 Landa, *The Alien Problem and its Remedy*, Chapter IX, p. 235 <http://archive.org/stream/alien>.

23 See Stevens, *UK Asylum Law and Policy*.

24 Landa, *The Alien Problem and its Remedy*.

25 *Morning Leader*, 17 March 1906.

'rights' and the citizen had extensive ones. What rights 'the alien' did have was a matter for the exercise of the Royal Prerogative and was not at that time thought to be capable of question by the courts (justiciable), although it has since been decided that it is.[26] The introduction of a review of decisions by the executive as to whether to admit or remove the foreigner was considered something of a revolution in 1905;[27] there had been no such opportunity to do so before, given the view that immigration fell entirely within the Royal Prerogative.

The First Tribunal

This right of review of the Minister's decision to refuse the 'right to land' (the term used to describe entry into the UK) was brought to a tribunal called the London Immigration Board. The Act also incidentally revived the Home Secretary's right to expel – but only with an order of the court or by way of extradition.[28] The 1836 Act, which imposed heavy penalties on carriers, was still in place. An alien passenger whose claim to land was rejected (almost invariably a steerage passenger), would have to be taken back free at the expense of the ship's master, who also, to add to his misery, was saddled with the passenger's own expenses during his or her stay!

The Board generally sat as a panel of three members, who had magisterial, business or administrative experience and were selected from a group appointed by the Home Secretary. At first, the Board sat in secret in an abandoned waterside office in Blackwall in east London. These premises must have been deemed unsuitable since the venue was soon moved to 141 Great Tower Street.

The Immigration Officer, however, seems to have been the 'boss' of this show. He would speak to the Board in the absence of the appellant, who, more often than not would not be present because they had not been told the date of the hearing. Anyway, even if the appellant *was* present, they were unlikely to have understood what was going on since the use of interpreters was rare.

The Board's comprehension of asylum seems to have been worse than dangerous and their decision could not be reviewed by the courts;[29] if, as was intended, the appellant was given the benefit of the doubt, it may have been of

---

26 *Secretary of State for Commonwealth Affairs v The Queen on application of Bancoult* [2007] ECWA Civ CA p. 498 (more familiarly known as the Chagos Islanders case).

27 Under Rules made under the Aliens Act 1905, c. 13.

28 Vaughan Bevan recites an interesting provision which no government today would welcome: that if a prosecution failed, the defendant must be paid treble his costs! See Development of British Immigration Law (1986) (London: Croom Helm) p. 61. Two writers at the time considered that this power contravened the Magna Carta and the Common Law. 'The right to asylum is writ in characters of fire on the tablets of our Constitution' Sibley and Elias Landa at p.125.

29 Landa, T*he Alien Problem and its Remedy*, chapters IX and X. Russians were returned to possible execution (*Morning Leader*, 17 March 1906), and in the House of

some comfort, but apparently they rarely were. Statistics can be dry fare but they illuminate the fact that a hefty proportion of appeals were, despite everything, successful. In 1906, 935 people were excluded and 796 appeals heard, of which 442 succeeded; in 1910, there were 1,066 people excluded, and 432 appeals, of which 144 were successful.

The provisions for an appeal to the Board were amended in 1910 to confirm that the appellant had a right to appear by counsel, but only at his or her own cost.[30]

By 1911, the whole Act had become totally reviled. The Sydney Street Siege in January led to an attack on the right of refuge and, at the time, Stephen Phillips wrote 'The right to asylum is being shamefully violated.'[31]

The First World War and Visas

With the outbreak of the First World War, this liberal yet legalistic approach collapsed and the right of review disappeared following the Emergency Powers Order in Council 1914, made under the Aliens Restriction Act 1914.[32] At the same time, visas were introduced for aliens. Today, the need for a visa still carries the stigma of not belonging, of being an outsider and an unwelcome foreigner.

Between the Wars

After the First World War, the League of Nations distilled the concept of refugee from European historical experience and institutionalized it.

Meanwhile the Aliens Restriction (Amendment) Act 1919[33] (which continued the visa regime, introduced in 1914 as emergency legislation, against anticipated pressure as a result of the 'disturbed state of Europe'), and the Aliens Order 1920 consolidated the continuation of the emergency sweeping powers, followed by the Special Restriction (Coloured Alien and Seamen) 1925. The 1919 Act, renewed under the expiring law's continuance system and born out of a period of military stress, was perpetuated for other reasons[34] and continued to govern policy up until 1967.

Commons on March 14 'the whole work of the Home Office was being disorganized and seriously interfered with by the administration of the Act.'

30 SR&O 565/1910, rule I.

31 *Westminster Gazette*, 12 January 1911.

32 Aliens Restriction Act 1914, c. 12; the Status of Aliens Act 1914 cap 17 and Order in Council SR&O 1374 .The seeds of conduct conducive to the public good as a reason for removal can be found as early as the legislation in Napoleonic times.

33 c. 92.

34 See Bob Morris, Public Relations Office Home Office 367/2 'History of Immigration and Nationality Department (IND)' He also mobilized Union support to

Between 1918 and 1939, it is said that there were several Conventions concerning the status of refugees coming from Germany. There appears to be no evidence of any Convention, but there *is* a body of literature which reveals conflicting opinions of British policies concerning Jewish refugees from Germany between the wars. Some are critical of the limits placed on numbers allowed to enter after 1933. Louise London posits that the control was based on what was good for the UK – a concept which she believes applies to modern-day approaches to immigration. Next came a short-lived Committee appointed by Sir Herbert Samuel on 29 February 1932.[35]This provided a judicial process which enabled an alien to 'show cause' (give reasons) why he should not be deported. This Committee had advisory powers only but the hearing was none the less still based on an adversarial (or non-interventionist) principle. In the four years of its existence, the Committee dealt with 33 cases, confirming the decision to deport in 19 of them.

Despite the fact that the Committee did not always agree with the Minister's policies, he did accept all 33 of the Committee's recommendations. However, perhaps counsel for the appellant's insistence that the case for deportation should be proved beyond all reasonable doubt went too far for the minister and placed an unacceptably heavy burden of proof upon him. The death knell of the Committee was sounded when an alien was found to have bribed an immigration officer to admit a relative.

Post-Second World War

Citizenship, Residence and Race

The history of the changes made to the rights to nationality in the Commonwealth and the right to live in the UK is relevant for three reasons; firstly, the changes in the status of members of the Commonwealth arose in many immigration appeals both directly and indirectly; secondly, the erosion of those rights enables one to understand the sense of betrayal and grievance felt by (particularly non-white) members of the Commonwealth,[36] and thirdly the complexities of the nationality laws would seem likely to give rise to a grievance which cannot be separated from the dislocation in society which, in part at least, has given rise to aspects of the security issues today.

Until 1949, when the British Nationality Act of 1948 came into force, any British subject, whether by birth within the Crown's allegiance or by descent

---

abolish the 'degrading and inhuman' voucher scheme for refugees: *The Times*, 15 April 2000, p. 17.

35 Known, as far as I am aware, simply as the 'Samuel Committee'.

36 See, for further reference, Select Committee of Race Relations and Immigration Session 1977/78: *Immigration*, Vol. 1 (London: HMSO), p. XXXI, paras 97–9.

was beyond question 'natural born'. This Act repealed all of the nationality acts previously referred to.[37] The Act retained the British Subject status and created the Citizen of the UK and Colonies (CUKC), citizenship of the Dominions Countries, Canada, Ceylon (Sri Lanka), Australia, India, New Zealand, Pakistan and Southern Rhodesia (Zimbabwe). Indigenes of the protectorates remained British Protected Persons. However many Asians and persons born in former trust territories could register under s 6(1) of the 1948 Act and did so and thereby became CUKCs.

The next legislative move was the Aliens Order in Council in 1953 (which paralleled the Commonwealth Immigrants Act 1953)[38] and gave further powers of deportation to the Minister.[39]

Following the independence of Uganda and Kenya, in particular, in 1960, there was a wholesale expulsion of Asians, who urgently wished to take advantage of their nationality and residence rights in the UK. Britain changed the law which, not surprisingly, was felt to be a deliberate step taken to deprive them of a right of abode in the UK which they had hitherto enjoyed.

The Commonwealth Immigrants Act 1962 rendered, at a stroke, all those (mainly from the Caribbean in this case) who had registered as CUKCs subject to immigration control.[40] This, not unnaturally brought howls of protest as being both treacherous and racially directed against the non-white members of the Commonwealth, particularly following as it did in the aftermath of a sudden rise in immigration to the UK from parts of the Commonwealth, notably the Caribbean and Uganda.[41] Between 1949 and 1962, there was no difference between a British subject and a Commonwealth citizen until the Commonwealth Immigrants Act 1962,[42] which introduced the distinction by adding the requirement of a right of

---

37 With one exception relating to the status of aliens: s. 34(3), Sched. 4, Pt II.

38 Commonwealth Immigrants Act 1952, cap. 21.

39 Article 20(2)(b) on the grounds that it was conducive to the public good. This power was later extended in the Immigration Act 1971, § 3(5)(b); see also *Chahal v United Kingdom* [1997] 23 Eur. H.R. Rep. 413; *R v Sec'y of State for the Home Department Ex parte Sivakumaran* 1 All E.R. 193 (HL 1988). For an early example showing the court's attitude toward protection of the liberty of the subject, see Ian A. Macdonald (1995) *Immigration Law and Practice* (London: Butterworth), p. 480.

40 S. 12(1). What was to add insult to injury was the right to deprive a person of the right to abode under s. 2 of the 1971 Act.

41 See, for an erudite treatment of nationality, L. Fransman (2011), *British Nationality Law* (London: Bloomsbury), and for a comprehensive treatment of the gradual erosion of citizenship rights, S. Juss, (2007), 'The Slow Death of Citizenship Rights', *KLJ* 18.1: 95–118.

42 c. 21.

abode. The Commonwealth Immigrants Act 1968[43] was aimed at those without any close connection with the UK – mainly Asians – which further soured relations.[44]

Then the Immigration Act 1971 (following the short-lived Immigration Appeals Act 1969,[45] which will be dealt with below in respect of the establishment of the IAA) introduced further restrictions in section 2, which was, in turn, further amended restrictively by the British Nationality Act 1981.[46] By this Act, the automatic right to citizenship of those born in the UK was removed and only those who were and continued to be Commonwealth citizens with a right of abode *before* the British Nationality Act 1981 had the right to live freely in the UK [47]

The question of a member of the Commonwealth claiming asylum appears not to have engaged the public, although on 13 March 1978, a Select Committee of the House of Commons in its report on the Commonwealth, did make reference to asylum and argued against further primary immigration. However, the report found that the quota system (which was already in operation for the Indian subcontinent) should be extended and more resources devoted to catching overstayers. It appeared that the Committee did not understand the effect of the 1951 Geneva Convention on Refugees too well when, with commendable patriotism but less foresight, it observed:

> … it seems inevitable that there will be a continuing need for such asylum and we regard the maintenance of the United Kingdom's historically long and proud record of generosity as of great importance and value … in the foreseeable future there will be no further major primary immigration.[48]

No thought appears to have been given to any need for a policy directed towards racial harmony and integration. This failure did nothing to help avoid the need for security legislation twenty years later, which, in the event, proved to be less than carefully thought through.[49]

An illustration of the need to educate the public on the subject of racial integration at that time arose in the case of one John Kingsley Read, who was

---

43 Commonwealth Immigrants Act 1968, c 38. The voucher system with an annual quota had been introduced in 1962. See London, 'British Immigration Control Procedures', on Union opposition to this scheme.

44 The Immigration Act 1971 put Commonwealth citizens on the same footing as aliens – to their great disadvantage.

45 Cmnd 4296 1969–70.

46 The current Nationality Act 1981 which reclassified patrial CUKCs only at British Citizens ('patrial' being later replaced by 'right of abode') came into force in 1983 and replaced the Nationality Act of 1948, which consolidated all earlier acts. This complex field is dealt with thoroughly by Laurie Fransman, see above and n. 41.

47 s. 2.

48 Select Committee of Race Relations and Immigration Session 1977/78, *Immigration* Vol. 1, p. XXXI, paras 97–9.

49 See Chapter 5.

arraigned before Judge McKinnon on a charge of racial hatred. The words, alleged to have been said following the death of an Asian, were 'one down and a million to go'.[50] The court acquitted him, but in the course of his direction to the jury, the appeal judge is reported to have said:

> Of course we cannot accommodate here unlimited numbers of immigrants, but it is not something to be ashamed of … homes are scarce. It is said that immigrants will occupy homes which are needed by ordinary English folk in this country. Members of the jury those are matters upon which people are entitled to hold and declare … expressed moderate terms.[51]

The leader of the opposition Margaret Thatcher, not content with this inflammatory approach by the judge, was reported to have said in an interview on Granada Television on 27 January 1978, 'people are rather afraid that this country may be rather swamped by people with a different culture … if you want good race relations you must allay peoples' fears.'[52] Her mailbag, it was reported, received 10,000 letters, predominantly thanking her for raising the subject!

Immigration is still the hot topic in Parliament, the media, on the international stage, on the streets and in many people's homes. One day, it is the Jews; on another day, the Roma, EU citizens, jobs, or if all else fails, simply 'there are too many foreigners'. The prevailing attitude seems to be: hospitality yes, but to the right people, at the right time – which is questionable when used to resile from international obligations such as the Refugee Convention.

Panic more than reason seems to have attended most legislative changes and, perhaps unsurprisingly, has never resolved matters. One writer described government policy thus: 'Fear and insecurity are a prominent theme in the secularization of migration policy management.'[53]

The Wilson Committee – The Conception of the Modern UK Tribunal

In 1967, the government appointed a Committee[54] to examine the lack of any remedy for those aggrieved by executive action over immigration and deportation.

---

50 Anti-fascism in the Northwest 1976–1981, online at http://www.dkrenton.co.uk/anl/northw.htm.

51 The case was heard on 6 January 1978 and reported in the press on 7/8 January. Online at http://discovery.nationalarchives.gov.uk/SearchUI/s/res?_q=john+kingsley+read; http://bunny.j12.org/kelman/attacknotracist.htm (accessed on: 17 July 2013).

52 *The Times*, 8 January 1978, p. 11.

53 Huysmans, J. (2006) *Politics of Insecurity Migration and Asylum in the EU* (London: Routledge).

54 Report 1967, Cmnd 3387, herein referred to as the 'Wilson Report', written following the Franks Committee Report which had recommended that decisions on immigration matters be subject to Tribunal review. See Report of the Committee on Tribunals and Enquiries, Cmnd 218, paras 47 and 48.

From this the Wilson Report emerged – taking its name from its chairman, Sir Roy Wilson QC.

The Committee interviewed and travelled widely. Some of those from whom they took evidence have maintained their close connection with this jurisdiction – for instance, Anthony Lester (now Lord Lester, whose wife later became an Immigration Judge), Ian Macdonald QC, Ann and Michael Dummett. There were others who were well known for their special wisdom, such as Tom Kellock QC, who became the Director of the Legal and Constitutional Section of the Commonwealth Secretariat

The Wilson Report was a very thorough examination of *all* incidents of immigration control, not just the right of review. The Committee looked at immigration control systems in many parts of the world and recognized that what was central to any system was the initial decision on right to entry. This had to be thorough and, hopefully, correct: it is unfortunate that this wise and detached opinion does not appear to have influenced the many changes which have been made over the ensuing 35 years.

The Committee emphasized the need for some informality (as had the Franks Committee before it and as subsequent writers were to do later),[55] and for a full and careful immediate *initial* hearing at or near the port of entry before an adjudicator (who would not necessarily be a lawyer nor full-time official). The recognition by the Committee of a need for both parties to be represented[56] implied an acceptance that whatever was recommended, it was still considered that the hearings would be set in an adversarial mode.

The purpose of having a second tier, the Immigration Appeals Tribunal (IAT),[57] was to give authoritative guidance to adjudicators on law and practice; the party line, as it were, was that an IAT decision was binding even though not all adjudicators accepted this position.

The Committee also gave careful thought to what issues any right to appeal from a ministerial decision should deal with; particularly to what extent such a right should deal with the exercise of ministerial discretion.[58] There were already

55 See, for example, J.M. Atkinson, 'Understanding Formality', *British Journal of Sociology* 33(1): 86–117.

56 In many countries, it is either not adversarial at all such as Australia and New Zealand, or the State is simply not represented but the appellant may be, as in the Netherlands and Belgium. In Switzerland, no oral evidence can be adduced. There is a view that oral evidence is preferable at all times to documentary, but surely that depends much upon just how complete that documentary evidence is – that is, what has been omitted or suppressed or just plain badly researched – and how well the judges are trained to evaluate oral evidence.

57 Wilson Report paras 110 et seq.

58 For a discussion of background and reasons for introducing the tribunal system, see L. Bridges (1975), 'Legality and Immigration Control' *BJLS* 2: 221.

'Instructions'[59] in place in relation to Commonwealth citizens, serving as private directions for immigration officers. They contained the policy and the discretion of the Home Secretary[60]. When the Immigration Appellate Authority came into being in 1969, these 'Statements of Changes', as they came to be known, became public as they had to be laid before Parliament which could review them, before they came into effect.

The Committee took the view that the Instructions would be justiciable, giving the tribunal the right to decide whether the *exercise* of any discretion in them conformed to such rules. The Wilson Report went on to say:

> This addition of a judicial element to the United Kingdom's system of immigration control will be a factor of importance if this country joins the European Economic Community, within which certain people are entitled to freedom of movement. It will also come nearer to realizing the ideal of 'due process of law' embodied in certain international conventions.[61]

The Report rejected the suggestion that appeals be heard by the ordinary courts of law, arguing that:

> The number of appeals … would impose an intolerable burden on the local courts. Neither the procedure followed by the ordinary courts, nor the rules of evidence … are … appropriate. The appeals would in any event relate to a special and highly technical code of rules [they went on to quote from the Franks Committee[62]] … there are demonstrably special reasons which make a tribunal more appropriate, namely the need for cheapness, accessibility, freedom from technicality, expedition and expert knowledge … .

---

59 See para. 65 of the Wilson Report. The Instructions to Immigration Officer 1966 then only related to Commonwealth citizens and not to aliens. Some argued it should stay that way to give it a desired flexibility. For more detailed discussions of the historical development of policy during the twentieth century, see R. Hansen (2000), *Citizenship and Immigration in Post-war Britain* (Oxford: Oxford University Press), and I.R.G Spencer. (1997), *British Immigration Policy since 1939* (London: Routledge).

60 But for just how far they are binding, see *NA and Others* [2009] UKAIT 00025.

61 But see the decisions on Article 6 ECHR *Salgado v Spain Appeal* No 65964/01 of 16 April 2002 and *Mraoui v France* in which it is held Article 6 does not extend to immigration hearings; and *The Sunday Times v UK* 1979 2 EHRR 245 para. 55. See further Chapter 8, p. 271.

62 This Report led directly to the modern tribunal system across the UK. Where once the tribunal had been regarded as an extension of the executive arm of government, Franks placed it firmly on the judicial side, with principles of openness, fairness and impartiality as the guiding watchwords. The question raised in this book is has that aim been achieved and can it be in immigration issues.

With the Immigration Appeals Act 1969,[63] the executive gave up its unfettered control over entry and stay in the country. Although the IAA, after 1987, fell under the management of the Lord Chancellor's Department (LCD), it was also under the supervision of the Council on Tribunals.[64]

The degree of 'independence' this independent tribunal actually exercises will be considered later, but the tribunal set up in 1969 was a new departure, which allowed much greater oversight and publicity about decisions regarding immigrants. The same structure was to serve all immigration matters including refugees, presumably because a single structure would be the most economic, but whether this was the best place for all manner of immigration appeals remains questionable.

The Council on Tribunals

The IAA became yet another administrative body added to the list of tribunals for which the then Council of Tribunals was responsible under the Tribunals and Inquiries Act 1958. Michael Sayers poetically explains how UK administrative law operates through a 'colourful tapestry',[65] of some 73 tribunals;[66] resolving disputes in every conceivable aspect of day-to-day life which gives a second look at ministerial decisions. As Sayers observed at the time, they keep the wheels of justice and administration moving well and swiftly.[67] In its own view, the Council believed its role was to promote a proper balance,[68] although the IAT and judicial appointments in the IAA came under the LCD from the outset.

Tribunals in administrative law in the UK are supposed to afford increased access and a less formal approach to justice than is to be found in the civil and criminal court system.[69] At one time, lawyers knew little about tribunals and the

---

63 Cmnd 4296 1969–70.

64 There are 75 tribunals in England and Wales, and 25 in Scotland. The Administrative Justice and Tribunals Service was been unified under the Tribunals Courts and Enforcement Act 2006 in 2005–2006: M Sayers (1990), 'Franks Revisited: a Model of the Ideal Tribunal', *Civil Justice Quarterly* 9: 36. There are also some references in the Patrick McNeill QC Report 1988, *All Souls Review of Administrative Law*.

65 Sayers, 'Franks Revisited'; Patrick McNeill QC Report, All Souls Review of Administrative Law, n. 90.

66 Twenty-five in Scotland. The Administrative Justice and Tribunals Service has been unified under the Tribunals Courts and Enforcement Act 2006.

67 Sayers, 'Franks Revisited'. Amusingly, he pondered whether the Council on Tribunal's control over its charges was more like a dog with a soggy bite, without a bark, or the bite of a toothless watchdog – the Lord Chancellor's poodle perhaps? From my dealings with it during Lord Archer's reign, not the case at all.

68 Special Report Cmd 7805 1980 10.3. For recommendations on legislation rejected by Parliament, see Parl. Debate, HL nV419 1980–81 and cc 1118–19 27 April 1981.

69 Mulholland, M. and Pullan, B. (2011), *Judicial Tribunals in England 1200–1700* (Manchester University Press) The Council on Tribunal's view was to use the advantages

general public even less, often regarding them as second-rate courts – which they are not. They are not courts as lawyers understand them. As quoted above, when the Wilson Committee was deliberating on whether to recommend that the courts should take on immigration appeals, they recognized that the procedure in a tribunal differed from that in the ordinary courts; the evidence and a need for special and highly technical code of rules called for a different – albeit still judicial – approach.[70] This is the point: to what extent can it be judicial, if by that term we mean independent of the executive? Whatever the answer, the caveat of Lord Justice Sedley[71] needs to be remembered whenever legislation is proposed which may impact on this independence.

In its Annual Report for 1970–71,[72] the Council remarked – again – that there should be a 'policy for organizing tribunals into fewer and stronger units'; the Tribunal Service was responsible for over 70 tribunals in England and Wales alone, by the time it was replaced by the new[73] Combined Tribunal Service.[74]

The Council on Tribunals had taken serious objection to the absence of any appeal in cases where national security was concerned, but it reluctantly had to accept that a reference to a non-statutory panel, which came to be known as the 'Three Wise Men'[75] had to suffice.

Refugees

Refugees and displaced persons (DPs) were the major source of migration in post-Second World War Europe. It was not, however, until the 1980s and 1990s that there became a need to distinguish between those who had lost the protection of their own country and needed a refuge from persecution and the ordinary (im) migrant.[76] This situation remains with us today.[77]

---

of a tribunal, informality, speed, independence, expertise, accessibility and efficiency and cheapness for the parties and for society as a whole.'

70 Which, as will be seen in Chapter 6, has happened in Sweden; and was proposed in South Africa.

71 See his speech to IARLJ New Zealand Conference Papers (2002), quoted more fully on p. 92; see also p. 42 and p. 68.

72 See *The Annual Report of the Council on Tribunals for 1970–71*, HMSO 26 (1 December 1971), especially paras 16 and 30–32.

73 Michael Huebner was keen that there should be a single Tribunal appointment providing the possibility for cross movement and a better opportunity for career progress.

74 Tribunals Courts and Enforcement Act 2007 c. 41.

75 *Annual Report of the Council on Tribunals for 1970–71*, paras 30–31. Later the panel was renamed the Special Committee on Asylum Appeals – SIAC. See Chapter 5.

76 See League of Nations; 1933 and 1938 Refugee Conventions. The ICRC had the care of some 1 million refugees.

77 In the sense that immigration and asylum has been allowed – if it ever could have been prevented except as a theory – to collapse one into the other.

The birth of the 'Nansen Passport' (named after the explorer and first UN High Commissioner for Refugees, Fridtjof Nansen) came about[78] because it was recognized that refugees were people in need of protection and in need for freedom of movement to enable their skills and energies to be put to productive use wherever they were.

The massive displacement of people in the aftermath of the Second World War led to 26 nations joining in a rare spirit of commitment to the 1951 Convention in order to cover refugees wherever they came from or to whichever country they went.[79]

The Organisation of African Unity (now the African Union) Charter on refugees was under discussion at the same time and was adopted in 1969.[80] This charter made provision for a claimant to benefit as an individual under 1951 Convention provisions and also applied to 'Any person compelled to leave his/her country owing to external aggression, occupation, foreign domination or events seriously disturbing public order in either part or the whole of his country of origin or nationality'. Protection was therefore extended for when flight or movement was triggered by conditions which cause people to lose the protection of their state due to man-made or natural disasters, such as internecine strife, flood, famine or earthquake.[81] The Charter contained two other significant differences from the 1951 Convention; firstly, there was an emphasis on burden sharing,[82] and secondly, there was explicit reference to repatriation:[83] not merely a prohibition

---

78 At that time, there was no need to justify reasons for flight. Regretfully then, just as much as now, though many recognized the need to remove the conditions causing flight, nothing was done about it. The second High Commissioner, James Macdonald (1933–35), in his resignation letter noted that 'The world refused to intervene to stop the existing impending tragedies of the Jews in Germany', see C.M. Skran (1995), *Refugees in Interwar Europe: The Emergence of a Regime* (Clarendon Press), pp. 148–56.

79 See 'Protocol relating to the Status of Refugees', entered into force, 4 October 1967 GA Resolution 2198 (XXI). But not all countries adopted the removal of the geographical limitation at the time, for example, Greece.

80 Organisation of African Unity (OAU), 'The Convention Governing the Specific Aspects of Refugee Problems in Africa' adopted a regional treaty based on the Convention, adding to the definition of a refugee: 1001 UNTS 45, 20 June 1974 (African Refugee Convention).

81 See, for a review of the root causes of refugee flows, 1998 Khartoum Recommendations by the Council of Ministers paras 1 and 2. This was debated by a joint UNHCR/OAU Conference to which the IARLJ were invited and participated in Addis Ababa in 1999. The Cartagena Declaration is drawn widely in a manner similar to the (0) AU Convention

82 Art. 5.

83 Art. 2.4.

on *refoulement* or return (to the country from which an individual had fled),[84] as contained in Article 33 of the 1951 Convention.

The original grant of asylum, at the whim of a particular ruler, was now governed by treaty; the global 1951 Geneva Convention, now signed by 145 nation states, and two regional treaties, the AU Charter and the South American Cartagena Declaration,[85] the latter being very similar in coverage to the AU Charter but drafted specifically for the South American States.

Outline of the Appeal System

The Immigration Act 1969 was the first legislative attempt to create the type of tribunal which the Wilson Committee had recommended in its report and it did re-establish a right of appeal from decisions by the Secretary of State for the Home Office from a refusal to enter or remain in the UK for Commonwealth citizens, but in a two-tier structure.[86] Aliens' rights to appeal were conferred in an Order in Council.[87] Could the glaring difference in approach be attributed to a view that aliens as 'foreigners' still fell under the Royal Prerogative? This Act, however, was very quickly replaced by another: so quickly in fact that there was no time to complete more than a handful of cases.

Since the next Act made little change to the structure of the 1969 Act, it is more convenient to give the outline of the structure based on the new Act, which is the Immigration Act 1971. An outline, which may be familiar to many readers, is still necessary in order to make the rest of the book more intelligible to those to whom it is new.[88]

First of all, the 1971 Act put Commonwealth citizens and aliens on the same footing. This was not good news for the former, because they lost their privileged exemption from being liable to deportation.

From thenceforth, everyone who did not have a right of abode in the UK was subject to immigration control, that is, broadly speaking, they needed permission to come in or stay in the country. They could be deported if they no longer had current permission to stay or if the Secretary of State deems it 'conducive to the public good'.

Deportation orders in the UK are very different from most other countries. Except when it is a court in a criminal case which makes the first step, it is for the Home Office (not the minister, the Home Secretary, him- or herself) to make

---

84 This is the technical term used to mean the return of a person to, or to the borders of, a country where he has a reasonable fear of persecution for a Convention reason.

85 The Cartagena Declaration on Refugees enlarges the definition of refugee to seek durable solutions which resulted from the conflicts during the 1980s: 19–22 November 1984.

86 To whom sections 1 or 6 of the Commonwealth Immigrants Act 1962 applied.

87 Aliens (Appeals) Order 1970 SI 151/1970.

88 See Appendix 1 for a diagram of the immigration appeals system.

a 'Decision to deport' and that is the order which may be appealed. If the appeal is unsuccessful and the Minister then makes a 'Deportation Order', that is not appealable.

Therefore having disposed of this anomaly, it is possible to say that virtually all other decisions, by the Home Office, or its representatives at missions abroad, who are termed either Entry Clearance or Visa Officers, did originally carry a right to appeal (from a refusal) to an adjudicator in the first instance. Over the years, this right of appeal has been curtailed from time to time in various ways, as will be seen – for example, by removing or limiting appeals in respect of a visit visa or short-term student visas. In addition, the immigration judges have power to release an immigrant who has been detained by the Home Office on bail.

In the case of applications for a visa (or Entry Clearance) to visit, study or to marry and settle in the UK, the initial decision is, as mentioned earlier in this chapter, taken by an officer stationed at a British Mission abroad. However, an application to come to the UK in order to apply to stay as a refugee cannot be made from outside of the country; the refugee must first get into the UK, although some countries do allow an application for refugee status to be made where the application has actually reached his Mission, on the principle that the Mission is technically a part of the country.

It was felt necessary to introduce some measure of uniformity in the interpretation of the law, which was the reason for a two-tier structure. The adjudicators were the first tier of the appeal system (then under the Home Office), and the Immigration Appeal Tribunal acted as the second or appeal tribunal (under the LCD). The adjudicators were mainly lawyers, though they did not need to be. It was intended that they would hear the appeals that came to them at or near ports of entry. An appeal, by either of the parties (that is whoever lost the first round) lay, with permission, to the Immigration Appeal Tribunal (IAT). The IAT was always staffed by lawyers, often former judges, or senior law officers, together with a panel of lay (that is, not legally qualified) men and women drawn from different backgrounds and cultures.

Where the Minister decided that a person should be deported because their presence in the UK was not conducive to the public good, the right of appeal went directly to the IAT and skipped the adjudicator level. Where the Secretary of State personally made the order to deport in the interests of national security, there was no appeal whatsoever.[89]

There was no further appeal from the tribunal to the courts at the time: that only came much later. Until it did, judicial review to the courts[90] was the only further opportunity for any supervision of the IAA's decisions and that judicial review would not deal with the facts nor would it substitute its own decision. If it

89 As to the present day issue of national security, this is dealt with in Chapter 5.

90 A major plank in the (un)written construction of the UK is the power of the court to review decisions by the executive. They were formerly termed 'Prerogative Writs' but are now 'Judicial Reviews'.

considered the earlier decision was not justifiable, it would simply (s)quash it and send it back.

The IAA could allow an appeal which was wrong in law and if any discretion should have been exercised differently, but even then not if the decision was simply a lawful refusal to depart from the rules made by the Home Office to be reversed. Directions could be made to give effect to the decision; an example of this was the direction to the Secretary of State for the Home Department (SSHD) in the *Sivakumaran* appeal[91] before the adjudicator in 1988, to bring the successful appellants back to the UK.

There was an interesting provision in the 1971 Act (section 21) which allowed the Home Office to refer back to the IAA for it to consider any matter connected with an appeal. There would not be another decision, only a Report. There is no record of this section ever having been used, despite proposals to implement it.

Growth of the IAA

The IAA grew from a quite insignificant acorn with but 19 full-time judicial members to be the second largest tree in the forest of tribunals in the UK; with over 600 members, it has been at the coal face in the development of administrative and then human rights law, especially in relation to the challenge to Ministers of the Crown and even to Parliament. It has a particularly high profile, upon which the attention, usually not too welcome, of Parliament and Press have frequently been focused.

The policy of recruitment was, at first, to find people with some foreign-service background, many of whom were retired and came to start on a new career, but one with little or no prospect of promotion. As time went on, all this was to change – as careers were carved out and promotion was sought.

In the beginning, everyone learned – or did not learn – on the job; they were fiercely independent, but perhaps a little too individualistic at times and not always as thoughtful as they could have been about the problems of those who appeared before them. There emerged an almost obsessive demand by adjudicators for recognition as judges and they resisted any suggestion that they were simply a part of the administrative machinery, which started off with a decision in the Home Office and only ended when all remedies before the IAA were exhausted.

This account of the development of the tribunal reveals the extent to which it has in general tried to maintain an openly fair balance between the individual claimant and the state, together with some of the lapses both at the level of the individual judge and in internal management or policy. That eternal enemy of justice – quantity not quality – was as pervasive then as it is today. Controls were imposed by procedural regulations at the expense of justice.

91 [1998] 1 All E R 193.

The tribunal was continually hedged, perhaps inevitably, by legislation into conflict with the very role it was established to perform. The conflicts between the judiciary and government, however, were to become more intense with the increase in terrorist activities, as Chapter 5 will discuss. Lord Donaldson's remark that 'The Government recognises that the judges are the great enemies of every government, because they are always supporting people who allege that they're being downtrodden by government' was given public expression in ministerial attacks on judges.[92] The original concept of an informal tribunal came to look more and more like any court – parties needed lawyers, the decision makers became judges and the red tape around a hearing became enough to satisfy a thousand bureaucrats. None of this made the task of assessing the risk to an asylum-seeker on return any easier – nor, it may be suspected, any more reliable, though some measures were clearly calculated to, and did, reduce caseloads. The sort of cases the tribunal heard included those who wish to come to or stay in this country for whatever reason; to study, visit, for family reunion and so on, although a significant part of the daily diet of the contemporary immigration judge now concerns issues of human rights in one form or another.

Strictly speaking, once an independent review of a decision made by the government is established, the dividing line between policy and that review should be clear. However, the courts have held that, determination, or decision, by the tribunal is not a clean break from the initial decision, rather it is a continuation of it, in that it replaces the original decision with its own and is the decision a court, on appeal (as opposed to judicial review) will look to. Within this analysis lie the views that the decision by the tribunal is, in one sense, merely part of an overall administrative process and that the immigration judge can be seen as complicit in carrying out government policy. To many members of the immigration judiciary who think about it at all, the first is an unwelcome conclusion. They see it as a yet further confirmation of the opinion, often voiced, that the adjudicators were 'only adjudicating officers'. As to the second, the idea of being an additional 'gatekeeper' is anathema to any judge, but as will be seen, in practice, there is the constant potential for this to occur, usually unwittingly.[93]

---

92 See Chapter 8, p. 255.

93 The coercive content of controls is seen in every aspect, even in the sort of indirect pressures on the tribunal present in the *Mohammed AS Al Mass'ari v SSHD (in its second round) 5 March 1996 BILS issue 15 2E 221i*. For Dominica's response to his proposed deportation to the island see http://www.independent.co.uk/news/exile-faces-cool-reception-on-dominica-1322409.html (accessed on: 16 July 2013). This case is referred to in Chapter 2.

No In-Country Appeal against Refusal of Asylum

Until 1993, there was no right to appeal from refusal of asylum as such in the UK at all. The applicant would have to leave the country first (since he or she would be an illegal entrant) and then apply from outside the country before exercising any right to appeal.[94] Faced with this, some countries have extended preventive measures out to sea and beyond territorial waters. Others, such as the UK, have resorted to thc use of the carrier to pre-empt entry by imposing penalties on them, in effect making the carrier an extension of the immigration officer into the country of departure.

Venues of Hearings of Appeals

Whenever there is a right to appeal from a refusal of any application, the appeal always has been heard in the UK, although there have been murmurings about holding the hearing in the appellant's own country. Applications for extensions to a visa must be made whilst that visa is still current (and the appellant may stay in the country until the appeal is finally disposed of); otherwise, no right to appeal exists as long as the appellant remains in the UK.

The initial hearing before the adjudicator was, in the early days, usually held either at one of four hearing centres, which were at or near a port of entry, or at Thanet House, the IAT's headquarters on the Strand in London; this was in accordance with the intentions of the Wilson Committee. It was supposed to be quick and informal.

The appeal, to the IAT (described earlier), was then always heard at Thanet House by a panel usually comprised of a legally qualified chairman and two lay members, except where the appeal was on a point of law, when three legally qualified chairman would be on the panel. What is a little puzzling is why the lay members sat in the IAT, which was created mainly to keep some consistency of approach in legal issues by the lower tier of adjudicators.

Any appellant who was already in the country when the appeal came up for hearing (even if he or she actually had no right to appeal whilst in the country and perhaps was in the UK by chance) could attend it and call evidence. However, given that in many, indeed most cases, the decision will turn on the applicant's intentions, the views of the only person whom the immigration judge would be likely to hear (often the sponsor) will be of limited relevance.

In-Country and Out-of-Country Appeals

It is surprising therefore that up to 25 per cent of these appeals succeeded. Usually those were the appeals in which a sponsor attended. This success rate upset the

94 *R v SSHD ex parte Zamir* [1980] QB 378, which showed just how far-reaching was the power to treat someone as an illegal entrant.

Entry Clearance Officers and on one occasion an ECO, whose decision to refuse a visa to a young woman was reversed by an adjudicator, was heard to remark 'She must have shown a pretty leg – there was no other ground of appeal.'[95]

The Early Immigration 'Judges'

The first adjudicators and Tribunal chairmen and members to be appointed came from very varied backgrounds. Often they came from a colonial service background one had been an Air Vice Marshall, others had been magistrates, judges, Law Officers, or other colonial office administrators and in practice, most of them had some legal qualification.[96]

In later years, the Legal Action Group[97] opined that the workings of courts and tribunals are more similar than dissimilar, despite the perceived informality of the latter. It was, as is remarked, not so intended but has increasingly become so by a creeping judicialization and complex jurisprudence and legislation. The downside to more 'legalism', as it were, is that it can distract the judges from what the Wilson Committee had in mind when they conceived the IAA in 1967, which was a swift and fairly informal decision-making process. This became impossible when the nature of the enquiry in asylum and human rights-based appeals came on the scene. None the less, the resulting contribution to the development of administration law mainly as a result of such appeals has been significant.

The training of those involved, both judges and representatives, has been in an adversarial or non-interventionist system and has tended to banish informality. The courts sought to emphasize the on-going and administrative nature of the enquiry,[98] which was unpopular with many adjudicators because it was felt that, in effect, it reduced their role to one of administrators.

The IAT's lay membership tended to leaven its sometimes over-legalistic approach and often brought a more acceptable result to findings of fact. Successive governments have whittled away this lay presence, seemingly blissfully unaware that they were removing that very balance a tribunal needs.

Tribunals can exercise a profound influence in society, as does the lay magistracy. However, once the lay content is removed, all one is left with, in the

95 That was not the ground on which her appeal was allowed; the author can vouch for this personally!

96 Those appointed in 1969 were on an annual salary of £3,596 with a 42-hour week.

97 The purpose of the Legal Action Group (LAG), a national, independent charity, is to promote equal access to justice for all members of society who are socially, economically, or otherwise disadvantaged. To this end, it seeks to improve law and practice, the administration of justice and legal service. To quote Lord Justice Sedley: 'LAG's role has always been the same – to inform, to agitate, to critique, to point the way forward'; see more at http://www.lag.org.uk/advanced-search.aspx#sthash.1aCO6nlp.dpuf.

98 *Karanakaran v S SHD* [2000] 3 All ER 449, at p 479 b; [2000] INLR 122 and *R v Ravichandran* [1996] Imm AR 97, at 109.

case of this tribunal, is just another type of court. It is interesting that, following the creation of the Board in 1905, some critics suggested that appeals should be heard by magistrates sitting with two assessors. Sweden has adopted this type of approach, as is discussed in Chapter 6.[99]

Career opportunities within the tribunal service were few and the introduction of a combined tribunal structure would, it was thought, improve the attraction of an appointment to the tribunal, with its ever increasing complexities.[100]. This development was not to materialize until 2010.

Changes in Migratory Patterns

By the time the legislation, following the Wilson Report, came on the statute book in 1969, the exodus of Asians from Africa and the first migration from the Caribbean were well advanced. It was not anticipated that refugees from across the seas would seek refuge outside their own regions in significant numbers and that any 'burden' which had to be 'shared' would have to be shared by the West as well!

In fact, right up to 1991 when the Immigration and Asylum Bill was introduced to give an appeal to those refused refugee status, it seems that policy was dictated by a fear of creating a statutory class of those entitled to claim asylum, whilst at the same time ensuring compliance with the Refugee Convention.

Thus, although the likelihood of the IAA having to consider refugees was anticipated,[101] there was nothing in the primary legislation concerning refugees and it was left to subsidiary legislation (made under powers given to the SSHD under the Immigration Act 1971) known as 'the Rules', to deal with this issue in a perfunctory fashion. Whereas internal sanctuary and external asylum existed side-by-side in ancient Greece,[102] in modern Europe, sanctuary has always been a form of internal protection developed in ecclesiastical law.[103] In modern times, it did

99 There was a similar proposal in South Africa in 2002. Reasons vary for this approach but cost savings certainly is one possible advantage.

100 The complexities arose in the form of the hearing, its increased technicalities, the lack of a common information data base and a research centre (which was remarked upon in Part VII of the *Annual Report of the Council of Tribunals 1970–71*.

101 Para. 19, Wilson Report. From a reading of other parts of the Committee's deliberations, it appears it was thinking in terms of the Jewish pogroms and conflicts in Europe of the past. There was nothing to make them expect large flows of immigrants and asylum claimants which did not begin in the UK, until the 1980s. See the White Paper 'Immigration from the Commonwealth', Cmnd 2739.

102 For example, *Oedipus at Colonus*, Sophocles. Herodotus and Adrastus who fled to Croesus in Lydia (now Turkey)

103 T. Sutton (1966), 'Modern Sanctuary', *Ecclesiastical Law Journal* 8 (January): at p. 487: 'James I abolished the right of sanctuary, but churches throughout Europe have been solidly interventionist and the Churches Commission for Racial Justice felt constrained by conscience to offer sanctuary to those facing deportation … as a last resort".'

re-emerge with the churches' desire to use sanctuary to supplement what it saw to be a too harsh an approach by the State towards the asylum-seeker.[104] There were in fact several meetings between Mr JD Haslam, the secretary to the World Council of Churches, and others to seek to resolve the use of sanctuary for this purpose.

What had been initially fairly generous rights of review of executive decisions, at least compared with most other countries, was soon to be eroded, as successive governments started wresting those rights of review back, when the flow of migrants from every part of the world increased. The impression given by governments when new legislation was proposed seems to have been that a right of appeal was a significant cause of the (uncontrollable) immigration to the UK, since each (almost) bi-annual change to the laws restricted the right of appeal in new ways. The flow continued and continues. What started fairly mildly in the aftermath of decolonization, with the exit of many Ugandan Asians wishing to exercise their citizenship, took on a very different look with the collapse of democracies, famine and internecine wars on the one hand, and growth in prosperity in the developed world and greater ease of travel on the other.

This led to public and press reactions such as 'We're being swamped by crime waves of migrants', and 'so-called' was replaced by the epithet 'bogus'.

It was to get no better as time passed: 'Asylum Seekers milk legal aid', said the headline in *The Times*,[105] but the article was actually about British advisers who were doing the milking; solicitors in this case.

The inevitable effect on public opinion and government was increased restrictive legislation on immigrants to the UK, not only for the alien but Commonwealth citizens as well. The people it affected most were those from countries such as India, Pakistan, Sri Lanka and from Africa. This, on top of the other legislation affecting rights of abode and citizenship (also felt to be directed at the non-white Commonwealth) led to a sense of discrimination on racial lines. The resentment remains and many see the restrictive approach toward family members of Commonwealth citizens already admitted as a sort of 'Fair Weather Friends' attitude. That is, as long as they stayed where they were and presented no problem to the UK, they could enjoy the benefit of a Commonwealth brotherhood – but when they wanted to come to live and work in the UK, it was a different matter. Immigration controls have consistently impacted disproportionately (whether intentionally or not) upon minority populations and the more vulnerable, and inevitably have led to accusations of racially discriminatory measures. Consider, for example, the impact upon children of immigrants who are compelled to leave the country many years after first arrival, the children having had their entire education in the UK and often unable even to speak the language of their parents' home.

---

104 *Viraj Mendis* [1988] Imm AR 12.

105 *The Times*, 7 June 1998 headline: 'Asylum Tide costs Britain £2bn a Year', and p. 2 which alleges British solicitors were 'putting grinding paste into the gearbox of the immigration system'.

No action taken by government was able to curb the rise in asylum claims, whether policy plans such as the *Faster, Fairer and Firmer – Modern Approach to Immigration and Asylum* report,[106] or any new legislation, while backlogs in the Home Office continued to increase from 65,000 to 98,000 in the space of just eight months in 1998.

The European Union

The European Union has adopted an ever-invasive role in all aspects of immigration, from Directives which deal with procedural matters to the development of the jurisprudence through decisions by the European Court of Human Rights (not always to the liking of the individual countries' governments) in cases brought by immigrants dissatisfied with the decisions of a member country of the EU. The aim of EU policy is harmonization of immigration policies and procedures in the EU, even extending to a possible centralized appeal system.

The restructuring of government policies and general approach as a result of policy decisions in Europe, particularly following the Presidency Conclusion of October 1999 at Tampere, Finland,[107] only added to the complexity.

The EU policy of harmonization has itself been forced by the influx of refugees and other migrants into one member state or another, all of which have a land border. This in turn has influenced the UK domestic approach by the government and as a result of the Directives and the decisions in the European Court of Human Rights (ECtHR).

A judge of the Polish Supreme Administrative Court wrote 'the role of an administrative court (administrative tribunal) judge often does not attract much attention and is perceived as being rather peripheral.'[108] That has been far from the UK experience. Immigration and the decisions by the tribunal and the courts have hardly moved from being a major news item for the last 20 years. Successive governments saw the solution to 'the problem'[109] to be the appointment of more and more immigration judges at bigger and bigger salaries, with more and more hearing rooms and with administration machinery to match.[110]

---

106 Cmnd 4018, 27 July 1998.

107 Tampere, European Council, 1999.

108 The view of Judge Jacek Chlebny, Warsaw. See Chapter 8, p. 271.

109 The backlog, which had reached around 100,000 in 2002, had more or less been cleared by 2006. See Wagner J., *A Changing Immigration System; Immigration Policies under Tony Blair and George Brown* <http://pages.wustl.edu>.

110 The size of the tribunal had become large but nowhere as large as it was to become ten years later. In 2005–2006, it decided 167,000 appeals, against the Appeals Service (the welfare wing, as it were) who decided 262,856 cases. See Annual Report of the Department of Immigration and Citizenship Service 2006–2007.

Chapter 2
From the Home Office to the Lord Chancellor's Department

Britain remained wedded to deterrence: if word got out that you were kind to strangers more would come.

R. Winder, *Bloody Foreigners*[1]

How the Rights of Appeal Operated

The previous chapter introduced the image of the foreigner or a stranger as they were seen in the eyes of the press and many people in the UK up to the early twentieth century; the Huguenots from France, the émigrés from Russia and the Jews from everywhere – all of which form a background to the approach toward immigration control.

By 1960, it was feared that people from the Commonwealth countries that had recently become independent would move in large numbers to the UK. Active steps began in 1962 with the Commonwealth Immigrants Act to limit such a movement as we saw in the last chapter; this was followed by the 1971 Immigration Act and later the British Nationality Act 1981.

The Aliens Act 1905 may have purported to address a straightforward need to control numbers of immigrants but its effect and the debate and press reports all seem to confirm that its real purpose was to put a stop to the entry of the (allegedly) poor immigrant. The poor at that time were seen to be Jewish. Some 65 years later, in 1971,[2] however, it is the spouse and family of Commonwealth Citizens wishing to join their spouse or parent in the UK that the legislation aimed at limiting, if not preventing.[3] The link between poverty and immigration remains in the explicit wording of some UK immigration controls (such as family settlements and student visas), which demand a certain level of affluence in order, so the argument goes, to avoid becoming a charge on the state – the 'poverty line'

1 Winder, R. (2004), *Bloody Foreigners* (London: Abacus).

2 Immigration Act 1971, c.77.

3 The Israeli Supreme Court in a 6–5 decision, upheld the constitutionality of the Citizenship and Entry into Israel Law – 2003 (as amended 2007) which restricts Palestinian Arab citizens of Israel from living together in Israel with their Palestinian spouses from the Occupied Palestinian Territory (OPT) or from 'enemy states', viz. Syria, Lebanon, Iran and Iraq: HCJ 466/07, *MK Zahava Galon v. The Attorney General, et al.* (petition dismissed, 11 January 2012).

rule – even though the fear of being swamped figures well to the forefront of many speeches by politicians over the years.

The manner in which the poverty line was given effect to in family reunions of every sort is achieved by making it necessary to prove that the member(s) of the family who seek entry to the UK must not expect to rely on public welfare support. The introduction of DNA testing, which enabled blood relationships to be established in most cases with reasonable accuracy, should have reduced refusals of entry clearance to children; it did not do so because the 'poverty line' rule was applied by the Home Office with greater strictness. The judge must apply the law when it requires a specified minimum level of affluence, but needs to be aware of historical background to the poverty line approach when assessing an appellant's own story.[4]

The removal of the rights to live in the UK for Commonwealth Citizens, in the light of decolonization and Harold Macmillan's 'Winds of Change' speech, was brought up in the last chapter. From the Commonwealth Immigrants Act 1962 onward,[5] powers to deport any Commonwealth citizen who had been sentenced to imprisonment and recommended by the court for deportation were added to the loss of freedom to come and go in the UK. The Immigration Act 1971[6] was not only a creation of the IAA, it consolidated control measures and their management of immigration generally and added to the Minister's power to deport anyone who did not have a right of abode in the UK. This put Commonwealth citizens and aliens on the same basis.[7]

When the Immigration Act 1971 succeeded the Immigration Appeals Act 1969, there 647 appeals were still outstanding, awaiting a decision. The 1971 Act did not change the basic structure of the system although a general right of appeal under the 1969 Act against exclusion at the ports, exercisable whilst the appellant remained in the UK, was not reproduced in the 1971 Act. Thenceforth the right of appeal was only exercisable after departure from the country, unless the immigrant had obtained a visa, entry clearance, or a work permit. Hence the distinction was created between 'in-country' rights of appeal and 'out-of country' appeals. Anyone who arrived without the required authorization was regarded as an illegal entrant.

The Act itself does not go into details of policy, which is left to the SSHD in Instructions to his immigration officers (and everyone else including the IAA) on how he wished his discretions to be exercised. The 'Instructions to Immigration

4 Consider, for example, Barcott, R. (2011), *It Happened on the Way to War* (USA: Bloomsbury)

5 Commonwealth Immigration Act 1962. c. 21.

6 c. 77

7 Commonwealth Citizens, sections 1 or 6 .of the Commonwealth Immigration Act 1962.

Officers'[8] were 'Secret', but after the 1971 Act,[9] they were required to be laid before Parliament for 40 days before they could come into effect and then they bind both the immigration officers and the IAA even though they are not delegated legislation as such.[10] The first instructions and the procedural rules differentiated between on- and after-entry claims. The first, which was under the 1969 Act, came into force on 23 October 1972. The next, henceforth to be known as 'Statements of Changes' under the 1971 Act, came into force on 30 January 1973[11] and have appeared regularly to make changes in the way in which the minister wished his officials to operate the system of control, and exercise any discretion.[12]

The first discrete right of appeal from a decision by the Secretary of State for Home Affairs (who will be referred to here as the 'Home Office' or the 'SSHD') to refuse asylum to anyone who did manage to reach the UK without entry clearance or a visa, did not reach the statute books until 1993; until then, the claimant would (generally) be in the country illegally and therefore liable to deportation.[13]

One case in particular which prompted a whole new approach to this position was *Sivakumaran* and his four co-appellants, who were refused asylum by the Home Office in 1987 and whose applications for judicial review of that decision were unsuccessful.[14] One newspaper depicted a photograph of the group undressing at the airport in protest at their removal. They were deported amid a flurry of publicity when they grabbed the headlines by removing their trousers at the airport. They then exercised the only further right of appeal which was left to them – an out-of-country one – whilst they were back in Sri Lanka. Their appeal was successful and the adjudicator ordered that they be returned to the UK with

8 They were recently examined in *Secretary of State for the Home Department v Pankina* [2010] EWCA Civ 719.

9 Section 3(2), Immigration Act 1971.

10 See Sedley, S. (2011), *Ashes and Sparks: Essays on Law and Justice* (Cambridge: Cambridge University Press), Chapter 7, which, among other chapters, addresses the development of public law. The ministerial directions play a role in this development of public law.

11 HC 79–82.

12 It was not until 2004 that some of their content began to influence legislation and affect how an immigration judge weighed the evidence before him and reached his findings of fact: Asylum and Immigration(Treatment of Claimants) Act 2004, s. 8, and Immigration (Treatment of Claimants) Regulations SI /2004.

13 Though of course any decision of the executive was subject to judicial review. 'Straw disowns refugee dispersal plan', Alan Travis, *The Guardian* 25 August 1999. Online at http://www.theguardian.com/uk/1999/aug/25/alantravis.

14 [1988] AC 958.

the minimum delay.[15] An application for leave to appeal to the IAT, made to the Divisional Court, failed, as it had been wrongly served and was out of time.[16]

Although the asylum-seeker did not have an in-country right of appeal the Instructions did include a measure of protection by requiring any claim to asylum at a border to be passed on to the Home Office by the immigration officer at the port of entry (now called a 'Border Guard' with a nice uniform like his Continental cousins), who (hopefully) had more experience.[17] The importance of this provision was that it prevented the instant removal of a person arriving at the border and claiming asylum by any, possibly untrained, official acting off his own bat without affording any opportunity to have the asylum-seeker's story carefully evaluated, or to be able to apply for a review of that decision.[18]

The *Sivakumaran* case, along with the repeated success of some 25 per cent of short-term visitor appeals, confirmed that a right to appeal even from outside the country did have a value. This was surprising when the outcome of most appeals turned on the appellants' intentions for applying for entry and not the intentions of his or her sponsor. It therefore paid an appellant to ask for an oral hearing at which he could appear by a representative and call evidence – usually his sponsor.

It came as no surprise that the government saw the removal of this right of appeal to be a way of making a significant reduction in the load of appeals and was one of the first rights to be was removed in 1993, while at the same time an appeal was made available to refused asylum-seekers[19].

In this instance, the IAA was consulted by the LCD on the removal of the right of appeal for short-term visitors. The Chief Adjudicator's somewhat laconic response was 'we make no comment in respect of removal of appeal rights of visitors, prospective students and short-term students. No doubt the probability of an increased number of judicial review applications and the burden on the courts have been taken into account … .'

---

15 The appeals were allowed by an adjudicator (the author) in the out-of-country appeal. The facts, which for the most part were uncontested by the Home Office, included testimony obtained through visits by their solicitors to Sri Lanka, the Home Office having been asked to adduce evidence, but failing to do so. (The BHC informed the author in February 1988 that the mission had supplied information to the Home Office which may have affected the outcome of the appeal.) The appeal is an unreported case, but details are recited at para. 44 for *Sivakumaran* in *Vilvarajah et al. v. The United Kingdom* (Application no. 13163/87; 13164/87; 13165/87; 13447/87; 13448/87). See the *Independent*, 17 May 1989, in an article by Sarah Helm, and in *The Times*, 1989, in an article by Lucy Hodges.

16 *The Times*, 18 May1989

17 Rule 58 of the Immigration Rules 1973 (and policies within the Home Office itself).

18 One ECO in Bangladesh commenting on this opined that the UK's lax immigration laws 'ought to be more like Denmark – who just throws them out at the border!'

19 By the Immigration and Asylum Act 1993, c. 23. It was restored in part but has recently been limited yet again.

This was intended to be an oblique way of indicating disapproval but avoiding the judiciary being seen to be involved in matters of policy; but it did not inhibit the regional adjudicator at Harmondsworth from expressing the views most adjudicators at the time felt privately:[20] that it was a bad move

The IAA was also consulted on the likely effect of proposed changes to an already procedurally complex scenario after the introduction of an asylum appeal. Two examples illustrate such issues. The first proposed that both asylum and non-asylum appeals should be heard contemporaneously and before the same adjudicator. The other was a proposal to make the same rules cover both asylum and non-asylum appeals.

The approaches in the two appeals – asylum and non-asylum – are different; in the non-asylum appeal (as a general rule), the tribunal could only consider the facts as they had been at the time of the original refusal, which may have been many months, if not years earlier. On the other hand, in asylum appeals, every time a hearing took place the facts at that time had to be reconsidered. The duty of the adjudicator in asylum appeals was to hear any evidence which was perceived to be necessary to reach the truth. In non-asylum appeals, the adjudicator had to rely on facts in existence as at the date of the decision. The standard of proof was also different, in that it was on the balance of probabilities, whereas in an asylum appeal the question is 'Is the claim substantially likely to be true?'

The same procedural rules apply in general to both types of appeal and therefore seemed difficult to apply, and when only those adjudicators who had been designated as Special Adjudicators by the Lord Chancellor were allowed to hear asylum appeals, it became impossible in practice. An appeal may start off as non-asylum and then develop into an asylum appeal as well – the adjudicator would have no alternative but to carry on and deal with the non-asylum part and adjourn the asylum part, or adjourn both.

The rights of appeal in the UK were certainly more extensive than in many other countries,[21] but those advantages could be rendered illusory; the case of Harwant Singh, a 17-year-old student is an example. He wished to visit his family in the UK for exceptional family celebrations in 1990. Having overcome the ordeal of the journey from his home in the Punjab to the British High Commission in Delhi, he was refused his application for entry clearance. His appeal (from outside the country) was successful but by the time he was able to go back to the Entry Clearance Officer (ECO) and get his leave to come, the celebrations he was to attend would be over. In an attempt to avoid such an outcome, the adjudicator

---

20 Victor Callender Regional Adjudicator at Harmondsworth wrote to *The Times* on 2 March 1995, noting the warning given explicitly to Foreign Office Entry Clearance Officers of the effects of a removal of such rights of appeal, especially on them. A form of supervision was introduced later in 1999 with the Independent Monitor of Entry Clearance Refusals, which it appears is to be subsumed under the UK Border Agency Inspectorate.

21 Such as in the United States, where there was never any right to appeal against a decision to refuse entry to a visitor.

may give directions to expedite a positive decision on a reapplication. This was then met by an ECO or visa officer refusing the re-application on the grounds that 'circumstances had changed'.

Hearing Centres

When the IAA was first created, the majority of appeals were heard at ports of entry such as Gatwick, Dover, Southampton and, a little later, Harmondsworth (which served Heathrow) and were quickly disposed by adjudicators, which is what the Wilson Report envisaged.

The other centres at Dover, Southampton and Gatwick had on average a low monthly use of hearing rooms. The use of hearing rooms, which were shared with the courts, for nine months in 1983 for Gatwick, varied from 12 to 30 hours in a month when a total of 118 cases were heard, to 1.5 to 8.25 hours in the month when a total of 47 cases were heard.

Those decisions were generally upheld on appeal to the IAT since most decisions turned purely on issues of fact. This picture began to change around 1977, when more and more appeals raised new and often complex issues of law.

In 1983, some of the early centres such as Dover and Gatwick were closed, since the government took the view that they were uneconomic to run;[22] the appeals were then sent to Southampton (which was also closed soon after, when the adjudicator, Air Vice-Marshal Ayling, retired). The Harmondsworth centre was opened, and became, along with Thanet House, the IAA headquarters, one of the two centres where all appeals in the South were heard. This building also housed the IAT, in prime position on the top floor (provided the lift was working, which it often did not). The part-time adjudicators, on the other hand, occupied two windowless and rather airless rooms in a basement, shared with a noisy old central heating system and the first aid room, which doubled as the night watchman's sleeping quarters.

Nevertheless, the part-time adjudicator's life was a communal and not at all unpleasant one, if rather more isolated from their full-time colleagues than is the case today. The full timers occupied superior accommodation on the upper floors – as befitted their station!

Other centres in Birmingham, Manchester and Leeds handled appeals in the rest of England; appeals in Scotland were heard in Glasgow, but administered from Leeds, and when security allowed, appeals in Northern Ireland were heard in Belfast behind locked doors and curtained windows.

22 This view did not go unchallenged. An adjudicator wrote in on 23 October 1984 pointing out the costs of accommodating an adjudicator in London as against the provinces according to Home Office Notice 252/1980, p. 19, was 54 per cent of salary as against 21 per cent. The way the Chief Adjudicator handled the proposed closures also caused irritation.

Some adjudicators, and particularly the Chief (and later the Deputy Chief) Adjudicator frequently travelled to hear appeals at all centres; otherwise, at the time, an adjudicator was attached to a particular centre and rarely sat anywhere else. When asylum appeals were introduced, it was felt that they should be heard by those with some overseas experience or exposure. The government made it necessary for further hearing centres to be opened by dispersing asylum-seekers around the UK (often without warning, especially to the local authority).

In the *New Law Journal*, Sharon Wallach described Thanet House as the 'Home of Immigration Appeals'. She wrote, 'If fried breakfasts were a symbol of the British way of life, the proximity of Thanet House to Lite Bite is appropriate.' Before her article, the fire exit was actually through the 'Lite Bite', a haunt for coffee for all.

She goes on to describe the building, a little shabby and unremarkable at that time, as 'just like magistrates' courts', with tatty handwritten notices warning the public to use the toilets in the basement; she finished off by writing that 'so unemotional were the hearings that adjudicators could be issuing nothing more important than dog licences'![23]

When disputes arose with the landlord over repairs and renewals, a search ensued for other premises, preferably within close range of all the facilities near to Thanet House. The favourite was an empty former newspaper office just to the east of Kings Bench Walk, which had parking space and was in all but one respect suitable – what killed the project was the modern requirements regarding the use of asbestos in buildings – hence the tribunal landed up in Taylor House[24] in Islington.

Further centres were opened after asylum appeals were introduced in 1993, and the intake of appeals increased, which will be dealt with in Chapter 3.

Administrative Staff

The Wilson Report had recommended that the IAT should be attached to the LCD, but the adjudicators should be under the Home Office. It was a usual practice at that time to attach tribunals to the same government department from which they would hear appeals as there were practical advantages of staffing and finance (later it was felt that this did not make for the transparency of an independent appeal). In the case of the IAA, the support staff included a manager, two personal secretaries, some typists, a number of clerks, and a most valuable, but now long-lost category of support staff called 'court messengers'. These were few in number but were fiercely independent and jealous of their position; they exercised authority over all who came into the building; they kept order in the hearing rooms, among

23 S. Wallach, 'Appealing to Stay', *New Law Journal* 141 (18 January 1991): 67

24 A suggestion that the building should be named in memory of Mark Patey was rejected in favour of naming it after the former Lord Chief Justice.

representatives, appellants, press – and adjudicators when they were late! They made the hearings run smoothly, and had the right, which none dared question, to walk into one's room without knocking.

The Home Office made a point of never appearing to influence the IAA and the relationship between the judiciary and the administration became professionally cordial and cooperative, acquiring the same degree of unity of purpose enjoyed, for example, in Denmark, Belgium, Sweden and the Netherlands.

As tribunals built up their judicial role it became clear that the control, whether exercised or not, of the very ministry against whose decisions they were hearing appeals would be perceived as undermining the independence of a review which was supposed to be independent. It was determined therefore that their proper place should be under the LCD, and the IAA was duly transferred from the Home Office to the LCD on 1 April 1987.

The Impact and Influence of the Early Immigration Judges

History becomes attractive for the people and the personalities of those who make it. Apart from the anecdotal interest of their stories, which lends a little colour to often colourless details, the early appointments were writing on a blank canvas and some of what they wrote remained with the tribunal after their departure.

The first adjudicators appointed under the 1969 Act had been designated to sit at hearing centres close to their homes, but their letters of appointment required that they be willing to sit elsewhere if required to do so. When the south coast centres were closed and south coast-residing adjudicators were required to sit in London, some took the view that this changed their terms of appointment and a group of them banded together to challenge the government, claiming compensation for a repudiation of their contract of employment. They argued that when they took on the job it was to sit at a centre close to where they lived, and if they were now required to travel to London every day, it would be both costly and inconvenient for them.

The Chief Adjudicator wrote to Mr Bohan[25] at the Home Office referring to three aspects of the adjudicator's challenge, firstly, that '... it was accepted that the Adjudicators were not civil servants', secondly that '... they had been appointed to a specific place', but thirdly that there was '... no question of offering compensation on abolition of office as ... if they were civil servants ... [they] would be readily transferable and compensation would not have entered into it'.

The adjudicators enlisted the aid of the Civil Servants Union in their challenge, despite the fact that they were not classed as civil servants, as there was no other union available at the time to represent their interests. This challenge was eventually, and very reluctantly, dropped on their counsel's advice but resentment and a feeling of victimization lingered on. They considered that the Lord

25 The correspondence is available in the archived papers for any interested reader.

Chancellor, Viscount Hailsham harboured a resentment against those who had the temerity to consider suing his department. Be that as it may, they remained sure their challenge dogged their steps for the rest of their days with the IAA.

Most of the earlier appointments had very varied backgrounds but shared one thing in common: they had lived abroad serving in senior positions, or had seen active service. For example, one was a former attorney general from Uganda (George Farmer who was later to become President of the IAT), three judges were from Zambia (Martin McCall, who had also been Solicitor General, John Housden, a District Officer, and a practitioner, Tom Healy), another two judges from Zambia were followed by two more in the 1980s and 1990s (the author and Dick Lawrence), and later the former Chief Justice of Botswana, Aidan O'Brien Quinn, and two judges from Zimbabwe. Some adjudicators resented it when their decisions were overturned by the IAT – though few can have taken it as badly as did Air Vice-Marshal Ayling, who never to spoke to Professor David Jackson[26] again, after Jackson had allowed an appeal from his decision. Sir John Pestell (who served with the last Governor of Rhodesia) Sir Norman Costar, Sir John Cotton (the one who liked to hear his cases in Urdu if possible) and Clem Richards OBE were all early appointments.

The pool of those with overseas experience ('the old Colonialists' some called them) dwindled; but other service arms, usually drawn from senior ranks of retired army or navy legal services, as well as those who had former diplomatic service, supplied future judges. Starting with David Jackson in 1984, academics also joined the judiciary in increasing numbers.

It was not until 1980 that there was a trawl for large numbers of part-time adjudicators. Forty-two were appointed but most soon dropped away over the next few years for a variety of reasons (including finding the work too onerous), so that by 1989, there were still only 70 part-time adjudicators for the whole of the UK.

The IAT started with one full-time president, Sir Derek Hilton, and two legal members, John Hooton, from Hong Kong, and David Neve, who had been a magistrate, also from Hong Kong; Neve then became the next president of the IAT. He was known to hate lengthy meetings, or lengthy determinations. It is said that he would even write up his determinations in advance, except for the last paragraph which would await completion of the hearing. Another story has it that he arrived at a meeting of IAT members only to find there was no quorum, so he promptly left without even waiting to take off his bowler hat.

The legal members of the IAT were at first called just that, but Diana Phillips, an early editor of the Immigration Law Reports and herself an adjudicator, felt this title had insufficient dignity and rechristened them all 'vice presidents' – and even though the title never had any official recognition, it stuck until they all became judges.

In addition to part-time adjudicators, the IAT also had a small pool of part-time legal chairmen. One fully occupied part-timer doubled as editor of the Immigration

26 Vice President of the IAT.

Appeal Reports (colloquially christened the 'Green Books');[27] another was a legal manager to *The Times*. Only two (apart from David Jackson) were appointed full-time vice presidents from the ranks of the adjudicators. Legal members began to be appointed from the ranks of adjudicators beginning in 1966, the first two being the Chief Adjudicator and his Deputy (the author), followed by a few more in the next three years. But the dual role, which involved sitting on appeal from determinations of fellow adjudicators, caused more tension than when there was a strict separation of judicial roles.

Two complaints of a more serious nature made by most adjudicators were that the IAT was inconsistent in its decision making, which made it difficult for adjudicators to know which determination to follow, and that when granting leave (or permission) to appeal to the IAT, they very rarely gave any reasons for doing so.

George Farmer became the next president of the Tribunal in 1983 (the last president not to be at least a circuit judge). By the time of his appointment, appeals had begun to throw up even more complex issues of law, particularly involving European law and asylum decisions, which persuaded him to strengthen the IAT with the appointment of an academic as a full-time vice president. The recruitment procedures to the IAT of the day were a great deal more informal; there was no advertisement of the vacancy and George Farmer simply asked the Chief Adjudicator for one or two names, one of which was David Jackson. He was invited to accept the appointment, which he did. The Lord Chancellor then approved the appointment.

David Jackson's presence was well timed and he tackled many of the issues which had begun to arise. One issue in particular was whether immigration law stood in a compartment of its own, unaffected by any other law, including EU law. One Legal Member considered that it did, but Jackson firmly rejected this approach. In the same manner, he introduced the IAA to the importance of the EU and generally he injected fresh thinking into the immigration jurisprudence. One of the many contributions he made was to remind adjudicators that it did not necessarily follow that merely because an appellant had not told the truth in one area the rest of his or her testimony was to be rejected.[28] But a sore topic to some was Lord Justice Watkins' dicta in *Mumin* (which limited the adjudicator's power to say how the SSHD should exercise his discretion outside the rules) said 'I think it would be prudent of chairmen of tribunals to leave such matters [of public law] to this court.'[29]

The priorities of each president of the IAT will follow his perception of the needs of the times. George Farmer concentrated on listing, keeping the listing book carefully locked away from the administration. It is doubtful if anyone ever understood why, in the position of president, he attached so much importance

27 Raymond Maddison.

28 *Chiver* IAT (10758), see p. 39 below.

29 [1992] Imm AR 554. An impossible direction today, one would think

to listing, but his argument was that by doing so he protected the tribunal from unwelcome administrative interference and control. Naturally, time spent on this issue meant less time to spend in hearing appeals and writing decisions; therefore, when issues of law were involved, he usually left them to one of the other vice presidents.

The legally qualified members of the IAT who chaired all the hearings have been dealt with, but in addition, there were usually two lay members on each appeal when no major issues of law were involved. They were drawn from a pool of, at that time 17 lay members, which comprised men and women who had distinguished themselves in many walks of life, including trade unions, the diplomatic corps, and so on. Their backgrounds and cultures varied far more than did those of the legal members and vice presidents, and they have always commanded great respect. For example, George Brown was a JP, Naynesh Kumar was from the Indian subcontinent and Eddie Edinboro from the Caribbean; another lay member, Margaret Countess of Mar (whose title dates back to the twelfth century) continued to sit in the House of Lords.

It has never been easy to understand why the lay members of the tribunal sat at the appeal level, as the role of the IAT intended by the Wilson Committee was simply to maintain some consistency in the law. The Leggatt Report[30] seemed to recognize this when some years later they recommended the retention of lay judges, but at the first-tier level where their value in assisting in decisions of fact was most valuable. Their presence gave the tribunal a deeper level of humanity – 'street cred' in descriptive slang. The experience of sitting with people of that calibre changed the author's view of the value of having non-legal men and women with whom to share such important decisions, especially when there were issues of fact to be decided; the later emasculation of their role was at best retrogressive and thoughtless.

The Permanent Secretary at the Home Office just before the adjudicators were transferred to the responsibility of the LCD was Sir Hayden Phillips and it was he who later became Permanent Secretary in the LCD when Lord Irvine became Lord Chancellor, much to the surprise and disappointment of many adjudicators, who had hoped the deputy in the LCD Michael Huebner would take over.

Development in Tribunal Case Management and Decision Making

The way in which an appeal was managed depended upon several factors, namely, what the issues were; its place of origin; whether it was an in-country or out-of-country appeal; the parties, whether a single person or a family; where the appellant lived; whether an oral hearing was requested; the need for interpreters and what the original application had been for. Flawed listing led to wasted hearing-room space, a waste of staff and judges' time and frustration for the parties.

30 See Chapter 3, p. 77.

When the application to enter this country was first made to an entry clearance or visa officer in a British mission in the applicant's country, the ECO had to grapple with the credibility and plausibility of the applicant, just as much as adjudicators did. They often felt that adjudicators did not pay sufficient regard to their knowledge of local cultures and traditions gained from local contacts and village visits. They did have that advantage, but in the larger Missions such as New Delhi, they usually lived isolated lives in the station, whereas many adjudicators either themselves came from those backgrounds or had abroad for years and had as much, if not deeper, understanding of other cultures than any ECO posted to a mission for three years.

The ECOs and the adjudicators both had valid points and the wiser adjudicator acknowledged this and used the knowledge gained from living overseas to assist in his comprehension, rather than pretend to any depth of understanding of individual traditions and cultural practices. The adjudicator's knowledge gained from a colonial background or solely in the familiarization tours which pairs of them went on every two or three years, known as the 'Grand Tours' (discussed in Chapter 4 under 'Fact finding'), was likely to be incomplete if not worse. The Grand Tour enabled the adjudicator to see what the ECO was referring to in his statements, the home environment of those who became appellants and where some of the pitfalls were to be found, such as in forged documents in some parts of the world, but not others.

In out-of-country appeals, the adjudicator often had to rely only on a statement from the ECO, accompanied by documents and the appellant's own statement. The Home Office representative (the Presenting Officer or 'HOPO', for short) would have little more to go on and the stronger minded ones would on occasion simply concede the appeal. The appellant could be represented and supplement what the ECO had sent or contest it. In-country appeals where the appellant was usually present were conducted much more like an ordinary adversarial contest.

In all appeals, the management skills rested in being able to have an appeal prepared to minimize adjournments, make accurate estimates of how long the appeal would last, for example, three hours for a primary purpose appeal,[31] 30 minutes for refusal of a visit and two hours for 40 cases for mention![32]

The adjudicators' determinations were each individually monitored by the Chief or Deputy Chief Adjudicator, or a Regional Adjudicator. This watchful eye often saved an adjudicator from embarrassment, if he had made a careless slip, and saved an appellant from having to pursue an appeal unnecessarily. Monitoring also revealed how often and why an adjudicator was being appealed, as well as the issues which were commonly arising, so that they could be addressed at seminars

31 An appeal to determine whether the primary purpose of a marriage was 'legitimate' or for immigration purposes alone.

32 A 'case for mention' was simply a short hearing to decide matters such as whether the appeal was ready for a full hearing or if not, what else remained to be done to get it ready.

or annual meetings of the adjudicators. The system could not survive the massive increase in appeals and numbers of adjudicators. The practice of monitoring could have become almost disciplinary similar to the Social Security Appeals (SSATS) practice where a policy of 'three strikes and you were up before the boss' operated, but it was not; it was a simple and informal process directed more at issues than personalities.

Types of Appeal

Some of the earliest migrants in any number after the Second World War were Bangladeshi seamen, who jumped ship from the jute boats on arrival at a UK port. They would stay on and settle down. Many others came initially as sojourners, but they and others following them were encouraged not to return home due to the poor and unsettled conditions in their country. This flow quite naturally was followed by applications from these men's families to join them. In the 1980s, there were some 5,000 wives from Bangladesh alone who were awaiting decisions. There was a similar flow of men from the Caribbean, followed later by their families.

One would expect applications by a member of the family of a person who had probably been settled in the UK for years to be straightforward, but they were far from simple and family reunion cases became highly contentious, and leave a sour taste even now. Family reunion and the maintenance of family ties in India or Africa is central to the cultural life in such regions.

The complexities arose in several ways. The first was christened 'Tax wives – and children'. This arose where the original immigrant, who was usually a man, in his application for leave to remain declared his marital and family status. He may have said that he was married with children. After he was settled and could afford to do so, he would want his family to join him. The family he sought for leave to join him may then not coincide with those in his original declaration: less children, different names, and so on. All these years, he had been claiming tax allowances for family he did not have. He sometimes included other relatives. To make up numbers, he might try to bring in someone else's family, claiming them to be his own. Naturally, he then had difficulty in proving relationships and ages of the children (males had to be under 18 and females unmarried). As his claim was tainted by the earlier deception, he was often not believed. To add to his problems, documentary evidence was also at best suspect. The robust warning by Professor Jackson not to allow earlier fraud to lead to automatic dismissal of the appeal should remain ringing in the ears of all decision makers.[33]

Whilst this fraud was practised from many places, one of the more common sources was Colombo. As a result, ECOs intensified their examination of each application and this led to increased delays and the overall backlog of cases at

---

33 *Chiver* IAT (10758), unreported until 1997 then sub nom *SSHD v Chiver* [1997] INLR 212.

missions with a knock-on effect of delay in an ultimate decision by the IAA. Given that the Home Office was in the habit of appealing many of the cases which they lost, there could be years between the original application and final clearance for a reunion.

The interpretative approach to the rules made by the Minister (the Statement of Changes) came to the fore early in the judgment of Lord Roskill that 'the immigration rules are not to be construed with all the strictness applicable to the construction of a statute or a statutory instrument'[34] nor do they enact a precise code.[35]

Issues of Culture and Country Conditions

It is impossible for all judges to be familiar with all cultures as well as all countries in a constantly changing world. Some adjudicators will be familiar with some either through having lived there, or because they come from that culture or country. But with those who spent time in Africa or on the Indian subcontinent during the colonial era or even after, that familiarity or that knowledge will be patchy or out of date. Some writings on the subject were regarded with respect, such as that by David Pearl (who was later to become Chief Adjudicator and then president of the IAT). Pearl, a professor and part-time adjudicator at the time, wrote in-depth and well-informed articles in which he examined the history of the families' (particularly Asian families) natural desire to be united.[36]

Zahir Chowdhury's report, 'Split Families' was written following an examination of the British immigration control system relating to dependants in Bangladesh in 1982.[37] Even today, his conclusions contain important messages for immigration judges. The criticism of a general lack of sociocultural background knowledge; a lack of confidence in the impartiality of the adjudicator,[38] and the need for more than one judge to hear cases which turned on facts were always in issue. However well-versed an outsider, the realities of life for the appellant in his

34 *Alexander v IAT* [1982] WLR 1076 at 1080G. as applied later.

35 *R v SSHD ex parte Bakhtar Singh* [1986] 1 WLR 910.

36 Pearl, D., 'English Family and the Immigrant Population: A New Challenge', in *Law in Context*, Vol 6:1 (1988), p. 50; Pearl, D. (1986), *Family Law and the Immigrant Communities* (Bristol: Jordan and Sons).

37 'The UK is a plural society … with a great diversity of immigrant communities, many of whom like to retain their own social, religious and cultural traits': Chowdhury, Z. (1982), *Split Families An Examination of the British Immigration Control System Relating to Dependants in Bangladesh* (London: UKIAS).

38 The criticism was not only of the adjudicator but the discriminatory manner in which the rules, for example, on family reunion, were administered both before and after the introduction of DNA testing: Ihenacho, J. (1991), 'The Effect of DNA Testing on Immigration Control Procedures: Case Studies of Bangladeshi Studies', Research Paper No. 16, Warwick University.

or her society are usually hidden from view, and there is bound to be some reliance on intuition: let it be informed intuition, if so.

A member of a local population in the Caribbean visited by two adjudicators commented to them that much of the immigration legislation was unfair. It was felt that, for example, in sole responsibility cases, the social and legal position of illegitimate children in the rules caused monstrous injustice. It seemed to baffle even the local social workers why children should be admitted to the UK, only if the parent had had sole responsibility for the child: it was, he said, as illogical as 'admitting the child on the size of his feet'.[39]

The new rules instated in 1980[40] allowed women who were born in the UK and were UK citizens, or with a UK-born parent, to join a husband or fiancé provided the couple intended to live together permanently and the marriage was not 'for immigration purposes'.[41] Fiancées did not need entry clearance; the male – husband or fiancé – always did.

The difficulty which the adjudicators had with this part of the rule was that, for perfectly sound reasons, the couple may have had to live apart for a long period after the spouse had arrived (because they could not afford to set up a home of their own in the UK), and this was seen by the Home Office as evidence of a lack of intention to live together permanently – an evidential problem.

Given the flawed system of age estimates and proof of relationships, the introduction of DNA testing[42] led to a lack of confidence in the system for too often it seemed that the IAA had got their decisions disastrously wrong and should have served as a timely warning, alongside Professor Jackson's decision in *Chiver*, and Sir Stephen Sedley's realism when he wrote, 'We plod on, judges and juries doing our best to discern the truth from the false.'[43]

The absence of formal training of any kind, let alone in instruction on appellants' cultures and/or any deep knowledge of the situation in any country, compounded this lack of confidence and frequently led to faulty conclusions, which had to be set aside and a fresh start made in the appeal. It is difficult to envisage a training programme which could possibly take in to any depth more than selected cultures, but it is not so much knowledge of the detail of a culture that is needed any more than one can be expected to have detailed knowledge about a country. What is necessary is an understanding of how these cultures can produce outcomes often beyond the decision-maker's comprehension. It is in this

39 Comment to George Farmer on his visit to the Caribbean, see Chapter 4, p. 120.

40 HC 394, replacing HC 169.

41 The intention to live together is now defined in HC 538 of 1 April 2003, so the ghost of Primary Purpose is still present at the feast. See also *Olofinusi v IAT* [2002] INLR 388.

42 See n. 41 above.

43 See Sedley, *Ashes and Sparks*, p. 218.

context that credibility must be understood.[44] In later years, when deciding on the very lives and safety of appellants in asylum appeals, there was often little comprehension of the situation which the appellant was trying to describe. In the search for a justifiable and transparently acceptable approach to the facts, there was a real danger of falling back on a scientific model, taking refuge in what Satvinder Juss calls the 'discrepancy approach'.[45]

The 'Primary Purpose' cases formed a predominant part of the lists in the 1980s. They were difficult cases and unpopular with the adjudicators. Notably in India, ECOs who were already sensitive to criticism by adjudicators felt it more in Primary Purpose appeals, where the ECOs felt there was a lack of understanding or appreciation by adjudicators of the difficulties they were facing; not to speak of the firm opinion that the adjudicators lacked the necessary knowledge of local conditions. Deciding a negative – that it was *not* the intention of the applicant in getting married to obtain entry into the UK – was difficult enough. The applicant himself or herself could not present to give evidence as to what their intention was and have it tested under cross-examination; it was on that testimony that the decision hung. It was perhaps as much in this type of appeal as any other that the decision-maker's fundamental approach to the rules played an important part. Were the rules 'facilitative' or were they' restrictive'? Were they there to define who could be admitted, or were they intended simply to keep people out? Lord Prosser in Scotland thought they were facilitative, that is, they were protecting and preserving the sponsor, a UK citizen, and allowing the ability to marry and live permanently with the man she wants, without being forced to leave the UK. This was not exactly the view taken by the Home Office – nor many adjudicators it seems, judging by the outcome of most appeals.[46]

A look at the debates in the House of Commons earlier in March 1984, which took place on the then proposed amendment to the rules, illustrates a bleak outlook for the immigrant, particularly in regard to any rights to family life: proposals which were considered by L. Kaufmann MP to have a 'devastating and oppressive' effect on family life.[47] Actually, these rules were intended to be seen as a liberalization method for wives and children.

As was noted in the last chapter in regard to the poverty line, the ability to maintain and accommodate the spouse had to be satisfied and assumed greater prominence when DNA testing appeared. But for now, the difficult task was

44 Credibility is dealt with elsewhere, but one of the most illuminating expositions of credibility in a cultural context is Kagan, M. (2009), 'Refugee Credibility Assessment and the "religious impostor" Problem', CMRS Working Paper 9 12/2009 <http://www.aucegypt.edu/GAPP/cmrs/Documents/KaganReligiousImposters.pdf>.

45 See Juss, *Discretion and Deviation in the Administration of Immigration Control*, p. 59.

46 *Mohd Safter v SS* [1992] Imm AR 513.

47 17 HC Deb 1 March 1984 V 55 cc 397-401. Followed into 5 March cc 659–708, where Jeremy Corbyn was just scathing, alleging that families are deliberately broken up.

intention; whose intention and how can it be demonstrated; what presumptions or assumptions were appropriate? The question was often put 'was it a genuine marriage or an immigration one'? However when put that way, the question was quite misleading. It is not surprising therefore that many adjudicators were unhappy about having to sit on such appeals as these. Certainly, there was force in the view that those with a family right of entry should not, on principle be subjected to the delay, cost, family separation and indignity which these rules brought and, furthermore, that it amounted to a denial of due process. This denial of due process rankled then, and perhaps still does, with the Asian community. Indeed, it will be recalled that the Wilson Report was opposed to any requirement for Commonwealth citizens to apply for entry clearance at all.

The discovery of DNA testing in 1985[48] allowed parties who so wished and could afford it, and the Home Office, to use this much more transparent and reliable method of determining relationships. Everyone fully expected see an end to appeals where relationships were in question; but they did not, at least to begin with, possibly because the Home Office then concentrated their efforts to show that there was inadequate support and/or maintenance. The figures are instructive: in 1985, before DNA testing, refusals ran at 50.2 per cent, but by 1989, they were down to 25.7 per cent. Unfortunately, it appears that there was selectivity in putting matters right later in cases where there had been clear errors in previous decisions.[49]

The doubts over the reliability of earlier pre-DNA testing decisions in primary purpose appeals also extended to doubts over decisions in tax fraud appeals. Perhaps this should have been a more penetrating lesson about any over-reliance on findings on an appellants' credibility.[50]

What was very surprising was the unwillingness of the Home Office to resort to the provisions of s. 21 of the Immigration Act 1971. This was inserted to allow the Home Office to refer a case to an adjudicator for an opinion. It was clearly designed for use when no appeal lay, or more precisely, when there had been an appeal which was dismissed but further facts came to light which justified reassessment – saving the expense and delay of forcing an appellant to apply all over again. This was exactly the position in *Uddin*; his claim to relationship and to join his family had been rejected twice, but DNA proved those decisions to have been wrong. The Home Office insisted that there should be a new application from abroad, which meant his going back to his country of origin and joining the end of

48 DNA fingerprinting was discovered by Dr (now Professor) Alec Jefferies in 1985; it was claimed to be the most precise means of establishing close relationships.

49 Jan Ihenacho's paper referred to in n. 38 above is interesting for the statistics and for some of the conclusions she draws from them relating to the implementation of UK immigration controls on family reunion – even in the eyes of a First Secretary appointed to the Dhaka Mission. She compares delays in Dhaka which can be months and years, with those in Eastern Europe of less than one week.

50 See Chapter 3.

a long queue – yet again. The Divisional Court was aware of this but still failed to recommend that a new application should be unnecessary.[51]

So far the types of appeal coming before the tribunal that have been examined have involved existing families. The formation of new families presented the next challenge. The approach of the Home Office to applications for new marriages differed according to whether it was the man or the woman who was in the UK and wanted to bring their future (or sometimes newly married) spouse, to live here. Added to this, some women were not always willing brides to the men chosen for them; or the new bride married abroad and became pregnant, or when the husband or wife arrived, the economics of establishing a home of their own prevented them from living together for long periods.

An example in this sort of category arose on judicial review before Mr Justice Henry in 1988. Ian Macdonald QC appeared for the applicant and David Pannick (now Lord Pannick) represented the Crown; nominally at least the Immigration Appeal Tribunal was the respondent (the other party) (as was the custom of the Treasury Solicitor's Department who would consult the President or Chief Adjudicator before conceding an appeal).[52]

The IAT had refused permission to appeal from the dismissal of an appeal from refusal of entry for the purpose of marriage by an adjudicator. When the case came before Mr Justice Henry, he applied the then recently enunciated principles laid down in *Hoque* and *Matwinder Singh*[53] and *Kumar*[54] (the case in which Lord Donaldson referred to evidence of behaviour which cast a 'flood of light' on intention) which drew attention to the dangers of compartmentalizing the various questions to be asked under the rules.

Mr Justice Henry was unhappy with the manner in which the adjudicator approached an assessment of the proposed spouse's credibility, and had described her behaviour as the 'whims of a girl of 17'. The judge thought capriciousness hardly described this girl's behaviour – a girl whom the adjudicator had already concluded was 'a young lady of very positive views'.

Kumar, *Hoque* and *Matwinder Singh* emphasized that the applicant had to prove a negative, that is to say, he or she must show that it was *not* the primary purpose of the marriage to obtain entry into the UK – but in carrying out this assessment, the immigration rules were not to be construed with all the strictness applicable to the construction of a statute or a statutory instrument.[55] One of the common facts which arose in these appeals was that the marriage was claimed to

51 *R v SSHD ex parte Uddin* Div Ct 1989.

52 In Scotland, Ian Harvie of the Solicitor's Office said 'I doubt if it would be competent for an adjudicator to be a party to the judicial proceedings since, as soon as their decision is made, they are *functus officio*': Memo to CA, 26 September 1991.

53 *R v IAT ex parte Hoque and Singh* CA [1988] 2 FLR 542.

54 *R v IAT ex parte Kumar* [1987] 1 FLR 444.

55 See Lord Roskill in *Alexander v IAT* [1982] WLR 1076 at 1080G; nor do they enact a precise code: *R v SSHD ex parte Bakhtar Singh* [1986] 1 WLR 910.

be a traditional marriage; if that was so, the adjudicator would ask, why was the man acceding to his intended bride's wishes to live in her country (when it was the UK) and not the other way round?

As with so many applications, they took so long in arriving on appeal before the tribunal that what had started out as a claim by a fiancé or fiancée had become a claim by a spouse, even a spouse with a child. Even when the parties had not married, the fact that the engagement had held up should be considered strong evidence that the couple were intending to live together as man and wife permanently. It was not enough simply to take any expressed intention by a fiancé that he wanted to live in the UK, at face value, it was the genuineness of the intentions which mattered and the adjudicator had to have regard to any fact that had occurred, even if it was *after* the decision by the Entry Clearance Officer. This was an exception to the cut-off date for the facts in non-asylum appeals.

Simon Brown J (as he then was) revisited the primary purpose case as late as 1987,[56] when Andrew Collins QC (as *he* then was) appeared for the Crown – and lost! The judge said:

> I am disposed to accept that in the light of *Kumar* entry clearance officers, and on appeal adjudicators, should not be astute to look for, and should not too readily find, that what they accept as a permanent marriage is nevertheless disqualified by reference to his [the husband's] motive.

Experienced practitioners and respected authors such as Ian Macdonald and Nicholas Blake[57] devoted considerable space and thought to this area. They posited the question: Why should a British woman who works in Bradford have to submit to the indignities of the primary purpose rule while one who has worked in Brussels does not? They urged practitioners to be astute in searching for an EC law solution to family reunion difficulties.

Applications by wives and children had largely given way by 1984 to applications by male fiancés and newly wedded husbands under the rather more liberal provisions then existing toward wives and dependent children.[58]

Mention has been made of the unwillingness of some women to be married to a man chosen *for* them rather than *by* them. This phenomenon is largely confined to traditional unions where the choice of the parties is made by the parents. Although such appeals are found mainly from the Indian subcontinent, there are child brides to be found in customary marriages in Africa, only they do not travel[59] and so do

56 *R v IAT ex parte Singh* [1986] WLR 910; 2 All ER 721.

57 Now Sir Nicholas Blake, a High Court judge and President of the Upper Tribunal of Immigration Appeals.

58 HC 395.

59 It is said that in Nigeria, for example, a child may be 'married' to a widow and would then live with the family until of marriageable age. But this is more an example of slavery and the 'marriage' could be of a female child – to the widow.

not figure in immigration appeals; interestingly, it was rare to find any case of a reluctant bride from Bangladesh.

It was in this situation that the phenomenon of the Reluctant Bride emerged. For both the Home Office and the tribunal, this presented difficulties. ECOs received a spate of 'confidential letters' from prospective brides complaining they were being forced into marriage. This was especially difficult for the tribunal, because it had to reconcile its role as an independent judicial arbiter when the decision maker had received evidence privately from a prospective bride who did not want to be married. If he disclosed this, it would put her at risk. If he did not, he could hardly put it out of his mind or tear up the letter.

Adjudicators solved this dilemma in a number of ways; that they had to find a solution became crucial with the news (though no one ever was able to establish whether this was true or false) that in one case the reluctant girl had been murdered.

Selected judges for selected cases, or selected courts for selected cases, puts a dangerous power in the hands of those who wield it. But it does happen and it happened in this tribunal in several areas at different times. In the case of reluctant brides, the author as Deputy Chief Adjudicator did try to direct appeals which were known to be sensitive in that way to adjudicators who had proved they could minimize the risks.

The topic was raised specifically at an adjudicator's conference in December 1984, following the suicides of two girls in Leeds who were being forced into marriage. The cases emerged due to the inquests being heard by an adjudicator, who was also a coroner. This debate was followed up in correspondence between the Chief Adjudicator and the Home Office over the next two years[60] and in the course of this exchange the Home Office admitted that it had been a problem which had been concerning them at their then headquarters at Lunar House in Croydon. This was not surprising in the light of a then recent report by a Commission to which the Home Affairs Minister gave evidence saying that 'the best that could be done was for the reluctant fiancées to persuade friends and others who would stand up for their rights outside immigration control.'[61]

The Regional Adjudicator at Manchester suggested that because we were unable to respect the confidentiality of any letter from the sponsor fiancée – at least officially – one way to work out a way round this, where the UKIAS and other representatives sympathetic to this approach were involved, was to hold a pre-hearing discussion of the appeal in an attempt to have the appeal withdrawn. This solution was not one which could be offered even semi-officially, since a representative was appearing for the appellant who was overseas and not for the sponsor who was (the bride) in the UK. If the appellant then wished to test the evidence, it could lead to fatal results to the bride.

60 See archival material.

61 C. 20 and article by Vallance-Webb, G. (2008), 'Family: Forcing the Issue', *Legal Week* (8 May). Online at www.legalweek.com (accessed 9 July 2009). See also Family Law Act 1996 c. 27 part 4 paras 63A and 63B.

Another somewhat intriguingly novel idea, which was proposed by an adjudicator, was that there should be a well-publicized prosecution of a relative for allegedly assaulting a young fiancée to force her into marriage against her will: likewise this did not appeal to the Home Office, being unlikely to have the desired – or any – effect.

The Forced Marriage (Civil Protection) Act 2007 was enacted to try to provide a solution. If theaccount of *Ranjit*'s case in *The Times* on the subject of forced marriages is anything to go by,[62] the judge, having accepted that the girl had been kidnapped, did not accept that the purpose was to force her into marriage and imposed a suspended prison sentence on the kidnapper. There are many examples of both forced marriage and honour killings but the recent conviction of the parents of Shafilea Ahmed illustrates that this danger remains in the UK.[63]

In other appeals, there was evidence of wife abuse, or the fiancée or wife was a minor. A wise adjudicator would try to hold a pre-hearing meeting to which the appropriate welfare authorities would be invited to attend – hopefully by the Home Office. Unfortunately, this approach received no cooperation from the Home Office, which refused the request, arguing that it was not part of its duty to call in welfare officers, and anyway, it would be a breach of the law so to act (though which law was never said). Another suggestion, that the Home Office should interview all fiancées separately and individually, was also rejected as too expensive – given that there had been 2,500 such applications in 1985 this was perhaps not surprising.

But these examples give some idea of the challenges a tribunal faces in trying to get at the truth and being hampered by an overly judicial mantle and, later, strict time limits. This forms part of one of the threads which the judiciary themselves could address.

The Home Office spoke out over the common practice in India of advertising for a bride (often for a light-skinned one). It would seem that it impacted on their policy concerning entry into the UK for fiancées, but when there was a protest by the Asian community who saw it as disastrous for innocent female victims, the Home Office admitted it was powerless to stamp out the practice of advertising for a bride, which of itself was of course perfectly lawful.

Following investigations by some newspapers, a story ran on immigrants seeking brides to skirt the Law. It was said that a journalist, posing as the brother of an eligible girl, met a man who had advertised for a bride in the *Daily Jang* and was at the time on a visit to the UK. The man is alleged to have told the reporter

62 See *The Times*, G. Langdon-Down, 12 June 2008, p. 59. Online at <http://www.thetimes.co.uk/tto/law/article2211347.ece.> (accessed on 5 July 2013).

63 Iftikar and Farzana Ahmed, strict Muslims who are first cousins from the same village in Pakistan, were jailed for life after being found guilty of the 2003 honour-killing of their 'determined' and 'ambitious' daughter, Shafilea. They were told they would serve at least 25 years. *The Telegraph*, 3 August 2012. Online at <http://www.telegraph.co.uk/news/uknews/law-and-order/9449374/> (accessed on 27 June 2013).

that he wanted to stay in Britain and was looking for a girl with a British passport who would marry him, so he could stay.[64]

Adoption, particularly of children from India or Pakistan, led to very difficult cases. First, the procedure of adoption is protracted, as is obtaining the necessary entry clearance. For a long time, there was the added problem that adoption was not a legal concept known to that part of the world and it was normal for children to join relatives' families to be brought up by them without any formal transfer of authority.[65]

Ingenuity to overcome barriers to the movement of people knows no limit. The desire to study abroad is common and, looked at from their own society's attitudes, understandable. Largely because there was no cooperation between the Home Office and the British Council in most parts of the world,[66] there was a loophole for bogus colleges to appear in the UK. Examples of these bogus colleges to get people into the country came to the fore between 1982 and 1988. Schools such as the London School of International Business (the LSIB) which opened in 1982, and the Academic College at New Cross which opened in 1984, were, effectively a front for this scam to obtain student visas. In all, the 'colleges attracted 250,000 students; again more than either the Home Office or the appellate authority could cope with.

There were hundreds (perhaps thousands) of appeals arising out of such colleges. In the case of the LSIB, the school's principal pleaded guilty to conspiracy to defraud. The Crown Court, for the purpose of sentence, accepted that LSIB was a genuine educational institution, a conclusion which the Immigration Appeals Tribunal did not regard as binding and held otherwise.

The Times received complaints from the ACE (another college) accusing them of 'gutter press reporting' and threatening proceedings if they published; they did publish with the headlines in the *Sunday Times* for 20 March 1988 'Bogus visa colleges open floodgates' – no action was ever taken.

Eleven years later, the fraud and floodgate theme reappeared in the press, with the appearance of headlines such as 'College faked record to fool immigration', and 'Immigration bodies are fooled as Pakistani-run colleges hide over 1,000 students on its register'.

The conclusion to be reached from this failure to prevent education and student scams on such a scale again must surely be that there is no inherited memory in the Home Office. One of the useful items of information to emerge from the adjudicators' 'Grand Tours' on how to avoid just this sort of debacle was also ignored. In Thailand, the British Embassy, the British Council, the Central Bank of Thailand and the Thai ministry responsible for study abroad devised a scheme to

---

64 Scam. See *Daily Mail* <http://www.dailymail.co.uk/news/article-2260822/Solicitors-ran-immigration-scam-arranging-thousands-sham-marriages-submitting-to> (accessed on 17 July 2013).

65 *R v SSHD ex parte Kahn* 1985; *R v IAT ex parte Tohur Ali* 1987.

66 Except Thailand, see Chapter 4.

ensure that only genuine students came to recognized UK colleges and then would return to Thailand. All colleges receiving overseas students in the UK were vetted and approved by the British Council, while family guarantees with a substantial deposit were taken in Thailand to ensure return. The scheme worked.

Appeals from decisions to deport an immigrant were also frequent, and perhaps too frequently allowed by adjudicators because, in 1988, the Immigration Act 1971 was amended for the first time,[67] which drastically curtailed the right to appeal against a decision to make an order to deport an immigrant.. Thenceforth the only two possibilities for a successful appeal were if the Home Office targeted the wrong person, or the issue involved asylum. The power to deport someone as an administrative act, however long he or she had been in the country, and even though he or she could not be prosecuted, had already been given under the 1971 Act. Thus the Minister in effect acquired draconian powers, which clearly was open to grave abuse, even if, thus far, those powers have never been used. This restriction on the right to appeal made such a weapon even more potent, when even children, who themselves could not otherwise be deported, ceased to have any protection.[68] It is necessary to remember that Lord Roskill said that such rules are not to be construed strictly.[69]

The Immigration Appeals (Amendment) Act 1988 therefore became another attack on the principle of family reunion by requiring evidence that there could be no reunion unless it was shown that family members would not become a 'charge on the rates'.[70]

Asylum Appeals

Chapter 1 took an initial look at refugees and the introduction of a discrete right of appeal was mentioned earlier in this chapter. Although there had a form of statutory appeal from refusal by the minister of a claim to asylum under the Aliens Act 1905, that had disappeared by 1920[71] and only re-introduced in 1993.[72] The mention of a right to make a claim under the Refugee Convention in Rule 58 of

67 Immigration Appeals (Amendment) Act 1988 c. 14.

68 S. 3(5) Immigration Act 1971.

69 Above n. 55.

70 HC 395 made under s. 3(2) of the Immigration Act 1971. Updated in June 2008 (HC 607). Pearl, D. (1988), 'English Family and the Immigrant Population: A New Challenge', in *Law in Context*, Vol 6:1, pp. 50*ff*; Pearl, D. (1986), *Family Law and the Immigrant Communities* (Bristol: Jordan and Sons).

71 Aliens Restriction (Amendment) Act 1919 c.92

72 By the Immigration and Asylum Act 1993 c. 23. Hitherto, there was no in-country appeal for anyone illegally in the UK and since most asylum-seekers were here illegally there was thus no effective appeal.

the Immigration Rules 1973 (and policies within the Home Office itself)[73] was the full extent of any formal protection.

None the less, the issue of asylum did arise very early and the first recorded appeal with any asylum content was in 1972. Between that year and 1992, there were 59 asylum appeals reported in the Immigration Appeals Reports, compared with 292 in the next decade. In 1988, out of 6,262 appeals in total, the few which involved refugee issues were heard by an adjudicator drawn from an informal panel of only three adjudicators.

Adjudicators were instinctively aware of the added risks to an appellant whose appeal involved any suggestion of persecution, and they tried to reach a decision which might afford some protection from removal. However, it was not until cases such as *Sivakumaran*[74] reached the House of Lords that the need for an entirely different approach to evidence and standard of proof came to be recognized. We should have been more aware than perhaps we were, as this quotation reminds us: 'Contemporary reflection about refugees begins in the shadow of the Holocaust. In discussing the topic of refugees, we should remember one fundamental truth: Jews fleeing Hitler deserved protection, and most of them did not get it.'[75]

The length of time which the claims were taking to be processed by the Home Office in the first instance alone usually meant that the facts could have changed from those which existed when the application was first made or decided by the Home Office. Unless the decision made at each stage reflected the facts as they existed, then the whole purpose of the Refugee Convention (to protect the person from return to persecution) would be thwarted.

Many of the issues which now form part of the jurisprudence in immigration were yet to appear, usually arising out of asylum and human rights appeals; for example, the point in the previous paragraph at what date the facts were to be assessed. Questions had to be answered concerning such issues as the 'standard of proof', the reception and evaluation of the evidence, the shared burden with the Secretary of State for the Home Department (theoretically, at least) of establishing the facts and, more fundamentally, the place of the tribunal in the decision-making process as it moved from Home Office to adjudicator, on to the IAT and then to the Court of Appeal and even the judicial arm of the House of Lords (the Supreme Court, as it is called now), all of which are addressed in later pages.

The Home Affairs correspondent on a newspaper acquired a copy of the Chief Adjudicator's directions issued in 1988 to adjudicators to 'take steps to be able to cope with the numbers of appeals which were overwhelming them'. The directions contained a request to adjudicators to streamline all appeals by making short, pro forma determination in appeals which were palpably devoid of merit. The

73 Public Record Office HO/45/14674.

74 *Sivakumaran v SSHD* [1988] AC 958.

75 Carens, J.H. (forthcoming), *The Dispossessed: Responsibilities for Refugees*, Chapter 9.

report continued by quoting the retort allegedly made by one adjudicator that 'any attempt to tell a judge how to do his job is quite off-limits'[76]

Home Office to Lord Chancellor's Department – More Developments

Mr Heath's confidence, in 1978, that the 1971 Act was all that was necessary to cope with immigration proved too optimistic a view for his successors to adopt, as they viewed migration patterns ten years later. A start was made by removing the right of appeal for short-term visitors and restricting the right to appeal from a decision to deport an immigrant.[77]

The increase in the movement of refugees which brought more immigrants to continental Europe and the UK, and who claimed asylum either on arrival or later, caused a shift in policy, in 1993,[78] to grant a definitive right of appeal to any claimant refused refugee status.

The Transfer to the LCD

The year 1988 was significant for more than just the removal of some rights of appeal from decisions to make deportation orders. Twenty years earlier, the Wilson Report had concluded that the only tier of the appellate system which needed to be put within the LCD was the upper tier, the IAT. The accepted thinking in the LCD had now changed and it was thought that the IAA as a whole should be made the responsibility of the LCD, and no longer the Home Office.[79] This would rationalize administrative arrangements and make more constitutional sense, since the attachment of tribunals to the ministry whose appeals they dealt with removed that semblance of independence now viewed to be desirable.[80] The practical advantages of a tribunal being staffed, financed and administered by such an attachment was outweighed by the concern that exercise of independent judicial functions by the tribunal was inconsistent with being in the same ministry which was one of the parties to any dispute before it.

This transfer was welcomed by the adjudicators, because it enhanced their status and they could look forward to better pay, pensions, career structure and conditions and ultimately, perhaps, the title of 'judge'. The pay at the time was

76 Michael Kerr, Home Affairs Correspondent, *The Times*, 'Immigration pleas should be cut short, judges told'.

77 Immigration Appeals (Amendment) Act 1988.

78 Asylum and Immigration Appeals Act 1993 c. 23.

79 The Transfer of Functions Order in Council, 1 April 1987, announced in Parliament, 12 March 1987.

80 Examples of this can be found in both employment and welfare appeals: the Employment Appeal Tribunal and the Social Security and Medical Appeals Tribunal.

considered too low to attract suitable (part-time) candidates. Part-time adjudicators were paid £104 a day;[81] the Immigration Appeals Tribunal lay members received £67 a day and legal chairmen (who were also part-time) £130 a day. The bulk of the appeals were dealt with by the part-time judiciary, both adjudicators and in the IAT.

The LCD was now to take on a body which operated in important different ways from the courts for which it was responsible. The tribunal differed from other civil law administrative tribunals in that every appeal was closely concerned with the liberty of the subject, bail, asylum, deportation and issues affecting the future of whole families. Rules needed to be tailor-made to ensure a transparency and a balance between fairness and efficiency: there were still only very few full-time adjudicators and only two (full-time) vice presidents in the IAT but the number of caseloads was growing rapidly.

Pure mechanics seems to have given rise to much of the tension which accompanied this changeover between the Immigration Appellate Authority[82] and the Lord Chancellor's Department (LCD) both in the period leading up to, and following the changeover. Those 'mechanics' were significant in that they often underpinned a struggle for control over matters which the judiciary saw to be central to its independence and the LCD saw the loss of which were a threat to their financial autonomy.

Meetings preparatory to the changeover began to take place between the Chief Adjudicator and the LCD in 1986. These meetings addressed the needs of each party in preparation for a smooth handover. Estimates were made of the anticipated additional resources required if, as was already being considered, a right of appeal was to be extended to asylum-seekers who had been recommended for deportation by the courts. The nature of those resources also occupied a great deal of time in these meetings.

The Permanent Secretary of the Home Office at the time of the transfer (and indeed at the time of the closures of the South Coast hearing centres) was Sir Hayden Phillips (later to become Permanent Secretary to the LCD,[83] when Lord Irvine became Lord Chancellor). One would have expected that his experience in that department, which had been responsible for the adjudicator tier of the IAA for nearly 20 years, would have of itself made for a smooth and seamless transition.

The administrative staff were of course supplied to the IAA by the Home Office and few of them saw a future for them if they remained with the IAA under

81 Letters to *The Times* from Judge Timothy Lawrence, Patrick Medd and the author urged a pay structure consistent with their responsibilities and the fact that many were also recorders, deputy circuit judges and coroners acting as adjudicators Correspondence 13 and 24 August, and 4 September 1992

82 The IAA became the AIT by the Asylum and Immigration (Treatment of Claimants) Act 2004 c. 19.

83 Michael Huebner as the deputy was passed over. This disappointed some adjudicators, since he had spearheaded the concept of a combined or unified tribunal service which would offer greater promotion opportunities.

the LCD. As a result, all but 78 left. Those 78 had to manage all the appeals in the UK[84] in the crucial period following the changeover. The gaps at all levels of administrative officers with experience in the workings of a tribunal created by this wholesale exodus were not easily filled. The LCD had no staff with any judicial experience in tribunals, only in the courts, and they had little or no idea of the different requirements of a tribunal, let alone a specialized one such as immigration. The senior members of the administrative staff appeared to find it especially difficult to adjust and the attitudes they brought to many cases seemed to the judiciary to keep an arrogant hold on ideas which were felt inappropriate in the tribunal; this led to tensions and frustrations on all sides.

The tribunal had to cope with records that rarely gave the judges what they wanted, letters going astray, files being taken apart and reassembled out of chronological order, with matters of record mixed up with administrative memoranda. A common cause of adjournments was due to missing files; on one particularly disastrous occasion, the author took on a search himself and, upon opening a cupboard, a mass of 'missing' files fell out. There was a more serious consequence of the failure to keep proper records, in the case of appeals allocated to adjudicators to determine without a hearing ('paper cases'). A part-time adjudicator had made claims for fees for determinations he said he had written but had not. Eventually his house was searched and about 400 files were found hidden, behind radiators! The adjudicator was convicted and sentenced to a term of imprisonment, but the mystery remains of how this could have happened.

Procedures for new asylum types of hearing had to be designed, and accurate forecasts made both for numbers of expected appeals and what sort they were, and then how long a hearing of each one might take. Mrs Pat Dews, the administrative manager at Hatton Cross, estimated that although there would be an increase in asylum appeals to 30,000 in 1994–97 (due in part to a backlog of 50,000 in the Home Office),[85] the removal of visit visa appeals and changes in Primary Purpose rules would reduce the overall total by about 6,000–8,000 appeals. This could take a year to have any effect – a visit appeal occupied a very short hearing if any at all, whilst one asylum appeal could take a day or more.

Of course, these increases would require more adjudicators. Based on an estimated disposal rate of 2.5 cases per day,[86] and a split of 50/50 part-time to full-time adjudicators, an additional 30 full-time and 117 part-time adjudicators would be required . The recruitment times the LCD needed could be up to 6–9 months between a decision being taken and an appointment made. Once appointed, they had to be trained, supplied with books and sets of reports. More hearing rooms were needed: Thanet House was already using former storage rooms and the basement.

84 David Hunt joined the IAA in 1970, and remained there until he died 25 years later.

85 In October 1993, at a meeting in Thanet House at which I was present, the Home Office estimated the numbers of appeals would be 10,000 per year.

86 The then Chief Adjudicator aimed at three appeals a day. The next Chief Adjudicator David Pearl was less optimistic and settled for 2.7 appeals each day.

The pressure on representatives for appellants and the Home Office meant that there were insufficient presenting officers (HOPOs) for the Home Office to staff all centres, and UKIAS,[87] which then represented around 40 per cent of appellants at all centres, was also short staffed, which delayed hearing of the appeals in which they were consulted.

The judiciary had been used to a very hands-off approach by the Home Office, where the relationship between the two was cordial yet professional – very similar to that which obtains today in other countries such as Denmark, Belgium, Sweden and the Netherlands, but the impression given to the judiciary was, rightly or wrongly, that the LCD wanted its hands on everything which it considered to be part of its administration, whether they understood the problems or not. Some of the difficulties have been mentioned and they had consequences for listing, courtroom usage, demands for interpreters and even the administration keeping personal records of the judiciary on their adjournment records. If the judiciary asked for a facility, such as recording devices, they may have been promised but rarely supplied.

The friction with the administration therefore arose essentially in defining the boundaries to administrative and judicial preserves, who was to be in charge of listing the cases, and the resources which the judiciary needed but which the administration did not supply. Sometimes the absence of funds was used as a reason, as in the case of adequate indexing and retrieving of cases and the ability to link types of appeal; at other times, it may simply have been foot dragging, such as the example cited of the lack of recording devices.[88]

The tension reached its zenith with the Mott Fisher Report, whose proposals predominantly concerned saving costs by the tribunal through peripheral and non-priority matters such as the abolition of full-time interpreters and personal secretaries (of which there were really only two). There was a petty attempt to interfere with the Callender Book of Precedents – which was the only case book of reference for adjudicators and had been produced by an adjudicator in his own time at a very small cost. That was accompanied by an unjustified accusation that part-timers were claiming fees to which they were not entitled.[89]

There was one positive suggestion: the creation of a Registrar's post with judicial duties. This would have proved a major asset, but unfortunately the post was to be under the control of the administration and as such was unacceptable to the Chief Adjudicator.

---

87 The UKIAS was split into the Immigration Advisory Service and the Refugee Legal Centre (now Refugee and Migrant Justice).

88 On one occasion, a senior member of the Court Circuit Administration insisted to the CA that the DCA be reprimanded because he had asked that a member of the administrative be disciplined for action affecting the judiciary.

89 One part-time adjudicator who had been a town clerk rarely claimed anyway, considering that it was his civic responsibility.

The Court Service Business Plan for 1988–89 assured the judiciary that it would be consulted in preparing plans before submission to the Lord Chancellor for approval but Mark Patey (then Chief Adjudicator) felt that the priorities of the administration would always win the day. Strategic Task 2 of the Commitments section of Plan included 'reviewing listing practice in association with the Tribunal judiciary to achieve longer sitting days and higher disposal rates'. It was because George Farmer anticipated what he saw as administrative interference like this that he kept such a tight control over listing, and the judiciary has always seen this as essentially within its own preserve.

Notwithstanding the grave concerns the Chief Adjudicator had over some aspects of resources provided by the LCD, he paid tribute at a regional conference in Leeds in 1991 to the Tribunals and Courts Administrator Peter Risk in 1990 who had brought additional resources and enabled a permanently staffed hearing centre in Glasgow.

The same plan contained other aims such as 92 per cent courtroom utilization and the disposal of at least three asylum appeals a day. The aims may have been laudable, but there had been no consultation with the judiciary whose task it was to achieve those aims. The Business Plan went on to identify delay and lack of control as two major and inherent problems, that is, delay in processing appeals, and the inability to monitor and control the progress of appeals in an effective manner. Very little of such comments were matters which the judiciary could do much about by themselves, except to keep to a minimum the length of their determinations and to produce them quickly.

A very sensible commitment under the Business Plan was that the IAT should sit in Birmingham and Leeds as well as London, but George Farmer opposed this, even, it was said, declining an offer by the Lord President in Scotland (Lord Hope) of a venue within the High Court of Judiciary in Edinburgh. It was not until David Pearl became president after George Farmer retired that the IAT started to sit in Scotland – but in Glasgow. The IAT also started sittings in Birmingham and Leeds.

The Business Plan was followed by other plans, all of which had optimism built into their titles (though rarely achieved in their application), for example, 'Invest to Save' in 1995 and 'Fairer and Faster' in 2004. The IAT had internal discussions over their concern about another plan – 'Quality amidst a Rising Tide', which arose out of a Consultant's Report in October 2002. The Chief Adjudicator's view of the Report was that it lacked any explanation of why more judges would help achieve the agreed 17-week target for a decision; nor did it address the length of sitting days, which had been on the agenda since the 1980s, nor even the thorny subject of remittals from the tribunal to the adjudicators, which were then running at 4,000 a year.

The output of the tribunal did continue to increase significantly, but judging from the numbers of remittals which had to be reheard, a sort of internal merry-go-round had been created. Raymond Maddison remarked[90] that if he were to be strict

90 In a conversation with the author.

on every application for leave to appeal, he would have to grant leave in 90 per cent of them. The number of successful applications was still large enough over many years to cause concern in many quarters.

The remittal of appeals for a further hearing after an appeal to the IAT naturally increased caseloads, which in turn affected overall throughput of finished cases: to counteract this, the government resorted to legislation to cure the problem whereas what was necessary was an improvement in the quality of the Home Office decision, more effective training for the judiciary and more consistency in representation especially from the Home Office. In 2003, the Legal and Research Unit sampled remittals and found 21 per cent were based on allegations of failure to make proper findings of fact or giving inadequate reasons, 22 per cent where it was alleged there had been a failure to take relevant evidence into account, and finally 15 per cent were cases which fell under the right to family life,[91] protected under Article 8 ECHR.[92]

The case management by the tribunal was in the hands of legislation, both primary and subordinate, which changed every two years or so, from 1988 onwards.[93] Apart from diluting its power to deal with certain categories of cases, time constraints were made increasingly stringent upon the judiciary, but never on the Home Office.[94] Other legislation affected the judiciary more indirectly in asylum appeals, by restricting claimants' rights to welfare, housing benefits and later legal aid.

The Home Office files relating to an application were of course never passed on to the tribunal and information upon which it relied was not always disclosed. This is the major effect in an adversarial system – in contrast to Belgium, for example. This issue arose in relation to the category of asylum appeal first created under the 1993 Act, which denied a substantive appeal to any asylum-seeker whose case was

91 The reliance on this Article, particularly by those who have been convicted of a serious criminal offence, has figured prominently; see Barrett, D. (16 June 2012), 'Judges who allow foreign criminals to stay in Britain', *Daily Telegraph* <http://www.telegraph.co.uk/news/uknews/immigration/9335689/Judges-who-allow-foreign-criminals-to-stay-in-Britain.html>.

92 'Article 8 – Right to respect for private and family life 1. Everyone has the right to respect for his private and family life, his home and his correspondence. There shall be no interference by a public authority with the exercise of this right except such as is in accordance with the law and is necessary in a democratic society in the interests of national security, public safety or the economic well-being of the country, for the prevention of disorder or crime, for the protection of health or morals, or for the protection of the rights and freedoms of others.'

93 The Immigration Appeals Act 1988 c. 14. This was the first of a continuous line of new primary legislation apart from the subsidiary legislation which dealt with every aspect of practice, procedure, welfare.

94 The Home Office consistently removed less than 20 per cent of unsuccessful appellants, and even less according to the Countess of Mar, 14 December 2006 <http://www.publications.parliament.uk/> col. 1688 et seq.

certified as 'manifestly without foundation', for example, when the claimant had last been in an EU country and could be sent back there.[95]

In theory, attachment to the LCD should have given greater independence and stature to the IAT. In practice, the procedure rules as well as some of the substantive legislation increasingly restricted the judges in the discharge of a judicial role; fairness and quality gave way to efficiency and quantity, and there was more interference in the day-to-day life of the judiciary, who had no say, let alone control, over their support staff, who from time to time encroached on the periphery of the judge's preserves.

The complexity and ever-increasing amount of appeals and pressure to decide them quickly was obvious and so was the need for more resources, which included computerization. In 1995, consultants were appointed by the LCD, which came up with a figure of £874,000.[96] Notwithstanding this, little or no notice was taken of the judiciary's needs either for hardware or supporting data of a kind which could help the decision maker, rather than just the administration.[97] What was not, it seemed so obvious, was the *type* of additional resources needed to handle the issues facing the tribunal; which could only be addressed effectively if there was cooperation between the LCD and the tribunal. More adjudicators, particularly part-time ones, were needed and were appointed, but they had little experience of handling immigration appeals, little training and came from backgrounds devoid of advocacy experience.

The appointment of Professor David Pearl, a Circuit Court judge, as the next Chief Adjudicator, was a step in the right direction to give the tribunal a higher profile to match the importance of its role. The next step would be to appoint a High Court Judge as president. The author had indeed suggested this to Mr Holmes in the LCD in 1996, but clearly the suggestion was premature, as the response was 'such a step is not now contemplated.' The intentions then and later, when the appointment was made, were to encourage greater uniformity in the law and supply clear leadership to adjudicators. Optimistically, also it might give the tribunal's decisions added weight, both nationally and internationally.

None the less, bringing in an outsider as Chief Adjudicator upset the adjudicators to such an extent that most of them signed a letter of protest to the Lord Chancellor Lord Mackay, pointing out the provisions of the Immigration Act 1971, which required that the Chief Adjudicator be appointed from among the adjudicators. Ironically, it was to the author of this book, merely one of many signatories, to whom the Lord Chancellor addressed his reply, stating that 'I will appoint whomsoever I like', which he did, by making David Pearl, then a part-time adjudicator, a Circuit Judge before appointing him as Chief Adjudicator.

95 *Abdi & Anor, R (on the application of) v Secretary of State for the Home Department & Anor* [1996] Imm AR 46 HL. See Chapter 2.

96 The consultants' fees were £41,600.

97 See Report 6.1.95 and Memo DCA to CA 29.7.95.

The most serious gap in the resources was the absence of any training budget, which the LCD consistently neglected to fill; it was only when chairman of the Tribunals Section of the Judicial Studies Board, Judge Machin, leant on the LCD and a threat was made to complain to the Lord Chancellor, when he came to open the new hearing centre at Hatton Cross; funds were then made available for a three-day Training Programme at Warwick University.

Growth – Globalization

Professor Anthony Richmond sums up the implications of globalization admirably as follows:

> Globalization is not a new process. It is an acceleration of changes induced by the post-industrial revolution in transport and communication. The rapid growth of population in less developed countries combines with a reduction in barriers to migration from formerly authoritarian regimes to induce mobility. Economic inequality combines with demographic pressures and environmental crises to generate ethnic conflict and terrorist threats. Wealthier countries are placing restrictions on the admission of those seeking to improve their economic prospects and/or to escape persecution. Despite the number of asylum seekers in Europe and North America, African and Asian countries bear the greatest burden of refugees. Temporary migration, business travel and tourism have added to the numbers crossing state boundaries, making effective control difficult.[98]

Such implications for both the immigrant and the refugee have accelerated, as increasing populations of the less wealthy countries have been accompanied by a lowering in standards of living and tyrannous regimes, and the ease of transport to the wealthier nations, all factors which have led to increased restriction on migration and ultimately to attempts by the wealthier countries to renege on the protections for refugees contained in the 1951 Refugee Convention.

By 1988, asylum appeals were running at the rate of 35,000 a year. There was little increase by the year 2000 but, taking a quick glance ahead, in 2002 the backlog of appeals stood at 84,148. In 1991, the Foreign and Commonwealth Office made a contribution to information concerning numbers and origins of immigrants.[99] First of all, its opinion was that there would be 17,000 non-asylum appeals (not applications, which could be very different when an application covered a whole family), and that this figure could increase by 1,000 every year. The reason they gave for these startling figures was that most would be coming from China.

---

98 Richmond, A. (2002), 'Globalization; Implications for Immigrants and Refugees', *Ethnic and Racial Studies* 25.5: 707–27.

99 A letter dated 25 July 1991 enclosed a league table (in archives).

Additions to the list of countries requiring a visa to enter the UK contributed to the increase in numbers of appeals. None the less, the tribunal still managed a 50 per cent increase in productivity, but the backlog also still continued to increase, leading the Chief Adjudicator to write to the Lord Chancellor's Department, with a request for a supplemental budget of £20,000: 'I regret I must inform you that the Immigration Appellate Authority at Adjudicator level has now been placed in the position that it is unable to discharge its statutory function.'[100]

Backlogs, however, can be deceptive, especially when the bulk of them consists of short visitor and 'paper' appeals.[101] In such a case, the tribunal worked on the basis that a backlog of around 6,000 ensured that there always were enough appeals available to list to keep the hearing rooms in use (if not fully so) and everybody busy. If and when there was a blitz, it could if necessary, in theory at least, be reduced almost to zero in a matter of weeks.[102]

In 1988, the majority of applications were granted by the Home Office; however, the numbers of applications for asylum on the Continent signalled many applications could be expected in the UK in the future. The absence of any stand-alone right of appeal seemed to preclude large numbers of appeals in the UK but created a flood of applications for review by the courts, that is, judicial review. There was no immediate need to increase numbers of adjudicators. However, applications for asylum did increase to 2,000 in 1990, and by autumn 1991 had almost doubled; appeals were being received at a rate of around 60–80 each month.[103] A combination of *Vilvarajah*, then before the European Court of Human Rights (ECtHR),[104] and the increasing global movement of people forced the government to respond.

To set the decision of the ECtHR in *Vilvarajah* in context, we need to go back to *Sivakumaran*, the case of the five Tamil asylum-seekers, referred to in Chapter 1, whose applications to stay in the UK were rejected by the Home Office, who branded them cheats and liars. The House of Lords rejected their applications and they returned to Sri Lanka where, so the evidence went, at least two of them were beaten by soldiers. Their solicitors travelled to Sri Lanka and obtained evidence of their mistreatment and lodged an appeal with the IAA on behalf of two of the five that their removal had been in breach of the Refugee Convention. The Home Office brought no evidence in rebuttal and their appeals were successful before

100 Letter from CA to Permanent Secretary LCD 15 January 1990 (archival material).

101 This was the term given to appeals in which there had been no request for an oral hearing and the adjudicator made the decision on the basis of whatever papers there were in the file before him. This meant there was no courtroom use.

102 The Immigration Appeal Reports (Green Books) show only 13 reported cases involving asylum.

103 Estimates from different sources for future appeals as well as HO backlogs. One estimate by the HO was 350 decisions a month in May 1993 when hitherto it had managed no more than 167: Memo and office note, 5 April and 4 May 1993.

104 *Vilvarajah and others v UK* (1991) 14 EHRR 248.

an adjudicator who ordered the Secretary of State for the Home Department, Mr Hurd, to bring them back to the UK. The Home Office appealed and lost again and subsequently issued visas.[105]

The IAA's decision in *Sivakumaran*[106] was part of the process which led to the introduction of the right to appeal, but it was due mainly to the anticipation by the government that the appeal to the ECtHR in *Vilvarajah*[107] would decide that the UK was in breach of its obligations under the 1951 Refugee Convention by the absence of an appeal. To its surprise but too late to change course, the ECtHR decided, by a majority, that the remedy of judicial review satisfied the requirements of the 1951 Convention.

The response was, ultimately, the Asylum and Immigration Act 1993,[108] the most important section (2) being uncharacteristically brief: 'Nothing in the Immigration Rules (within the meaning of the Immigration Act 1971) shall lay down any practice which would be contrary to the [1951 Geneva] Convention.'

The earlier, much more detailed, Bill required the leave of an adjudicator for, broadly, all asylum-law appeals to the IAT and any appeal to the IAT (also with permission) was to be only on a material question of law.[109]

On 2 January 1991, the *Daily Telegraph* published an article by Maurice Weaver, 'After the Frontiers Fall', in which he argued in favour of firm immigration controls to stem the threat to western European stability and prosperity resulting from the freedom of movement within (an expanded) Europe. He called the signatories to Schengen 'the Schengen guinea-pigs'!' Weaver saw this as the new threat overtaking the military menace of former times which he thought (somewhat misguidedly) had by now receded. He asked the question 'Can the EC combine immigration policy with its proposals for free movement?', followed by another question which was to return to haunt the government of the day: 'How are we to sieve out terrorists if we have no checks at all?' Weaver also pointed to European countries, which he seemed to think justified his opining 'Britain stands alone.' What seemed obvious to him, and to many others[110] at the time, was that an expanded EU would mean a large increase in (economic?) migrants.

Such influences are illustrated by two articles about refugees in the *Evening Standard* on 17 September 1988. The first, on the front page, carried the bold headline 'Refugee Crime Wave in London', and the second one warned of the 'Imminent danger of collapse of the system'. The 'crimes' referred to were begging

---

105 See n. 15 above.

106 *Sivakumaran v SSHD* [1998] AC 958.

107 *Vilvarajah v UK* 1991 EHRR 248.

108 c. 23.

109 This earlier Bill printed 1 November 1991 50/5, fell through lack of Parliamentary time.

110 Matthew Parris, for example, could not resist even recently either: 'We must harden our hearts and our borders', he wrote in *The Times*, 10 July 2010, Comment p. 21. <http://www.thetimes.co.uk/tto/opinion/columnists/matthewparris/article2637836.ece>.

and pickpocketing; a photo of one 'persistent' Romanian beggar on page 6 seems to suggest the culprits were Romanians (presumably Romany), but what 'system' it was that the paper thought was about to collapse is not clear.

One would have expected that most claims for asylum would be made immediately upon an asylum-seeker's arrival in the country. Only when there is no in-country right of appeal (the only remedy being Judicial Review) would a claim be made later. With the introduction of a right of appeal in 1993, that was no longer necessary.

The Home Office announced that they had 40,000 applications sitting in its office,[111] with 150 new applications arriving every week and that it granted refugee status to 25 per cent of applicants, Exceptional Leave to Remain (ELR) to 45 per cent,[112] and the rest were refused altogether. Since the majority of outright refusals and large numbers of ELRs led to appeals, the backlog alone should have produced 30,000 appeals.

Current receipts on the same basis should have produced a further 37 appeals a week for the IAA to deal with. What made any predictions so difficult was that no one knew where the next large batch might come from. An outbreak of violence in the Middle East? A coup in Nigeria? But the problem seemed to lie with the Home Office allowing a backlog of cases which kept on rising (and falling). A worst-case scenario estimate in 1996 was that the IAA backlog alone could reach 100,000 by the turn of the century, if effective steps were not taken soon. These measures were not taken until 2002, when the backlog reached 107,174.[113]

Plans were made to cope with an estimated flow of 30,000 appeals each year up to 1998, and then fall back to 23–25,000 in each following year. The numbers of refugees entering continental Europe certainly seemed large and must have created some sense of panic, but a closer look at those large numbers reveals that about 325,000 people came from East Germany at the fall of the Berlin Wall and, so far as West Germany was concerned, these people were Germans, not refugees (as West Germany had never recognized the division of the Fatherland into East and West). They were regarded as 'Internally Displaced Persons' (IDPs) at most, since they had not crossed a political boundary and thus should not be included in statistics as refugees. The UNHCR did draw this distinction in a Global Trends Report, which showed a steady drop in refugees but a steady increase in IDPs.[114]

111 A paper on judicial resources, prepared around 1993, records that the HO still claimed to have 40,000 applications awaiting decisions. The real number was, however, generally recognized to be uncertain.

112 ELR: The applicant was allowed to stay for the time being for compassionate reasons, but the facts of the claim did not fall within the Convention.

113 Statistics taken from the Records of the IAA. UNHCR statistics available on <www.unhcr.ch>.

114 Divisional Operational Services UNHCR (June/July 2007), *2006 Global Trends*, at p. 476. Timothy Kirkhope wrote to *The Times* in January 1996 justifying the latest legislation, relying on the fact that the Immigration Appellate Authority were only

However, as noted elsewhere, the IAA at the time treated all Home Office statistics with scepticism, the more so when they were trotted out to justify, for example, stricter immigration policies.

Where statistics were valuable, however, was to show discernible trends for the future rather than for any other purpose, for example, an increase from 740 appeals in 1970 to 37,660 in 1997 means little without having far more information, but it does show the growth of the tribunal. On the political front, however, figures seemed all-important despite being sometimes misleading or inaccurate. In Luxembourg, in 1991, John Major warned of excessive immigration and Kenneth Baker, then Home Secretary, said the UK expected 60,000,000 people to come in 1995. Of course, they would not all be refugees and few may want to stay indefinitely![115]

Thought had been given as to how to make predictions of how many and from where migrants might come in the short and long term, but they were not pursued; though sometimes there were signals to go by, such as the situation in Iran and Iraq in the 1980s, most flows of migrants defy accurate prophecy since there are too many unknowns.

The use of a claim to refugee status offered a way to circumvent restrictions on entry. The complexity of the UK system, with its opportunities for re-hearings, coupled with the incredible slowness of the Home Office in dealing with cases, could delay a final outcome for years;[116] even when all opportunities for further appeal were exhausted, the Home Office never managed to remove more than about 17–20 per cent of those who no longer had any right to remain in the country.[117]

The burden on the industrialized and richer countries has affected on welfare budgets and the entire immigration system, but perhaps the longer-term effect has been to worsen the relations between native and incomer, black and white, Christian and Muslim, and is very much linked to public perceptions of security.

---

overturning 4 per cent of HO decisions, and, in the case of Nigeria, 1 per cent. He alleged that measures taken in the early 1990s resulted 'in a fall … from a peak of nearly 45000 in 1991'. But the only measure is HC 251 and this added Algeria, not Nigeria to the visa regime and dealt with returning residents. The big increase came after the break-up of Yugoslavia. Nigerians always needed visas.

115 The Home Secretary went on to add that his opposite numbers in Africa had said the country was 'crazy' to offer such generous welfare opportunities: *The Times*, 20 October 1995 As late as 1998, Mike O'Brien, Immigration Minister, told MPs 'asylum-seekers will pack one jumbo jet every day for 275 days unless measures are taken now', *The Times*, 13 May 1998.

116 *NA v UK* ECHR 25904/07 is an example. The claim was made on entry in 1999, the HO decision was first made in 2002, appeal dismissed in 2003, and first removal directions made in 2006. The ECtHR reversed decisions by three judges and the AIT, in 2008.

117 The delays in entry clearances were endemic in the 1980s (and for that matter in the 1990s as well) and were the greatest source of grievance within the Asian community ... and soured relations.

But the impact on the less-developed and poorer host states in Africa is to threaten their fragile stability. To illustrate the extent of their burden, in 1993, 600,000 fled from Burundi to neighbouring states and another 600,000 landed up in Togo, which has a population of under 7 million, of whom 39 per cent live below the breadline.[118]

The steps the industrialized nations have or have not taken to address the root causes of flight[119] or disasters of one kind or another which create refugees and IDPs (whose numbers are forecast to reach 250–300 million by 2050[120]), is a topic of its own, but such countries are a reservoir storing up uncountable numbers[121] of refugees to be released in future years, if no effective solution can be found. One of the unknowns for Europe was what has become known as the global 'warehouse' of refugees and displaced people once estimated at some 60,000,000 people.[122]

The growth of migration to the EU, especially of those claiming asylum, never failed to present new practical problems to be solved whatever system was put in place. A migrant may lay claim to a false nationality. Of course, this presents a problem if there is an attempt to return the claimant, but the problem can arise on arrival, as the following story illustrates. In 1992, the Deputy German Ambassador to Nigeria was explaining to the Second Secretary to the UK High Commission the headlines in German newspapers which stated that the large number of asylum-seekers arriving via Bulgaria were Nigerians. It was so alarming that even when the UK officer assured him that they could not be Nigerians alone, he replied, 'We cannot find out where they come from and it would be dangerous to do so.' Why it was dangerous, he seemed unable to tell us.

The churches were from time to time eloquent in their condemnation of many aspects of the immigration laws, from 'Primary Purpose' to asylum. The

118 <http://www.unicef.org/infobycountry/togo_statistics.html>.

119 Julius Nyerere said, as chief mediator in the Burundi conflict (in 1996), 'The international community will be spending less money eventually if they help these countries to develop than if they wait to watch these most horrible pictures on their television screen. It is a part of any democratic process to explain what needs to be done': 'Refugee Law in the International Context and the role of the IARLJ', *Refugees*. Online at <http://www.refugee.org.nz/Reference/IARLJ3-00Care.html. No real attention has been paid to this comment which points the way to a solution to most of the evils which give rise to refugees and IDPs.

120 IPPC Report 1990; Stern Review 2006, online at <http://www.hm-treasury.gov.uk/>; and Professor N. Myers *Environmental Refugees: An Emergent Security Issue,* 13th Economic Forum Prague (2005), online at <www.osce.org>. Also Boano, C. et al, *Environmentally Displaced People: Understanding the Linkages between Environmental Change Livelihood and Forced Migration,* Forced Migration Policy Briefing 1, Refugee Studies Centre Oxford, para. 4; Christian Aid (2007), 'Human Tide: The Real Migration <http://www.christianaid.org.uk/images/human-tide.pdf>.

121 Possibly 60,000,000 refugees: Glover, S. et al. (2001) 'Migration: An Economic and Social Analysis' Home Office Research Development and Statistics Directorate Paper 67 (ISBN 1 84082 599 5).

122 Glover et al., 'Migration: An Economic and Social Analysis' above.

Methodist Conference Immigration and Asylum Report adopted by Conference in 1996 reviewed all aspects of immigration law and carefully catalogued its views of the Christian approach.[123] Meetings between the Deputy Chief Adjudicator and the Reverend David Haslam of the Churches Commission for Racial Justice in 1996 kept the IAA informed about the discussions and correspondence between the Lord Chancellor and the Primus Bishop Holloway and the General Secretary of the Action for Churches in Scotland, the Reverend Maxwell Craig, concerning delays in appeals and the churches' attitude toward the tight time limits for appeals, as well as the removal of the right of adjudicators to refer cases back to the Home Office and the safe third-country provisions. Interestingly, the churches also criticized what African leaders were supposed to have told Nicholas Baker, that is, that Britain was a 'soft touch', adding 'Ministers are often told what they want to hear!'[124]

In the case of the asylum-seeker, the churches' position did not end with supporting the homeless and giving sanctuary. Christianity and evangelism cannot be separated, and for a judge to refuse asylum on the basis that the asylum-seeker would be safe in the country of origin if he holds his tongue – as happened in Australia in 2005 – is, to put it in mildly, unbelievably naïve.

Flows of Migrants

The movement of people has become a matter of major concern in every country. Apart from those who have traditionally moved to and fro for all the more common reasons, this movement has over the last thirty years involved increasingly large numbers of people, often moving all at once in many parts of the globe, and for so many reasons, and with different intentions. Sometimes, the movement was voluntary, but more often involuntary. Sometimes the refugees' intentions were to move on, or eventually back home, but frequently any such intention changed and the migrant settled where he came to rest and made his home there.[125] This has imposed unsupportable burdens on receiving states with few facilities; as a result, the African tradition of hospitality has worn thin of late.

The burden, or 'responsibility' as the European Commission labelled it, has become so much heavier on a larger number of countries than when the 1951 Convention was first conceived and signed, that it has led to persistent demands to

---

123 <www.methodist.org.uk/downloads/re_imm_asylum_1996_report>.

124 Minutes of Meetings with the Churches Commission for Racial Justice on 27 June 1996 (retailed by the then LC, Lord Mackay) and also17 June 1996 and letters, 16 July and 16 August 1996. (archive material). The role of the churches reappears with 'Sanctuary', see for example, Sutton, T., 18 *Ecclesiastical Law Journal* Jan 1996, p. 487, especially at p. 491.

125 Glover et al., 'Migration: An Economic and Social Analysis'Home Office Research Development and Statistics Directorate Occasional paper No. 67.

reform, or even abandon, the Convention as being 'out of sync with the times', or anachronistic. The Convention, which arose from the horrors of the Second World War (on top of another world war which had ended just over 25 years earlier), was a compromise, and was limited to Europe. It does have shortcomings. The AU Charter[126] and the Cartagena Agreement[127] both testify to wider forms of protection, but the real risk is that if the Convention's measure of protection is abandoned, it will not be replaced by anything better, and perhaps by nothing at all.

A Further Look at Handling Appeals

The offer of a Registrar's post, noted earlier in this chapter and one which Mark Patey rejected, would have helped greatly in managing the volume of appeals to come later. It was not merely a question of numbers alone but the sorting, preparing for hearings, recording in a manner which enabled ready retrieval of information as well as listing. There was a need to interpose someone with registrar experience between the clerks and the judiciary. There were also many interlocutory functions a registrar could perform to reduce the burden on the judiciary and maximize the economic use of hearing-room time. One would have thought that providing such a post would not have been an insuperable hurdle.

A solution was finally agreed with the administration to train up some suitable members of the administrative to act side-by-side with the judiciary. In 1992, a Registrar's post was therefore created informally and Lesley Armes, an executive officer at the time, became an extremely valuable member of the team in this capacity, sifting through asylum appeals and making them ready for listing. This also gave the staff an added dimension to their own work and, if left in place, would have helped built up a closer relationship between judiciary and administration.

Unfortunately, it became yet another casualty of the regular round of position changes amongst the staff. The argument advanced by the senior staff was that it gave the staff experience of (and training for) all the tasks in the office. But it created disruption for the adjudicators, since the changes were made without consultation with the Chief Adjudicator, even in defiance of his wishes, and were therefore unknown to the judiciary. The adjudicators christened this 'a game of musical chairs'.

---

126 The Organisation of African Unity (OAU) Convention Governing the Specific Aspects of Refugee Problems in Africa adopted a regional treaty based on the Convention, adding to the definition of a refugee: 1001 UNTS 45, 20 June 1974 (*African Refugee Convention*, Chapter 1, n. 81).

127 Cartagena Declaration on Refugees enlarges the definition of refugee to seek durable solutions which resulted from the conflicts during the 1980s, 19–22 November 1984, Chapter 1, n. 82.

The Home Office continued to make unreliable first decisions added to which, when no Home Office representative appeared[128] and it lost, it still appealed – and still complained the courts were taking too much time. The blame for any delay has invariably been placed at the tribunal's door and the legislation has proceeded on that assumption, as will emerge as the story progresses. The Home Office was never visited with the type of constraints which have been imposed on the appeal system. The Courts have themselves levied severe criticism at Home Office delays: Munby J in *Reg (G) v SSHD129* viewed delays caused by the Home Office as inimical to justice and accused it of 'unacceptable disdain for the rule of law';[130] even John Reidas Home Secretary held the Home Office up to ridicule in 2006, as not being fit for purpose.[131] The introduction of equality of treatment of women applicants unexpectedly caused even more delays in processing applications at the missions, when the rigorous approach to male applicants was applied to females as well.

Asylum appeals were not the only factor in the rise in levels of immigration but forecasts of how many there would be, where they would be coming from and for what reasons, were exceptionally difficult. This information was important in order to estimate the length of time an appeal would take and therefore what resources would be required. In Home Office discussions around 1994, it was agreed that a future likely source of asylum-seekers could be Nigeria, and if that were so, numbers could be very large and sudden.

The inadequacy of the 'Explanatory Statement'[132] produced by the Home Office on any refusal became even more noticeable by 1994. That coupled with the abandonment of the 'Minded to Refuse' (MTR) procedure led to strong complaints from the Coordinator of Asylum Aid, a major source for immigrants of free advice and representation from barristers and solicitors.

The pressures to over-list before immigration judges will remain and with the already severe restriction on adjournments[133] (both in the legislation and psychologically on the immigration judge), lack of real opportunity to read the

---

128 See *SSHD v Qosja* [2002] UKIAT 05673 and *Subesh and others v SSHD* [2004] Imm AR 1 at para [72] per Laws L.J.

129 *Reg (G) v SSHD*, see report in *The Times*, 12 May 2006.

130 *R (on the application of Karas and Miladinovic) v SSHD* [2007] EWHC 747, at p. 87.

131 Home Secretary John Reid has damned his department's immigration operation as 'not fit for purpose' with 'inadequate' leadership and management systems. Tuesday, 23 May 2006. Online at <http://news.bbc.co.uk/1/hi/uk_politics/5007148.stm> (last accessed on 30 June 2013).

132 This told the claimant the reasons for refusal and often little more. Even the tribunal, who had urged shorter such statements in 1990 were forced to criticize the uninformative and less than clear statements on occasion.

133 Doubtful perhaps that today Alper Riza QC would have got his adjournment to get married as he did before Mark Patey years ago!

papers beforehand coupled with the need to reach the decision within ten days,[134] all will add to the threat to sound decisions.

The Practice Directions in 2005[135] had more teeth to them than in earlier days, but still they relate to matters which the adjudicator observes automatically: it would seem doubtful if the immigration judge of today even knows of their existence. None the less, when the judge felt interference with his judicial duties as he did when an attempt was made to straitjacket judges in the *form* of their judgments or the more reasonable request to streamline them and get a move on, one judge said it was an infringement of judicial independence.

In October 1995, the Refugee Legal Group questioned the then Chief Adjudicator on four issues: first, the publication of practice directions; secondly, the poor quality of Home Office decisions (though not the CA's responsibility); third, the siting of hearing centres convenient to detention centres, but inconvenient for representatives, and last, but hardly least, the prejudiced adjudicator. This last complaint led to a call for a record to be kept of refusal rates by individual adjudicators!

The Franks Report[136] set as a major requirements for a tribunal, that it should exercise openness, fairness, impartiality and be (and be *allowed* to be) transparently independent. In the realm of immigration – more perhaps regarding refugees than others – these requirements have presented successive governments with the claim to be able to act with transparent independence on the part of the tribunal, on the one hand, and the demand to limit immigration, especially immigration by people who would be difficult to remove later, on the other. Much of the legislation referred to in this book demonstrates the continuous attempt to do this – unsuccessfully.

To obtain the disposal rate needed to keep up with the caseload, a daily disposal rate for each adjudicator of 2.7 cases in a four-hour sitting day was essential. But high-quality decisions by adjudicators had to be matched with a sufficient number of typists dedicated to asylum work to allow promulgation within ten days,[137] and adjournments disrupted the entire process.

The time regimes imposed by rules may well have been thought necessary by successive governments intent on satisfying their electorate that something was being done, but the IAA had been drawing up much more effective methods of streamlining appeals in relation to listing, such as 'Warned' lists,[138] adjournments (which required notice), bail applications, pre-hearing Motions Days orders, and so on. These still left judges free to carry out their proper function. The IAT was consistently refused any powers to apply any sanctions. The adjudicators

134 See Adjudicator Guidance, n. 4, February 2003 'Delayed Promulgations'.

135 [2005] INLR p. 357 Reg 21(2) intended to discourage adjournments.

136 Franks Report Cmnd 218 (1957).

137 6 March 1996 – a call by David Pearl as Chief Adjudicator.

138 A 'Warned List' was a notice to the parties and their representatives indicating when their appeal was likely to be heard. It *warned* them to be ready.

themselves were then dismissing 73 per cent of the appeals in 1989, and the IAT dismissed 60 per cent of those that went to them from the adjudicators. Remittals from the IAT to the adjudicators, a matter which greatly concerned both the LCD and the Home Office, had dropped since 1987.[139]

Because of the importance of being able to handle the old cases without delaying the new ones, it was suggested that Recorders and Circuit Judges be recruited on a temporary basis to deal with the backlog as a separate issue under the management of the Deputy Chief Adjudicator, leaving the adjudicators themselves to handle all new cases. There would be no need for appointment boards and at the time the judges were being under-utilized. The Treasury were happy to fund at least a month's training for the judges. The proposal was not followed up until later, but then it was implemented not to clear the backlogs, but to handle current appeals.

The major question mark which hangs over any discussion of the system is this; the inherently confrontational[140] nature of the system starts with the party-political approach to immigration, which makes immigration policy a party-political matter as well. This in turn invites taunts of racism, unfairness and the common conception that there was a climate of disbelief on the part of the Home Office. The suitability or otherwise of an adversarial type of appeal was referred to by the tribunal in 2004,[141] and will be dealt with further in the next chapter

From time to time, the tribunal (both the IAA and the AIT) cooperated with the Home Office to hold back the listing of some classes of appeal, expediting other categories. This allowed the Home Office to massage its own figures, but at the expense of non-asylum appeals which were deferred. This caused dissatisfaction among many non-asylum appellants and sponsors with visit, student, or other family appeals, of urgent concern to them, awaiting decisions. They saw this as queue-jumping and it brought the tribunal into disrepute.

The autonomy and the independence of tribunals is ruled to a large extent by statute,[142] which explains the reason for the earlier reference to achieving some sort of balance; the question mark hangs over the extent to which a tribunal exercising jurisdiction in such a sensitive area can be independent. What seems the most astonishing interference into its independence is the requirement that judges shall treat certain behaviour by an appellant as an adverse indicator of credibility,

---

139 See Appendix 2: 'Statistics of adjudicator appeals'. See Glover et al., 'Migration: An Economic and Social Analysis'; Home Office (25 October 1990), *Immigration and Nationality and Passports Annual Report*.

140 Though C. Harlow and R. Rawlings, writing in their book, *Law and Administration*, saw 'adversarial procedures and the right of access to the courts as the ultimate protection the law can bestow' (Cambridge: Cambridge University Press; 3rd edn, 1998), p. 404.

141 *WN (Surendran, Credibility, New Evidence)* [2004] UKIAT 00213 (Surendran Guidelines). See also Sir Stephen Sedley's 'Asylum: Can the Judiciary Maintain Its Independence?' (Working Paper, IARLJ World Conference, 21 April 2005).

142 See Care, G. (2005), 'The Judiciary the State and the Refugee – the Evolution of Protection in Asylum. A UK perspective', *Fordham International Law Journal* 28.5 (May).

thus purporting to direct how the judge discharges their fact-finding duties.[143] This lessens their own credibility as independent judges. The results flowing from the preponderance of asylum cases meant that it became increasingly difficult to give the adjudicators a mixed diet of cases. Asylum appeals are sometimes incredibly stressful and the fear of judicial burn-out occupied much concern on the part of senior adjudicators.

It will be recalled that those adjudicators who challenged the LCD over their conditions of service had no union to turn to for help. That deficiency has now been remedied with the formation of the Council of Immigration Judges (CIJ) for the legal members and the Association of Members of the Immigration Appeal Tribunal (AMIAT), mainly for lay members, which has provided voices for representations to be made by the judiciary themselves to Government. Both were welcomed by the president of the Immigration Appeal Tribunal and both seem to have earned the respect of the Ministry of Justice.

Despite efforts to keep asylum and non-asylum cases apart, the collapse of one into the other seemed unavoidable and this inability to keep them locked into separate compartments affected legislation, and in turn indirectly, the decision-making processes. No government has been able to design a system which would sort out who was genuinely in need of protection and who was not in a morally justifiable manner.

However, the tribunal has had time to be less parochial. For example, the International Association of Refugee Law Judges (IARLJ) brokered agreements between the Republic of South Africa, the UNHCR, the Lord Chancellor's Department and the governments of Australia and NZ to second judges to South Africa to support and help to train the new judges there.[144]

---

143 S. 8, Asylum and Immigration (Treatment of Claimants, etc.) Act 2004 and Immigration (Claimant's Credibility) Regulations, SI 2004/3263. A closely reasoned commentary on the proposed changes was submitted both in writing and in evidence by the Council of Immigration Judges. There is much written on this topic. one example is Herlihy, J. (2006), 'Should Discrepant Accounts given by an Asylum Seeker be Taken as Proof of Deceit?', *Torture* 16.

144 The late Eddie Edinboro, a lay member of the IAT, spent several weeks in South Africa under this scheme.

Chapter 3
The Development of the Tribunal Structures

> Courts in States party to the Convention vary in effectiveness – often depending on the strength of implementing legislation – which is often subject to restrictive reservations – [depending on] … the overall strength of the rule of law in countries of asylum.[1]

Ringing the Changes

Countries face many competing interests when it comes to the control over their borders; as patterns of migration change, so do countries' responses change toward the migrant. However, the responses, as that word implies, tend to be reactive rather than proactive, which perhaps explains why the measures taken so often appear piecemeal, poorly thought through and crisis driven. As the quotation above points out: 'Courts in States party to the Convention vary in effectiveness – often depending on the strength of implementing legislation – which is often subject to restrictive reservations – [depending on] … the overall strength of the rule of law in countries of asylum.' It is difficult to predict just how effective any legislation will be, especially in such an uncertain area.

But need this necessarily be the case? One reason may be that it is difficult to predict when, from where and how big any change in migratory patterns will be. The tribunal had been monitoring the few claims to asylum it had been receiving mainly from the Middle East and later from parts of Africa as well, from the middle of the 1980s, and by 1988, had already delegated the management of anticipated flows of appeals likely to involve asylum issues to three adjudicators. This preceded any formal right of appeal as such.

Perhaps the root explanation, derived from the legislation and its constant revisions, is that no government has ever tried to conceptualize the problem of controlling the influx of asylum-seekers as being primarily one of preventing abuse by economic migrants or of restricting the number of successful claimants among people with potentially strong claims.[2]

---

1 M. Smith, 'Development without Refugee Rights? A Civil Society Response', *Fordham International Law Journal* 28(5): 1479–1503. In the same edition, the author addresses the role and the responsibility of the courts in judicial protection in 'The Judiciary, the State, and the Refugee: The Evolution of Judicial Protection in Asylum – A UK Perspective', pp. 1421–56.

2 T. Hayter's 2004 book, *Open Borders: The Case against Immigration Controls* (Pluto Press. 2nd edition) contains a comprehensive account of the growth of earlier and current political approaches to containing immigration.

The massive displacement of people in Europe following the Second World War awakened the conscience of the world to the need to protect those displaced by persecution in their own countries; in turn, this led to the Refugee Convention of 1951 which was limited both in time and geographically – to Europe. The next, anticipated, mass movement was that which was expected following decolonization and this which brought about the legislation restricting Commonwealth citizens' rights to enter and stay in the UK.

Thereafter the next significant migration began in continental Europe in about 1980, but only reached the UK eight years later. This movement arose from increasingly large numbers of immigrants from outside Europe, who claimed asylum. They came from a volatile Middle East, or from the newly independent countries in Africa and generally from countries disrupted by civil wars, ethnic and religious strife, and tyrannical and repressive regimes. This exodus of people who were escaping everything from economic deprivation to persecution inevitably demanded that the Refugee Convention be extended to cover them as well, so in 1967 when it was realized that the Convention needed to deal with those displaced due to persecution at *any* time and in *any* part of the world, the Protocol Relating to the Status of Refugees was added.[3]

In 2002, the pattern changed yet again, this time as terrorism became globalized after 9/11. The terrorist proved that the borders of no country were safe from attack without warning, and smuggling of would-be illegal immigrants, coming in via the Adriatic, the Balkans, Spain and Poland, became a $32-billion-a-year business.[4]

These were major shock waves to the system in every country and few of them could have been predicted, except perhaps in the case of the movements as a consequence of decolonization. However, whether predictable or not, each wave stirred up discontent at some part of the changes, which followed so quickly one after the other. The management of immigration therefore was disrupted by these frequent changes,[5] from the 1962 Commonwealth Immigrants up to the present day.[6]

---

3 UN General Assembly (1967), Protocol Relating to the Status of Refugees, 31 January, UN, Treaty Series, vol. 606, p. 267.

4 With a real flood if the predicted 250 million IDPs by 2050 comes about, the seriousness of the situation could far outstrip this sum, which the All Party Parliamentary Group on Human Trafficking estimated and the profits from arms dealing and drug smuggling. *The Guardian* 2 July 201. Online at <http://www.theguardian.co.uk/law/2011/jul/02> (accessed on 2 July 13).

5 See p. 77 below and the use Lord Carnwath made of this expression.

6 Commonwealth Immigrants Acts 1962, 1968; British Nationality Acts 1958, 1964, 1965; Immigration Act 1971 and latterly the Asylum and Nationality Immigration (Treatment of Claimants) Appeals Act 2002.

On 30 January 1978, Margaret Thatcher was interviewed on ITV's *World in Action* programme and said 'If you want good race relations, you have got to allay peoples' fears [of immigration].[7]

The first example of a piecemeal approach to immigration legislation was with the replacement of the 1969 Immigration Appeals Act with the Immigration Act in 1971. The next example was a Bill in 1991 to give right of appeal, but this failed and was quickly followed by the 1993 Act. For the next ten years, primary and subordinate legislation followed so rapidly that there was never enough time between one set of legislative measures and the next to gain any knowledge of how the most recent changes could be made to produce a 'good' outcome.

The tribunal has attempted to speed up the throughput of appeals by whatever means at its disposal, but as mentioned below, any attempt at a smooth process was often thwarted by the manner in which the Home Office released its decisions. We have seen how they wished to massage their statistics but they also refused to cooperate over the release of the 'manifestly unfounded claims' for which the tribunal was compelled to keep empty hearing rooms available. However, the worst and most consistent hurdle the tribunal faced was the poor quality of the initial decisions themselves.

Offers to make things easier for the Home Office were consistently rejected by it. One example occurred when the tribunal offered to accept in manuscript the records of overseas missions appeals when they became overwhelmed by backlogs. The tribunal heard appeals, which all involved the same basic issue en bloc – for example, the bogus college appeals – and suggested that the outcome in one typical case should then be applied in all other cases, but this suggestion was not taken up. A more radical proposal put to the head of Asylum and Special Cases Division of the Home Office (the predecessor to the Immigration and Nationality Department (IND) in 1996, suggesting that the Home Office should make positive decisions only and leave disposal of the rest to the tribunal, was more understandably summarily rejected.

When it came to the attempts by the Asylum and Immigration Appeal Tribunal (AIT) to speed up the process, it encountered problems for which it was not responsible. For example, the Home Office assumed the responsibility for sending the determination to the appellant. It did not, however, always keep a record of service and did not prompt the appellant when time to appeal was about to expire.

7 Thatcher expressed sympathy with people who felt immigration was too high and who were 'really rather afraid that this country might be rather swamped by people with a different culture'… 'If you want good race relations, you have got to allay peoples' fears about numbers.' Rather than doing so, she proceeded to misreport figures in an upward direction, asserting that:.'There was a committee which ... said that if we went on as we are then by the end of the century there would be 4 million people of the New Commonwealth or Pakistan here. ... The moment the minority threatens to become a big one, people get frightened.' Online at <www.margaretthatcher.org/document/103485> (accessed on 18 July 2013).

Due to the already short time limits in which to appeal, the result could be the appellant falling out of time to appeal and an application for an extension of time becoming necessary and being likely to be granted. Apart from a transparent injustice in giving the decision in a case to one party before the other, this added extra work and caused further delay.

The Home Office Policy Mantra

The reactive nature of successive government's responses to the need for a comprehensive immigration policy with effective management is demonstrated by a succession of management 'mantras', such as 'Invest to Save' in 1995, or the 'Fairer Faster Firmer' approach set out in a White Paper in July 1998[8] and which led to the Immigration and Asylum Act 1999, and 'Secure Borders, Safe Havens – Citizens, Guest Workers and Asylum Seekers' – in February/2002, or yet again the Consultant's report in October 2002 entitled *Quality amidst a Rising Tide*[9] and the 2004 report *Delivering Justice, Rights and Democracy.*[10] Each slogan or report was an attempt to succeed where the last one failed. The last aimed to speed up immigration appeals by the 'Fast Track' process (detaining the applicant) and introducing the 'single-tier appeal structure' which did not last long. This was supposed to deter weak appeals and contribute to a faster, fairer and more effective overall process referred to earlier which ensured a high quality to judicial decision making. However, it was the Home Office's decision making which needed to be high quality.

Comments which followed from both sides of the House of Commons, as well as outside Parliament, on what was, at least from the government's point of view, a sensible and comprehensive attempt at managing the flow of immigrants whether asylum-seekers or not, were not always helpful. The Home Secretary, Jack Straw described the asylum-seeker as 'Bogus'. UNHCR welcomed his speech as a basis for discussion but objected to the use of the term 'abuser', applied by the Minister to asylum seekers[11] and accusations by Ann Widdecombe that the UK was 'a soft

8 Home Office (1998), Home Office, *Fairer, Faster, Firmer, A Modern Approach to Immigration and Asylum*, Cm.4018 (London: TSO, 1998).

9 KPMG (Peat Marwick) Report, especially paras 3.2.1/2 and 3.6, expressing concern at the demotivation of Vice Presidents.

10 Department of Constitutional Affairs (2004), *Delivering Justice, Rights and Democracy DCA Strategy 2004–2009* <www.dca.gov.uk>.

11 The Director of International Protection's Reaction – (see a note in archives). But the government could not meet its own targets for removal: *The Times*, 26 April 2001, 'Parliament and Politics'. On 14 February 2001, the *Sun* published an article entitled 'About Turn', with a cartoon by Doug Gaskill *'I'd try counting deportees but there's just not enough of them'*.

touch'.[12] The continued delays in dealing with asylum applications – sometimes whilst asylum seekers were detained – could hardly be deemed 'fair, firm, or fast'.[13]

Changes within the Tribunal

The confrontational approach which is to be found throughout immigration control is not an approach which is confined to the UK; it is to be found from those working on the borders and right on up, as most travellers will be able to testify. However when it comes to the asylum application, the confrontational approach is inconsistent with the nature of the enquiry which calls for a sharing of the facts and a joint duty to find and evaluate the facts. The decision is one made by the judge (and should have been made by the Home Office) based on an inquiry into the *truth* of the story and not just a more narrowly based decision on whatever *evidence may be produced.*[14] This approach was that adopted by the Court of Appeal in *Ravichandran* and *Karanakaran*[15].

However, other decisions by the courts at times seem to conflict with this approach. For example, the House of Lords in *Abdi and Gawe,*[16] which said, broadly, that the government cannot be compelled to make full disclosure of all the information on which it relied to make a decision – an approach which most countries on the Continent could not by definition ever accept.[17]

One must perhaps accept such decisions but they still seem out of tune with decision making in this jurisdiction. It leaves the observer to wonder why the judges as a whole have not come out with a clearer lead to the tribunal to adopt a much more interventionist approach in the hearing of all immigration appeals, especially in asylum appeals – and even, perhaps, abandoning the adversarial approach completely.

Moses J (as he then was) referring to the decision by Mr Justice Collins in *Muwyinyi*[18] does agree that an adjudicator may put questions to a witness, but he says so in the context that if the Home Office is not represented. In doing so, he must be careful not to don the mantle of the Home Office Presenting Officer (HOPO). He went on to agree with counsel (who was a young Raza Husain at the

12 Widdecombe savages government's law and order policy Ros Taylor http://www.guardian.co.uk/politics/1999/oct/05/conservatives1999.conservatives18

13 The author heard an appeal in Glasgow from an appellant who had been held in Barlinnie Prison for several years awaiting the determination of his case in circumstances where no one understood him, his diet was strange and there was no family to visit him.

14 *Handbook and Guidelines on Procedures and Criteria for Determining Refugee Status* (the *UNHCR Handbook*) (UNHCR, rev Dec 2011), paras 195–205.

15 [1996] Imm AR 97 (CA) and [2000] 3 All ER 449 (CA).

16 *Abdi & Anor (on the application of) v Secretary of State for the Home Department & Anor* [1996] Imm ARHL.

17 German Federal Administrative Court BVerG 10 C48 07.

18 Muwyinyi (00052), 24 November 1999

time, now a QC) that, furthermore, an adjudicator should not adjourn an appeal merely because the Home Office was not represented.[19]

A major boost to the authority of the president of the tribunal was the appointment of a serving High Court Judge as President. Mr Justice (Andrew) Collins proved to be an inspired choice.[20] He promptly tackled the delays in the appeals section of the system and, by emphasizing the binding nature of IAT decisions put the first stamp of the authority on them. This gave a clear lead to the removal of conflicting decisions by the differently constituted benches of the tribunal long complained of by adjudicators by 'starring' decisions, which had to be followed in all other cases by the AIT.

During Collins's presidency, the tribunal found itself having to deal with numerous asylum appeals brought by nationals of Turkey and it decided to try and outline a set of risk categories. Collins himself sat on a case involving asylum-seekers from the former Yugoslavia and that led on appeal to John Laws in the Court of Appeal A in *S & Others*,[21] approving the idea of the tribunal giving guidance on country conditions so long as it was comprehensive guidance. When Mr Justice Ouseley became president, discussions took place between himself, Hugo Storey and other Senior Immigration Judges over the general need to shorten the length of appeal hearings where much of the time was spent by immigration judges in going over the same ground time after time. Many cases involved appellants from the same countries and if the final forum for dealing with facts was able to spend the time considering all information then available and reaching some generally applicable conclusions, those conclusions could be used in all other appeals emanating from the same country. The unique formalization of the Country Guidance Case (CGC)[22] was to take place under the next president, Mr Justice Ouseley.

A president with the authority of a High Court Judge was in a better position to push through changes generally and he tackled another cause of delay by encouraging shorter and off-the-cuff or *ex tempore* determinations and more rapid promulgation of them by the administration.

Unfortunately, he could not force the Home Office to accept the authority of the CGCs any more than he or anyone else has so far been able to dissuade the Home Office to confine its own appeals to important issues and not to abandon those which may advance the jurisprudence, lest they lose the appeal and it creates 'a precedent'.[23]

---

19 *R v a Special Adjudicator ex parte Demeter* [2000] Imm AR 424, at p. 430.

20 A Circuit Judge, David Pearl, had been appointed as Chief Adjudicator which added stature to the first tier.

21 See S (01/TH/00632), which went to the Court of Appeal as S & ors [2002] INLR 416, in which Laws LJ held that the notion of a 'factual precedent' could be 'benign and practical'.

22 See also Chapter 4., p.116ff.

23 The current President Mr Justice Blake is clearly determined to change this.

A New Look?

The Review in the Leggatt Report in 2001[24] had four main objects: to make the 70 tribunals in England and Wales[25] into one Tribunals System, to render the tribunals independent of their sponsoring, to improve training, and to enable unrepresented users to participate effectively.

The Franks Report[26] and the Tribunals and Enquiries Act 1958 were considered no longer sufficient to create a coherent tribunals system. Lord Carnwath[27] remarked, 'Tribunals have come to play a central part in the UK civil justice system, particularly in relation to administrative law. Their principal distinguishing features, as compared to the courts, are flexibility, specialisation, and accessibility. The present system is the result of piecemeal and incoherent development of many decades. The TCEA has provided the statutory framework for a radical restructuring'.[28] The Leggatt Report considered that a two-tier structure was the best option for some tribunals and approved of the retention of lay members in the tribunals, albeit only at a first hearing.[29]

In 1999, the government had published a White Paper,[30] which maintained the need to retain judicial review and so it seems that the LCD considered that the IAT was an essential engine for refining and developing immigration and asylum jurisprudence, whose authority should be reinforced.

In 2002, the government also published the report by the consultants, PA Consulting Group,[31] a report which was considered disappointing by the IAT judiciary. Amongst other deficiencies remarked on was that it lacked any suggestion as to how more judges would help achieve a 17-week target for a decision to be made and sent out. Neither did it address the length of sitting days which had been on the agenda since the 1980s, or the even thornier subject of remittals from the tribunal to the adjudicators, which were then running at 4,000 a year. Inevitably, those 4,000 added to the caseload, as well as to the government's dissatisfaction.

---

24 The Report of the Review of Tribunals by Sir Andrew Leggatt (2001) <www.tribunal-review.org.uk>.

25 Only now in 2011 is Scotland looking at their approach.

26 Cmnd 218, 1957. This Report put tribunals on the judicial side in administrative reviews.

27 Appointed a Senior President of Tribunals in 2010.

28 Tribunal Justice – A new start (Carnwath LJ – Senior President of Tribunals) ajtc.justice.gov.uk/adjust/articles/LordCarnwathSpeech2008.pdf (last visited 2 July 2013).

29 The Leggatt Report considered a single Tribunal Structure would provide better career opportunities. For the AIT, it did so formally on 10 February 2010 when the Upper and First-Tier tribunal became the Immigration and Asylum Chamber and the AIT ceased to exist. See *Tribunals for Users One System, One Service* Report of Tribunals by Sir Andrew Leggatt, March 2001.

30 White Paper LCD, Cmnd 4018, 1998.

31 PA Consultant's Report following a review of the judicial processes of the IAT, published October 1992.

The government published its response to the Leggatt Report in July 2004 as a White Paper called 'Transforming Public Service Complaints, Redress and Tribunals', which made three important recommendations, which are relevant at this point. The Leggatt vision was to achieve: '... a system that is independent, coherent, professional, cost-effective and user-friendly… a service fit for the users for whom they were intended.'[32]

It was recommended that first, there should be a single-tier judicial appeal in the AIT; secondly, there should be a single judicial office with the overall Tribunal Service, and third, judicial review (the method by which excessive use of executive power is controlled by the courts) should, in part, be removed[33] – whatever the Leggatt Report opined. The response by the Association of Members of the Immigration Tribunal (AMIAT) and the Council of Immigration Judges (CIJ) was that a change to a single-tier tribunal would be premature. In respect of the further proposal to abolish judicial review, they pointed out it was a volte-face from 1999 – all a decision in a vacuum they said.[34] This met with strong opposition from the judges, especially in the House of Lords, and the proposal was defeated.[35]

There were also proposals to empower the president of the AIT to make Directions, which could include a right to discipline immigration judges for a breach of a rule or regulation. The first was unacceptable to the judiciary as a whole, and condemned in the House of Lords. Lord Woolf added his objection to this, but what was worrying is that it was ever proposed in the first place. The provision in section 8 concerning what evidence should be regarded as damaging to credibility slipped though unnoticed, it seems. Whoever conceived and suggested these measures and whatever motivated those behind the scenes to put them forward should be a warning to all that the battle for independence of the judiciary must be fought, and won, every day.

The administration of the AIT was to be transferred into the Tribunals Service, but was to maintain its existing jurisdiction as a separate 'pillar' of the new tribunal system. The report also heralded a curtailed role for the lay members. It was not long after the changes to the role of the lay members that Margaret (Countess) Mar, one of the most senior and very highly valued lay members, announced her

32 As referred to in L.J. Carnwath's speech, see n. 29 above.

33 Cmnd 6243, 2004.

34 Reports by Ouseley J, Collins J, HH H Hodge and CIJ and AMIAT and Evidence to the House of Commons Constitutional Affairs Committee Second Report of Session 2003–2004, Vol 1 HC 211-1 24.2.04 as well as to IND Legislative Unit 17 November 2003.

35 See Rawlings, R. (2005), 'Review, Revenge and Retreat', *Modern Law Review* 68.3: 378–410 for a very comprehensive explanation of the defeat of the government proposal to abolish judicial review. See the chapters 'Everything and Nothing' and 'Bringing Rights Home:Time to start a Family', in Sedley, S. (2011), *Ashes and Sparks: Essays on Law and Justice* (Cambridge: Cambridge University Press).

resignation from the Tribunal with a resounding condemnation of the changes to the system in the House of Lords.[36]

The transfer of the AIT to the new Tribunal Service eventually took place in 2010; the Asylum Chamber and Upper Tribunal became part of the Unified Tribunals framework created by the Tribunals, Courts and Enforcement Act 2007. The Upper Tribunal of the Chamber is a superior court of record dealing with appeals against decisions made by the first (lower) tier.[37]

New Hearing Centres

The issue of hearing centres reappears repeatedly, either they become under-used and are closed, or new ones need to be opened due to increases in cases in other regions. So the topic of hearing centres goes hand-in-hand with changes in the whole immigration appellate system. At first, the only centres in and around London were Thanet House and in Harmondsworth, but with the anticipated increase in asylum appeals, a dedicated building was considered necessary. A building was found close to Heathrow, plans were made and several site visits took place with all stakeholders before the internal alterations made. This became the first purpose-designed hearing centre for the tribunal.

The new centre at Dukes Green Feltham (also known as Hatton Cross – see Figure 3.1), was opened by the Lord Chancellor Lord Mackay on 29 April 1994, and was intended by the Lord Chancellor for the hearing solely of asylum appeals. At that time, this proved impractical since there were insufficient adjudicators in the London area and not enough representatives, either for appellants or the Home Office. It was also obviously impractical to compel appellants who lived far away to come to Hatton Cross. By 1999, there were 100 AIT tribunal rooms then sitting each day throughout the UK.

The few appeals which were heard by adjudicators in Scotland in the early days took place in cramped quarters in Merchant House, George Square in Glasgow. Khurshid Drabu, then deputy director of UKIAS, wrote to the Chief Adjudicator in 1989 complaining of 'an enormous backlog of appeals' due in part, it seems, to administrative hiccups between Leeds and Glasgow. The problem was partly due to the inadequacy of the accommodation at the time and partly the lack of locally based staff, since the administration took place in Leeds. The move to the Customs and Excise building at Charing Cross in Glasgow, and recruitment of excellent local staff made the Scottish centre the smoothest running administrative machine in the entire IAA. The building itself, however, was less suitable. Both the office manager, Mrs Hedden, and the Chief Adjudicator were so concerned and irritated

36 See Appendix 6, 'Resignation of Lady Mar, House of Lords'.

37 Tribunals, Courts and Enforcement Act 2007 c. 27.

that the landlords' promise of free public access to the building was denied, that the Chief Adjudicator suspended all hearings.[38]

3.1 The Opening of Hatton Cross by the Lord Chancellor Lord Mackay, pictured here with President IAT George Farmer, Regional Adjudicator Victor Callender, H.H.J. Machin QC and Geoffrey Care, Deputy and Acting Chief Adjudicator

The opening of the centre was delayed until 28 March 1994 due to the difficulty in obtaining free and ready access. Even the Lord President of the Scottish Court of Session, Lord Hope, when he arrived to open the new hearing rooms (see Figure 3.2), was refused admittance by security guards employed by the landlords, HM Customs and Excise. Although this was speedily resolved on that day, there were continuous difficulties arising from the conflict between the need of Customs for tight security in the building and a need for the hearings of the tribunal to be open to the public.[39] This was to come to an end as soon as the administration was centralized in England, following a move to a new building. This centre,

38 Donald Dewar MP made a protest, to which the Regional Adjudicator responded by letter on 26 July 1993 (archives).

39 See Minutes of meeting, 2 December 1993, CA7, vol. III; and letter DCA to J. Davidson, 24 January 1994 (Archives).

in Glasgow, became the second purpose-designed hearing centre, this time for appeals originating in Scotland. Unfortunately the experienced staff who had been with the tribunal for several years departed.

3.2 Lord Hope (Lord President), Mrs Judith Davidson (Regional Adjudicator) and Geoffrey Care (Deputy and Acting Chief Adjudicator) opening the new Hearing Rooms at the Glasgow Centre

Mention was made above of Lord Hope's offer to accommodate the IAT within the precincts of the Court of Session in Edinburgh in order, one supposes, to encourage appeals originating in Scotland to be heard in the country. As we saw, that offer was rejected but then at the time, there were few appeals from cases originating in Scotland anyway.

The Home Office took up dispersal in another form. The Minister Mr Jack Straw proposed what the press described as a 'Crisis law to disperse refugees'[40] His proposal was to give the Home Secretary the power to impose quotas on areas around the country in order to spread the load of immigrants. The trouble lay in the detail, which was primarily a lack of communication. The County Council of Cumbria, for example, said it had received no warning that they were about to receive a batch of immigrants whom they were to be expected to house and feed. Similarly, Glasgow refused to keep refugees begging on their streets and promptly

40 *The Times*, 24 August 1999. But Straw also quickly disowned the plan.

bussed them back to London.[41] A proposal to house refugees in a city hotel in Sauchiehall Street, Glasgow was met with fury from local residents.

The EU and Harmonization – 'Creating a Level Playing Field'

The Paris Summit in 1974 urged legislation concerning foreigners to be made 'in stages', and prophesied that the uneven distribution of refugees will become more burdensome on those countries least able to cope: not helped so it would seem, with the richer and the poorer countries having contiguous borders one with the other, the economically poorer wanting to join the EU club: a prophesy which came true.

The EC (or EU) was preparing to assume an increasing role in immigration controls in general, and human rights and refugee status appeals, in particular. David Jackson's prescience was therefore rewarded, since by the time the first EU Directives affected decision making in the UK, adjudicators had begun to look beyond any narrow view of immigration law. The tribunal owes much of its initiation into the intricacies of EU law to the efforts of Hugo Storey, who is now a Senior Immigration Judge.

EC (EU) directives aimed at harmonization[42] of procedures and the interpretation of the 1951 Refugee Convention were introduced[43] following the policies set at Tampere.[44] Some of the Directives did not pass without criticism from the UNHCR, for example, the London Directive on Manifestly Unfounded Cases, which, it argued, was wider than the Executive Committee of the UNHCR (EXCOM)[45] had recommended.

41 The *Evening Standard* carried two articles about refugees on 17 September 1988. The first on the front page carried bold headlines 'Refugee Crime Wave in London' and the second 'Imminent Danger of Collapse of the System'. The 'crimes' referred to were begging and pick-pocketing. The actual system that was about to collapse is not clear, but a picture of one particular 'persistent' Romanian beggar was shown on p. 6. The police accused the East Europeans – they meant Romany, of course – of drugging their children with Night Nurse and calpol and thought that to keep on arresting and releasing them would be pointless. This came on the heels of the government's scheme for 'dispersal' to, for example, Glasgow, coming on-stream, which eventually led to Glasgow sending refugees back to London.

42 Resolution 30/11 and 1/12 1992; 2–3/1995; Joint position 4 March 1996 L.63/2 guidelines; Joint action 28 October 96 L287/3.

43 For example, Directive on common standards and procedures in Member States for returning illegally staying third-country nationals COM(2005)0391, and minimum standards in 2005/85/EC/1205.

44 European Council – Presidency Conclusions, Tampere, Finland, 15–16 October 1999. The Council reaffirmed the importance of a common European asylum system.

45 The Executive Committee of the UNHCR, which consists of 85 members, meets annually to review programmes and budgets and advise on international protection; see <www.unhcr.org>.

The EU also proposed rational guidelines and general aims for policy in immigration and information procedures in 1991.[46]

In 1991, the Lord Chancellor's Department 'UK Working Party 6' put a number of questions to the tribunal concerning their views about the effect of harmonization with European immigration law and procedure, to which the tribunal gave the warning that there were significant differences between the UK and other EU countries. Among the differences pointed out were that the UK does not have a written constitution and none of the conventions normally regarded as being of constitutional relevance contain provisions, which directly or exclusively affect immigration issues. UK immigration officers abroad handle visas applied for abroad, and the Home Office deal with all 'after entry' matters and all asylum applications.

What is more, in the UK, a multiplicity of appeal opportunities exist, all in an adversarial or accusatorial type of hearing (even though the tribunals were not supposed to be thus for asylum appeals), whereas the tribunals on the Continent were inquisitorial (or interventionist). Furthermore, in 1991, there was no appeal in the UK as such from a refusal of asylum, and the European Convention on Human Rights (ECHR) could not be applied directly by a UK tribunal or court.

Another technical difference lay in the distinction drawn in the UK between a 'deportation order' and a 'decision to make a deportation order': the first being made by the Minister (the Secretary of State) and not subject to appeal, and the second being made by some official in the Ministry of Home Affairs which was (subject to some restrictions) appealable. What is more, immigration control operates all over the UK, even though Scotland has a separate court system and different laws.[47]

The EU also required the same visa regime to be imposed by every member state, not only in order to enter the country but to pass through it in transit as well, which ignored the special relationships that existed within the Commonwealth; for example, Zambians now required a visa to enter or transit to the UK. The Zambian ir foreign minister was outraged, and retaliated by imposing a visa requirement for British visitors to Zambia.[48]

The International Association of Refugee Law Judges (IARLJ) was formed to encourage the judges themselves to take positive steps to harmonize the jurisprudence and develop consistent and fair practices. The IARLJ set out to achieve these objectives by promoting a 'worldwide understanding of refugee law principles',[49] encouraging reliance at all times on The Rule of Law. It was hoped

46 C339/15.

47 The police are rarely involved in immigration matters. Additionally, the police forces of England, Wales, Scotland and Northern Ireland are separate entities.

48 Immigration and Nationality Directorate of the Home Office (26 February 2003), Appendix 1 to Law and Policy.

49 *Li, Yi Mei v M.C.I.* (F.C.A., no. A-31–4), 5 January 2005.

that this would head off harmonization by legislative (or Directive in the case of the EU) coercion.[50]

In the mid-1990s, there were wide disparities in the way asylum applications were dealt with in many parts of the world, even among co-members of the EU. This led to applicants being rejected in one country, when they may have been accepted in another. There were remarkable disparities between the recognition rates one country had against another, even in respect of the same nationalities. This 'lottery' was seen to be inimical to fair practice. The other political objections to a harmonized system are beyond the scope of this book, but the view of Professor Joe Carens is that 'In practice, in recent years, harmonisation seems to have meant mainly a reduction in procedural protections for refugee claimants.'[51]

The variations in countries' systems can concern anything, from detention practices or welfare benefits to tight time limits, from an absence of proper interpreters to unavailability of suitable representation and advice, to differing approaches to law and fact by the judges. All these factors can lead to vast differentials in outcomes; and this is not to mention the particularly worrisome disparities in the views taken by governments of the safety or otherwise of a country of origin or transit.[52]

Issues of EU law, which arose in a domestic tribunal, were rarely referred to the European Court under Article 177 of the Treaty of Rome, but occasionally justice and urgency demanded a reference be made, even at adjudicator level, in order to try to avoid delay.

The Human Rights Act 1998[53] when it came into force (mostly) on 2 October 2000, required the important provisions of the European Convention of Human Rights to be applied in immigration appeals where human right issues arose, most commonly under article 3 (in short, where removal may put the appellant at risk of torture on return to their country).

Immigration judges were unsure of how this would affect the length of hearings and their approach. The IARLJ arranged for a study tour for the immigration judges to observe how judges in the Netherlands and from other parts of Europe handled this situation as asylum judges. On the Continent, the judiciary had been handling the combination of human rights and refugee issues for years and their UK counterparts found it surprising just how effortless it was. The only problem

50 The harmonization process has been criticized by Jane Herlihy (2006), 'Should Discrepant Accounts given by an Asylum Seeker be taken as Proof of Deceit?', *Torture* 16.

51 Carens, J.H. (1998), 'The Ethics of Refugee Policy: The Problem of Asylum in Western States' Refugee Studies Council, pp. 16–17.

52 The principle of 'first safe country' arises out of the view that if someone is fleeing persecution, a claim to asylum should be made in the first country reached, but when the asylum-seeker does not do so and arrives in the UK, a decision must be made as to whether that first country can be relied on not to send the asylum-seeker back to where they came from, without regard for the Refugee Convention.

53 c. 42.

which arose was due to the Home Office being unable to handle both asylum and human rights appeals at the same time.[54]

Issues of Law and Development of the Jurisprudence

The jurisprudence in immigration law has had to respond quickly to all manner of categories of appeals and the issues arising in them. This book is not intended to trace all these developments and is confined to those which seemed to have a relevance to the way in which the tribunal was developing. Some examples are referred to throughout, relating both to asylum and non-asylum appeals.

Jonah[55] was the earliest reported refugee case which dealt with what Professor James Hathaway later described as 'the third category of rights';[56] that is to say, a denial of those rights the infringement of which *may* amount to persecution if it amounted to a denial of basic living standards. This issue continues to engage the academics and the judges, as it should, if only to provide some counterbalance to the labelling of refuges en masse as economic refugees, as if seeking to escape from starvation were a crime.[57]

Whilst the UNHCR Handbook clearly has this situation in mind when it says that 'measures of discrimination [which] lead to consequences of a substantially prejudicial nature … e.g. serious restrictions on his right to earn his livelihood'[58] may amount to persecution, this aspect was not revisited, at least in any discoverable cases in the UK,[59] until it came up before the Tribunal, first of all in *Chiver*, and then in two cases in 1994 and 1995. Several more were to follow between then and 1999.[60]

Chiver held that dismissal from employment could, if serious enough, amount to persecution and he followed Nolan J's definition of persecution in *Jonah* 'to pursue with malignancy'. Incidentally, there is an important reminder in *Chiver*

54 *Pardeepan* [2000] INLR 445.

55 *Jonah v SSHD ex p Jonah* 2000 INLR 15.

56 Hathaway, J. (1991), *The Law of Refugee Status* (Toronto: Butterworths), p. 108.

57 More cases have been decided in this area, relating to discrimination in employment and education, in a much less restrictive approach, for example, in Australia where McHugh J. defined refusal of government employment in a country where there was little else as 'an act of oppression', and the US.

58 Para. 54 of 3.19.

59 There are innumerable cases from 1977, at least in the US, Canada, Australia and New Zealand addressing this issue.

60 *Chiver*) [1997] INLR 212 before a panel with Professor Jackson in the chair. In *Grahovac* (11761) again in *SSHD v Baglan* (126200) before a strong panel with David Jackson, Naresh Kumar and (the now late) Eddie Edinboro. Then in *Lily Woldesmaet v SSHD* (12892) with the very experienced Mrs Jasu Chatwani in the chair and later in a series of cases following *Gashi and Niqshiqi* (1997) INLR 97 and *Horvath* (1999) INLR and *Horvath v SSHD* [2001] AC HL 489.

that merely because a claimant is believed to have been dishonest in some matters (for example, the tax fraud cases), that must not preclude acceptance of the centrepiece of a witness's testimony in another appeal.

Woldesmaet is interesting because the question was whether the loss of her post as a High Court Judge and her certificate to practice as an advocate was such a serious restriction on her right to earn her livelihood as to amount to persecution.[61] The adjudicator decided that it was, but the tribunal simply found the adjudicator had applied the wrong standard of proof and sent it back for a rehearing– the ultimate outcome of the appeal is lost.

The grounds for granting leave to appeal, apart from where asylum or a matter of law was concerned, were envisaged to be 'if it appears … that there is a principle of importance involved in the case, or there are other special circumstances'. Otherwise, it was to be left to the tribunal to decide on what basis an appeal would be entertained. As noted, such an approach was premised on the basis that by the time it had reached the tribunal, the case would have been 'fully and carefully considered twice', once by the Home Office and once by an adjudicator. The distressing aspect of a provision in the rules, which reduced the ability of the tribunal to give the appeal the careful consideration required, was that the original decision was poor then and still is now.[62]

Brief mention was made in Chapter 1 of claims to asylum certified by the SSHD to be without foundation. Certificates were routinely granted in respect of France, Belgium and the Netherlands – all of whom had ports on the Channel to whom asylum-seekers were regularly returned. In a succession of 'Manifestly Unfounded' (MU) appeals, adjudicators had accepted evidence from the appellants that each one of these countries may have '*refouled*', or sent asylum-seekers onwards, either to their own countries or to another country without being able to know whether in doing so they were in breach of the Refugee Convention. The result was that at one point the Home Office was unable to send anyone to any Channel port on the Continent.

A well-documented example was *Kwita*. Belgium had what was called 'the eight-day rule'. Briefly, this meant that if the asylum-seeker (in Belgium) did not lodge their claim within eight days of arrival in Belgium, they lost completely the right to claim asylum. *Kwita* came to the UK from Belgium and claimed asylum. He was refused and returned to Belgium, but outside the eight days from his *original* entry into that country. He was therefore debarred from making a claim to asylum

61 See *Gujda* (18231), 5 August 1999 where there was a concatenation of consistent denials of human rights, including the right to work; *Harakal v SSHD* [2001] EWCA Civ 884.

62 See the Independent Monitor Report 2010: 'it is still quantity first and quality second', referring to ECO decisions: <www.independent.gov.uk/icinspector> and <www.official-documents.gov.uk>.

in Belgium. There was correspondence between the UNHCR and Belgium (which was made available to the tribunal) to see if this was really the case – it was.[63]

Three cases in particular illustrate what happened when the courts intervened in 'Manifestly Unfounded' cases. Justice Laws in *R v SSHD ex p Mehari*[64] dealt with a case which certified that it was a claim without foundation on the grounds that it was intended to return him to a country, which had been designated as safe. The judge held that such a certificate could only be made when a country to which the applicant was to be return was safe.

The time limits in the claims that were certified as being without foundation were strict; the notice of hearing had to be given within three days, determination of the appeal within a further seven days and, if the adjudicator agreed with the certificate, he was required to pronounce his satisfaction at the end of the hearing with reasons. In this type of appeal, the time limits were imposed on the tribunal and not on the Home Office. The result was that the Home Office could and did release such appeals erratically – some weeks there may have 60 or even more, but the next week as few as 15 – but the tribunal had to keep hearing rooms and adjudicators (both in short supply) available and the staff had to be ready to receive and deal with them instantly; representatives were also needed for both parties and might not be available.

The ability of a tribunal, especially one which adopts the adversarial approach, to reach a just and fair decision can be severely limited by the decision in *Abdi and Gawe*, which allows the Home Office to withhold all the information on which it made its first (and frequently poor) decision.[65] What makes the case important lies in what the judges said and how it can apply generally even though the majority decision was founded on the narrow interpretation of the 'Manifestly Unfounded' provisions. The burden of proving whether the 'MU' – as a claim which had been certified as unfounded came to be known – was justified or not rested with the Home Office; but there was no right to appeal further.

The circumstances were these. Messrs Abdi and Gawe arrived in the UK having transited in Spain. The Home Office certified both claims to asylum to be without foundation on the grounds that Spain would not send them back to Somalia without considering their claims to asylum.

The information on which the Home Office based their decision was challenged, but it refused to disclose the detail of how it reached its conclusion. The appellants lost their appeals to the adjudicator, but won them in the High Court before

63 Correspondence with the UNHCR, Ministry of External Affairs Belgium and *Kwita M v Faustin*, a decision of the Conseil D'Etat January to March 1994: (Archive material).

64 *R v SSHD ex parte Mehari* [1994] Imm AR, p. 151.

65 *Abdi & Anor, R (on the application of) v Secretary of State for the Home Department & Anor* [1996] Imm AR 46 HL. [1996] 1WLR 298.

Mr Justice Sedley (as he was then) who relied on *Musisi* in 1987.[66] The case was important, more perhaps for what Lord Mustill said in disagreement; this is dealt with below.

The Court of Appeal overturned Mr Justice Sedley's decision and the House of Lords upheld that decision. There were powerful opinions expressed by the judges along the way, but with a dissent (or disagreement) by Lord Mustill, whose judgment in part is set out below. The remarks of Lord Slynn, who said, also in agreement with Lord Steyn in the Court of Appeal, 'The current procedure is not such as to enable the special adjudicators (immigration judges) fully to perform their task and is calculated to produce unfairness'. The majority decision was based on a narrow or strict interpretation of the Rules, which their Lordships held were very specific about what documents the Home Office was obliged to serve upon the appellant. The only substantive papers included were the notice of decision, any documents referred to therein and the notes taken of any interview.

Lord Mustill also said:

> On the first question concerning the suggested duty of the Secretary of State to disclose all material information … I am persuaded that in the very special context of this abbreviated procedure no such duty can be implied … I must however disagree on the remaining question, which … is in my judgment of very real general importance. It will be recalled that the only evidence adduced in support of the assertion by the Secretary of State that the claim for asylum was "without foundation" was a letter written on his own behalf to the following effect, at p. 420:
>
> "The Secretary of State, on the basis of his knowledge of the immigration policies and practices of Spain, and on previous experiences in returning passengers to Spain, has no reason to believe that, in the circumstances of your particular case, the authorities there would not comply with their obligations under the Convention."
>
> My Lords, to contend that such a statement is evidence sufficient to justify a finding favourable to the Secretary of State in his contest with the appellant before the Special Adjudicator amounts to … the Secretary of State [saying he] knows what he is talking about and that the Adjudicator should take his word for it … the procedure was none the less adversarial … the Secretary of State cannot be contending that, in the absence of express statutory provision, a bare statement of honest belief by one party to an adversarial procedure is sufficient to prove the fact asserted … It must therefore be the proposition that there is something unique in the position of the Secretary of State which transmutes a statement of belief into an item of evidence. No authority was cited in support of this notion, which I find disturbing … I do not accept it. …'

66 Lord Bridge of Harwich, in *R. v. Home Secretary, Ex parte Bugdaycay* [1987] AC 514 at p. 531, ('*Re Musisi*').

This appeal was one of the rare (possibly unique) instances in which the tribunal itself sought to be joined as a party to the appeal. It did so in this case in order to present the argument that 'having regard to the contents of the statutory scheme, the purpose of the appeals procedure, the scope of the duties and responsibilities of Special Adjudicators in such cases', the adjudicators had a need to be supplied with all relevant information in order to reach decisions which were consistent with international practice, as well as in compliance with the guidance laid down in the UNHCR Handbook (and probably in *Karanakaran*).

Other EU member states could not have reached the same decision as that in *Abdi and Gawe* because the entire file from the first instance generally travels with the case until completion. Transparency is recognized as part of the system of justice.

It was not foreseen how important a general power to order disclosure and production could be. This was the more so after the House of Lords, in *Abdi and Gawe and Musisi* had decided that there was no obligation to make full disclosure of all the information upon which it reached its decision. It is the absence of a right to order disclosure that distanced the tribunal yet further from any development toward an interventionist structure.

That inadequacy (of the rules) combined with the need for all relevant material, not just what a party wanted to put before the judge, arose in one respect in 1989 *R v SSHD ex parte an adjudicator R.G. Care.*[67] The Divisional Court held that the tribunal had no power to make an order for the production of documents, including those held at missions abroad, even if justice and fairness called for them to be considered. The nature of evidence which counsel for the appellants was trying to introduce related to discussions about this case, which the British Foreign Secretary Geoffrey Howe had in India.[68] It is interesting that there was no suggestion of State Privilege being claimed. The appeal had involved a Sikh who, it was suggested, had been responsible for burning a cow's head close by a Hindu temple – and possibly being implicated in the then recent hijack of an aeroplane.[69]

A further example of the efforts of the government on the one hand to discourage asylum-seekers and the courts on the other hand to protect those who managed to come to the UK from severe deprivation whilst awaiting (often for years) the outcome of their applications for asylum is to be found in a case arising out of the restrictions on housing benefit imposed by regulation:[70] Lord Justice Simon Brown, as he then was, condemned the legislation as 'so uncompromisingly draconian [that] Parliament could not have intended a significant number of genuine asylum-seekers to be impaled on the horns of so intolerable a dilemma',

67 [1996] 1 WLR 298.

68 *R v SSHD ex parte an adjudicator R.G. Care* [1994] Imm AR.

69 Victor Callender proposed amendments to the rules in this and other respects with a view to reducing abuse of the system, rationalizing bail and removing appeals which were not pursued: Memorandum P.A. CA8. (archives).

70 Asylum and Immigration Act 1996, c. 49.

either to abandon their claims or to carry on in utter destitution.[71] Having struck down the subordinate legislation, the Conservative Social Security Secretary, Peter Lilley, proceeded to demonstrate that that was exactly parliament's intention. He asked parliament to reverse the Court of Appeal's ruling by passing new primary legislation. In spite of strong opposition in the House of Lords[72], Parliament promptly restored it in primary legislation.

Another example was *R v Borough of Kensington ex parte Kehara & Westminster City Council ex parte A*,[73] which arose out of regulations which denied housing to an impoverished group that did not have the means to improve its condition: homeless refugees not legally allowed to work, who were thus becoming part of what was eventually known as the 'black economy'. Regulations purporting to remove the right of homeless refugees to be housed did not operate retrospectively to affect a right, which had already been acquired.

High-profile cases were no rarity in the tribunal caseloads but the appeals of *Mohammed Al Mass'ari* were prominent for two major reasons. First, Saudi Arabia, whence Al Mass'ari came, had told the British government that if Al Mass'ari were granted asylum, the UK would lose a multimillion-pound aircraft contract. Secondly, after an unsuccessful attempt to refuse asylum before the author, the Home Office sought removal directions which appeal was heard by David Pearl, the British government having obtained the consent of the government of the Dominican Republic to allow Al Mass'ari entry and grant him asylum. Thus, Saudi Arabia was not the only country to which he might be removed. The evidence before Judge Pearl was, in short, that the Dominican Republic was 'as safe as a dark night on the backstreets of Bombay'. Therefore, his decision was that the Dominican Republic was not a safe country to which Al Mas'ari could be removed and held that the UK would be in breach of its obligations under the 1951 Convention if they sent him there.[74]

This gave an unusual insight into how behind-the-scenes politics operate in some high-profile cases. The UNHCR had been in the habit of having itself joined as a party to asylum appeals when there were few and the law was being looked at for the first time. As the numbers increased, they would only appear when there was an issue of particular importance. The author was warned in advance by the local representative of UNHCR of the intended attempt to remove *Al Mass'ari* and had specifically told him not to intervene in the appeal. He disclosed that

---

71 *R v SSSS ex p JCWI* [1997] 1 WLR 275.

72 Achieved in the Asylum and Immigration Act 1996.

73 See *R v Westminster CC ex p M.P.A. and X 1CCLR 85* (1997) and *Lismane v Hammersmith & Fulham LBC* [1999] 31 HLR 427.

74 '*Secret Deals in Arms and bananas that condemned a man to exile*, *Independent*, 5 January 1996 front page. Whether the success of Al Mass'ari in his appeals did in fact jeopardise Babcock's £200 million engineering deal with the Saudis may be questionable but the anger of the UK and Saudi governments was not, and led the author to believe that he rather than the CA should be best in the firing line to hear the (second) appeal (archives).

the UK had personally spoken to the High Commissioner. It seemed at the time that there was no purpose to be served in disclosing this information even to the Chief Adjudicator, when he considered it was his duty to take on the next hearing of the appeal.

Somalia was well known from 1991 to be a country of endemic civil war without any effective government. It produced many refugees who fled to surrounding countries as well as to Europe and Australia and all gave rise to the same question: whether they were Convention refugees. The only reason for introducing this (well-known decision of the House of Lords at this point) is to demonstrate the extent to which the interpretation of the same provisions of the Convention can differ from one country to another. The Court held in *Adan*[75] that he was not a Convention refugee since he could not show a *differential impact* from any other mere bystander in the country. A joint judgment of the full court of the Australian Federal Court disagreed.[76]

The latitude for different approaches is pointed out in *R v Mohamed* and *R v Osman*, where the Court of Appeal was dealing with section 2(4)(c) of the 2004 Act, which provides a defence for an individual who has reasonable excuse, for example, for not being in possession of a genuine document. The court pointed to Article 31 of the Refugee Convention and said the provisions must be interpreted generously. The case may have been a criminal one, but the rationale seems to apply equally in human rights related cases.

The court's reasoning would seem so to suggest:

> When refugees arrived in the UK without documents or using false ones, a compromise had to be maintained between legislative control over entry, with arrangements reflecting the stark realities faced by refugees with genuine claims, taking into account of refugees with bogus claims.

The comment on the effectiveness of legislation in the quotation at the head of this chapter takes on relevance in the light of the present global conflicts, which affect the security of any country. As early as 1977, the courts said 'Great as is the public interest in the freedom of the individual. In the last resort it must take second place to the security of the country itself.'[77]

The Human Rights Act 1998,[78] and decisions of the European Court of Human Rights, cleared the way for the House of Lords to strike down a decision by the Secretary of State for the Home Department for the indefinite detention without trial of non-British subjects believed to be involved in terrorist activities.[79] This action was discriminatory because it only applied to aliens, despite argument

---

75 *R v SSHD ex p Adan* [1998] INLR 325.

76 *MIMA v Abdi* (1999) 162 ALR 105.

77 *R v SSHD ex parte Hosenball.*

78 C. 42.

79 *A & others v. SSHD , X & Another v SSHD 2 WLR 87* (HL 2005)

that international law recognized the right of any country to control aliens. In his judgment, Lord Bingham stated:[80]

> I would allow the appeals. There will be a quashing order in respect of the Human Rights Act 1998 (Designated Derogation) Order 2001. There will also be a declaration under [s]ection 4 of the Human Rights Act 1998 that [s]ection 23 of the Anti-terrorism, Crime and Security Act 2001 is incompatible with [A]rticles 5 and 14 of the European Convention in so far as it is disproportionate and permits detention of suspected international terrorists in a way that discriminates on the ground of nationality or immigration status.

Lord Steyn, a member of the House of Lords and an earlier member of the ECtHR, said at p. 201:

> Courts will sometimes have to balance the protection of the fundamental rights of individuals against the general interests of the community. Individualized justice and the stability needed in any democratic society may be in contention … Often courts will have to choose between competing values and make sophisticated judgments as to their relative weights.

In 1996, the IARLJ began to bring judges from all over the world to meet together every two years and discuss every aspect of immigration appeals in order to try to find a common approach to the interpretation and application of the Refugee Conventions, and, where differences remain, to understand why this should be so.

The addresses by Judge Stephen Reinhardt (of the 9th Circuit Court USA) and Sir Stephen Sedley in two papers at IALJ Conference in Wellington, New Zealand, where they examined the freedom from influence of judges, are clear warnings.[81] The US immigration judge and board member is the more overtly vulnerable because they hold office at the pleasure of the Attorney General. But the full-time UK immigration judge, although appointed for life, is beset by overt and covert pressures which renders their independence correspondingly 'fragile'.

The overt pressures on the immigration judges to adhere to strict time limits in the conduct of the appeals are obvious, but there are unseen pressures which are difficult to identify, much less prove. The attempt to endow a president with disciplinary powers indicates the climate, experienced by both the legislator and some senior figures in the judiciary at the time.

80 *A & others 2 WLR*, at 130. See also, Arthur Chaskalson (then Chief Justice South Africa) (1998), 'Human Dignity as a Foundational Value of our Constitutional Order', *South African Journal of Human Rights* 16: 193–201.

81 IARLJ 5th Conference Papers, Wellington, New Zealand, Stemming the Tide or Keeping the Balance – the Role of the Judiciary October 2002 Victoria University

The 'Guidance' from the Chief Adjudicator,[82] which was aimed at discouraging all but the most essential adjournments, is itself a sensible measure, but it had the potential for hidden pressures, particularly on a part-time judge. Generally, the judge must be trusted in the exercise of their judicial duties and to put any judicial officer in jeopardy of direct or indirect disciplining for being in breach of a practice direction or a Guideline must be unacceptable.[83]

One of the last cases to be heard in the Court of Appeal, prior to the limitation of the right to have the decision at first instance reconsidered, brought a warning from the Bench:

> Thirdly, we permit ourselves a final historical observation. If the Asylum and Immigration (Treatment of Claimants) Bill ... is enacted in its present form and the appeal system is unified, the present ability of the IAT to provide guidance will be lost. A first instance determination would only be reviewable within the proposed Asylum and Immigration Tribunal on paper and then only on the basis that the decision 'depended upon an erroneous construction or application of a ... provision of an Act'. It seems to us that this would be a recipe for more ... irremediable inconsistencies.[84]

When promulgated, the Act allowed reconsideration only on a point of law. The essence of the difference between the law as it was in *Subesh* and after 2002 is that before there was another separate tribunal to hear an appeal.

Tribunal or Court – Adversarial or Interventionist?

There are several terms used to describe two recognized approaches to the manner in which a dispute between two parties is resolved. The one used for the approach in the UK is 'adversarial'. The other used generally to describe that employed on the Continent is 'inquisitorial'. The term 'adversarial' seems always to connote a confrontational or a non-interventional approach, but in practice, it is doubtful if any experienced judge in a common-law country slavishly adopts one approach or the other.[85] The limits to a system, which calls itself adversarial, are not clearly defined and will often depend on how expertly a judge can manage to get away with an intervention without it being noticed. Thus, wherever in this book the

82 The Adjudicator's Guidance note of 4 February 2003, in ' Delayed Promulgations'.

83 Immigration and Asylum Appeals (Procedure) Rules 2000 SI 2333, r. 31; then SI 2003/652, r.13 (1), which limits the powers to adjourn yet further by closure dates. Whether this is truly a proper disciplinary matter is dealt with in Chapter 8.

84 *Subesh and others v SSHD* [2004] Imm AR 1 at para [72] per Laws LJ.

85 An erudite treatment of the historical background to the origins of the adversarial approach is to be found in various chapters of Sedley's *Ashes and Sparks; Essays on Law and Justice*; see especially Chapter 3, p. 32.

alternative to an adversarial system or approach is being examined, it is not labelled 'inquisitorial' but 'interventionist'.

When it comes to immigration appeals, especially those relating to refugees and human rights, which will almost always turn on fact at some point, how the judge is able to approach the fact-finding task may turn on *how* they are allowed to conduct it, as much as on expertise.

In 2004, the suitability or otherwise of an adversarial type of appeal was examined by the IAT.[86] This was one of the few occasions where a judge in this jurisdiction has taken a long hard look at something so crucial to decision making by the AIT. The pity is that this initiative remains finally unresolved and some courts still hold to the view that the best approach for a tribunal is an adversarial one.

The peculiarity of asylum cases, from the forensic point of view, is that there is normally only one side (the asylum-seeker's) with evidence to give on the facts of the individual case. This does not fit in well with the adversarial procedure used in most common-law countries, and, in Scotland, on appeals against negative decisions. It fits in even worse with the situation in the United Kingdom, where the other side (the Home Office) is often not represented at all, at least on first-instance appeals. This has been recognized for some time[87].

The standard of proof for subsidiary protection[88] was not 'more than a mere possibility', but 'whether there are substantial grounds for believing' the claim. This issue rose to the surface when the State stopped being present at appeals at the first instance and then appealing when it lost. The judge was left alone with one part of the adversarial system missing; what can and should be done?

The *Surendran Guidelines*

The topic is mentioned again in the next chapter, but the seminal decision of the AIT chaired by SIJ John Freeman concerned a review of what had come to be known as the *Surendran Guidelines*[89] and what follows is a close examination of that decision.[90]

86 WN (Surendran, Credibility, New Evidence) [2004] UKIAT 00213 (Surendran Guidelines). See also Sedley, 'Asylum: Can the Judiciary Maintain Its Independence?'.

87 See Care, 'The Judiciary, the State and the Refugee: The Evolution of Judicial Protection in Asylum – A UK Perspective', *Fordham International Law Journal*, 28(5): 1438, n. 99.

88 Basically, the exercise of a discretion by the SSHD to allow someone to remain in the country even though his or her circumstances may not fall within any Convention.

89 *WN (Surendran, Credibility, New Evidence)* [2004] UKIAT 00213 (hereinafter the *Surendran Guidelines*).

90 For this, I am indebted to John Freeman himself.

The decision, which gave its name to those guidelines (*Surendran* (19197), perished in the Field House[91] fire of 2009. Ironic or not as its physical fate might seem, its electronic immortality had been ensured by the guidelines themselves being appended to a decision which did appear on the appellate authority's website as a 'reported'[92] case. This was *MNM (Surendran Guidelines for Adjudicators) Kenya** [2000] UKIAT 00005. Despite the asterisk in the long title, indicating a still higher level of official endorsement as a 'starred' decision, to be followed by all immigration judges on the point referred to, much of *MNM* was taken up with a learned discussion of whether article 6 (1) of the European Convention on Human Rights[93] applied to statutory immigration appeals (the conclusion being that it did not).

In *MNM*, the Tribunal[94] referred at paragraph 18 to the problems caused where the Home Office were not represented, and at paragraph 19 to the *Surendran Guidelines*. They went on to refer to another decision (*Muwyinyi*, not 'reported'), where it had been said that 'adjudicators were not bound to accept accounts at face value but could and should probe apparent improbabilities.' However, they must not involve themselves directly in questioning appellants or witnesses save as was necessary to enable them to ascertain the truth and must never adopt or 'appear to adopt' a hostile attitude.

Given a purposive interpretation of 'absolutely necessary', this need not have caused any problems. However, the tribunal went on to refer to the *Guidelines*, and concluded 'They must be observed. If they are not, there is a real danger that the hearing will be regarded as having been conducted unfairly'.

The *Guidelines* themselves, not written by the draftsman of *MNM*,[95] (abridged) provided

> 4. Where matters of credibility are raised in the letter of refusal, the special adjudicator[96] should request the representative to address these matters, particularly in his examination of the appellant or, if the appellant is not

---

91 The home of what had been the Immigration Appellate Authority library, and what was until April 2005 the Immigration Appeal Tribunal, then effectively the appellate division of the Asylum and Immigration Tribunal, and since February 2010, the Upper Tribunal (Immigration and Asylum Chamber): the frequent changes of name tell their own story of legislative intervention.

92 Thus officially endorsed as citable.

93 Article 6 of the European Convention on Human Rights is a provision of the Convention which protects the 'right to a fair trial … [and] it protects the right to a public hearing before an independent and impartial tribunal within reasonable time, the presumption of innocence, and other minimum rights'.

94 In this case, the Immigration Appeal Tribunal; but see n. 30 for the designation of the Tribunal.

95 Sir Andrew Collins President.

96 Then the designation of an immigration judge (not their formal title until 2005, but used here generically throughout) authorized to hear asylum appeals.

giving evidence, in his submissions. Whether or not these matters are addressed by the representative, and whether or not the special adjudicator has himself expressed any particular concern, he is entitled to form his own view as to credibility on the basis of the material before him.

5. Where no matters of credibility are raised in the letter of refusal but, from a reading of the papers, the special adjudicator himself considers that there are matters of credibility arising therefrom, he should similarly point these matters out to the representative and ask that they be dealt with, either in examination of the appellant or in submissions.
6. It is our view that it is not the function of a special adjudicator to adopt an inquisitorial role in cases of this nature. The system pertaining at present is essentially an adversarial system and the special adjudicator is at impartial judge and assessor of the evidence before him. Where the Home Office does not appear the Home Office's argument and basis of refusal, as contained in the letter of refusal, is the Home Office's case purely and simply, subject to any other representations which the Home Office may make to the special adjudicator. It is not the function of the special adjudicator to expand upon that document, nor is it his function to raise matters which are not raised in it, unless these are matters which are apparent to him from a reading of the papers, in which case these matters should be drawn to the attention of the appellant's representative who should then be invited to make submissions or call evidence in relation thereto. We would add that this is not necessarily the same function which has to be performed by a special adjudicator where he has refused to adjourn a case in the absence of a representative for the appellant, and the appellant is virtually conducting his own appeal. In such event, it is the duty of the special adjudicator to give every assistance, which he can give, to the appellant.
7. Where, having received the evidence or submissions in relation to matters which he has drawn to the attention of the representatives, the special adjudicator considers clarification is necessary, then he should be at liberty to ask questions for the purposes of seeking clarification. We would emphasise, however, that it is not his function to raise matters which a Presenting Officer might have raised in cross-examination had he been present.
8. There might well be matters which are not raised in the letter of refusal which the special adjudicator considers to be relevant and of importance. [Examples are given of internal relocation or civil war.] Where these are matters which clearly the special adjudicator considers he may well wish to deal with in his determination, then he should raise these with the representative and invite submissions to be made in relation thereto.

It may well be imagined that the standard of representation available to asylum-seekers, whether publicly funded or not, is not always of the highest. Where a whole relevant topic has not been covered by the asylum-seeker or their representative – and internal relocation may be a good example here – then there may be little alternative for the judge, at least in the first place, to asking that it should be dealt with. However, a guideline obliging the judge to raise detailed points of concern through a representative as intermediary (often with an interpreter involved as well) who was not familiar with other fields of law, was particularly likely to lead to problems.

The sheer prolixity of the *Guidelines* also carried its own difficulties for hard-pressed immigration judges sitting at first instance. Inevitably, their appearance in *MNM* was understood as a general inhibition on any judicial intervention at all, other than through a representative whose professional skills might well make it more trouble than it was worth. Some idea of the scale of the resulting problems, at least in terms of the guidelines provoking 15 further 'reported' decisions,[97] which appeared on the tribunal's website between *MNM* and the end of 2004.

These decisions varied in their approach, and in their potential helpfulness to immigration judges. On the one hand, there was *KH (Fair Trial – Surendran Guidelines) Iraq*,[98] still on the website as a 'reported' decision, whose *ratio* (or major reason) consisted of the following passage:

> We are concerned that in the course of a lengthy cross examination which was carried out by the respondent's representative, the Adjudicator has asked a number of questions. The timing, the content and the nature of some of these questions could lead to a perception of bias. An Adjudicator has every right to ask questions and to seek clarifications of evidence but he must not enter the arena and his questions must be formulated in such a way and asked at such a time as to ensure that he is not seen to be taking sides. We do not make any criticism of the Adjudicator in this case but it is clear to us that the hearing before her was not a very happy one and it was not assisted by the fact that it took place during the month of Ramadan and the appellant as well as his Counsel were fasting.

Impeccable as the statement of principle in the third sentence undoubtedly was, the decision as a whole, which said nothing about what specifically should not have been asked in this case, left immigration judges no clearer as to what questions they could legitimately ask, or when. While this is a question of general judge-craft in any field, the problems already mentioned (the inevitably one-sided view of the facts, the frequent lack of any representation for one side, and the variable quality of it for the other) made the problem particularly acute in this one.

There were, on the other hand, worthwhile attempts to set the *Guidelines* in the context of the general law: one such was *HT (Surendran Guidelines – Questioning – Test for Bias) Algeria*.[99] There the tribunal referred to the (still fairly recent)

---

97 Four of them are Country Guidance cases,

98 *KH (Fair Trial – Surendran Guidelines) Iraq* [2003] UKIAT 00048.

99 *HT (Surendran Guidelines – Questioning – Test for Bias) Algeria* [2003] UKIAT 00128.

decision of the House of Lords in *Porter & another v Magill*.[100] *Porter*, a decision on a very different subject – the surcharging of a well-known local politician by the district auditor – had re-stated the test for apparent bias, as 'whether the fair-minded and informed observer, having considered the facts, would conclude that there was a real possibility that the Tribunal was biased'.

The tribunal, in *HT*, took the view that the practice (of referring to another decision, not 'reported') was that:

> where there has been a failure to follow the Surendran guidelines the better course is to remit the hearing afresh before a different Adjudicator, cannot be regarded as authoritative following the decision of the House of Lords. It may be that it will be the right course but the Tribunal must first consider the existence of any apparent bias in accordance with the guidance of the House of Lords.

This put the *Surendran Guidelines* back where they belonged – in the context of the general law on bias – but their effect in practice continued, apparently unabated, until *WN (Surendran; credibility; new evidence) Democratic Republic of Congo*.[101]

Meanwhile, in another part of the United Kingdom,[102] the problem was being approached from the other side. In *Koca*,[103] Lord Carloway was dealing in the Outer House, by way of a challenge to the tribunal's refusal of leave to appeal, with the decision of an adjudicator sitting in Scotland. He referred to *MNM* and the *Guidelines*, and also to the effect on the proceedings of the practice, apparently new to him, of the appellant's witness statement,[104] standing as evidence in chief. He went on to point out that 'The somewhat unusual situation was then that there would be virtually no oral testimony from the petitioner at all in a case in which his credibility appeared to be a, if not the, live issue.'

However, in this case, the adjudicator had asked 32 questions, many of which Lord Carloway set out. He noted that the application for leave to appeal had managed both to blame her for not following the *Guidelines*, by stepping too far into the ring; and for not putting to the appellant a particular discrepancy between his interview and statement to the Home Office, and his witness statement, as to his membership of a political party in Turkey. Lord Carloway referred to the

100 *Porter & another v Magill* [2001] UKHL 67.

101 *WN (Surendran; credibility; new evidence) Democratic Republic of Congo* [2004] UKIAT 00213.

102 Scotland, which shares the same system of statutory appeals as England and Wales (and Northern Ireland), but where challenges to their decisions go to the Court of Session (Outer House at first instance, and Inner House on appeal).

103 *Koca* [2002] Scot CS 300.

104 Described as 'something akin to a precognition … In a very limited number of fori, and proceedings before an adjudicator is one of them, it appears to have been to a large extent abolished in favour of the written, and presumably to a degree tailored, "witness statement" or more commonly "precognition".' One has to express some surprise at a Senator of the College of Justice thinking that the plural of 'forum' should be 'fori'.

'traditional passive role' of the judge, and held that this did not change when a party's opponent was not present to cross-examine:

> ... albeit that in certain situations the adjudicator may have to ask more questions than he might have done with a contradictor present. It is not the function of an adjudicator, or indeed of any other court or tribunal, to assume the role of contradictor when a party's opponent has elected not to appear at an oral hearing.

In the case in hand, Lord Carloway held that the hearing had been fair, since the judge had invited the appellant's representative to address her on credibility: she was not required to go further and prepare and put to the appellant 'a list of potential problem areas', which might influence her decision on credibility. The particular discrepancy referred to had in any case been created by the appellant and his representative in drawing up the witness statement.

By 2005, the case had wound its leisurely way through the Scottish legal system to arrive on appeal[105] in the Inner House.[106] The appeal was allowed (see paragraph 19), on the basis that the immigration judge had not given proper reasons for rejecting part of the 'country-expert' evidence relied on by the appellant. However, the court went on to deal (at para. 20) with the point already discussed and after an extensive review of the authorities, both domestic (including *MNM*) and transatlantic, they reached the decision that:

> Nevertheless the litmus test remains whether or not in the particular circumstances of the case the Adjudicator has provided the applicant with a fair hearing. In this case we consider that the reclaimer has reason to consider that the Adjudicator's failure to put her concerns regarding what she perceived as contradictions or discrepancies of importance in his evidence to him, meant that the hearing was conducted unfairly.

This decision, while not binding on immigration judges in England and Wales, might have been hard for them to deal with in any spirit of comity, if it had not been for *WN*,[107] written by Sir Duncan Ouseley sitting as president of the AIT. After discussing *MNM* and Lord Carloway's decision in *Koca*, it goes on:

> 37 ... The Adjudicator can properly put, without it becoming a cross-examination, questions which trouble him or inferences from answers given which he might wish to draw adversely to a party. These questions should not be disproportionate in length to the evidence given as to the complexity of the case, and, we repeat, an Adjudicator should be careful to avoid developing his own theory of the case.

105 On a 'reclaiming motion'.
106 See *Koca* [2005] CSIH 41.
107 Referred to above in n. 85.

> 38. There is a tension, reflected in the guidelines, between fairness in enabling a party to know the points on which an Adjudicator may be minded to reach conclusions adverse to him where they have not directly otherwise been raised, and fairness in the Adjudicator not appearing to be partisan, asking questions that no-one else has thought it necessary to ask. This has proved troublesome on a number of occasions.
>
> 39. The tension should be resolved, so far as practicable, by recognising the following:
>
>   1. It is not necessary for obvious points on credibility to be put, where credibility is generally at issue in the light of the refusal letter or obviously at issue as a result of later evidence.
>   2. Where the point is important to the decision but not obvious or where the issue of credibility has not been raised or does not obviously arise on new material, or where an Appellant is unrepresented, it is generally better for the Adjudicator to raise the point if it is not otherwise raised. He can do so by direct questioning of a witness in an appropriate manner …
>
> 4. There is no hard and fast rule embodied in (1) and (2). It is a question in each case for a judgment as to what is fair and properly perceived as fair.
>
> The *Surendran* guidelines and *MNM* should be read with what we have set out above.

This left the field clear for immigration judges in any part of the United Kingdom to raise their concerns on the facts with appellants, and the decision of the Inner House in *Koca* positively encouraged them to do so, at least in Scotland. The practical effect of *WN* can be gauged by another glance at the results of a *Surendran* search on the tribunal's website: the *Guidelines* had been cited in no less than 15 cases between *MNM* in 2000, and *WN* in 2004 (and another, heard before *WN*, but not published till afterwards), and *WN* was followed by four other cases, heard in 2005.

One of these was *SW (Adjudicator's questions) Somalia*:[108] here the tribunal (Mr Justice Ouseley again presiding) found it necessary, not only to repeat the whole of paragraphs 38–40 from *WN* (above), but to add that '*Surendran* and *MNM* should not be cited to us or to Adjudicators without *WN* (DRC) also being cited.'

There could have been no clearer illustration of the continuing pervasive effect of the *Guidelines*: the tribunal also took the opportunity to give detailed guidance, previously lacking, about what sort of questions could be asked, and when. The next decision, by a different panel, also reaffirmed *WN*, while the last was almost, if not entirely concerned with the operation of the exclusion clause at article 1F of the Refugee Convention.[109]

---

108 [2005] UKIAT 00037.

109 See more on this in Rikhof, J. (2012), 'The Criminal Refugee: the Treatment of Asylum Seekers with a Criminal Background in International and Domestic Law (PB)', *Human Rights Series*, 3 (Library of Human Rights).

Only *XS (Adjudicator's conduct – Psychiatric report)*,[110] calls for any comment here: despite the unfortunate impression given in the long title, the psychiatric report had not been called for to explain the adjudicator's conduct of the case. The tribunal (Ouseley P, again) said this:

> … the Adjudicator with his approach to nationality, frontiers, mode of travel and source of money and, seemingly inaccurately, as to when the Appellant declared himself to the police, was developing his own theory of the case. This was very different from the Secretary of State's refusal letter or the Home Office Presenting Officer questions. Again, no absolute rule can be laid down; an obvious issue may have been omitted; credibility may be at issue but a facet not otherwise explicitly identified may call for examination. However, in what remains an essentially adversarial system, for an Adjudicator to develop a hostile theory, in addition to the Secretary of State's different opposition can create a real possibility of the Adjudicator appearing biased. Warning bells should be sounding.

This was a development of a point made in previous decisions. While the immigration judge was entitled to play his own part in the examination of the appellant's credibility, he was not to take on the role of investigator. This will be looked at later.

SW and *WN* clearly had the intended affect, because there is not a single citation of the *Surendran Guidelines* in any reported case between 2005 and 2010. They next appear in *TR (CCOL cases)*.[111] The impenetrable looking acronym in the long title refers to the Cambridge College of Learning, which on investigation by the Home Office had turned out, to put it neutrally, not to be running the courses for which it had issued post-graduate diplomas, with which a considerable number of overseas students had secured extensions to their leave from the Home Office. A guideline decision of the tribunal[112] had upheld the results of the investigation.

However, *TR* had persuaded the immigration judge at first instance to allow his appeal on the basis of his own evidence that his diploma was genuine: as the tribunal said at paragraph 13, the judge had been:

> taking that evidence very much at face value. He stated that the appellant had been able to give a relatively detailed account of modules, assignments etc. But he did not show that he had in any way sought to ask the claimant any obvious questions designed to test his evidence. Of course, given that the SSHD was not represented, he was required by the *Surendran* guidelines [contained in an annex to *MNM*] not to enter into the arena, but he had to ensure that the claimant had at least tried to answer the substance of the respondent's case. If it was not

110 [2005] UKIAT 00093.

111 [2011] UKUT (IAC) 33.

112 *NA & others (Cambridge College of Learning) Pakistan* [2009] UKAIT 00031)

> dealt with in the claimant's witness statement he, in the absence of a Presenting Officer, had a responsibility to ask a limited number of questions designed to test the evidence … .

This was not so much the sound of the *Surendran Guidelines* clanking their chains, as of their being put in their place once and for all. Far from Lord Carloway's 'traditional passive role' of the judge not changing even when one side is not represented, the immigration judge now has a positive responsibility to test the other side's evidence..[113]

Meanwhile, north of the border, the Scottish Court of Session (Inner House) had decided *HA & TD*.[114] Before turning to the facts of the cases, they had reviewed a number of authorities, both English and Scottish and referred (at para. 4) to the need to make an intuitive judgment on fairness, in context[115] and then (in para. 5) there were the practical problems caused by late introduction of evidence,[116] with the need for immigration judges to consider it critically for themselves, while still avoiding the appearance of stepping into the fray. Notably (at para. 6), they made this point:

> One factor which has been emphasized in numerous cases is the specialist nature of the Tribunal.[117] This has implications for procedure before the Tribunal: although the procedure is adversarial,[118] the Tribunal is not confined to a consideration of the evidence and submissions presented to it by the parties. In that regard, the observations made by Sedley J (as he then was) and cited in *Secretary of State for the Home Department v Abdi*[119] in relation to adjudicators appointed under the previous legislation, remain apposite:
> "Adjudicators are not recruited from the Clapham omnibus. They are skilled and specialised office-holders carrying out an independent and, in many respects, judicial function of profound importance to the individuals who come before them. From case to case they will build up a fund of information about different third countries. It would be wrong, of course, for them to decide cases upon the basis of private information of this kind; but it would also, in my judgment, be wrong for them to ignore such information and close their minds to everything

113 This is not limited to situations where the unrepresented side's evidence is of a generic kind, and has been the subject of an authoritative judicial decision: see *TR*, para. 11, where the Tribunal said 'We consider that the IJ [immigration judge]'s decision is vitiated by legal error even without reference to the case of NA and Others.' (which had not been 'reported' until after the hearing in *TR*).

114 [2010] CSIH 28.

115 *Doody* [1993] UKHL 8.

116 *Maheshwaran* [2004] Imm AR 176.

117 For example, *AH (Sudan) v SSHD* [2008] 1 AC 678).

118 *R v Secretary of SSHD, ex parte Abdi* [1996] 1 WLR 298 at p. 301 per Lord Mustill).

119 [1994] Imm AR 402 at p. 412.

> except the evidence that the Home Office chose or the applicant was able to put before them."

In that case (per Steyn LJ at p. 420), and in subsequent cases (for example, *Gnanavarathan v A Special Adjudicator*[120]), it was accepted that the adjudicator was entitled to rely on matters within their own knowledge, provided such matters were disclosed to the parties so as to afford them a fair opportunity to deal with them.

The Inner House (in Scotland) went on to make the following points:

> [7] Similarly, the Tribunal may identify an issue which has not been raised by the parties to the proceedings, but it will be unfair, ordinarily at least, for it to base its decision upon its view of that issue without giving the parties an opportunity to address it upon the matter …
>
> [8] As an expert body, the Tribunal is entitled to reject evidence notwithstanding that the evidence has not been challenged before it. Fairness may however require it to disclose its concerns about the evidence so as to afford the parties an opportunity to address them …
>
> [13] Given the judicial nature of the Tribunal's function, it is generally inappropriate for it to become involved in challenging the evidence placed before it. As Moses J observed in *R v Special Adjudicator, ex parte Demete*.[121]
>
> "The appeal should be, and is, adversarial. It is important that the special adjudicator should avoid, if possible, giving any appearance of entering into the arena by challenging the account that the applicant gives himself."
>
> There are however circumstances where, as a matter of fairness, the Tribunal cannot remain silent in the face of the evidence presented to it … It is however necessary to emphasize that such circumstances are fact-sensitive. The Tribunal is not under a general obligation to air its concerns about the evidence presented to it, even if the evidence is unchallenged.
>
> [14] As we have indicated, however, circumstances can arise in which the Tribunal cannot fairly adopt the passive role which a judge or a jury would ordinarily adopt. Such circumstances are particularly apt to arise in situations where the Secretary of State is unrepresented at the hearing before the Tribunal.

The results of the individual cases in *HA & TD* show the approach likely to be taken in practice by the Court of Session. In *HA*, they concluded (para. 23) that the points which it was said should have been put to the appellant should have been obvious to him and his representatives:

---

120 [1995] Imm AR 64.

121 R [2000] Imm AR 424 at p. 430.

> … the inconsistencies on which the Tribunal founded were apparent from the documents before the Tribunal, of which the first appellant and his representatives had prior notice; and it appears that the other difficulties relating to the arrest warrant were raised in the course of cross-examination. The reliability of the accounts which the first appellant had given, and the genuineness of the arrest warrant, were plainly matters of importance. In the circumstances, we are satisfied that there was no violation by the Tribunal of the first appellant's right to a fair hearing.

In *TD*, on the other hand, the discrepancy on which the immigration judge had disbelieved the appellant turned on what the judge saw as the difference in his signature, as it appeared on the party membership card relied on to support his account of events in Nigeria, and the witness statement[122] and other documents used in the course of his application for asylum in this country. The court took the view (para. 31) that while:

> The parties can be taken to anticipate that the immigration judge will consider the contents of the documents and may attach significance to differences or inconsistencies which are to be found there … The parties would not however ordinarily anticipate that the immigration judge would compare the signature on a document relied on as evidence with the signatures to be found on the documents prepared for the purposes of the asylum claim, such as the asylum application and the interview form. In reality, the immigration judge was raising an issue – the genuineness of the signature on the membership card – and reaching a decision on that issue, without giving the parties any notice of that issue or affording them an opportunity to address it. To do so was in our view procedurally unfair.

It may not be immediately obvious why discrepancies in the contents of documents needed to be put to the appellant and his representatives, so that they could deal with them; but the signatures on them did. The answer may be that a document is normally relied for its contents, and the signature serves no purpose beyond helping to verify it, if that issue arises at all.

At the start of the millennium, many immigration judges, and many of those who appeared before them, clearly felt that they were inhibited by the *Surendran Guidelines* set out in *MNM* from asking questions in the course of the evidence. This not only made it harder (not to mention less interesting) for judges, who felt constrained in this way, to do justice on the facts of the case before them; but it also generated a parallel stream of litigation, most visible in Scotland, with extensive discussion of what points nevertheless needed to be put to appellants.

---

122 It seems that by now the Court of Session had digested this unfamiliar foreign term.

Lord Carloway's 2002 decision in *Koca* discouraged them from appearing to act as 'contradictors'.

In the course of the last decade, immigration judges were not only encouraged to raise points of difficulty which were not otherwise obvious (*WN*), but given detailed guidance (*SW*) as to how they should do it. They were still not to act as cross-examiners, or to develop their own theory of the case (for example, *XS*: though the gloss of 'hostile' on the word 'theory' may be important); but they were encouraged to take a broad view of what fairness required in the individual case.[123]

By the end of the decade (2010), immigration judges were under a positive duty to probe evidence which was in issue before them, even where the opposite party had chosen not to be represented (*TR*). They were encouraged not only to use their judicial common sense in deciding which points needed to be put (see the individual cases in *HA & TD*), and which not; but also to use their expertise as a specialist tribunal, not only in the relevant law, but in the 'fund of information about different third countries' which they had acquired.[124] Naturally, they needed to put such information to the parties.

Thus as has been seen, whilst asylum (and other immigration) appeals are still adversarial in form in England and Wales and Scotland,[125] the immigration judge intervenes more than it was formerly thought to be proper. If a judge feels it necessary to intervene, it must not seem hostile or partial and clearly requires skill and experience, but that is part of the craft for judges.

---

123 *Koca* (in the Inner House).

124 See the reference by the Court of Session in *HA & TD* to what Sedley J had said, in what eventually became *DS Abdi* [1996] Imm AR 148.

125 There is a lack of reported cases from Northern Ireland; but no doubt the same applies there.

Chapter 4
Getting the Facts – Interpreting the Evidence, Credibility

> We should be constantly aware that the study of the products is vastly more important than the study of the production.
>
> Karl Popper[1]

Part I: Getting the Facts

It is a bit unlikely that the immigration judges themselves would ever have thought of describing themselves as 'road builders', but given the dangers on many roads today it is a picturesque way of illustrating the immigration judge's responsibility to make 'possible life-and-death decision[s] extracted from shreds of evidence and subjective impressions'.[2]

Any decision maker's need for information is obvious enough, but what is not immediately quite so obvious to the outside observer is where the decision maker can acquire information without compromising judicial independence and fairness to all parties. And, having acquired it, what limitations are there on how that information is used and the manner in which it is evaluated?

The judge, and those who are familiar with any ordinary domestic court, will be well aware of the answers to all such questions, but a judge coming fresh to decision making in an immigration context will soon discover that those answers will not suffice.

The differences between an ordinary civil or criminal trial lie in the nature and approach to the evidence, in the level to which the judge must be satisfied and in the type of the inquiry or hearing itself; and these differences are discussed in more detail. The nature of the hearing was addressed in Chapter 3, the level of satisfaction, or standard of proof, appear at various points mainly in connection with asylum and human rights cases and the evidence is dealt with later in this chapter. Put differently, the immigration judge is both judge and jury (the more so since the role of the lay members has been largely cut out by successive governments) and the aim of the decision to be reached (that is, the truth),[3] is determined by the

---

1 Taken from Popper, K. (1979), *Objective Knowledge: An Evolutionary Approach* (Oxford: Oxford University Press), p. 114, from a lecture he delivered 25 August 1967.

2 Sedley, 'Asylum: Can the judiciary maintain its independence?'.

3 'The court's search is not for truth but for verisimilitude' This is but an extract from a more comprehensive treatment of the 'system' in England by Sir Stephen Sedley in the collection of essays and talks he has given over the years in *Ashes and Sparks*.

diversity of the information required, how to weigh the evidence and to apply it ('the standard of proof') and the type of hearing, that is to say, whether it is to be an 'adversarial' or 'interventionist' contest, or a mixture of both.

The evidence in immigration appeals, whether it is documentary, or oral (including expert reports) will in part relate to general information provided in order to familiarize the judge with the background from which the appellant comes, which may sustain or detract from the reliability of the personal story told. There will also be oral evidence which focuses on the appellant's actual personal story.

The judge in an immigration case does not, or should not, reach a decision merely on what the parties are pleased to produce. The decision here, unlike in the normal case, is designed to reach the truth. That may mean calling for more evidence to fill any gaps. It also may mean asking questions, that is, 'intervening', not just sitting back and listening. There is an art to doing this while still remaining dispassionate. There is also an element of solving a crime, but it is not a detective thriller where the reader is left to ferret out clues – in other words, it is not a 'whodunnit'. The system within which the judges operate either provides the tools to acquire what they need, or it may hinder them. By and large, it half does the job, in the sense that all the outward trappings are in place: a court room, reference books, clerks, interpreters and typists, and a mass of papers supplied by the parties.

There are some universally applicable matters to watch out for, such as contamination of memory or observation, quite apart from plain dishonesty, but for the immigration judge the task is more complex for the reasons explained earlier. It is well known that recalling events of the past, especially traumatic events, are rarely a rational, ordered story of what happened.[4]

The witness will probably not look familiar, may not bear himself or herself in a recognizable manner, nor react as expected. In most cases, the judge will not hear one single word spoken by the witness since it will be all through at least one interpreter and the story may sound implausible. Hearing the same story with or without variations does not necessarily make it more or less plausible; it simply makes it more familiar.

Beyond 'learning on the job' and the adjudicators' occasional seminars and annual meetings, there was no training as such until after 1989 when the asylum appeals demanded something more. There is much more help available to the immigration judge today than there was then. There are more sourced country information databases, there are Country Guidance Cases (CGC),[5] Guidance Notes and Practice Directions. The judge has access to decisions from courts in many parts of the world and much more.

The role judges in general have to play is clear enough, that is, to hear a case fairly, without fear or favour; they must give the parties an opportunity to present their case and give a reasoned decision quickly.

---

4 The article edited by Jane Herlihy, 'Should Discrepant Accounts given by an Asylum Seeker be Taken as Proof of Deceit?' is an example.

5 See Chapter 3.

The real challenges to the judge have deepened as governments increasingly have played the political card to keep control over immigration and at the same time make it appear that the review was truly independent to all. This intrusion into the role of a judge came to the fore when the 'Instructions to Immigration Officers' on how to approach claims was given the force of law by section 8 of the Asylum and Immigration (Treatment of Claimants)Act 2004.[6] This in effect told the judges what conclusions they must draw from certain specified behaviour of the appellant – for example, producing false documents. This came on top of earlier legislation removing some categories of cases the judges were permitted to hear (the 'Manifestly Unfounded' (MU) and those from EU or so-called 'white countries' (ironic since the appellants were predominantly black).

For a moment, let us return to the Wilson Report of 1967, which envisaged a relatively informal enquiry into issues which at the time covered quite a small spectrum of situations with minimal law and on sets of facts which were fairly recognizable to the judges of the day. The original decision by the Home Office would have been thorough and presumably professional. The caseloads were light and there were few restrictions on how the judge conducted the appeal.

But caseloads increased and the jurisprudence expanded. With international conventions governing the position of asylum-seekers and regional treaties governing every issue of life within the EU, appeals demanded more expertise and frequently wheelbarrow loads of papers which, even if one had unlimited time, could never be absorbed nor analysed by judges to know whether what they distilled from it all was correct or not.

The form of the enquiry for immigration, particularly asylum appeals, is not simply to decide on the evidence as presented but decide where the truth lies – elusive as such an aim may be, none the less that is still what the Immigration Judge keeps in mind. The expectation of a 'good' decision which has such an aim seems inconsistent with the strict time constraints which inhibits powers to try to correct the inadequacies of inadequate Home Office decisions, being required to decide facts in prescribed ways, and so on.

The Home Office, on the other hand were under no such legislative time constraints but had already succumbed to the pressures, being unable to produce carefully constructed decisions in a thorough and professional form, within anything like reasonable time limits When cases came on appeal, the Home Office did not have enough presenting officers to present the cases before the adjudicators, and they still appealed when they lost.

Dealing with the Evidence

The judge, when dealing with any immigration case will, in Stephen Sedley's words, be '[doing his] honest best to discern truth from falsehood [which] is a

6 c. 19.

grim and exhausting business and is not helped by the pressure of time';[7] the responsibility is a heavy one since the consequences to the appellant (and the appellant's family) if the judge gets it wrong can be disastrous, even fatal in asylum and human rights appeals. Certainly, many of the Rules, Guidance and Practice Directions are helpful, but others limit discretion on adjournments to get evidence, and even what the judge should deduce from certain behaviour[8] or, in the case of the CGC, accept a statement of fact as binding even though one may suspect it may be inaccurate.[9]

Judges in England and Scotland have dilated on the expert character of the tribunal. Some judges even consider that they 'are not recruited from the Clapham Omnibus'; they are skilled and specialist and will build up a fund of information about different countries. The danger in thinking that experience necessarily leads to better decisions is that in fact it may simply lead to making the wrong decision over and over again.

The predominant part which factual evidence plays in the immigration appeal is clear: get the facts right and the likelihood of a good decision is high. Misread the facts and, however well the law is interpreted, or however hard the judge tries to do his or her honest best, the decision will be flawed, in the sense that it looks good but that the conclusion is wrong.

For all anyone knows, every decision made could be wrong, because there is no means of knowing when it is right. The only two instances known to the author where the tribunal in the UK has learnt the outcome of a decision were when a reluctant bride ended up dead, and when the Tamil refugees in the *Sivakumaran* case either disappeared or were tortured after being sent back to Sri Lanka.

Before turning to sources of evidence, Professor Leroy Certoma, formerly a senior member of the Immigration Review Tribunal in Australia, remarked on how procedures and the type of hearing can be either a help or a hindrance:

> There is a balance to be struck between the speed and the quality of procedures. While legislation should help accelerate the asylum procedure, good quality decision-making, particularly at first instance is also important to ensure the integrity of the system (and this can reduce the number of appeals allowed thereby saving more time and resources). Any legislative measure should take account of this balance. In the mid to long term the EU should agree on key principles of good practice for administrative acts such as interviewing and decision making and could even establish a Centre of Excellence for asylum practitioners which promulgates best practice and provides training on these

7 Sedley, 'Asylum: Can the judiciary maintain its independence?'.

8 S. 8 Asylum and Immigration (Treatment of Claimants, etc.) Act 2004: Immigration.

9 Does such a Practice Direction as 18(2) April 2005 not implicitly exert such a pressure?

> issues as well as acting as a key resource for the sharing and exchange of Country of Origin Information.[10]

What may or may not be relevant as evidence can mystify the lay person. In asylum appeals, the decision cannot rest just on what evidence the parties may choose to lay before a judge as is the position in a court of law; being able to take it further within time constraints does come with experience, and often not a little courage. Some skill is called for in eliciting more information without seeming to take sides, as we saw in the observations about the *Surendran Guidelines* in Chapter 3.

The rules of evidence are relaxed in this jurisdiction but still there are limits. One of these limits is the extent to which the judge may rely on their acquired personal knowledge. Broadly it is accepted that this knowledge may be used, but only if both parties are given an opportunity to question it.[11] Information-gathering exercises during the 'Grand Tours', and indeed in the course of any other visit or tour by an individual or a group of individuals, encountered this problem – and no doubt will continue to do so as long as the appeals follow an adversarial judicial pattern[12]

There was timely advice in what the Court of Appeal said of the unusual nature of this jurisdiction, in so far as it concerns asylum appeals, in *Karanakaran* and in *Shah and Islam:*[13]

> The civil standard of proof which treats anything which probably happened as having definitely happened is part of a pragmatic legal fiction. It has no logical bearing on the likelihood of future events or (by parity of reasoning) the quality of past ones.

The immigration judge's enquiry is not simply to decide the outcome on the balance of probabilities and upon whatever may be presented to him, which is what lawyers are used to. Consider again what is spelt out in the UNHCR Handbook:[14] 'the duty to ascertain and evaluate all the relevant facts is shared between the applicant and the examiner, and the examiner should be qualified by having the necessary knowledge and experience.'

The Home Office makes the first examination of the facts and is in the best position to assemble all the facts and make a reasonably sound decision, given it has all the time to do so. Frequently, however, it has given bizarre reasons for

---

10 See unpublished paper 'The Non-adversarial Administrative Process and the IRT' (1991) by Professor Leroy Certoma, once Senior Member of the Immigration Review Tribunal Australia.

11 *Hettiarachchi* [1991] Imm AR 499.

12 See Appendix 3 for other examples.

13 *Shah and Islam v Home Secretary* [1999] 2AC 629.

14 UNHCR Handbook on Procedures and Criteria for Determining Refugee Status (1992), HCR/IP/Eng/REV.1, Geneva, especially at paras 195–205.

refusing asylum claims. If the Home Office does not carry out its duty in accordance with the UNHCR Handbook, is it not unreasonable to expect the judge to be able to make a better decision? Sedley J said, commenting on the unique complexity of issues in asylum appeals:

> Its adjudication is not a conventional lawyer's exercise of applying a legal litmus test to ascertain facts; it is a global appraisal of an individual's past and prospective situation in a particular cultural, social, political and legal milieu, judged by a test which, though it has legal and linguistic limits, has a broad humanitarian purpose.[15]

But the Home Office decision was often based on inadequate research, or poor understanding and little knowledge of the law. As Lord Carnwarth remarked:

> Ideally the process should start and finish within the department responsible. The initial decision needs be made, or action taken, on the basis of the fullest appreciation of the facts and the law. If not, internal review procedures may bridge the gap. Tribunals can help to improve the internal decision-making by constructive feedback from the cases before them[16]

This inevitably presents every decision maker from the start to the finish with a daunting task. It is particularly daunting when it is a single judge to decide the facts; there is no jury[17] to insulate the judge or provide a balance of 'street credibility'.

The Background Material

When the tribunal first started, and for many years afterwards, there was no budget for books or for training. Somehow, the Chief Adjudicator found resources to provide the Immigration Appeal Reports and from 1985 Callender's Book of Precedents (later referred to as a Handbook), which was updated by him roughly every three months and distributed to adjudicators. With the arrival of asylum appeals, the Amnesty International Yearbooks, the US State Department Reports and the UNHCR Handbook were provided. Those Reports were at first vetted

---

15 *Reg. v. Immigration Appeal Tribunal and Secretary of State for the Home Department, Ex parte Shah* [1997] Imm.A.R. 1 at 145, 153.

16 *Tribunal Justice – A new start* (Carnwath LJ – Senior President of Tribunals), para. 21, ajtc.justice.gov.uk/adjust/articles/LordCarnwathSpeech2008.pdf (last visited 2 July 2013).

17 I will return below to the absence of a jury in dealing with representation. The removal of the nearest the tribunal ever had attained street cred approaches, the Lay Members on the Tribunal and the emasculation of the ability to challenge factual errors compounds the doubt that the decision is 'good'.

by a very prestigious Committee on Human Rights, which issued a critique of them,[18] giving the Reports both authenticity and some independence from the State Department. That vetting process was abandoned and the Reports can no longer be regarded as independent.

The Foreign Office started producing Fact Sheets at least as far back as 1978, but they were no more than one or two roneo'd sheets, covering 25 countries, with little more than information gathered at missions or in the Foreign and Commonwealth Office with an edited version of Keesing's Archives. But they gave adjudicators ready access to some hard facts – such as how many *biggahs* there were to the acre (three), or the value of land in the Punjab and how governments operated. The Fact Sheets were gradually extended[19] to cover political information for asylum appeals but there were hiccups; first, the Home Office did not want some of the information shared with appellants, thus they were or little use and later the citation of background material was suspended[20] for a while to avoid misleading adjudicators because the information was unsourced.

A proposal in 1993 that the tribunal should produce its own sources of information in the public domain (of which a list would be given to the parties inviting them to supplement them) in the absence of support never got off the ground – but it was successfully introduced in Cape Town when a group of adjudicators was seconded to assist South Africa.

In 1993, John Housden, one of the first adjudicators to be appointed, prepared a Benchbook, which was intended mainly for new adjudicators, and was later issued in loose-leaf form. This handbook contained what was contained in earlier handbooks, together with information on other practice matters such as bail and CA's Practice Directions. This supplemented minimal information given to adjudicators in any other way. It contained both law and references to factual material.

Ann Dummett and Jan Niessen of the Churches Commission for Migrants in Europe produced Briefing Reports in the 1980s and early 1990s. They lost nothing to their practical value by being succinct. When there was a paucity of any information at all, these Reports often proved most valuable.

---

18 Lawyers Committee for Human Rights (1991), *Uncertain Haven* (New York: LCHR), p. 141. Arthur Helton was the Director of the Refugee Project for 12 years until, in 1994, he joined SOROS. He was also a staunch friend of the IARLJ until his tragic death in Baghdad.

19 The CA visited the FCO on 21 September 1988 and persuaded it to extend the service for adjudicators, generally in effect from the South Asia and Middle East desks preparatory to the overseas tour by Lady Anson and the author.

20 By the author, in order to protect the adjudicators and prevent time wasting. See correspondence, including letter from IND 5 June 1995 (archives).

The search for more reliable information and safer ways to evaluate it is no doubt what the Home Office would say it has been consistently trying to do.[21] The Home Office rejected the idea of an Independent Documentation Centre, but prepared a more complete and sourced body of information on those countries producing the most refugees. It is produced biannually by the Country Information and Policy Unit (CIPU), which was established by the Home Office in 2003.[22] Some information may be included which has been supplied by fact-finding missions – presumably by people from the UK.

Later, an Advisory Panel on Country Information (ACPI) was established. The intention behind this would seem to be to give some added weight to the reliability of information which had been produced by one party to the appeal but its powers were only advisory.[23] The Home Office's own Country of Origin Information (COI) does not appear to claim to be totally objective and a refusal to allow an independent database must leave the impression that all their information is likely to be policy driven.[24]

The Intergovernmental Consultation on Asylum, Refugee and Migration Policies in Europe, North America and Australia (IGC, for short) is an informal, non-decision-making forum for country of origin information.[25]

A transparent Europe-wide independent documentation centre remains a dream to this day.[26] The Action Plan of the EU Council and Commission in December 1998 on the implementation of the Amsterdam Treaty encouraged a proposal for a continuous process of information gathering and analysis by a joint and independent European Research and Documentation Centre as part of a uniform European asylum system.

CIREA (the Centre for Information, Discussion and Exchange on Asylum) was another initiative, which was established in 1992 as an informal meeting-point for the exchange, documentation and dissemination of information on matters relating

21 And it seems to have satisfied the Tribunal that it is discharging its duty under the Handbook: *RK v SSHD (DRC)* [2004] UKIAT 00129.

22 Now the Home Office Country of Origin Information Service (COI) <www.ind.homeoffice.gov.uk>.

23 Transferred in 2009 to a new Independent Advisory Group on Country Information.

24 For an interesting critique of the subject, see Pettit, J. et al. (2008), 'The use of COI in the Refugee Status Determination Process in the UK: Looking Back, Reaching Forward', *Refuge* 25/2 (Fall): 182.

25 <www.igc.ch>.

26 Sources: 'Communication of the Commission to the Council of Parliament on the right to asylum', (SEC(91) 1857). Also the work by the scientific committee set up in 1993 at the European University of Namur with a very illustrious panel from the UNHCR and twelve countries. See Laeken European Council 12/01 <ec.europa.eu/governance/impact/background/docs/laeken_concl_en.pdf>, which established a system for exchange of information on asylum and migration and countries of origin – now the European Migration Network. It would have had a single reference point and would be broader than CIREFI and others.

to asylum in EU member states.[27] It was also intended that it should contribute to the development of EU policy and claims that it has shared information about the political, social, religious and economic situation in countries of origin since 1993. Whilst not doubting that claim, the immigration judges had no knowledge of its existence and if government circles in the UK knew of it, the information was not shared with the immigration tribunal. Indeed, it only came to light when a report was used in an appeal before the author, who caused a question to be asked in the House of Lords.[28] In many European countries – Germany for example – the country was represented on the CIREA council by a judge as well as civil servants, but it was only after the question was raised in the Lords was the then Chief Adjudicator His Honour Hubert Dunne asked to sit on CIREA's board.[29]

As the adjudicators began to understand what was required of them in deciding asylum appeals, particularly on facts regarding the country from which the appellant came, the sheer volume of material became overwhelming. The task of limiting what was almost 'wheelbarrow loads' of references and making access to information easier was more urgently needed when caseloads increased and the time allowed to make a decision decreased. It was only when the Country Guidance cases came on the scene that it was possible to limit this burden, but, as was remarked earlier, the Home Office does not seem to regard itself as bound by the findings of the AIT, whether relating to the factual position in a country or on the law. One example could be changes in circumstances and situations in a country which could enable a refugee to return home safely.[30] When the Home Office thinks that by pursuing a particular case, the AIT may reach a finding which will be an unwelcome precedent, it simply concedes the appeal. It is therefore encouraging to see that the new president Nicholas Blake has pledged to try to change this whole attitude adopted by the Home Office; he has said, 'My vision for the Upper Tribunal is a body of case law of high quality, consistency and clarity. We must … earn the respect of … politicians and the public and in doing so no doubt persuade the Home Office to consider itself bound by the tribunal.'[31]

With the growth into a veritable empire of more than 600 decision makers, the resources needed to ensure that decisions involving someone's future are in safe

---

27 A full explanation, together with a list of EU directives is to be found at <http://aei.pitt.edu/7061/1/000431.pdf>.

28 See Hansard, 3 August 1998, an oral answer by Lord Williams of Mostyn to a question by Lord Lester of Herne Hill.

29 For a list of formal and informal bodies tabulating the increasing role played by the EU, see *Chronological Overview: Europeanisation in the Field of Immigration and Asylum* <www.network-migration.org>.

30 The facts (on which *Arif v SSHD* [1999] Imm AR 271 were based) in 1996 could, according to his lawyer, affect 50,000 other refugees. Such a scenario was not unusual and yet there has never been any known example of the Home Office making 'block' or 'bulk' decisions which could save time, money and much heartache.

31 <www.freemovement.org>.

hands have had to expand; as the cost rises, so does the attention paid to the system by politicians and public.

The need for the best objective (but what is 'objective' in this context?) support should not, as has been noted, stop at what is offered by the parties themselves. It also has resource implications.

The International Association of Refugee Law Judges (IARLJ), through its working parties, has devoted much time and thought to both country background information and expert evidence. In respect of both it has produced Guidelines and Reports.[32] These guidelines are intended for use by judges and decision-makers in any country. They are intended as a guide only and not all countries regard the UK approach to the method of gathering and using country information as suitable to their jurisdictions.

But whatever material is placed before the judge, oral or documentary statement of facts, expert evidence, even the judges' own knowledge where it can be used, he or she is to a large extent but an observer, an observer who has rarely had any training in observing though some experience in evaluation of oral testimony.

The Country Guidance Cases

Facts are an integral part of the approach in the UK to the use to which country information is put by the immigration judge; hence the importance of trying to get the facts right and to make decisions as consistently as possible – quite apart from saving time from constantly going over the same ground every time in every case which bears some similarity.

The origins of the Country Guidance Cases (CGC) has been dealt with in Chapter 3. Here, we look at their function.

The Upper Tribunal selects an appeal which involves a country which recurs frequently in appeals and thoroughly examines all the available relevant evidence on that country. When it has done so and reached a decision on the situation there, the decision is then reported and must be applied to all other cases involving the same facts until any change takes place.[33]

The CGC, though not binding as such at the time (since it involves matters of fact only), should be followed unless there has been some change in circumstances of the country in question. The best the president could do at the beginning was to rely on his authority and the intrinsic practicality of this innovative approach. If it was not followed, it was considered that it may well be considered an error of law.[34] On 4 April 2005, the then president made Practice Directions under a

32 'Judicial Criteria for Assessing Country of Origin Information: A Checklist', 21 IJRL 149 and Report 2009 <http://www.iarlj.org/general/images/stories/wp_papers_cape_town/hugo_storey_bostjan_zalar_-_coicg_working_party.pdf> and 'Expert Medical Evidence Guidelines', see Appendix 5.

33 See *S and others v SSHD* [2002] EWCA Civ 539; [2002] INLR 416.

34 *R (Iran)* [2005] EWCA Civ 982.

power given him by the Asylum and Immigration (Treatment of Claimants, etc.) Act 2004, one of which (Practice Direction 18.2) required the tribunal to treat a case marked 'CG' as authoritative and not merely strongly persuasive.

Authoritative or not, is it a 'fact' that there is or is not a risk to failed asylum-seekers on return to the Democratic Republic of the Congo,[35] or is it a conclusion which each judge must draw from the CGC? Which part of these cases will a judge be 'in error' not to follow? Situations in countries also change with great rapidity – a country or part of a country may be safe today, but not tomorrow. A problem related to the authoritative nature of the CGC would seem to lie in the point of time at which knowledge of a past change in circumstances may become known.

There will inevitably be different views by different judges about *how* the situation in any particular country applies to the case before them and they must rely on their experience in other appeals and on common sense to reach a decision. The CGC is a tool, but only a tool which by and large judges can welcome in the face of time constraints. It is possibly an improvement, too, on the Canadian practice of giving the judge a precis of all the information, which amounts to someone else's opinion of what the material means.

The usage of the CGC was a courageous step to take since it is, as Sir John Laws said, 'foreign to the Common Law', but for all the CGCs' pitfalls[36] (some of which are mentioned above), it kept the facts of some of the most commonly recurring countries under constant review by a panel of senior immigration judges, who, supposedly, had more time on their hands than the individual immigration judge.[37] This absolved other more time-pressed immigration judges from having to trudge through the same wheelbarrow of documents every time they heard a case from the same country. The CGC now covers some 60 countries or more.[38]

Given that facts are at the root of most asylum and human rights-based decisions, mere 'Guidebook knowledge' of a country is not of much use for the decision maker in an immigration appeal, and the real expertise of the immigration judge lies perhaps in knowing where to look for that which others do not know or may want to conceal, as well as knowing what to look for in the information obtained. This is not just for cases where someone claims he will be tortured if he is returned to his country; it is just as important – though the consequences may be milder – in deciding why spending a small fortune on a qualification in the

35 *VL(risk-failed Asylum Seekers) DRC CG* [2004] UKIAT 0007, and *MM [DRC] v SSHD* [2005] UKIAT 19; [2005] ImmAR 198.

36 'Assessing which accounts are reasonably likely to be true may often come down to intuitive evaluation', from Talbot, T. (2004), 'Credibility and Risk: One Adjudicator's View', *Immigration Law Digest*: 29.

37 Dealt with in more detail in Chapter 3.

38 For a substantial critique of the Country Guidance Cases system, see Immigration Advisory Service Report 2004 and also see Thomas, R. (2011), *Administrative Justice and Asylum Appeals* (Oxford: Hart).

UK, when there are good schools back home, is logical and justifiable. The sort of enquiring mind Martin Buber speaks of here is vital: 'The observer is wholly intent in fixing the observed man in his mind, on "noting" him. He probes him and writes him up … .'[39]

Without being able to see behind the public image and interpret the unrevealed, sifting the plausible from the implausible story, the real from the imaginary will always be difficult.

The 'Grand Tours' and Own Knowledge

The familiarization tours (the so-called 'Grand Tours') were introduced shortly after the IAA came into existence, in an enlightened hope that they would be sources of useful information for the adjudicators generally, and at the same time break down mental barriers as to how the rest of the world lives and add to the 'specialist' knowledge which today's immigration judges are said to have.

In principle, it was a good idea, but it was never thought through. The adjudicators on the tour may benefit, but how could they use that knowledge in any case they heard? And how could they share it in such a way that other adjudicators could use it? Only two adjudicators would visit different regions of the world every two or three years – a maximum of about ten in a decade.

Those who went on these tours, which normally lasted from two to four weeks, did come back with a better understanding at the very least of decision making by visa and entry clearance officers in the missions themselves, the often difficult circumstances in which they had to work and the lack of feedback information they received concerning the outcome of their and other decisions. The adjudicator may not have the advantage of what happened after their decision but at least the ECOs in the mission could have been told the outcome of their decisions.

The reports made after every visit were never routinely distributed nor even discussed.[40] It was not until 1988, when the then Permanent Secretary, Sir Derek Oulton,[41] suggested that seminars should be held by those who went on the tours, which would add to their value. But this never happened, perhaps due to the fear that a seminar might influence a decision, perhaps unwittingly, without having been disclosed to the parties.

It is not intended to repeat here the detail of the reports – though many of them make interesting and amusing reading – but what follows are some of the highlights which are relevant to some of the issues which face an immigration judge. Adjudicators generally made a point of meeting the local communities; on the first of such tours in 1973 (to Pakistan, Bangladesh and India), whilst in India,

---

39 Buber, M. (1947), *Between Man and Man* (London: Collins Fontana), Chapter 1 'Dialogue', p. 25. Buber was dilating on 'Observing, Looking on, Becoming aware'.

40 A copy of every Report has been kept by the author and is available for anyone to see.

41 Through Steve Orchard, then Circuit Administrator.

one of the adjudicators was hauled out of bed at midnight by Dr Patel of the British Passport Holders Association demanding an immediate audience with the adjudicator on some issue which was never recorded. He got his interview despite the late hour, but with the, adjudicator in his pyjamas *chota hazri*[42] in hand.

Stories abound about diplomatic missions abroad; many portray them as figures of fun. Some, like the one that follows, have their amusing sides but are practical examples of British diplomacy in action. In Dhaka, after the departure of some Russian envoys, the British considered that the Russians had ruined the international tea market for Bangladeshi tea due to their own (peculiar) tastes. The British High Commission therefore cloned a replacement, which subsequently became popular and highly marketable, stocked in many shops and sold under the label 'Genuine Bangladesh Clone Tea'.

The evidence of age estimates given in many hearings was regarded by adjudicators with suspicion. An event which demonstrated the unreliability of age estimates of older people better than any technical evidence was the test carried out on Mr Peterkin the Chief Adjudicator at the time; an estimate of his age recorded him as being eight years older than he actually was.

But whether discussed or not, or openly relied upon or not, some of the information obtained from the visits did become received 'wisdom' amongst adjudicators, in a sort of 'grapevine' manner, especially when the information simply concerned customs, geopolitical facts and economic conditions which were in the public domain already – if you knew where to look and had the time.

The value of the presence (or absence) of particular documents, the corroborative value of school certificates and the use and value of documentary evidence of a marriage which was regarded as purely a religious ceremony, for example in Mirpur, was all useful background and came up time and again. Possibly this too sunk into a subconscious expertise. Even the attitudes of the local courts to challenges to documents – who proved as suspicious of them as did the adjudicators – was relied on in making judgments on the plausibility of a story or the truthfulness of a witness.

All who went on the tours met with officials, the mission and the judiciary. The extent to which they had any close contact with local people tended to vary. One judge had recently visited the UK, and met the Lord Chief Justice and attended the House of Lords. He related that none the less his exposure remained inadequate and that an acquaintance with the peculiarly English institution of the pub would give him a better feel for the ordinary people. He started his pub crawl at the 'Prospect of Whitby' at Wapping Stairs – sad to say, the record does not tell us at what pub he remembered reaching at the end of his own familiarization tour.

The Entry Clearance Officers (ECOs) obtained much of their information in village visits, although they took place in less than 1 per cent of the applications in Bangladesh. Adjudicators who went to India, Pakistan and Bangladesh would usually accompany the ECOs on one such trip. The importance of these visits

42 A drink.

diminished in most theatres, when genetic fingerprinting (DNA testing) became more common to determine relationships – and the villagers became more practised in deceiving the ECOs. DNA was not universally regarded as reliable and the reason, so it was claimed in Pakistan, was the practice of marriage to first cousins.

ECOs generally objected to adjudicators, having allowed an appeal, say from a refusal of a visit visa, giving a direction that the visa be issued. Their point was that the situation may have changed; the adjudicator's concern was that failing such a direction, by the time the successful appellant got his visit visa, the reason for it would long since have passed As a result, the form of the direction usually given was 'if the circumstances have not changed' and gave a right to apply for further directions if a visa was not granted on reapplication.

An example of the need to have 'street knowledge', not just country information, came up in a visit to Ghana. It was inexplicable to the adjudicators why such a populous region as any country in West Africa should produce, relatively, so few appeals. They learned that the reason was that applicants frequently gave accommodation addresses and as a result, the notice of hearing never reached them.

In Accra, for example, the locals assured their visitors that all the beggars they saw on the streets were not Ghanaians but came from Chad. As a matter of fact, this is much closer to the truth than a Bulgarian judge's opinion that all the crime in his country was committed by Gypsies.

In one visit to the West Indies, the UK was taken to task by local people for applying its own standards of morality to a totally different West Indian society, when it came to the question of whether a parent who wanted a child to join him or her, who had control and had supported the child sometimes over many years. This has echoed down the years when gender issues arose in asylum appeals. Recommendations in the Report that changes be made to recognize this situation and bring the law into line with Canada and the US went unheeded.

George Farmer, who was on this tour and who later became President of the IAT, was asked to give evidence on what he had seen or heard in the West Indies. He declined on the grounds that it was not 'evidence', especially in the context of a tribunal which has become so 'Judicial'. It is supposed to acquire an expert knowledge of both the law and the country profiles: but how can such acquired knowledge be shared with others – inside or outside the judiciary? Even in Sweden, a former director of the Swedish Asylum Board who went on a familiarization tour himself was taken to task by the press in Sweden for relying on what he discovered when hearing subsequent appeals.

The first occasion when the adjudicators were briefed to look out for potential areas which may produce refugees ('political activists', as the government then regarded potential refugees) was January 1984, when Mark Patey and Sir John Pestell, who had been chief secretary to the governor in Zimbabwe (Southern

Rhodesia) during the UDI period,[43] went to India, Pakistan, Bangladesh and Sri Lanka.

In regard to the hostilities between Tamil and Sinhalese in Sri Lanka, the source of information was largely obtained from the British High Commission and later proved wildly optimistic. The mission concluded there was no reason why any Tamil need have any fear of return to Sri Lanka.[44] An example of 'mindsets and prejudices' emerged at lunch one day, when a Sinhala adjudicator opined that 'no Tamil could ever claim to be a refugee.' He did not remain an adjudicator for much longer.

Another pair of adjudicators was given some of the treatment many complain of when they come to the UK – they were refused leave to enter India and their passports were impounded! No appeal from this decision existed in India, but their discomfiture did not last for long. There is a picture of one of them, Victor Callender, doing a very creditable high-wire walk in Bangladesh.

Figure 4.1 Victor Callender in Bangladesh – practising for the high wire?

43 Unilateral Declaration of Independence by the Smith regime. This appointment further demonstrates the variety in backgrounds of adjudicators at the time.

44 Some idea of this thinking emerges in the course of the judgments in *Sivakumaran v SSHD* AC 958 [1998].

Short visits can be revealing to those trained to observe and who do not stick to the guided tour route but, to demonstrate how adjudicators have failed to get it right, those who went to West Africa saw no signs of future conflict and assessed military or 'chieftainship' or any other form of restrictive (undemocratic?) rule to be the best guarantee of basic stability in all West African countries, thereby avoiding difficulties of a political nature. This was long before Sierra Leone, Liberia, or anywhere else.

That there was no visit to Iran or Iraq was due to Mark Patey's fear that two valuable adjudicators might be taken hostage.

The longest and most comprehensive visits were the last major ones. Lady Elizabeth Anson and the author spent over four weeks in the Middle East, India, Pakistan, Sri Lanka and Thailand in early 1988.

The advantage this pair had over most others was that they had their own contacts in India, Pakistan and Sri Lanka, and hosts in each country who enabled them to get out and meet the people. There were some hair-raising and interesting journeys, such as Baroda (a city famed as the seat of the Maharaj of Baroda) from Mumbai (Bombay) by minibus through the market junction at Navsari famed as the meeting place where everyone met his bride-to-be 'by chance' (there is a similar venue in the Philippines). The roads were crowded; the lorries claimed unquestioned full occupation of the road, and at night time, no one dipped their lights.

Again we went from Peshawar up the Khyber Pass through the settlement of Landikotal, a sort of free port where one could buy almost anything, from bicycles to radios, fridges, watches, all without duty and nearly everyone, children included, carried an AK47. What followed was a terrifying journey (fortunately with an armed guard from the North West Frontier Police), when an oncoming lorry struck the Land-rover and nearly tipped it into the ravine. The policeman was able to calm the irate lorry driver – with help of his rifle. This was followed by another, even worse ride, in the assistant political agent's Land-rover to the last military outpost, where a major in the Khyber Rifles indicated the lie of the land out to the front into Afghanistan.

Chief Justice Naseem Hassan Shah issued an invitation to attend a seminar at the Centre for Islamic Studies in Islamabad, the day a fatwa was pronounced on Salman Rushdie. The subject was the Islamicization of the Law and was addressed by very senior Muslim scholars, including a much-revered Egyptian cleric who in effect told everyone to calm down as Rushdie had not even been arraigned, let alone convicted, and death at human hands was not what the Quran prescribed.

Colombo and Kandy yielded evidence of extensive training institutions in all manner of commercial activities awarding UK qualifications – and at very reasonable rates. So why, the ECOs very logically asked, should there be a need to go to the UK for the same course at a much higher cost?

Not for the first, nor the last, time there were adverse comparisons voiced concerning the modern facilities afforded to missions from other countries, such as Canada, Australia and the US and the penny-pinching attitude of the Foreign and Commonwealth Office and Home office toward the facilities provided for their own offices abroad. Things have improved perhaps, if a recent visit to the Chancery in Abuja, Nigeria is anything to go by.

A suggestion by the Swedish ambassador to Pakistan, to hold appeals from refusals at the missions which made them, appeared to have great appeal to the two adjudicators. Both the applicant and the decision maker could be heard, which made much more sense since it was usually the intention of the former which is important. (Also a tour of duty abroad would be a welcome break from Doncaster in midwinter!)

Far from dismissing this out of hand, the circuit administrator, John Heritage, remarked to the Chief Adjudicator, 'The points which you and I may usefully pursue include the possibility of the local hearing of appeals.' Nothing came of it, as we know, but maybe this idea could be revisited – it may solve some problems both for the Home Office and the Asylum and Immigration Tribunal – who already go on circuit in the UK. The risk is due to the inevitable proximity of the judge to the original decision makers and in their own somewhat closed society of the mission – particularly in large centres, such as New Delhi.

On another occasion, in pursuit of information on refugees from Afghanistan, the adjudicators visited Peshawar. There they ran into a riot, in which the offices of the *Frontier Post*, a local newspaper, were ransacked. The cause apparently was an article about Adam and Eve in which the paper had lifted a painting of Eve in a fig leaf and Adam draped in a vine. The local Muslim students were incensed by this insult to a revered *hazrat* (saint), not only portraying him at all, but showing both of them in a state of undress.

The twist to the tale, which today may not be so surprising, is that the police filed a case against the paper for publishing sacrilegious material – but none against the students.

The earlier opinions of Elisabeth Anson and Geoffrey Hawthorne[45], that visits to the Middle and the Far East (even China) could be useful, showed great insight.

A separate report relating to asylum was 'Restricted'. But what use was the knowledge obtained, if it could not be shared? As far as we know, not even the Home Office was told what we said. There was a general feeling that the Home Office took little notice of what the tribunal said anyway – a downside to the overall air of confrontation in this area of administrative justice.

Eighteen substantive recommendations were made (much to the Chief Adjudicator's concern, since in his view they lay outside the adjudicator's remit) on matters which, if implemented, could have led to a faster, better and cheaper

45 'It is more important that adjudicators should be informed about the social background to their appeals. It is disappointing … To learn that we are limited to the subcontinent where adjudicators have the benefit of their own experiences over the years, which in my view is invaluable, as well as reports and documents from colleagues and other individuals visiting those countries.' Disley and Hatt did indeed go to China later. See correspondence Hawthorne to CA in archives and further correspondence with Migration and Visa Department.

disposal of appeals. Among those recommendations was a closer involvement of the British Council in student visa applications, on the lines of the approach adopted in Thailand. There was also a suggestion regarding the reluctant spouse issue, emerging from discussions with the Indian community in Bombay (Mumbai). The Asian community were sympathetic towards a closer connection in spouse visa applications. However, the suggestion was never followed up and the dangers to the reluctant bride remain.

Another suggestion was a fast-track appeal for visit visas instead of a total abandonment, a recommendation which Sir Thomas Legg (the permanent secretary to the Lord Chancellor's Department) promised to 'consider'. That it was not adopted was doubtless due to Home Office determination to rid itself of such appeals completely.

Generally the ECOs told us that our decisions were frequently inconsistent. They were not the only ones to take that view, but then the adjudicators also felt that the Immigration Appeal Tribunal had failed to do its job in bringing about uniformity – which is what they were there for.

None of the missions appeared to receive the Immigration Appeal Reports (the Green Book) nor any feedback of adjudicators' decisions from the Home Office in London. When the Chief Adjudicator raised this with Terry Evans in the Migration and Visa Department, Evans responded, forgetting perhaps that the tribunal was no longer under the Home Office: 'I have no money for them, perhaps the tribunal may consider paying for them'!

The adjudicators on a tour in Sri Lanka got a local flavour of the dangers attendant on the hustings in that country when, five days before the elections, they stopped to listen to a politician address a meeting – barely an hour later, the meeting was bombed.

The author had heard the out-of-country appeal by *Sivakumaran* and two others, and had written the determination before travelling to Sri Lanka. It had not, deliberately, been promulgated since the decision was to allow the asylum appeals of the Tamils (who had lost their appeals in the House of Lords). The High Commissioner said that none of the information which he had fed back to London had ever reached the hearing of the *Sivakumaran* case.

Although there was nothing seen of persecution of groups, individuals were at risk in Sri Lanka and there was evidence which clearly suggested extreme insecurity for all young people in Colombo. The risk of arrest for young Tamils in Colombo was made quite clear, as was the risk to any lawyer who took on a habeas corpus case to try to secure the release of a detained Tamil from custody. However the UNHCR representative considered that European countries – who had received between them 90,000 Sri Lankans between 1988 and 1992 – were far too generous

In Thailand, there was a remarkable degree of practical cooperation between a commercially conscious ambassador and the Thai authorities and the Bangkok Bank, as a result of which there were few if any student overstayers. The British Council encouraged students in what seemed like a spirit of enlightened self-interest. It was thought that this may have been due to the cash guarantees obtained from the students' families. The embassy officials pointed out the drug haunts and drug rehabilitation centres – as well as the bar girls in Pat Pong.

What was a frequent recurring discovery from most reports was the lack of feedback from the adjudicators and the courts to the ECO. This explained why the ECOs continued to repeat the same mistakes.

The admission of husbands and fiancés and reluctant fiancées were still present on the Indian subcontinent – but as to the latter, not elsewhere. The adjudicators thought that the ECOs in Pakistan were exaggerating when they claimed that between 5 and 20 per cent of all UK sponsor marriage applications involved coercion, but agreed that the situation had been worsened when the Home Office relaxed the Primary Purpose rules and where a British sponsor had borne a child. The ECOs said they knew of cases of ill-treatment, detention and even rape to ensure a child would be born and had on numbers of occasions given refuge to reluctant female sponsors and facilitated their return to the UK – unbeknown to the relatives.

Because Ahmadi asylum-seekers regularly appeared before adjudicators, enquiries were made to try to find out just how much truth there lay behind their claims of persecution. It was discovered that there was a list identifying Ahmadis, and that when there was an Ahmadi Conference held outside Pakistan, the delegates who went to it would nearly always return home. The German embassy had told them that only four out of 120 Ahmadi asylum-seekers were recorded as genuine in Germany.

The Punjab was quiet when the adjudicators went to India, so they were able to visit this fertile part of India, where land could fetch up to £8,000 per acre, the same value as Grade 1 silt land in Lincolnshire. Police were stationed at the embassy gates so no one without their authority could get in – and given the need for a visa to travel and the great distances to be covered even to lodge an application for one, it must have made the experience expensive and frustrating.

John Disley and Tony Hatt were the last adjudicators to make a Grand Tour in the old style. They visited a raft of new countries such as China and the Philippines. They, too, encountered student visa cases but there is no record of how successful the Home Office was in persuading students to return to China when their studies were over. However, the Australians said that they had granted 40,000 student visas – and only between 100 and 800 ever went back to China!

One can perhaps see the beginnings of the current trouble with labourers upon whom the fast growth of China depends, but who are not being paid by their employers. Many arrived at railway stations and were ordered by the police to return home but potential employers simply scooped them up in busloads and took them off to work in factories.

In the Philippines, apart from the usual story of forged documents, there was a Commission for Filipinos Overseas who usually advised marriage applicants not to go abroad, advice ignored in 90 per cent of the cases. Robinson's Gallenia

Centre was the Filipino equivalent to Navsaria in Surat, India, that is, the generally acknowledged meeting place if you were looking for a bride.

David Pearl, as Chief Adjudicator, reported on a visit to Ghana and he shared this report with other judges in the tribunal. In doing so, he emphasized that it was confidential and could not to be disclosed to any party to an appeal – and that it was not usable in decision-making. But how could an adjudicator, once seized of something which may be germane to an appeal before him, eradicate it altogether from his mind?

David Pearl advised that an adjudicator's duty was to listen carefully to the position laid before him and then embark on (the unenviable) task of deciding whether the background framework he heard in the case before him makes it reasonably likely that the claimant may be persecuted on return. The adjudicator should eliminate from any final assessment the observation (by David) that he had been told that young Tamils are rounded up in Colombo and that it is no better and no worse for a returned Tamil. Or that, in India, the majority of people with whom he spoke considered that few Punjabis might have a bona fide claim to refugee status.

He made it clear that it was an ECO's view that asylum claims from Ghana were not likely to be successful, and he was not expressing a personal view. David raised the issues explicitly when he said:

> I suppose the important issue is how much personal knowledge a decision maker can take into account when making a decision. The point arises in other contexts, for example in the Employment Appeal Tribunal (EAT) and also in the Care Standards Tribunal (CST). In the EAT, there is judicial authority for saying that a lay member cannot take account of personal knowledge of a particular industry, for example, without putting that knowledge to the parties for them to comment on. But in the CST, the knowledge of a medical member may contradict the expert evidence brought on the part of one of the parties. The lay member's opinion must be put before the parties' expert for him or her to comment on. Surely the same should apply in the Immigration and Asylum context.

Once he had decided to circulate the report, that advice which may well have been good advice and the best he could give in the circumstances raises yet again the question about the sort of body the immigration tribunal is and the type of evidence it may be allowed to admit and rely upon. If the information it contains is relied upon by a judge, the source must be disclosed.

The West Africa tour in 2006 probably came as near as it is possible to sharing useful observations which help other adjudicators toward a better appreciation of the depth of understanding their role calls for, without any risk of the sort of fears and criticisms made in the past. For this reason I have included in this volume an abridged version of Catriona Jarvis's report,[46] which provides a sympathetic insight to what she found.

Is it possible to make any assessment of the worth of such visits, either then or now? Assuming we are stuck with the present tribunal system, perhaps the only messages which come across are that whatever information adjudicators have and cannot or should not put out of their minds must be revealed to both parties at the hearing.

Putting to Use Judges' Own Acquired Information

Allied to the information gained in the course of the familiarization or similar tours by others is the judges' knowledge gained from other sources.

It is inevitable that the immigration judges collectively will acquire some familiarity with the situations in many countries which they cannot help but share to some degree with other judges. It could be said that the CGC cases institutionalize this unspoken situation and put it on a more transparent and complete level.

But what about information gained in other ways, for example on some familiarization tour? The opinion so far has been that it could only be introduced if it is disclosed to the parties and an opportunity given to contest it.[47]

To the extent that knowledge amassed collectively can be used in the individual appeal provided certain procedures are followed, it would seem that the tribunal as a whole can be regarded as specialist.

Additionally, expertise can no doubt be acquired in other aspects of the immigration judges' role; for example, on how to deal with an expert, or how to handle evidence through an interpreter or intervene without taking sides; even perhaps how to read a person's body language and know when to do so may be misleading.

Of course if the consequences of the decisions were ever known, a better judgment of expertise would be possible, but any feedback is usually apocryphal; though events leading to the out-of-country asylum appeal in *Sivakumaran* in 1988 contained evidence of abuse on return to Sri Lanka.

In regard to the use of one's own knowledge, part of the difficulty seems to lie in the nature of the hearing. So long as the present adversarial system remains, the judge must balance on the one hand his role as judge in judicial or quasi-judicial proceedings (who would normally decide on the evidence presented to him), with what seems to be the overriding duty, at least in so far as Refugee Convention appeals are concerned, to do everything possible to reach the truth.[48] Almost all courts and judges consider that the tribunal is adversarial to some (undefined) degree.

46 See Appendix 3.

47 *Gnanavarathan v Special Adjudicator* [1995], p. 64 The court also considered that the adjudicator may not must (as Ouseley J said), identify an issue not raised by either party.

48 UNHCR Handbook, 1992 edn, p. 204.

The tribunal has held to the view that it should not produce evidence itself and only rely on what it is told. In other words, it should not be proactive. But then what happens when it acquires a body of expertise (and knowledge)? If there is to be consistency, that knowledge must somehow be collectivized. Indeed, it must be generally recognized that in this field it is impossible to separate the judge from the experience gained. How can this be recognized, exploited and made transparent?

Examples of reliance on personal knowledge must abound, but as there is no recorded appeal from anyone doing so, the examples given here can be personal. A young villager without political credentials fled Angola claiming to be at risk as a known and wanted opponent of the ruling party. He arrived in Lagos and said that within a half-hour he was smuggled aboard a flight to London. The story was rejected, not because it was inherently implausible, but because the adjudicator personally was familiar with the airport and its internal workings in Lagos and was satisfied that for this appellant his story was not possible within the timescale given. All this was put to the appellant at the time and included in the determination rejecting his appeal.

Another example occurred where an adjudicator had decided that the appellant's story was implausible. Extracting a very limited part of the determination (which is not reported), the judge said: 'I find the appellant's account of her escape from the DRC completely incredible. I find her account of walking through the forest and surviving on bananas and cassava implausible.' There is nothing to indicate in his determination whether he himself had any experience of walking through a forest in Africa nor whether he asked what type of forest, which may have suggested whether there were likely to be any bananas at all. If he did have such an experience, then it was undisclosed knowledge and he was wrong to rely on it. The case also illustrates some judges' approach to credibility and the sort of fallback position used to reach a negative decision.

With the formation of the IARLJ,[49] there is an increasing opportunity for immigration judges to travel widely, meet their colleagues and see the situations in many different countries of the world for themselves, in company with other judges. The IARLJ has assisted in sending judges from many countries to participate in training and seminars all over the world. Databases have been created of both facts and law as well as of procedures. As a result, judges' experience and understanding of the task they perform has widened immensely.

Judges from the UK, Australia and New Zealand were seconded to help with refugee decision making in South Africa; they brought to South Africa their experience and had the opportunity to take away a wider perception of the refugee. It is a pity that those in control do not yet see these opportunities as essential parts of the judge's training.

49 Formally established in Warsaw in 1998.

Expert Evidence

In the UK, it is not the practice for the tribunal itself to call for expert evidence, as it is in the Netherlands. Given this situation, the immigration judge needs to know how to handle any expert and this expertise can seem to clash with the judges' perception of their role as final arbiter. Certainly judges do become familiar with the approaches of some experts which may help weigh the value of their opinion. But when, as is usually the case, the expert is not present, it can be difficult, in adversarial or judicial-type proceedings, to cast doubt upon the reliability of the word of someone who is not present and to whom the doubts cannot be expressed.[50]

The IARLJ has been concerned about the need to give assistance to decision makers in this field and several years ago established an ongoing working party to identify whether some general guidance can be given. The guidelines it produced are now published on the IARLJ website.

In addition to the *Instanbul Protocol*, outlined below, the IARLJ have now published working guidelines for judges.[51]

The Istanbul Protocol provides in paragraphs 103 and 104 for guidance on medical examinations, assessment of the need for treatment and a psychological evaluation and goes on to suggest six questions to ask:

> (a) Are the physical and psychological findings consistent? (b) What physical conditions contribute to the clinical picture? (c) Are the psychological findings expected or typical reactions to extreme stress within the cultural and social context of the individual? (d) Given the fluctuating course of trauma-related mental disorders over time, what is the time-frame in relation to the torture events? Where in the course of recovery is the individual? (e) What other stressful factors are affecting the individual and what impact do these issues have on the victim? (f) Does the clinical picture suggest a false allegation of torture?

The reception of expert evidence[52] has become relatively well understood in civil or criminal litigation. But in immigration matters, the attitude adopted by the appellate tribunals has been the subject of extensive criticism in such areas as

---

50 Barnes, J. (2004), 'Expert Evidence: The Judicial Perception in Asylum and Human Rights Appeals', *International Journal of Refugee Law* 16.3: 349–57. It is proposed to follow these guidelines up with others for expert evidence on country situations. See also Barnes, 'Expert Evidence'. It has also a working party on Vulnerable Persons Guidelines

51 See Appendix 3, Catriona Jarvis's report on trip to West Africa 2006, also in <www.iarlj.nl>.

52 UNHCR REF World also provides list of expert COI: <http://www.coi-training.net/content/doc/en-COI>.

age determination, psychiatric reports[53] and the opinions of anthropologists. An example of how post-traumatic stress disorder (PTSD) is sometimes perceived by immigration judges (at tribunal level in Canada, in this instance) appears in *Appiah v Canada* in 1997. The judge, in overturning the Immigration and Refugee Board decision, said:

> The tribunal committed a reviewable error in assessing the applicant's credibility in that it accepted that the applicant had been sexually assaulted and that he suffered from post-traumatic stress syndrome as a result but did not evaluate or consider how the post-traumatic stress disorder could influence the applicant's recall of events or his demeanour before the tribunal.[54]

Form of the Hearing – To Intervene or Not to Intervene

The approach by a judge to the evidence credibility, their own attitudes, expert evince, and so on, cannot be divorced from views about what form the hearing should take, given the aims especially in asylum appeals.

The adversarial approach[55] was recognized by the Court of Appeal to be in need of modification at least.[56] The more interventionist the system is, for example in Australia or Canada, the more transparent its fairness seems to be – but this does not seem to be a universally accepted view.

The dilemmas in the use of 'own knowledge', referred to above is, as has been noted, bound up with the type of hearing and the nature of the position of the tribunal throughout; whether it is solely administrative, solely judicial, or a mixture of both. Most lawyers familiar with the common law courts would not approve of judges relying on their own knowledge as part of the evidence used to reach a decision. But adjudicators appointed in the early days were expected to draw from their own knowledge and experience; this familiarity with other countries was partly the reason why they were recruited from among those with service abroad. (Though one adjudicator, whose foreign service had been in India, had the habit of conducting his hearings in Urdu – if that is what the appellant spoke; this was discouraged by the IAT.) The informality of approach by any tribunal sitting alongside an official adversarial view was easier to accept in the early days and worked perhaps because of the adjudicators' background experiences and attitudes. They may have brought with them prejudices of a colonial background, a mindset which could contaminate the ability to make dispassionate judgments

53 HE DRC Credibility and Psychiatric Reports GG [2004] UKIAT 00321, on the duty of the judge if he rejects a report.

54 *Appiah v. Canada (Minister of Citizenship & Immigration)* [1997] Carswell Nat 1498, 134 F.T.R. 232, 73 A.C.W.S. (3d) 654.

55 Referred to earlier in Chapter 3, especially in relation to the case on the *Surendran Guidelines*.

56 *S and others v SSHD* [2002] INLR 416, at para. 15.

regarding people from other cultures and vastly different conditions of life, which Posner refers to in *How Judges Think*. But that may affect any of us – usually unconsciously.

Turning from personal approaches to general cultural attitudes in other countries, a leader in *This Day*, a national newspaper circulating widely in Nigeria, on 14 July 14 2006, dilated on the practice of female circumcision.[57] It observed that if there is any cultural practice which has resisted western influence, despite campaigns against it by the World Health Organization and various Conventions, it is this one. The journalist did not ask, as one judge in Nigeria did of the author, why the (western) courts confined themselves to the practice of female circumcision but never male circumcision. Both Zahir Chowdhury in his book *Split Families*, and Walter Kälin emphasize that 'a fair application of the law requires a close and accurate understanding of the socio-cultural diversities ... of ... people' if distortion is to be avoided and a credible decision reached.'[58]

In Africa and the Middle East particularly, at least among the mass of people, Christian and Muslim, homosexuality is universally condemned and any imposition of western cultural beliefs on this matter is rejected. For the judge in UK, this will usually only be raised in an asylum appeal when the issue is not the culture itself, but the state's persecutory reaction.

The view of Robert Thomas, which is referred to in the Preface,[59] is that there is an element of complicity on the part of the immigration tribunal in government policy, with respect this is not in any material sense simply because it replaces the original decision by the executive. If the tribunal reaches the same conclusion as the Home Office did, it is merely holding that the decision was right in law and fact. Surely this is no more complicit than the decision of the House of Lords (now the Supreme Court) in *A v Secretary of State for the Home Department (No 2)*[60]. If, on the other hand, one is to have in mind the *manner* in which individual judges exercise a discretion or interpret the law, the decision may take on the look of being in support of government policy. The judge may become a 'gatekeeper', as it were, but it will be unlikely that this would be done consciously.

The balancing exercise required of a judge mentioned earlier, which can put the judge on a knife edge, is whether to raise an issue not taken by either party. This has occurred where the facts suggest that the appellant may have been guilty of an act of criminality justifying exclusion from protection under article 1F of the Refugee Convention. When the judge must raise it, was considered in a number of cases.

---

57 In some countries, for example, Mali (2012), practitioners of this act are being prosecuted.

58 Kälin, W. (1986), 'Troubled Communication: Cross-Cultural Misunderstandings in the Asylum-Hearing' *International Migration Review* 20.2: 230–41; Professor Walter Kälin is at the University of Bern, Switzerland. Chowdhury, *Split Families*.

59 Thomas, *Administrative Justice and Asylum Appeals*.

60 [2005] UKHL 71, [2006] 2 AC 221, and dealt with at p. 157 in Chapter 5.

The latest was the decision of the AIT in *Arokiyanathan* in 2006,[61] which dealt with the law as to when the duty of the tribunal to take up the issue of exclusion regardless of whether either party has raised it, arose. The tribunal explained that it followed from *A (Iraq)*[62] that this is not optional: it is an integral part of the refugee determination assessment. But (since this was not the subject of argument), the decision in *Gurung*[63] must be read subject to two qualifications:

1. the exclusion point must be obvious on order for it to require the tribunal to take it into account of its own motion (refer to *Robinson*[64]); and
2. it must not require the finding of any further facts at the stage where the Upper Tribunal is deciding whether the First-tier Tribunal made an error of law, at least where it was the Home Office that sought permission to appeal.

The view that countries have demonised the asylum-seeker through their security-motivated legislation is of course linked to exclusion, and the judge cannot avoid being accused, rightly or wrongly, of coming down on the side of policies which give rise to that view. Mr Justice Ouseley himself said in *XS*:[65] 'However, in what remains an essentially adversarial system, for an Adjudicator to develop a hostile theory, in addition to the Secretary of State's different opposition can create a real possibility of the Adjudicator appearing biased. Warning bells should be sounding.'

A recent book by Joseph Rikhof of Canada, examines the extensive jurisprudence at the international and domestic level, which has attempted to balance the right of asylum for an individual versus the right of the state of refuge to restrict this right in situations of criminality (under the exclusion clauses of the Refugee Convention).[66]

At the end of the day, what may be viewed from the outside as 'complicity' may amount to no more than acting judicially within the permissible range of differing approaches; judges are expected to have the ability to be *de*tached from but not *un*attached to the society they serve – a judge does not operate outside society.

There are dangers in the judge going along with an administrative decision made to achieve a politically desirable end, such as the retention of a large engineering order from Saudi Arabia,[67] but that goes for all appellate decision makers and means only that judges must be trusted. This comes back to the Ministry of Justice

61 Arokiyanathan Appeal no. AA 09777-06.

62 A (Iraq) [2005] EWCA Civ 1438 (Court of Appeal).

63 IG (Exclusion – Risk - Maoists) Nepal * [2002] UKIAT 04870) (abbreviated to *Gurung*).

64 [1997] EWCA Civ 3090.

65 [2005] UKIAT 00093.

66 Rikhof, J. (2012), 'The Criminal Refugee: the Treatment of Asylum Seekers with a Criminal Background in International and Domestic Law (PB)', *Human Rights Series*, 3 (Library of Human Rights).

67 *Al Mass'ari*, Chapter 3, p. 81.

finding judges with the right approach to decision making, a difficult task given that there is no real means of measuring who is suitable and who is not for the role of immigration judge. Previous experience in some other sphere is unlikely to be a sure guide. Richard Posner in his book *How Judges Think*[68] did not think many judges even understand why they act as they frequently do.

Credibility

The observations above bring us neatly to deciding who is lying and who is not, or, much more frequently, whose story can be accepted as reasonably likely to reflect the situation on the ground. 'Credibility' is a word which has achieved such doctrinal authenticity that it is almost heresy to suggest that its pre-eminence of position may be misplaced. It figures in almost every decision, because it has achieved such a measure of acceptance, but no experienced judge is under any illusion about the fallibility of discerning the truth from the false – especially in a witness from an alien culture, telling a story in a foreign language. In many hands, it can be minefield. This predominance given to the word makes it an arrogance best avoided. Hence the support by many experienced trial judges for the jury.[69] Where credibility must be used, let it be with studied care. Usually the issue is the plausibility of a tale and this a matter of reliability where the benefit of the doubt can more easily be given.

It is indeed used in of the UNHCR Handbook, but paragraph 195 does state that *after* the claimant has furnished the relevant facts 'it will then be up to the person charged with determining his status … to assess the validity of any evidence and the credibility of the applicant's statements.'

The wording of paragraph 195 puts the assessment of *validity* of the evidence *before* credibility, which seems to support the Canadian approach that, if a story seems plausible, the judge should be very careful about disbelieving the appellant. Basing a decision on disbelief of the appellant is often a common fallback, a counsel of despair, when all else fails.

The EC Qualification Directive imposes duties to cooperate with an applicant and confront him with relevant Country of Origin Information (COI), which the party is intending to rely on, which seems to be in line with the Handbook.[70]

Training, if available, will of course help a judge to approach cultures with which they may have but second-hand experience and highlight the dangers of allowing one's concentration to dwell on the interpreter and not the witness.

---

68 Posner, R.A., (2008), *How Judges Think* (Cambridge, MA: Harvard University Press). Posner has written extensively from experience as a judge and an academic, and his views in many areas are not without their detractors, at least on this side of the Atlantic.

69 A graphic tale of this is recounted by Stephen Sedley in *Ashes and Sparks*, about Hone who, denied counsel, got three verdicts from three juries, against the judges' recommendations.

70 EC Qualification, etc. Directive 2004/83/EL Recital 23 and article 4(1).

Training may also give some guidance on how to approach the seemingly incredible and to empty one's minds of a lifetime of assumptions and presumptions, if not prejudices. But no training will teach the need for humility in face of the challenges. But do judges need instructions on how to interpret human behaviour, as the law has now directed in the 2004 legislation?[71] Rough rules of thumb may be thought enough for immigration officers. If innocent, it is an insult to their intelligence; if deliberate, it is a further attempt to wrest judicial oversight by the executive. It still suggests a judge does not know when to give such matters the value they deserve and implies the judge is not fit for the job.

Sorting the true from the false is, fairly obviously, central to the majority of decisions. There are still judges who argue that one can tell a liar by their demeanour. Even if you agree with Freud that body language is a giveaway, there is nothing to suggest Freud was thinking about reading the body language of someone from another culture speaking through an interpreter. Likewise, looking for total consistency in a story in this jurisdiction in order to support a finding of credibility is likely to lead to a flawed result.

Courts all over the English-speaking world have struggled to find a formula to guide the over- or under-credulous, and to counsel caution in being too ready to reject a story.[72]

Lord Bingham said, over 20 years ago, and Stephen Sedley repeated more recently that a veteran judge had once said, 'The longer I sat on the bench, the less certain I became that I could tell truth from falsehood.'[73]

To say that credible statements must be coherent and plausible and not run counter to generally known facts arguably begs the questions of how to assess plausibility and which facts are *generally known* facts. Geertz suggests credibility or plausibility is a cultural system resting on a conviction of its validity,[74] but how well qualified is that person to assess what is reasonable in the circumstances? How are we to separate systemic injustices from individual prejudices?

Credibility is neither an aim in itself nor some sort of points system of analysis. As Regina Graycar puts it, 'Credibility is not itself a valid end to the function of an adjudicator.'[75]

---

71 S. 8 Asylum and Immigration (Treatment of Claimants) Act 2004.

72 UNHCR Handbook, 1992 edn, p. 204. *MM [DRC] v SSHD* [2005] UKIAT19; [2005] Imm AR 198.

73 Sedley, 'Asylum: Can the judiciary maintain its independence?', pp. 323–4. See also Bingham, T. (2003), 'The Judge as Juror: The judicial determination of factual issues', in Rideout, P. and Jowell, J. (eds), *Current legal Problems* (London: Steven and Sons); Jarvis, C. (2003), 'The Judge as Juror revisited', *Immigration Law Digest* 7 (Winter).

74 Geertz, C. (1983), *Local Knowledge* (New York: Basic Books), p. 76.

75 *Asif* 1999 SCC. Graycar, R. 'The Gender of Judgments: An Introduction', in Thornton, M. (ed.), *Public and Private: Feminist Legal Debates* (Oxford: Oxford University Press).

It was indicated at the beginning of this volume that it is not intended to present an up-to-date picture of the tribunal or immigration law, but at times some matters occur which underline a point. Such an event arose which graphically illustrates the government's lack of concern for the independent role of the courts. The Secretary of State for Home Affairs, Teresa May, in an interview on BBC1's *The Andrew Marr Show*, accused the judges of not taking into account the wider public interest when applying Article 8 of the ECHR:

> This is not an absolute right. So in the interests of the economy or of controlling migration or of public order – those sort of issues – the state has a right to qualify this right to a family life, I would expect that judges will look at what Parliament will say and that they will take into account what Parliament has said.
>
> What I am going to do is actually set out the rules that say this is what Parliament, this is what the public, believe is how you balance the public interest against the individual's interest. I would expect that judges will look at what Parliament will say and that they will take into account what Parliament has said.

Geoffrey Robertson QC is reported in the *Sunday Times* to have responded that Parliament could not 'pre-determine' the outcome of individual cases, which all depend on careful and compassionate assessment of very different facts and cannot use subsidiary legislation such as immigration rules to dictate to judges their interpretation of Article 8, saying 'Hard cases make bad law and politicians make bad judges.'

Some supporting evidence, such as expert evidence, may call for its own separate evaluation before putting it into the credibility equation. Some judges seem to perceive a possible threat to their role as the final arbiter in the case by expert evidence and, when the evidence comes from psychiatrists and anthropologists, it seems that some judges are reluctant to see how their fields are complementary to a well-reasoned and well-informed judgment.

In relation to all findings, something may have been missed and Karl Popper reminds us that 'We should be constantly aware that the study of the products is vastly more important than the study of the production.' The facts as found can be regarded as the 'production' in Popper's mind, whereas the conclusion to be drawn is a 'product'. It is one thing in effect to make the first binding, but quite another to do so in respect of the second – if only in name. The danger is to 'conflate the evidence and the assertion to be proved and reject the law of the middle'.[76] Perhaps more thought needs to be put into training for all decision makers at all levels, who have evidence led before them.

76 Popper, *Objective Knowledge An Evolutionary Approach*. It seems to me that the influences behind this system are Cartesian.

Interpreters

Assessing a witness's story – that is, plausibility – is closely connected to interpretation. Adjudicators appointed in the early days were generally familiar with working with interpreters – it would come naturally to look at the witness whilst listening to the interpreter as it were. Nowadays, not every immigration judge comes with experience of handling evidence through an interpreter from one language to other, let alone multiple interpretations. It calls for training but no training was given in this area; the expertise was learned – or often not learned – on the job. Just how dependent a judge is on the ability and the reliability of the interpreter to render accurately what the witness is saying was illustrated in 1995 where the appellant was Polish, claiming to be at risk of persecution for political reasons in Poland. The interpreter which the tribunal used on a regular basis was an elderly lady who had left Poland before the Second World War. Appellant's Counsel – also Polish – complained that she was mistranslating, appearing to be unfamiliar with modern Polish expressions. Unless the judge is alert to such possibilities, of which he can know nothing for certain, an appeal is likely to succeed. The selection of interpreter is, therefore, of the utmost importance and the input of the judiciary in their selection can minimize such risks.

Another recent example, taken from South Africa, shows the interaction between belief in a story by the judge, evidence given through an interpreter (which it was claimed was at fault) and rejection of the claim by the judge. A Rwandan woman, Jeanne d'Arc Muberarugo, who alleged that she had fled persecution in her country due to membership of the Rwandan National Congress was disbelieved and her appeal was dismissed due to perceived discrepancies in her story. This, she claimed, was caused by a flawed interpretation by a translator.[77]

Interpreters make communication possible across language barriers. That much is obvious but what is less obvious is the identity and training of the interpreters themselves, how they can be used and their potential for influencing the outcome of an appeal. When the Lord Chancellor's Department (LCD) took over the Immigration Appellate Authority (IAA), one of the most hotly debated issues over the provision of adequate resources was that the LCD did not consider there was any call for full-time interpreters. The Chief Adjudicator considered that so much turned on the use of the interpreter that control over their management and abilities needed constant supervision. A large number of cases were from the Indian subcontinent, so it seemed practical to have at least one full-time interpreter from that region.[78] The LCD insisted that the interpreter manager need not be an interpreter herself and in later times she was not.

---

77 'South Africa: Rwandan Challenges Refugee Status Denial', International Bar Association *LegalBrief Africa*, 30 July 2012, No. 489.

78 Report by Staff Audit Branch No. 4 of 1989/90. The conclusions are based on assumptions that casual interpreters can be assessed for competence. With Ann Corsellis and others at the Nuffield Foundation, attempts were made to establish credible certification

The qualifications, pay and character of interpreters within the judicial system as a whole is so central that to allow interpretation to be franchised out to some private enterprise, without close supervision, threatens the administration of justice. At one time, a librarian in the Refugee Council began to compile a glossary of terms in common use with their equivalent translations in languages most often encountered. Some attempt was made at this with some interpreters, after it was discovered that there were four different versions of translations of the words 'Primary Purpose' in the Gujerati in use in Mumbai.

The translation of documents and the need for a glossary of common expressions and relationships (especially before representatives became more organized and expert) was a common feature in appeals. Most interpreters did not regard this as part of the work for which they were paid, though for short translations, they were usually willing to help.[79] The importance of good interpretation was recognized much more recently in the Leggatt Report.[80] But to get good interpreters calls for the right pay structure and a recognized qualification. Translation from one language to another is only reliably made if it is in a cultural context. The change in language over time can render the interpreter himself out of date.

In some appeals, it has been discovered that the interpreter was from a tribe or other group who was either a traditional enemy or from the other side of the political fence. For example, the interpreter may be a Saudi al-Wah'habi, in an appeal by a Shi'ite, and both from Pakistan or perhaps Afghanistan – not always a good mix! Then there is the question which faces judges from time to time, where they understand the language themselves and consider the interpretation is faulty.

It is clear, therefore, that unless the translator is well qualified and independent, assessments of plausibility and credibility are likely to be of questionable reliability. The opportunity for establishing habitual places of residence through language usage has received some attention, for example in 2004 by the International Association of Forensic Linguists (IAFL).[81] As the IAFL Report stated in its conclusion: 'we advise that language analysis should be used with considerable caution'. Guidelines set out in the Report by the Legal Research Unit make interesting reading:[82] dialect and use of language, as well as knowledge about a particular place can, with care, be additional useful tools to determine some of the

---

after training, but at the time the level of fees paid to casual interpreters was so low that most would not take the tribunal courses.

79 With effect from 1 March 1994, translation of documents would no longer be checked and time limits were to be rationalized for submitting verified translated documents. See Direction by DCA, 17 December 1993.

80 Leggatt, A. (2001), *The Report of the Review of Tribunals* <www.tribunal-review.org.uk>.

81 IAA Legal and Research Unit Update Issue 18/2004 (30 September 2004). Guidelines on Language Assessment: International Association of Forensic Linguists p. 29.

82 Guidelines for the use of Language Analysis in Relation to Questions of National Origin in Refugee Cases ibid at p. 30

issues which arise in asylum cases, such as credibility, but also, like credibility, they are tools which in the hands of the inexpert can lead to mistaken (and possibly unjust) decisions.

The first and eighth guideline could overcome the problem of whether an interpreter can be allowed, in effect, to give evidence: 'Rather, they [the linguists] should be asked to provide evidence which can be considered along with other evidence in the case' and it is important to remember that 'national borders are not the same as linguistic borders.'

Likewise, explanations of cultural aspects of a language may be essential to a complete understanding of the culture, but the judge may not ask the interpreter for any opinion in an adversarial context in the UK – as was done in South Africa – in order to decide whether the appellant came from the Sudanese side of the border or the Ugandan – as it may render the interpreter a witness.[83]

Libraries and Practice Databases

The Bench Book prepared in 1994 was by 1996 in serious need of updating .and David Pearl arranged for this to be done at considerable cost. The Determination Templates which had been tried before and had led to criticism were tried again but subsequently abandoned.

Victor Callender's Book of Precedents[84] was for many years the only source of ready reference for cases prior to 2000, but after Victor's retirement, it became out of date and Jim Latters' Book of Precedents replaced it. It seems Housden's Benchbook disappeared. The tribunal's own website within the LRU provided a link between training and the work of the LRU and in addition there was another web-based source, the Electronic Immigration Network (EIN).[85]

The EIN was started in 1997 and was conceived as a nationwide project to enable the voluntary sector to provide better-quality services to its immigration and asylum clients through the electronic dissemination of specialized legal information. After an initial pilot project, on which Hugo Storey made detailed suggestions, a re-designed database was launched in June 1998 with both an open access public site and a members' area accessible by password. It developed a Country Information Database, a Directory of Experts, Caselaw Headnotes and the *HeadlEINs* bulletin. The IARLJ assisted Dr Paul Tiedemann in creating an online database in four languages, English, German, French and Polish, to widen

83 Personal experience of decision making in Cape Town whilst on secondment.

84 This is futher referred to along with other material on p. 143 above. The Regional Adjudicator at Harmondsworth produced a roneo'd list of recent relevant cases on immigration, with some comment and a good indexing system. It supplemented the Green Books, the Immigration Law Reports which concentrated on decisions by the higher courts.

85 The Electronic Immigration Network: <www.ein.org.uk>.

access to decisions in Europe. This database now contains Court decisions in asylum law of many different countries.[86]

When the Hatton Cross hearing centre was opened, it was intended that the bulk of the asylum appeals would be heard there, which would seem to call for a library and database as there were none nearby, but there was no library there and no money provided for one. Electronic databases were becoming a recognized feature and the UNHCR asked that we be part of a pilot scheme for their intended database of country reference and case law materials.[87] But money was needed. A budget was prepared with the help of the Supreme Court librarian at the time, but it was based on a somewhat artificial list of books. It was expected that the judges would be consulted before purchases were made. In fact, they were not and quite a grand collection, of not altogether suitable material books, appeared at Hatton Cross one day in 1995.

The provision of modern techniques of information technology was slow to be provided by the administration. The benefits of computer literate adjudicators using modern equipment was proposed but not implemented until after 2000. The new computer system at Thanet House in the mid-1990s took no account of the judiciary. Access to the internet was long resisted, because administration considered the judges would spend too much time surfing online! The judiciary did initially provide one computer in order to participate in a UNHCR experiment which involved putting data online. This was the result of a judicial initiative flowing from a close liaison with the UNHCR's regional office and the head office in Geneva.[88] After a number of hitches and some pressure, an online facility was in operation by the time the Lord Chancellor opened Hatton Cross.

A Consultants' Report commissioned by the Lord Chancellor's Department priced computerization at £873,600, which would have put the entire tribunal on the internet and give access to databases such as the UNHCR Refworld[89] and the EIN. Unfortunately, the tribunal's administration went off on a venture of its own in 1995 and tried to establish a relationship with an organization (in which a lecturer at SOAS was involved). This proved abortive but it set back the achievement of a unified database which would have been of assistance to the judges as well as the administration. The Information Technology subgroup of the Training Administrative Group, which was an in-house judicial initiative created in the absence of any finance to create a better system for training immigration adjudicators at the time. This group co-operated with outside groups such as the Immigration Law Practitioners Association (ILPA), and through it the Electronic Information Network (EIN), on how to put determinations on a database using the

86 See <http://www.iarlj.org/general/database> and <http://www.eear.eu/>.

87 The Tribunal now has its own case report database <www.ait.gov.uk>.

88 Professor Guy Goodwin Gill's wife Sharon Rusu was at the time re-establishing UNHCR databases. The cooperation was thrashed out between her, Hans Thoolen, Rick Towle, Victor Callender and the author.

89 <http://www.refworld.org/>.

discs from which the determinations were prepared. Unfortunately, someone in administration wiped them all out.

As Canada discovered, having a good information database for the tribunal is essential, but it has the disadvantage that the judges can be saturated with too much information. The dilemma was how to summarize it without taking away from the judge the duty to reach their own conclusions independently and not on the view of the available information taken by someone else.

Part II: Training and Representation

The days when judges were often heard to say they were judges and did not need training has thankfully passed – no longer is there any to resistance to training.

The IARLJ developed a training manual which has been used increasingly over the last 12 years for judges and others dealing with refugee issues in most parts of the world. The EU has also used the IARLJ to train judges in this jurisdiction.

The questions of how to address the evidence likely to be led in the context of what the issues are and who has to prove what and to what level, how to handle expert evidence interpretation, credibility, and so on, are not always familiar even to experienced advocates or judges from other fields. The law itself has become more and more complex as well.[90]

As late as 1988, when there were only 13 full-time (and 43 part-time) adjudicators and three full-time vice presidents, the induction of adjudicators was very basic, compared with the programme for immigration judges today; the IAT members did not seem to think they needed any training at all and there was no training in the use of interpreters by adjudicators.

From the very beginning, it was a case of learning on the job, but at least many of the early appointments had already served in some often senior judicial posts and had experience abroad, though to what extent this benefited the claimant is often questioned. Also at the time, a number of adjudicators were also fortunate enough to go on tours abroad.

Otherwise one had to rely on assistance from the UNHCR and talks by experienced and respected medical consultants at the Medical Foundation for the Care of Victims of Torture and the experience and expertise of judges and counsel.

The absence of any long-term budget, or in later years an insufficient one, was one reason for the absence of formal training, but another was that new

90 Fortunately, there are a few good, practically oriented textbooks and writers such as Macdonald, I. and Blake, N., *Immigration Law and Practice* (London: Butterworths); Fransman, L. (2011), *British Nationality Law* (London: Bloomsbury); Guild, E., *European Community Law from a Migrant's Perspective* (London: Kluwer Law International); a most useful handbook by Phelan, M. and J. Gillespie (2013), *Immigration Law Handbook* (Oxford: Oxford University Press), and Symes, M. and Jorro, P. (2001), *Asylum Law and Practice* (London: Butterworths), just to name a few.

adjudicators were appointed on a replacement basis, often only one or two at a time. Where three or more were appointed at any centre, the regional adjudicator would conduct a three-day seminar for them, but otherwise informal meetings and monitoring had to suffice.

A Training Advisory Group (TAG) was formed[91] to manage training, comprising adjudicators with experience, contacts in Europe and those with academic backgrounds, such as Hugo Storey and Mark Ockelton.[92] TAG's programme and functions are set out succinctly in a letter prepared by Hugo:

1. To identify training needs of all adjudicators
2. To determine training to be provided and training procedures
3. To construct and publish an annual and rolling programme of training events integrating national and regional courses
4. To monitor and evaluate the quality of training. Tasks here will include:
   (a) Maintaining oversight over the designing of courses, their preparation and the production of course materials
   (b) Maintaining accurate records of all training undertaken
5. To liaise with other bodies concerned with the adjudicator tribunal and its standards and workings, in particular, the Judicial Studies Board (the Board itself and the Tribunals Committee) LCD; Council on Tribunals
6. To ensure accountability for realization of suitable training.

This initiative was another example where lack of support from the administration prevented the judiciary from taking essential steps to ensure it could carry out its role; TAG did not even have enough money for meetings and resorted to fixing hearing days at some centre for all members, so their travel costs could be met.

In regard to monitoring, it had been fairly informal but at the time relatively effective by the Chief and Regional Adjudicators; one could say it was institutionalized in the 2004 Act,[93] with a revised Complaints Protocol.

The absence of judicial and advocacy experience may not be compensated just by classroom training, or even doing the job for a long time, when one never knows the outcome of an appeal (was the appellant tortured, imprisoned, or even killed when was sent back home?); it is difficult to know just how reliable are our decisions. Although there was little formal training in the early days, some cross-cultural knowledge was obtained from talks by those with experience or who were themselves from backgrounds other than in the UK.

The jurisdiction has greatly expanded and the law grown more complex. The solution has usually been to appoint more and more judges. Certainly not many

91 Minutes, Southern Regional Conference, 11 May 1990.

92 Mark Ockelton, now Deputy President, offered his help in regard to judicial functions in Europe in a trans-national context and the possible exchange of judicial personnel – an exciting idea which seems not to have been pursued.

93 Sched. 4 (3) c (i).

have had earlier judicial experience and fewer have had experience of practising before the courts. Fortunately, some do come with earlier immigration-related experience having served with bodies such as UKIAS, and also there are part-time adjudicators who carry out immigration work in their practices.

Training has become increasingly sophisticated; the calibre and the impact of representation, databases and interpretation have gained more attention. The days of circulars may not have disappeared, but the content has changed somewhat from, for example, one in 1987 sent to all adjudicators at Thanet House titled 'Notes for Dictators'.

The importance of cross-cultural communications received official encouragement with the formation of the Ethnic Minorities Advisory Committee of the Judicial Studies Board under the chairmanship of Lord Justice Brooke.

Early on it was realized that asylum appeals would require special skills and some experience, possibly of other cultures and countries and it was only fair to the adjudicator and the parties to nominate those with this sort of experience or sometimes previous judicial experience. This caused some resentment and the reasoning was not accepted by other adjudicators.

When Mark Patey was Chief Adjudicator he considered it irresponsible to expect adjudicators to assimilate the constantly changing new legislation and decisions and generally to perform their duties to the necessary standard without ongoing training coupled with frequent and regular sittings. But there was neither a budget for training, nor any promise of one. The offer of some 200 more judges seemed to him like good money after not so good and was not an answer.

In 1993, a budget was prepared in readiness for the day the 1993 Act came into force. It was only with the strong support from the Tribunals Committee of the Judicial Studies Board and its chair Judge Machin and a promise to raise the matter with the Lord Chancellor at the opening of Hatton Cross on 29 April 1994, that funds were obtained to hold a two-day conference for the first time at Warwick University where one could also attract speakers of the calibre of Professor (now Lord) Bhiku Parekh on 'Differing Cultural Perceptions'.[94] Judge Machin found it astonishing that funds were not forthcoming; the author, when Acting Chief Adjudicator had a somewhat forthright exchange of correspondence and discussions with Peter Risk, the tribunal's administrator, who said, 'it was not intended that Circuit, or the Lord Chancellor's Department would be the purse-holder for training funds for tribunals.' Without realistic estimates of appeals or new adjudicators, it was something of a stab in the dark to assess additional

94 'While cherishing cultural diversity Britain must remain a cohesive society with shared national culture': Parekh Report. He also considers that the nation state is being eroded by globalization from within by increasing cultural diversity brought by the immigrant as well as from without: *The Times of India* (9 April 2007), Interview with Amrit Lal, Editorial Opinion.

resources required for judicial training in order to be ready for the first Bill, which was expected to be on the statute book in 1992.[95]

Eventually an estimate was made that a total of 90 new adjudicators would be required to be appointed in two separate batches – which at the time it seemed a lot.

Until some training was in place, new adjudicators had to rely on an Asylum handbook,[96] a case law database (to include EU cases in due course) and country background sheets (updated from time to time). A pamphlet, 'Best Judicial Standards', was prepared which opened with the warning 'getting the law right is not the only criteria', addressed natural justice in such diverse areas as delay, administration representation and of course – training.

A fresh, managed approach and new thoughts to the training of those occupying judicial positions was brought by the Tribunals Committee of the Judicial Studies Board, which consisted of the heads of all the tribunals. The 'Tribunal', a new publication, became a valuable form of communication for members of all tribunals.

From April 1994, training and necessary funding did not look back and residential conferences became common practice. There were, of course, light moments in lectures and discussion of complex and often new issues. At one in Oxford, an evening reception was held at the natural history museum among the dinosaurs, which one wag described 'as an appropriate setting for the assembled judiciary'!

The year 2000 saw a review of training programmes with each adjudicator being required to attend three training days a year. With a budget of £1 million for over 500 immigration judges and a head of training appointed by competition, by 2002 residential conferences could be planned in advance.

Staff also became available, and it was no longer necessary to take Janice Cotton, the Deputy Chief Adjudicator's secretary, away from her regular duties nor make the training officer lick the stamps for the notices.

Ongoing education programmes, and four-day inductions were being held every time there were enough new adjudicators to justify them.

Many plans for training were suggested, some new and others restored and polished up with the benefit of some money. A rolling agenda for training for all judiciary, consisting of day courses every year interspersed with residential courses every two or three years, was thought ideal and an annual conference for full-time judiciary was another particularly visionary idea.

With the appointment of adjudicators with little or no practice behind them, and even for the experienced judges in an ever-changing scenario, such ideas were not extravagant. What was taught in the programme, however, was even more

95 See letters, 13 and 19 April 1994 to G. Calvett and P.N. Risk respectively. Archives held by author.

96 A looseleaf volume for use by adjudicators as a Bench Book, compiled by adjudicator, John Housden. Referred to at p. 138 above.

important. A training methodology was agreed, concentrating on skills, discussion and small group sessions.

Representation[97]

Representation of parties before the tribunal is of great importance, possibly even more so than in the civil or criminal courts, due to the ever-increasing complexities in the law, the dangers of not getting the facts right first time and the manner in which such crucial issues are to be resolved. The worse the representation for a claimant (or, even, its absence), the greater the need for a judge (who is jury as well) to be well-versed in how to handle appeals in every way.

From the outset, the Immigration Act and the rules prescribed who had rights of appearance,[98] with the intention of preserving standards. But they did not regulate who could give advice, and in most cases good advice right from the start was as valuable as at a hearing – probably more so.

The Immigration Act 1971 guaranteed that any immigrant who needed advice or representation should have it free. Many of those who joined the United Kingdom Immigrants Advisory Service came with some immigration-related background or experience. The adjudicators did not then have any at all, but many of them had judicial experience and some familiarity with other countries and cultures.

The Wilson Report gave a lot of thought to an immigrant's need for advice and said that the State should always be represented. The report concluded that in something as important as deportation, associated with the liberty of the subject, there should be legal aid but for the rest a new organization closely linked to other welfare organizations was proposed. This was to be United Kingdom Immigrants Advisory Service (UKIAS).[99]

UKIAS was founded in 1969 with a central office in Bloomsbury.[100] The first chairman was Lord Foote, then David Winnick and Alf (now Lord) Dubs, and John Ennals was the first Director. Many counsellors have moved into politics or become judges such as the late Larry Grant, also late Clem Richards, Jasu Chatwani, Kate Eshun, Esme Martins, (now Her Honour) Barbara Mensah and Dick Lawrence, as well as Harriet Harman and Patricia Hewitt.

---

97 See Care, G. (1991), 'Representation in Immigration appeals: an adjudicator's view', *Immigration and Nationality Law and Practice* 5(2). Another adjudicator, Dr H.M.G. Concannon of Manchester also wrote of this (and other matters) in 1987, in an unpublished paper 'Some Comparative Observations of the Immigration Appeal Process'.

98 The Immigration Appeals (Procedure) Rules 1984: Rule 26 repeating the provisions of the 1972 Rules was eventually replaced by Rule 35 of the Immigration and Asylum Appeals (Procedure) Rules 2000. By that time, the Immigration Advisers and Immigration Service Providers provisions had been enacted in Part V of the Immigration and Asylum Act 1999.

99 Paras 175–8, Wilson Report; Part VIII, Wilson Report.

100 S. 23 Immigration Act 1971.

An allegation by the UKIAS that 75 per cent of the decisions by adjudicators were either quashed or remitted on appeal indicated poor-quality decisions by the adjudicators. This seemed to the Chief Adjudicator to have been based on a 'score' kept by UKIAS and was badly received by the CA and led to a meeting between himself and the author with the then Director and his Deputy (Khurshid Drabu) in an attempt to restore a harmonious relationship.

Apart from establishing offices in the UK and advising both appellants and their sponsors within the country, the UKIAS also sought to provide reliable advisory centres where there was a concentration of potential applicants for entry clearance to the UK. Examples are offices in Mirpur in Azad Kashmir and in Sylhet, Bangladesh. This was an early and important step in the battle against local shady 'travel agents'. Much later, Keith Best when executive director of the IAS[101] tried to do the same by franchising an office in Lagos and another in Abuja, but neither was successful. In the first few years of the 1990s, UKIAS represented around 48 per cent of all appellants But in 1992, it was facing a threat to its grant aid due to allegations of bribery and conspiracy by two of its staff in Leeds.

In 1993, UKIAS was split up, following a high-powered report by a committee which included Lord Dubs and Humphrey Malins MP, Baroness Feather, Dr Z.U. Khan and Rachel Pickavance. The new bodies were at first called the Immigration Advisory Service (IAS) taking on the non-asylum work, and the Asylum Advisory Service, which was soon renamed the Refugee Legal Centre (RLC) (now renamed Refugee and Migrant Justice). At first, all asylum work was channelled through the RLC and it became successful very quickly – at least in the eyes of the appellants – who won 22 per cent of their cases in 1996–97.[102]

There were other bodies representing appellants, five of them charities or welfare groups providing representation in those areas of the law not covered by legal aid. The Joint Committee for the Welfare of Immigrants is one which figured in some ground-breaking appeals.

Many who were involved as representatives in those early days – some for the Crown, but most for appellants – cut their teeth on this area and brought knowledge and experience which set a tone for the jurisprudence today. They have become judges[103] and recognized authors and senior counsel.

---

101 By then, UKIAS had been divided into two: the IAS and the Refugee Legal Centre, primarily to handle asylum appeals.

102 See the report by Justice, Immigration Law Practitioners' Association (ILPA) and Asylum Rights Campaign (ARC) (July 1997), 'Providing Protection: The Joint Report'. See also a very thorough, and critical, report by the Refugee Legal Centre (RLC) (1997), 'Reviewing the Asylum Determination Procedure A Casework Study'. This will be referred to in other contexts but it did deal with the role of the HOPO and adversarial systems, p. 130.

103 Lord Slynn appeared in *Syed Bashir Hussain* in 1975 in the Divisional Court as did Eugene Cotran. Colin Manchip (now CBE).appeared for the Home Office before the adjudicator as the Presenting Officer.

A development of great significance at the time and now for the future was the foundation of the Immigration Legal Practitioners Association (ILPA),[104] in which all or nearly all of those regularly appearing in immigration matters participate. Many of those practitioners, both solicitors and barristers, however have now left the ranks of those entitled to represent appellants, which not only deprives the appellant of help, but also deprives the jurisdiction of the research and advocacy which goes into decisions of depth and lasting merit.

The original decision by the Home Office can largely dictate the ultimate result, in the sense that if there are insufficient numbers of trained staff, poor information and prejudicial attitudes at that level the outcome will be inadequate. The inadequacy often lay in the 'Explanatory Statement'[105] which was produced by the Home Office when an application was refused. The Explanatory Statement became shorter by 1994, which was not in itself an unwelcome move, provided it still gave all essential details, but when the 'Minded to Refuse' (MTR) procedure was abandoned,[106] this led to strong complaints from the coordinator of Asylum Aid, a major source of immigration free advice and representation provided by barristers and solicitors.

The adjudicators adopted a pragmatic approach and gave advisers, who could not appear as of right under the law and who regularly appeared before them, an automatic right of audience. New ones tended to be given a chance to prove themselves. Many independent advisers or immigration counsellors, as well as solicitors and barristers, charged for their services.

The quality of the representative was very variable and the need for some regulation has never been far from peoples' minds but the Immigration Appellate Authority had few weapons in its armoury to exercise any control or to provide any criteria for transparent refusals. Neither the Bar nor the Law Society was in a position to help very much and there was no official controlling body for the unqualified immigration advisers. The Lord Chancellor's Department did not think that the Courts and Legal Services Act 1990 applied,[107] if it did, perhaps some separate and expensive body would have been unnecessary.

The Royal Commission on Legal Services concluded that the availability of advice and assistance to tribunal applicants was unsatisfactory. In 1987, the LCD

---

104 Justice, ILPA and ARC, 'Providing Protection'; ILPA (1999) 'Breaking Down the Barriers', p. 33: The refugee community organizations and private firms each accounted for 40 per cent of those from whom advice had been sought.

105 This told the claimant the reasons for refusal and often little more. Even the tribunal, which had urged shorter statements in 1990 were forced to criticize the uninformative and less than clear statements on occasion.

106 An preliminary intimation of the proposed decision.

107 The Lord Chancellor's Advisory Committee on Legal Education and Conduct published a report in July 1998 'Improving the Quality of Immigration Advice and Representation'. Surprisingly enough, the Committee was established under the Courts and Legal Services Act 1990.

recommended a more coordinated provision for tribunal representation. It was observed that success and representation went hand-in-hand, but no one knew why and questions were raised as to whether a change in the adversarial nature of hearings should take place. The right to representation is not usually removed in non-adversarial-type proceedings, but it is limited – usually no cross-examination is allowed. Although not strictly related to representation, the introduction in 1992 of the Users' Consultative Committee by the adjudicators met with enthusiastic support from ILPA and others, as a major step to bring the representatives on board to discuss hearing-related policies before they were introduced.

A former vice president of the Immigration Appeal Tribunal wrote in a paper given at a Training Seminar:

> What we as adjudicators are trying to do, is find the truth ... to do that, I consider that we should act in a more inquisitorial role. By that I mean that no matter how well represented the Home Office or the appellant before us is, we should not be satisfied until we are as certain as we possibly can [be], that all the evidence is before us.[108]

He went on to quote David Pannick QC (now Lord Pannick): 'The integrity of the criminal justice system depends upon the assumption that all defendants will receive competent advice and representation' – which does not include some incompetent barging around in a cloud of ignorance in the hope of something turning up. Again, the impact of an adversarial approach emerges. It is premised on equality of arms, as it were; but the fact that the inquiry is supposed to be a shared responsibility (at least in asylum cases) hardly stands up to scrutiny when there is no obligation on the Home Office to disclose what information it relied on to reach its decision.[109] and often simply does not appear at all.

As the law in this jurisdiction has become more complex, time constraints have been made more stringent, caseloads are heavier, the judges do not see the case papers until the day they go into the hearing and yet are expected not to adjourn and to produce a reasoned judgment within days – if not on the spot. More and more judges are appointed from a very limited pool of suitably experienced people.

It does not require a crystal ball to discern how all this escalates demands for more and better support with attendant cost implications. The most crucial support was good advocacy on both sides. But either government removed it or made it more difficult to obtain, and, in the case of the Home Office, simply did not provide it.

The representative of a party not only benefits him or her, but also helps the judge to do their job well. Hazel Genn (now Professor Dame Hazel Genn, QC) and Yvette Genn set out their conclusions from in-depth research of representation at

---

108 The occasion and the reference is lost, but the author was present at the time.

109 *Abdi and Gawe*: see Chapter 3. But also consider *Heteriachchi* (1991) Imm AR 499.

tribunals (or the lack of it) and its importance in a report to the Lord Chancellor entitled 'The Effectiveness of Representation at Tribunals'. The Report states 'Although legal or lay representation of applicants is permitted before most tribunals, the ability of applicants and appellants to obtain representation is restricted'. In its conclusions the Report expressed the view that 'it is clear that calling the adjudicative for a tribunal … does not constitute a sufficient justification for assuming representation is unnecessary. It is not the name that is important. It is the nature of the issues at stake'.[110]

It is fine to provide, as the UK does, a remedy to check on an earlier decision, but such a right may be illusory if a claimant cannot understand how to present their appeal nor have the time in which to do so. This need for experienced, well-trained and resourced people to represent the parties has increased, not decreased.

The Legal Action Group[111] remarked on the lack of knowledge about tribunals and their workings back in 1990. There is a much better understanding today, but still the less formal atmosphere intended with the use of the tribunal structure should not mislead parties into believing that they alone are the best people to present their own cases.

In 1996, the Lord Chancellor suggested that failing legal aid, a register of practitioners be set up and the KPMG Review of Asylum Appeals Procedure in 1994 took on board the unsatisfactory state of affairs and recommended regulation of all immigration advisers – but there was no suggestion that legal assistance of some kind was unnecessary. In 1998, the Home Office addressed the allegations of persistent overcharging, poor advice and poor service – and even deception – in a Report, 'The Control of Unscrupulous Immigration Advisers'.[112]

The tribunal had always lacked formal means to allow it have any effective control over representatives who were neither authorized by statute nor belonging to established charities or members of the Bar or the Law Society[113] – though whether another outside body was necessary is questionable. The establishment

110 Genn, H. and Genn, Y. (1989), 'The Effectiveness of Representation at Tribunals', Report to the Lord Chancellor. July 1989. Online at <http://www.ucl.ac.uk/laws/judicial-institute/docs/Effectiveness%20of%20Representation%20at%20Tribunals.pdf> (accessed on: 4 July 2013).

111 See Chapter 1, p. 23. The Legal Action Group is a charitable organization campaigning for equal access to justice for all members of society <www.lag.org.uk>.

112 Home Office IND Consultation Document -1 27.1.98. Online at <http://www.nationalarchives.gov.uk/ERORecords/HO/421/2/P2/ind/advisers.htm> (last visited 2 July 2013).

113 For example, the New Refugee Unit, or Free Representation Unit, which began with a group of socially conscious law students in a pub in Grays Inn in 1964. From the pub it moved (up market?) to the Bedford Row Camden Community Law Centre (and they would often represent the interests of many other similar law centres at user meetings); other groups include the JCWI and UKIAS.

of the Immigration Services Commissioner,[114] with an appeal to another tribunal (the Immigration Services Tribunal) to promote good practice among those who provide immigration advice or immigration services, was intended to rectify this lacuna.

The Legal Services Commission (Office of the Immigration Services Commissioner – OISC) [115] found100 firms abusing the system, regularly taking large sums to represent unwary immigrants and but providing little or nothing in return. The penal sanctions in section 79 of the 1999 Act were not then in force and later only a 'Certificate of Merit' was introduced.

The introduction of some method to regulate the abuses of indiscriminate and uncontrolled representation was, as noted above, necessary but whether yet another bureaucracy was necessary is questionable (the OISC cost the taxpayer up to £4.3 million in one year with but 14 people prosecuted,[116] and a Commissioner (admittedly employed part-time) being paid at the same rate as the SIJ). It seems to be part of an overall government policy to limit access to legal services.

Unfortunately, the requirement that only solicitors who accepted the option of being put on a panel could act in immigration appeals led to the best firms dropping out, because they could not afford to take the work at the rates paid; inevitably, the standard of representation generally has suffered.

The changes made to the legal aid funding provisions of the 2002 Act by the 2004 Act[117] made the situation even more unattractive to the representative and led Lawrence Saffer to see a 'gloomy prospect',[118] with more claimants representing themselves. The change made the grant of legal aid retrospective, which meant a representative took the chance that they would not get paid for the work done.[119] As *The Times* reported in an articled entitled: 'Need advice on asylum? Come back next month'.[120]

The debate in the House of Lords when the Immigration, Nationality and Asylum Bill was in progress is instructive for our purposes in two respects. First,

---

114 By the Immigration and Asylum Act 1999 as amended in the Nationality, Immigration and Asylum Act 2002.

115 The first appointment to run the OISC, Judge Cripps, had previously sat briefly as Legal Chairmen of the IAT. A later director was Steve Orchard, who was part of the circuit administration in 1989.

116 Though many more were investigated. OISC Annual Report 2011–12 <http://oisc.homeoffice.gov.uk/latest_information/press_releases/oisc_annual_report_2011>.

117 S. 8 Asylum and Immigration (Treatment of Claimants, etc.) Act 2004. Taking into account is one thing, doing so as damaging is an astonishing interference with the independence of the judiciary.

118 'The possible impact of legal aid changes' Saffer L Immigration Appellate Authority (2004)

119 The Community Legal Service (Asylum and Immigration Appeals) Regulations SI 2005/966.

120 *The Times*, Jon Robins 11 July 2000 where he was addressing the situation in northeast England.

the almost unanimous condemnation, supported with concrete examples, of the further removal of safeguards for the welfare of the asylum claimant included added limitation on legal assistance. This came on top of the resignation of Margaret Mar (the Countess of Mar) who had been a lay member of the tribunal for 24 years. Secondly, the debate revealed the vapid reasons given by the government side of the House for the provisions in the Bill.[121]

Little mention is heard nowadays of the 'Mckenzie friend' (MF) in the tribunal, despite quite detailed rules in Rules of the Supreme Court[122] about the use of an MF, who could offer advice but not actually represent a party. The Legal Aid Administration was in the habit of allowing extensions to enable a solicitor to act as a Mckenzie friend and the LCD suggested that this be brought to the attention of tribunal staff, but cautioned against double payment of travel and subsistence – one by legal aid fund, and one by the tribunal. This notwithstanding, Iain Donnell, an adjudicator, considered that the 'Mckenzie friend' had no place in immigration proceedings, which was a view not held by all his colleagues.

If we think of the decision-making process as an ongoing process from application to final outcome and liken that to the image of a pyramid where the base is wide and the top is narrow, each step towards the top should involve less time and cost until the summit is reached. This presumes the absence of repetition at each step. If the pyramid is turned on its head, and at each step there must be more and more time spent, the outcome will be less reliable, public opinion becomes more hostile and legislation more restrictive.

121 14 December 2006, col. 1688 et seq. <http://www.publications.parliament.uk/>.

122 RSC 53.

Chapter 5
What Price State Security?

with Frances Webber

> Terrorist violence, serious as it is, does not threaten our institutions of government or our existence as a civil community … The real threat to the life of the nation, in the sense of a people living in accordance with its traditional laws and political values, comes not from terrorism but from laws such as these.
>
> Lord Hoffmann[1]

The Special Immigration Appeals Commission (SIAC) was set up in 1998 in response to the European Court of Human Rights' condemnation of the lack of judicial safeguards for those facing deportation from the United Kingdom for national security reasons.

National security deportees had been expressly excluded from the right of appeal within the immigration appellate system since 1971, and the extra-statutory review procedure by a special advisory panel – known as the 'three wise men' – featured no real legal safeguards at all; there was no right to know what the allegations were which underlay the decision to deport, and deportees had no right even to know whether they had 'succeeded' before the advisers, whose powers were limited to making a recommendation which the Home Secretary was free to reject.

The 'three wise men' system came under increasing scrutiny as a result of high-profile cases such as that of Phil Agee, the former CIA spy who became a campaigning journalist and who fought his deportation unsuccessfully all the way to the European Court.[2] Palestinians detained for deportation during the first Gulf War of 1991 included Abbas Cheblak, who unsuccessfully sought judicial review of the special adviser system.[3] However, it was the case of Indian Sikh activist Karamjit Singh Chahal, detained without trial for six years in Bedford Prison pending deportation as a suspected terrorist, which led the European Court in 1996 to condemn the adviser system as not providing detainees with the opportunity of judicial oversight.[4] The advisory panel was not a court, the European judges said.

The European Court's judgment referred to a 'more effective form of judicial control' used in Canada, employing techniques which 'both accommodate legitimate

---

1 Lord Hoffmann, in *A v Secretary of State for the Home Department* [2005] 2 AC 68, para. 97.

2 *Agee v United Kingdom* (Application no. 7729/76), 7 DR 164 (1976).

3 *R v Secretary of State for the Home Department ex p Cheblak* [1991] WLR 890, CA.

4 *Chahal v United Kingdom* (1996) 23 EHRR 413.

security concerns about the nature and sources of intelligence information and yet accord the individual a substantial measure of procedural justice'. The Canadian model was followed in SIAC, and its procedural and substantive justice have been in contention ever since.

The Special Immigration Appeals Commission Act 1997, which came into force on 1 August 1998, gave a right of appeal to the Commission to those formerly excluded from rights of appeal against immigration decisions. Those subject to a decision to refuse entry or leave to remain, or to remove or deport them, who had been excluded from the ordinary appeals process because of national security or diplomatic grounds for the decision, now appealed to SIAC, a court comprising a High Court judge, a senior immigration judge, and a lay person (generally a security service representative). The main distinguishing feature of SIAC's procedure derives from the requirement not to disclose information to appellants or their lawyers where disclosure is deemed contrary to the public interest.[5] This duty is enshrined as an overriding duty in the Commission's procedure rules:

> When exercising its functions, the Commission shall secure that information is not disclosed contrary to the interests of national security, the international relations of the United Kingdom, the detection and prevention of crime, or in any other circumstances where disclosure is likely to harm the public interest.[6]

The Act and the Rules clarify that the Home Office may not let appellants to SIAC or their representatives know details of the case against them, or serve them with material whose disclosure is believed to pose a risk to national security.[7] In recognition of the inroads this provision makes into rules of natural justice, the rules require that non-disclosure is justified to the Commission.[8] 'Closed' allegations and material are served on the special advocate, appointed by the Attorney-General (or the Lord Advocate in Scotland),[9] who can challenge it in closed hearings from which the appellant and representative are excluded.[10] The special advocate may also use the closed hearing to argue for more disclosure to the appellant. But once he or she has seen the closed material, the special advocate can have no further contact with the appellant (save with the permission of SIAC), and may not ask the appellant for their comments on the 'closed' allegations.[11] In SIAC hearings, as in other immigration proceedings, the normal rules of evidence

5 Special Immigration Appeals Commission Act 1997 s. 5(6).

6 Special Immigration Appeals Commission (Procedure) Rules 2003, SI 2003/1034 as amended

7 SIACA 1997 s. 5(3); SI 2003/1034 r 37.

8 SI 2003/1034 r 38.

9 Ibid., r 34.

10 Ibid., r 43.

11 Ibid., r 36.

do not apply, so that hearsay evidence may be relied on.[12] The rules provide that before releasing a public determination, the Commission must send a draft to the Secretary of State, to enable him or her to apply to have parts of it removed from the public domain.[13] The Commission generally issues both 'open' and 'closed' versions of their decisions – and once again, the appellants see only the 'open' decision.[14]

These rules effectively prevent SIAC from doing justice. As the higher courts have acknowledged in other contexts, allegations and evidence which 'has been insulated from challenge may positively mislead'.[15] Ignorance of the detail of allegations frequently prevents their rebuttal. A joint statement signed by 57 special advocates, including eleven QCs, responding to a government consultation on its proposals to extend the regime to other civil cases and inquests involving sensitive material, argued that, even when attempts were made to give appellants the gist of the case against them, the procedures remained 'fundamentally unfair' and 'represent a departure from the foundational principle of natural justice that all parties are entitled to see and challenge all the evidence relied upon before the court and to combat that evidence by calling evidence of their own'.[16]

The problem is exacerbated when so much of the evidence is fragmentary. It is not simply a question of providing an alibi for a particular event on a particular day. Very few national security deportation cases are based on clear, unambiguous evidence of particular terrorist acts; the overwhelming majority depend on a 'mosaic' of fragments of intelligence and information which might relate to travel, acquaintances and associations, study and financial transactions. The security services put the fragments together, perhaps in accordance with preconceptions and prejudices, to make a pattern which points to involvement in or support for terrorist activity. Without an appellant's explanation for apparently suspect behaviour, associations etc., SIAC is likely to accept the security services' interpretation, and is unlikely to find the Secretary of State's suspicion unreasonable. (SIAC does not have to find the allegations proved, only that the Secretary of State's suspicion is reasonable.)

The limitations of SIAC's powers were set down in its very first case. SIAC allowed its first appeal against a decision to deport[17] – only to have its wings clipped by the Court of Appeal and the judicial committee of the House of Lords (replaced in 2009 by the Supreme Court). The appellant, Shafiq ur Rehman, was

---

12 Ibid., r 44.

13 Ibid., rr 47–8.

14 A procedure mandated by the rules, rr 47–8.

15 Lord Kerr, in *Al Rawi v Security Service* [2011] UKSC 34, para. 93.

16 Justice and Security Green Paper: Response to consultation by special advocates, 16 December 2011. Despite the strength and cogency of the objections, the Government proceeded with legislation (the Justice and Security Act 2013) extending closed material procedures to any civil case engaging national security.

17 *Rehman v Secretary of State for the Home Department* [1999] INLR 517.

said by the Home Secretary to have been involved in training and funding fighters in Kashmir against Indian rule. SIAC did not find the allegations proved, and in any event did not see how such activities could affect the national security of the UK, since they were not targeted at the UK, its government, or its people. On both counts, the Commission was roundly rebuked and its decision reversed by the higher courts.

On SIAC's demand for proof of the allegations, the Court of Appeal held that the point was not whether specific matters had been proved against the appellant:

> ... it is also necessary to examine the case as a whole against an individual and then ask whether on a global approach that individual is a danger to national security, taking into account the Executive's policy with regard to national security. When this is done, the cumulative effect may establish that the individual is to be treated as a danger, although it cannot be proved to a high degree of probability that he has performed any individual act which would justify this conclusion.[18]

The Court of Appeal held that SIAC was also wrong to reject the Secretary of State's national security case on the grounds that the acts Mr Rehman was accused of were not targeted at the UK. Acts endangering the national security of a friendly state were capable of endangering Britain's national security, the court ruled, since the targeted country might retaliate against British interests. This was a definition of the UK's national security of unprecedented breadth. But on Mr Rehman's appeal to the House of Lords, the law lords not only upheld the Court of Appeal's decision on the burden of proof, but also ruled that if the Secretary of State said that acts targeted at another state endangered the UK's national security, that should be good enough for SIAC. It was not the Commission's business to override a ministerial assessment. Lord Hoffmann said in terms that 'the Commission is not entitled to differ from the opinion of the Secretary of State on the question of whether, for example, the promotion of terrorism in a foreign country by a United Kingdom resident would be contrary to the interests of national security'.[19]

The *Rehman* judgment was of enormous significance. It confirmed a shift from proving specific acts to assessing risk, a much more subjective exercise and one more easily susceptible to error and bias.[20] Its endorsement of the idea that the UK's national security could be affected by acts directed against 'friendly' states eroded the principles underlying refugee protection (a 'friendly' state was often a torturing state, and thereafter persecution by such a state could be recast as

---

18 *Secretary of State v Rehman* [2000] EWCA Civ 168 para. 44, per Lord Woolf MR.

19 *Rehman v Secretary of State* [2003] 1 AC 153.

20 See Hornqvist, M. (2005),'The birth of public order policy', *Race & Class* 46.1, on the growth of 'a concept of security that has broken away from the logic of the law. The focus is shifted to what a person might do instead of what the person has done.'

legitimate investigation of suspected terrorism[21] – and any ill-treatment attributed to rogue officers). It opened the door to much closer cooperation between British and foreign security services and thus to the reception of torture evidence. The judgment also represented a huge and very dangerous abdication of judicial responsibility to the executive, and was a body blow to SIAC's independence, from which it has arguably never recovered.

The Introduction of Internment

In December 2001, Parliament passed the Anti-Terrorism, Crime and Security Act (ATCSA), which allowed for indefinite detention without charge or trial – internment – of 'suspected international terrorists' who were not British citizens and could not be deported because they risked being tortured on return to their own countries. Within days, eight people were arrested, and shortly after, they were joined by another six detainees. Most were North Africans, nearly all recognized refugees, and none had been or were questioned by police or security services. They spent the next three years in Belmarsh high security prison, where eight of them were driven into mental illness, and four had to be transferred to Broadmoor special hospital.[22] But as the government somewhat cynically pointed out, they were free to leave the country – they could go home, or try to find a safe country which would take them.

In a report published in February 2003, following an unannounced visit by investigators the previous year, the European Committee for the Prevention of Torture and Inhuman or Degrading Treatment or Punishment (CPT) condemned the suggestion that the men could end their detention by going home, saying:

> The UK authorities consider that the detainees in question would be at risk of serious human rights violations, including death or torture, in case of return to their countries of origin; indeed, this is the declared reason why they cannot be removed from the United Kingdom.[23]

21 See, for example, *R (Sivakumar) v Secretary of State for the Home Department* [2003] UKHL 14.

22 In January 2005, the Royal College of Psychiatrists was moved to issue a statement pointing out the serious effects of indefinite detention on detainees' mental health <http://www.rcpsych.ac.uk/pdf/StatementAntiTerror_01.pdf>.

23 Report to the Government of the United Kingdom on the visit to the United Kingdom carried out by the European Committee for the Prevention of Torture and Inhuman or Degrading Treatment or Punishment (CPT) from 17 to 21 February 2002, Strasbourg, February 2003, para 25. Online at <http://www.cpt.coe.int/documents/gbr/2003-18-inf-eng.pdf>.

The CPT also expressed concerns about the treatment of those detained under ATCSA, noting in particular that 'the belief that [the ATCSA detainees] had no means to contest the broad accusations made against them was a source of considerable distress, as was the indefinite nature of detention.'[24]

Such indefinite detention was clearly in breach of the fundamental right to liberty guaranteed by Article 5 of the European Convention on Human Rights, brought into UK law through the Human Rights Act 1998. The government therefore issued a derogation under Article 15 of the Convention, declaring that a 'public emergency threatening the life of the nation' justified derogating from the right to liberty. The jurisdiction of SIAC was enlarged to enable it to hear appeals against the derogation, the men's detention, and their designation as suspected international terrorists.

In July 2002, the Commission, headed by Mr Justice Andrew Collins (who is not easily cowed by the executive), ruled that the men's detention breached the anti-discrimination provisions in Article 14 of the Human Rights Convention, since they applied only to foreign nationals and not to British terrorist suspects and there was no justification for this difference in treatment. Once again, however, the Commission was overruled by the Court of Appeal, who in October 2002 held that there was no unlawful discrimination. Their reasoning was that since the men were foreign, and subject to immigration control, they could be treated differently from British nationals, although they could not be deported (because of the acknowledged risk of torture).

In December 2003, the Privy Council Review Committee strongly recommended that 'the powers which allow foreign nationals to be detained potentially indefinitely should be replaced as a matter of urgency', and that Part 4 of the Anti-Terrorism Crime and Security Act should be replaced with a measure that 'does not require the UK to derogate from the right to liberty under the European Convention on Human Rights'.[25]

Meanwhile, in October 2003, SIAC, now headed by Mr Justice Ouseley, dismissed the consolidated appeals of a number of Algerian detainees against their designation as 'suspected international terrorists' – a designation which, as noted, did not require the Secretary of State to prove that they were in fact terrorists or had carried out any terrorist acts. In fact, none of the appellants was, the Home Office conceded, actually involved in terrorism; the case against each of them rested on (suspected) links with (suspected) terrorist groups. The Commission said, in *Ajouaou and others*, that 'reasonable grounds for suspicion is some way short of proof … and reasonable grounds can be based on material which would not be admissible in a normal trial in Court, such as hearsay evidence.'[26]

---

24 Ibid.

25 Report of the Privy Counsellors' Review Committee on the Anti-Terrorism Crime and Security Act 2001, 12 December 2003, HC 100.

26 *Ajouaou, A, B, C and D v Secretary of State* (generic determination), 29 October 2003, para. 41; available on the SIAC website <http://www.justice.gov.uk/tribunals/special-

The 'hearsay evidence' would include information from the security services alleging that third parties in foreign countries had implicated one or other of the appellants. There was thus a grave risk that the third-party 'evidence' incorporated in such intelligence might have been obtained by torture or violent ill-treatment. However, the Commission refused to state that as a matter of principle it would exclude evidence which might have been obtained by such means,[27] despite the fact that the UN Convention against Torture requires all evidence obtained by torture to be excluded and not to be used in evidence against a suspect. The Court of Appeal upheld the refusal of the Commission to exclude evidence obtained by torture, holding that the Secretary of State was entitled to rely on such evidence so long as neither he nor any agent of his was implicated in the torture, when determining whether to detain a suspected foreign terrorist under the 2001 anti-terrorism legislation, and SIAC was entitled to admit it.[28]

In December 2005, a seven-judge judicial committee of the House of Lords overruled SIAC and the Court of Appeal, ruling in *A v Secretary of State for the Home Department* (No 2)[29] that torture evidence was never admissible – although the majority held that the Commission would need to have it established that torture had in fact been used to obtain the relevant evidence before excluding it. Lord Bingham dissented powerfully on the issue of the standard of proof, arguing that a real risk that torture had been used should be enough to exclude the evidence:

> The foreign torturer does not boast of his trade. The security services … do not wish to imperil their relations with regimes where torture is practised. The special advocates have no means or resources to investigate. The detainee is in the dark. It is inconsistent with the most rudimentary notions of fairness to blindfold a man and then impose a standard which only the sighted could hope to meet.[30]

The majority's ruling was applied three years later to overturn the Court of Appeal's decision quashing the deportation of Abu Qatada to Jordan on the basis that he would face a real risk of trial based on torture evidence. The House of Lords held in *Othman* in February 2009 that such a risk was not enough to preclude his return.[31] The European Court of Human Rights however ruled that Othman could not be returned to Jordan because of the risk, characterizing the use of torture evidence in a trial as a flagrant denial of fair trial rights.[32]

---

immigration-appeals-commission>.

27 *Ajouaou* above, para. 83.

28 *A and nine others v Secretary of State for the Home Department* [2004] EWCA Civ 1123, 11 August 2004.

29 [2005] UKHL 71, [2006] 2 AC 221, 8 December 2005.

30 *A v Secretary of State for the Home Department* (No. 2) above, para. 59.

31 *OO (Jordan) v Secretary of State for the Home Department* [2009] UKHL 10.

32 *Othman v United Kingdom* [2012] ECHR 56, 17 January 2012.

Back in May 2004, the Commission's perceived lack of independence from the executive, the draconian legislation it was obliged to enforce, and the concealment of so much vital evidence from appellants in secret hearings led to the resignation of the first appointed national security representative on the Commission, Sir Brian Barder KCMG. He said:

> It is perhaps a measure of the extent to which SIAC has been hobbled by the legal imperatives handed down by the higher courts that the commission has not so far allowed a single appeal by any of the dozen or more people who have been imprisoned under the Anti-Terrorism, Crime and Security Act …
>
> In a press statement on 25 February, David Blunkett claimed that the existence of SIAC as a court of appeal helped to justify the continuation of the government's extraordinary powers. Given SIAC's current emasculation, this claim looks distinctly disingenuous. It is questionable whether SIAC, now buckled into the legal straitjacket imposed on it by the two highest courts, can really act as an effective champion against error or abuse by the executive.[33]

Two special advocates, Ian Macdonald QC and Rick Scannell, later resigned from SIAC, citing similar reasons.

In December 2004, a nine-judge judicial committee of the House of Lords[34] overruled the Court of Appeal, and held that the statutory scheme for the detention of foreign terrorist suspects under ATCSA was unlawful. The law lords upheld SIAC's 2002 judgment that there was no lawful justification for treating foreign terrorist suspects differently from British ones, and ruled that if the Home Secretary wanted to intern suspected terrorists, he or she would have to include British nationals in the powers to detain.[35] Lord Hoffmann went even further. The law lord who in 2001 had disallowed SIAC's entitlement to challenge the Home Secretary's definition of a danger to UK national security, now, three years later, declared:

> Terrorist violence, serious as it is, does not threaten our institutions of government or our existence as a civil community … The real threat to the life of the nation, in the sense of a people living in accordance with its traditional laws and political values, comes not from terrorism but from laws such as these.[36]

A stand-off ensued between the country's most senior judges and the Home Secretary. The Human Rights Act 1998 did not allow the judges to strike the legislation down, merely to declare it incompatible with the European Human

33 Barder, B. (2004), 'On SIAC', *London Review of Books* 26:6.

34 Normally, the House of Lords' judicial committee sat with five members.

35 *A and others v Secretary of State for the Home Department* [2004] UKHL 56, [2005] 2 AC 68.

36 *A and others*, at paras 96–7.

Rights Convention. It was for the government in Parliament to decide whether to remedy the incompatibility. For three months, the government did nothing, and the men remained in (unlawful) detention in Belmarsh. Then, in March 2005, Parliament repealed the offending sections of the Anti-Terrorism Crime and Security Act, and passed the Prevention of Terrorism Act 2005. This replaced internment with 'control orders', which could be imposed on British terrorist suspects and on foreign nationals who cannot be deported because of a real risk of torture at home. In 2011, control orders were in their turn replaced by terrorism prevention and investigation measures (TPIMs),[37] which contained more safeguards (dubbed by some 'control orders lite'). But in 2005, SIAC's jurisdiction over non-deportable foreign terrorist suspects came to an end.

Return to Torturing States via Diplomatic Assurances

Within months of the end of internment of foreign nationals, the government had decided to deal with the so-called 'non-deportables' by deporting them. For this purpose, urgent negotiations were started with some of the world's torture regimes. British diplomats in Libya, Jordan, Egypt, Tunisia and Algeria worked to persuade these governments to sign diplomatic assurances that they would not subject to torture those of their nationals deported from the UK as suspected terrorists. In this, the government ignored (and continues to ignore) the serious concerns expressed by (among others) the UN High Commissioner for Human Rights,[38] the UN Special Rapporteur Against Torture,[39] the Council of Europe Human Rights Commissioner,[40] Human Rights Watch[41] and Amnesty International,[42] to the effect that such assurances weakened the general prohibition against torture and did not work.

By August 2005, the Home Office was sufficiently confident that it could obtain assurances against torture from the Algerian authorities to re-detain the Algerian ATCSA detainees for deportation to Algeria. The appeals in the new batch of cases involving such deportations to Algeria were repeatedly deferred, as

37 Under the Terrorism Prevention and Investigation Measures Act 2011.

38 Statement to the Council of Europe, March 2006.

39 'Diplomatic assurances not an adequate safeguard for deportees', Manfred Novak, UN press release 23 August 2005.

40 'Torture can never be accepted', Thomas Hammarberg, 27 June 2006.

41 Human Rights Watch, 'Empty promises: Diplomatic assurances no safeguard against torture' (April 2004), 'Still at risk' (April 2005), 'Not worth the paper they're written on' (August 2005), 'Dangerous ambivalence: UK policy on torture since 9/11' (November 2005): all reports from HRW <www.hrw.org/reports>.

42 Amnesty International, 'Diplomatic assurances no protection against torture or ill-treatment' (December 2005), 'UK human rights: a broken promise' (February 2006), 'Europe and Central Asia: summary of concerns UK' (July 2007): all Amnesty International reports <www.amnesty.org/en/library/info/>.

diplomats sought vainly to secure formal assurances with independent monitoring of the men's treatment, which the Algerian side repeatedly refused to allow. Eventually, the British side withdrew the request for independent monitoring of the assurances, and brazened it out with the Commission, saying that monitoring was unnecessary as the security situation in Algeria was improving, torture was no longer routine (although they conceded it happened with 'distressing frequency' on national security detainees), and the Algerians' new trade and diplomatic links with Britain provided incentives not to break their word.[43] SIAC gratefully accepted the defective assurances, putting the Algerians' resistance to monitoring down to post-colonial sensitivity.

Adding insult to injury, so far as Algerian national security deportees were concerned, was the fact that a number of them had been tried and acquitted in the UK, on the same allegations on which the Secretary of State now sought to deport them. In 2002, a large number of Algerians had been arrested on suspicion of involvement in a plot to manufacture ricin, a poison derived from cooking castor oil beans, allegedly intending to smear it on door handles in north London. The subsequent 'ricin trial' collapsed when the main prosecution evidence was found to have come from the tortured mind of an Algerian interrogated under torture in Algeria, and the jury acquitted the defendants. No ricin had ever been found.[44] Almost all of those acquitted (or whose charges were dropped) owing to the collapse of the first 'ricin trial' were subsequently arrested for deportation on exactly the same evidence which the jury rejected. Of those, only one, Mouloud Sihali,[45] had his SIAC appeal allowed on the grounds that he was not a danger to national security – although he lost a later appeal against his deportation for the commission of 'ordinary' criminal offences, this time on the ground that he would be adequately protected by the assurances against the risk of torture.

In its decision on the first Algerian 'deportation with assurances' appeal, delivered in August 2006,[46] the Commission sidestepped the issue by finding that the appellant, Y, who had been tried in absentia for terrorist offences and sentenced to death, would obtain the benefit of an amnesty under national reconciliation provisions. Therefore, they held, there was no reason to believe that he would be detained by the notorious military intelligence, the DRS, to whom torture was

43 An earlier, pre-SIAC illustration of the importance of trade and diplomatic links was provided by the attempted deportation of Saudi dissident Al-Mass'ari in 1996. See Chapter 3, p. 21, p. 90 and p. 132.

44 See, for example, 'Questions over ricin conspiracy', BBC News, 13 April 2005; Archer, L. (2010), *Ricin! The inside story of the plot that never was* (London: Pluto); Peirce, G. (2010), 'Was it like this for the Irish?', in *idem*, *Dispatches from the Dark Side: On Torture and the Death of Justice* (London: Verso).

45 Sihali (SC/38/2005), 14 May 2007, available on SIAC website <http://www.justice.gov.uk/tribunals/special-immigration-appeals-commission>.

46 Y (SC/36/2005). Since about 2002, cases have been anonymized unless appellants waive anonymity.

generally attributed – and even if he were briefly detained by them, there was no incentive to torture him, since torture was used in the main to extract confessions.[47] Somewhat rashly, the Commission concluded by considering what the situation would be if after all and contrary to the assurances, the appellant was found not to be eligible for the amnesty:

> … it would mean that what the UK government had been told by Algeria at all levels was worthless or had been completely misunderstood … the prospect that Y would be detained by the DRS would become a real one on this hypothesis; there would be greater incentives to torture him, the period of detention would be far longer than has been envisaged by us, and the ability of interested parties to maintain his profile would diminish. The context in which those issues would be considered is wholly different … .[48]

Perhaps not altogether surprisingly, it transpired that what the Commission had been told was not reliable and there was indeed a real prospect that Y would face trial. By the time this was revealed, however, the first judgment's overall conclusion that Y would not be tortured had been so reinforced by its repetition, re-use and extension in other appeals on wholly different facts,[49] that it had turned into a sort of general mantra which could not be dislodged by correction of the facts of Y's situation and his prospects of detention and trial on return. By now, SIAC's conclusion – that the informal assurances given by the Algerian authorities would obviate the otherwise grave risks of torture – could not be displaced even by explicit and desperate evidence of exposure to torture and ill-treatment by Algerians who, sick and tired of waiting in maximum-security detention for the distant prospect of a hopeless appeal, had withdrawn appeals and returned home, and had promptly been detained incommunicado by the DRS in barracks to which even the International Committee of the Red Cross do not have access.[50] It was quite shocking to see this evidence of ill-treatment, smuggled out at great personal risk to the witnesses concerned, brushed aside by the Commission – the same Commission who had said there was no need for independent monitoring in Algeria because human rights lawyers, NGOs and others could be relied on to reveal ill-treatment.[51] And to add insult to injury, the Home Office refused to ensure the confidentiality of this material. Lawyers for other Algerian appellants sought to protect the identities of informants by a 'reverse closed' procedure

47 Y judgment, paras 381–4.

48 Ibid., paras 381–4.

49 Ibid., para. 399; *BB v SSHD* SC/39/2005; December 2006; *G v SSHD* SC/02/2005, February 2007.

50 See Amnesty International, 'UK: deportations to Algeria at all costs', 26 February 2007, available at <http://asiapacific.amnesty.org/library/Index/ENGEUR450012007?open&of=ENG-GBR>.

51 SIAC dealt with this evidence in the U judgment, at paras 14–42.

whereby appellants' lawyers presented the sensitive evidence to the judge at an *ex parte* hearing, and sought an order guaranteeing total confidentiality before revealing it to the Home Office. SIAC refused to countenance the idea. Its refusal was upheld by the Court of Appeal in July 2010.[52] In March 2012, the Supreme Court ruled that SIAC could and in certain circumstances should make orders binding the Home Office to complete and irrevocable confidentiality in relation to this sort of evidence, on the basis of *ex parte* applications from which Home Office lawyers would be excluded.[53]

Meanwhile, the categories of evidence which the Secretary of State was allowed to give to SIAC while withholding it from appellants and their lawyers had been spreading. When the Bill creating SIAC went through Parliament, the minister gave an explicit assurance that secrecy would be resorted to only when national security was at stake.[54] But ignoring this parliamentary assurance, the Secretary of State presented secret evidence about the risks of torture for returnees to Algeria, not to protect national security but for diplomatic reasons: British government assessments of Algeria's record on torture might harm the relationship between the UK and Algeria. This extension of the use of secret evidence was upheld by the House of Lords' judicial committee in 2009.[55] The law lords saw no irony in their condoning a breach of an assurance by a British minister while upholding the reliance on an assurance given by Algerian officials.

In the same hearing, the law lords upheld SIAC's acceptance of diplomatic assurances as obviating a real risk of torture in Algeria. The sunny optimism shown by the Commission and the higher courts towards Algeria's likely compliance with flimsy, unmonitored and unenforceable assurances against torture was on display again in relation to human rights in Jordan, where torture and inhuman and degrading treatment was if anything even more entrenched, in the appeal of Omar Othman (popularly known as Abu Qatada), decided in February 2007,[56] and the later appeal of 'VV' decided in November 2007.[57] Jordan, unlike Algeria, had agreed to monitoring of its assurances; for the purpose, the Foreign Office pumped money into a small, unknown and untried organization, Adaleh, which had no experience in the field, whose founder had never visited a prison, and which was not trusted by Jordan's long-established human rights organizations. In VV's deportation appeal, the Commission heard extremely disturbing eye-witness evidence from a Human Rights Watch observer who had made a prison inspection just weeks earlier, and had returned after a couple of days to find

52 *W (Algeria) and others v SSHD* [2010] EWCA Civ 898.

53 *W (Algeria) and others v SSHD* [2012] UKSC 8.

54 The terms of the assurance are set out in *RB (Algeria) v SSHD* [2009] UKHL 10, [2010] 2 AC 110, at para. 80.

55 *RB (Algeria)*, above.

56 Reported as OO (SC/15/2005), available on SIAC website <http://www.justice.gov.uk/tribunals/special-immigration-appeals-commission>.

57 SC/59/2006.

inmates bloodied, beaten and forcibly shaved as a punishment for communicating with the HRW team. Despite finding the human rights situation in Jordan's prisons 'appalling' and torture for national security detainees systematic, and in the face of compelling evidence of contempt for human rights organizations or monitors, the Commission expressed itself satisfied that the Jordanian government would comply with its human rights assurances. The Court of Appeal and subsequently the Supreme Court upheld SIAC's findings in *OO (Jordan)* in February 2009,[58] emphasizing that these were questions of fact in which the higher courts would rarely interfere. Regrettably, the European Court of Human Rights too upheld the assurances given by Jordan in Othman's case as sufficient to remove any real risk of torture (while refusing his deportation because of the lack of similar assurances covering the use of torture evidence in his retrial).[59] The Algerian assurances have not yet been tested in Europe.

The Commission found assurances by Libya a step too far, however, and rejected the Secretary of State's proposal to return alleged members of a Libyan terrorist group back there under cover of such assurances, monitored by a human rights organization run by one of Gaddafi's sons.[60] Unlike the president of Algeria and the king of Jordan, Colonel Gaddafi was not someone the UK authorities could trust to keep his word, according to the Commission. The Secretary of State's appeal to the Court of Appeal was rejected.[61] And in May 2010, SIAC ruled against the proposed deportation of terrorist suspect Abid Naseer to Pakistan because of the unacceptable risk of torture. In that case, assurances had apparently been given, but in secret. SIAC held that since the Secretary of State refused to disclose the material, it could not be relied on: assurances against ill-treatment must be openly given and received.[62]

58 [2009] UKHL 10, [2010] 2 AC 110. The judgment also deals with Algeria, under the heading RB (Algeria); see above.

59 *Othman v United Kingdom* (8139/09), 17 January 2012. The issue of Abu Qatada's deportation became a trial of strength for the coalition, with prime minister, David Cameron, threatening temporary withdrawal from the European Human Rights Convention in order to deport him (see 'Britain may squander human rights for the sake of deporting Abu Qatada', *Our Kingdom* 1 May 2013, <http://www.opendemocracy.net/ourkingdom/frances-webber/britain-may-squander-human-rights-for-sake-of-deporting-abu-qatada>). The cleric prevented that disaster by saying he would leave voluntarily once Jordan signed a treaty banning torture evidence from its courts.

60 DD and AS (SC/42/2005 and SC/50/2005), appeals allowed 27 April 2007.

61 [2008] EWCA Civ 289, 9 April 2008.

62 SC/77/80/81/82/83/2009, 18 May 2010, available on SIAC website <http://www.justice.gov.uk/tribunals/special-immigration-appeals-commission>.

Detention and Bail

Proposed national security deportees are generally not released willingly by the Secretary of State. Some have been in detention for years; Omar Othman or Abu Qatada, for example, the radical cleric whose deportation to Jordan was stopped by the European Court because of the risk of a terrorist retrial based on torture evidence, had been detained for six-and-a-half years for deportation before the European Court's judgment made his further detention impossible and he was given bail.[63] SIAC has jurisdiction to grant, refuse, or revoke bail in national security cases, but there is no right of onward appeal against its refusal or revocation of bail, and in U and XC's joined cases, the High Court ruled against the Secretary of State's argument that SIAC's decision on bail was final, holding that its bail decisions can be challenged by judicial review.[64]

Partly because of the significant delays in hearing appeals, SIAC has shown itself increasingly willing to release appellants on bail to await appeal hearings, at least where the allegations against them are not very serious. Those who have been granted bail by SIAC, however, often find themselves so controlled as to be to all intents and purposes under house arrest. Extremely strict conditions can last for several years, as deportation appeals wend their way slowly from SIAC through the higher courts. Conditions of bail normally imposed by SIAC on those awaiting deportation include:

- a curfew of between 12 and 24 hours,[65] during which time they must remain in their room, flat, or house. If they are in a house, they may not use the garden during this time (although SIAC has modified this condition in recent years, particularly for family men; if in a flat, they must not use the 'common parts'; if they have a room, they may not leave it;
- a 'bail zone', generally of about a mile square, which they are not allowed to leave at any time without prior permission;
- an electronic tagging device, worn round the ankle, to ensure compliance;
- reporting to a local police station at least daily;
- telephoning the curfew monitoring company before first leaving the house and on return;
- no visitors to the premises except those vetted in advance;
- no pre-arranged meetings outside the premises except with people vetted in advance;

63 He was subsequently re-detained for unauthorized possession of mobile phones, and at time of writing remains in detention.

64 *R (Rex C, U, XC) v the Upper Tribunal, Special Immigration Appeals Commission* [2009] EWHC 3052.

65 Frequently, the Commission starts with a curfew of at least 16 hours and then reduces it on evidence of compliance with the strict conditions. A 22- or 24-hour curfew is rare, but has been imposed.

- no mobile phone, computer, or any equipment capable of connecting to the Internet;
- right of admission to police, immigration officials and monitoring company employees 24 hours a day, 7 days a week for searches of premises and seizure of suspect items.

This kind of package of conditions, with an 18-hour curfew, was held by the House of Lords to be an unlawful derogation from liberty for those subject to control orders (in *JJ and others*, in October 2007).[66] But immigration bail presupposes the right to detain, so it is far more difficult to challenge such conditions in the context of national security deportation.

'A Substantial Measure of Procedural Justice'

The system of control orders introduced by the Prevention of Terrorism Act 2005 contained High Court review procedures which mirrored those in SIAC, with special 'closed' procedures to ensure that disclosure of allegations or evidence was not given to appellants or their lawyers where it could prejudice the security services' operations. But in 2007, the House of Lords held[67] that the right to know the case against you was so fundamental to the requirements of fairness embodied in Article 6 ECHR, that the duty of non-disclosure had to be read subject to the requirements of a fair trial, which required at least the gist of the case to be disclosed to the appellant. The Secretary of State claimed that the ruling was ambiguous and did not require an irreducible minimum of information to be given to appellants, but the Lords repeated its ruling two years later,[68] following a clear statement from the European Court that fairness required the gist of the allegations to be given to enable them to be effectively rebutted. In the context of detention, and control orders, which impinged on civil rights and obligations, the special advocate procedure was not enough to ensure fairness.[69] The belated acknowledgement by the higher courts of the basic requirements of a fair trial – the right to know what is said against you – resulted in a number of control orders being quashed, as the Secretary of State was ordered either to reveal more or to withdraw the secret allegations, and generally elected to withdraw the allegations.

But those subject to immigration decisions have no such rights. The courts have ruled that none of the fair trial guarantees apply to proceedings before SIAC;[70] Article 6 of the Human Rights Convention does not apply to deportation

66 *JJ v Secretary of State for the Home Department* [2007] UKHL 45.
67 *MB v SSHD* [2007] UKHL 46, see, for example, para. 72.
68 *AF v SSHD* [2009] UKHL 28, [2009] 3 All ER 643, 10 June 2009.
69 *A v United Kingdom* (Application 3455/05) 49 EHRR 625 (Grand Chamber).
70 See, for example, *W Algeria v SSHD* [2010] EWCA Civ 898, 29 July 2010.

proceedings,[71] which have been held to be fundamentally different from control order proceedings (a conclusion based on a European Court of Human Rights case, *Maaouia v France*).[72] The UK courts have also ruled that SIAC's procedures cannot import common law fairness obligations either[73] – meaning that SIAC appellants are unprotected by common law and human rights law alike, in attempting to fight vague accusations of support for terrorism which might lead to deportation to torturing states.[74] There is an extraordinary and unjustifiable disparity between British and undeportable foreign nationals on the one hand, who have the right to know the essence of the case against them, and foreign nationals facing deportation on the other, who can be deported on evidence they cannot know or offer a response to.

The secret evidence regime has also been applied to decisions to exclude from refugee status those deemed to have committed acts contrary to the principles and purposes of the United Nations. SS, a Libyan, could not be deported because of the real risk of torture in Libya, against which diplomatic assurances would not provide protection. But his asylum claim was rejected on the basis that he was excluded under Article 1F of the Refugee Convention. All he was told was that he was believed to be a member of the Libyan Islamic Fighting Group (LIFG) – which he denied. On wholly secret evidence, SIAC held that he had been guilty of acts justifying his exclusion. The Court of Appeal quashed SIAC's decision – but not because of the secrecy, or the unfairness, but because from the open case against him, it seemed SIAC had focused on his time in the UK rather than his conduct before arriving, as required by the Convention.[75] But the fact that refugee status – and exclusion from it – is now dealt with in EU law (by the 2004 Qualification Directive)[76] may provide a remedy for excessive secrecy. In another case, involving the exclusion from the UK of a long-resident, dual French-Algerian national with a British wife and eight children, referred by the Court of Appeal, the Court of Justice of the European Communities (CJEU) ruled that the principle of effective judicial protection required courts considering exclusion of an EU national to ensure that the individual concerned was informed of the essence of the grounds against him notwithstanding security concerns.[77]

---

71 Article 6(1) (right to a fair trial) states: 'In the determination of his civil rights and obligations or of any criminal charge against him, everyone is entitled to a fair and public hearing within a reasonable time by an independent and impartial tribunal established by law.'

72 33 EHRR 42, para. 40.

73 Fair trial rights at common law, such as the right to know the allegations against you, pre-date the Human Rights Convention by centuries.

74 In *W Algeria* above (CA).

75 *SS (Libya) v SSHD* [2011] EWCA Civ 1547.

76 2004/83.

77 *ZZ v SSHD* (Case C-300/11), CJEU 4 June 2013.

Residual fair trial rights apply in the context of detention. The European Court of Human Rights[78] upheld the rights of interned suspected international terrorists to the fair trial guarantees implicit in the right to liberty,[79] so that the Secretary of State was obliged to disclose enough of the allegation founding the detention to enable it to be effectively challenged. The High Court applied the principle to detention pending deportation,[80] ruling that SIAC's revocation of the bail of a proposed national security deportee on wholly closed evidence was unlawful. But the use of wholly secret evidence to impose onerous bail conditions was upheld, provided they did not amount to a deprivation of liberty.[81] BB had been granted bail, but on extremely stringent conditions, including an 18-hour curfew. When the curfew was reduced to 16 hours, SIAC upheld the bail conditions on closed evidence, and the Divisional Court refused to interfere, ruling that since liberty was not in issue, and bail was ancillary to deportation proceedings, none of the fair trial guarantees of the Convention applied.

Appellants facing deportation on secret evidence have sought to rely on the procedural guarantees contained in Article 8 (rights to family life),[82] in cases where deportation would separate them from families in the UK, to seek more disclosure of the allegations against them. But the attempt was defeated in the Court of Appeal;[83] the only procedural rights associated with family life were to have independent scrutiny of the decision in an adversarial proceedings – that is, an appeal against deportation to an independent tribunal.[84] The protection of family life threatened by deportation did not extend to having allegations particularized so that appellants know what they are supposed to have done to merit deportation.

In this absurd situation, where national security deportees have no rights to fair procedures despite what is at stake for them and for their families, it is worth noting that the stand by the European Court in *Maaouia* excluding all immigration-related proceedings from fair trial guarantees was not unanimous. There was a powerful dissenting opinion by Judge Loucaides, joined by Judge Traja, to the effect that it was 'absurd not to extend an interpretation to enhance individual rights where independent judicial control is especially required'.

In so far as the European Court of Human Rights – perhaps the regional human rights court with the strongest track record – has steadfastly set its face against

78 In *A v United Kingdom* (2009) 49 EHRR 625.

79 Article 5(4) (which requires court supervision of detention).

80 In *R (U, XC) v SIAC* [2009] EWHC 3052 (Admin).

81 *BB v Secretary of State for the Home Department* [2011] EWHC 2129 (Admin).

82 Article 8 protects the right to respect for family and private life, home and reputation. It carries with it certain procedural guarantees, to ensure that someone is not deprived of family life unfairly, without a hearing.

83 *IR (Sri Lanka) v SSHD* [2011] EWCA Civ 704, followed in *BB v SSHD* [2012] EWCA Civ 1499 and *AHK v SSHD* [2013] EWHC 1426 (Admin) .

84 The Court of Appeal relied on the ECtHR case of *Al-Nashif v Bulgaria* (2003) 36 EHRR 37.

applying Article 6 of the ECHR to cases involving immigration or deportation, it has limited its influence on governments in this crucially important area of human rights. This means that apart from committees such as the UN Committee Against Torture (UNCAT) and its European equivalent the Committee on the Prevention of Torture (CPT), which can comment and condemn but cannot issue binding judgments, there is no steadying hand available to restrain governments in times such as these when it is especially needed. This control is, as Judge Loucaides himself notes, particularly important in the absence of an International Tribunal, where domestic laws are arguably in conflict with the Conventions and where review methods have been weakened.

Events have moved further since Judge Loucaides uttered his warning, with the domestic courts providing less and less protection to those who may be returned to persecution on what may often be doubtful evidence of some link, however tenuous, with terrorism – regardless of how long ago and whatever the evidence of an exemplary life since.

Association with any group which a government designates as 'terrorist' is frequently now hardly justiciable, and therefore a 2008 judgment of the Court of Appeal, *Alton and others*,[85] is of particular importance. In brief, the court held that an organization which had no capacity nor was carrying out any steps to promote or encourage terrorism could not be held to be concerned in terrorism just because its leaders had a future contingent interest to resort to it. The court demanded 'significant justification' for any interference with human rights and ruled that in this case, the Home Office was acting perversely in refusing to remove the People's Mujahadin Organization of Iran (PMOI) from the list of proscribed organizations under the Terrorism Act 2000.[86] It should not be too much to ask that the rigorous scrutiny of the Home Office's case for keeping the PMOI on the terror list, seen in this case, be brought to bear on the suspicions of 'terrorism-related activity' used to found deportation decisions, and on its assertions that the countries to which it seeks to deport suspects are safe.

Getting and Losing Citizenship

There is no appeal to SIAC (or anywhere else) against refusal of naturalization as a British citizen, whether on national security or any other grounds, and the remedy is judicial review. This can be something of a farce where the reasons for refusal are not disclosed, since the Court of Appeal ruled that in some cases the Home Office will be permitted to present secret evidence to the judge explaining

85 *Alton and others v SSHD* [2009] 3 WLR 74.

86 Under Schedule 2 of the Terrorism Act 2000 (as amended by the Terrorism Act 2000 (Proscribed Organisations) (Amendment) Order, SI 2001/1261.

the decision, while the applicant will not even have the limited protection of a special advocate.[87]

There is, though, an appeal against deprivation of citizenship, which goes to SIAC if the decision is based on evidence which 'should not be made public' on national security, diplomatic or other public interest grounds.[88] Since 2002, a wider range of British citizens can be deprived of their citizenship, the grounds for deprivation have broadened and the threshold has lowered, at the same time as procedural protections have been withdrawn. In an appeal against deprivation of citizenship, the lack of disclosure of evidence or detailed reasons is not the only handicap for appellants.

In 2002, the law was changed to enable British citizens by birth to be deprived of citizenship if they are dual nationals. At the same time, it was no longer necessary for the Secretary of State to show 'act or speech ... disloyal or disaffected towards her Majesty', or 'trading with the enemy', as before, but 'serious prejudice to the UK's vital interests'.[89] In 2006, the grounds for deprivation of citizenship were amended once more,[90] so that the Secretary of State merely had to show that deprivation was conducive to the public good – the same test as for deportation of foreign nationals, although citizens' stake in the UK is far greater and arguably, their rights should be correspondingly greater.

A British citizen served with a notice of deprivation of citizenship remained a British citizen pending appeal, and only if the decision was upheld was citizenship finally removed. But an amendment to the provisions, hardly noticed when it went through Parliament in 2004, removed that protection,[91] meaning that citizenship could be cancelled immediately on service of the notice of deprivation. The amendment has caused untold injustice and misery to those affected, hugely exacerbated by the practice of the Secretary of State to wait until the subject of the decision is abroad before serving the deprivation notice. So from one day to the next, British citizens, who may have gone abroad with family members for a short holiday, leaving homes and belongings in the UK, find themselves no longer British, with no right of return and with allegations which cannot be properly responded to but which are likely to keep them out of the country permanently. The victims of this practice can find themselves stranded abroad, as passports are no longer valid and exclusion orders prevent return to the UK. Clearly this makes the exercise of the right of appeal extremely difficult – there is no right of re-entry for the appeal. But SIAC's former lead judge, Sir John Mitting, sitting

87 *MH and others v Secretary of State* [2009] 1 WLR 2049.

88 British Nationality Act 1981 s. 40A; Special Immigration Appeals Commission Act s. 2B.

89 British Nationality Act 1981 s. 40 as amended by the Nationality, Immigration and Asylum Act 2002.

90 By the Immigration, Asylum and Nationality Act 2006 s. 56.

91 The Asylum and Immigration (Treatment of Claimants, etc.) Act 2004, Schedule 2, repealed s. 40A(6) which provided this protection.

as a High Court judge in judicial review, saw nothing unfair or untoward in the practice, upholding the Secretary of State's prerogative powers of exclusion in this situation.[92] Foreign nationals whose leave to remain in the UK is cancelled while they are abroad were better off, since their leave to remain continued for a period, enabling an appeal to be lodged, and they could return to the UK to exercise in-country appeal rights here[93] – until Parliament legislated to do away with this right in the Crime and Courts Act 2013.[94]

92 *R (GI Sudan) v SSHD* [2011] EWHC 1875.

93 *MK (Tunisia) v SSHD* [2011] EWCA Civ 333.

94 Section 53, which amends the Nationality, Immigration and Asylum Act 2002.

Chapter 6
How Other Countries Do It: Belgium, North Africa, South Africa and Sweden

With Katelijne Declerck, Amor Boubakri, Ahmed Arbee and Göran Hakansson

The world's a Stage … '
Shakespeare, *As You Like It* 2/7

Everyone who is concerned with decisions affecting the lives and well-being of people moving, willingly or unwillingly, away from their homes, should be left in no doubt about the potential for damage their decisions have for the people who appear before them, as well as their families and the possible repercussions on others elsewhere in the world.

No country would, at least openly, deny some need to provide sanctuary – even if only to ones 'friends' – but in practice there are those who either fail to give any such protection or hedge it with such restrictions as to make a mockery of the principle. The Conventions (such as the 1951 Refugee Convention) provide a universal approach to such protection but do not prescribe any particular structure for doing so. Generally, where any system exists at all, an initial adverse decision may be reviewed, hopefully by someone or some body independent of the person who made that first decision.

When someone moves away from their home, the move may be just next door as it were,[1] but sometimes the neighbouring country may have a treaty to return any refugee – as was the case between Saudi Arabia and the Yemen which emerged in the *Al Mas'sari* appeal – or the country may not be safe for other reasons, in which case the move may be thousands of miles away to a country thought to be safer and more congenial, even if the language is different and the culture alien. We have looked at how the system of review in the UK came about in some detail and how it has been affected when the country received more immigrants than it felt it could cope with, especially those with totally different habits and languages.

1 And in many instances where countries have one or more land borders, constant boundary disputes, often hangovers from past colonial times, may cloud any decision as to whether someone has fled their country or just joined their brother over the road. Is he an IDP or a refugee?

This chapter and the next describe the regimes in place in five other nation or regions. In most cases, these systems apply only to refugees and not, as in the UK, immigrants as a whole. Hopefully, they will not only prove of interest but will help decision makers understand a little of what may be happening beyond the borders of their own state or region. There are illustrations of extra-territorial means of discouraging the immigrant, anything from interception on the high seas, to safe havens, or bilateral agreements with countries who are well known to provide no protection from onward transmission to another country where no protection can be assured.

The 1951 Refugee Convention, and any other similar convention,[2] is, as we have seen, intended to prevent that onward transmission or *refoulement*; that is, to ensure that anyone who needs protection is not sent back, directly or indirectly, to the country they is trying to escape from – either directly or indirectly. Decision makers cannot be sure there is no risk of indirect *refoulement*, unless they know something about the system in a country to which the claimant may be returned. This much is fairly obvious and the five countries covered in these two chapters are examples of some of those other systems. It is often not enough to know just the system but also something of the law; for example, not every country takes the same view of what is a fundamental human right. The right to family union is one example. In Israel, a spouse from the Occupied Palestinian Territory (OPT) or from enemy states viz. Syria, Lebanon, Iran and Iraq, may not join his or her spouse to live in the country as of right[3]. Or, better known, homosexuality in most countries in the Middle East and Africa is frowned upon, if not unlawful. But in these chapters it is only systems which are addressed.

The choice of countries in this chapter was made for their variety and potentials for security or insecurity, for policed and for porous borders, and even for possessing no system of refugee-status determination at all. They are also systems which any UK judge may encounter in appeals coming before them. Such knowledge is necessary in order to realize that if pressed, any country is not beyond, in effect, bribing another country to accept or to take back someone.

The EU Commission founded partnerships in 2005 with Mauritania, Morocco, Algeria, Tunisia and Libya and, with the Dutch government, are financing five UN pilot projects. Will the existence of asylum systems make it possible to designate those countries safe first countries of asylum and hence to return people who transit them en route to Europe? As we will see, five years later there are still no systems but there are returnees whose situation on return is not monitored. 'The

2 See Chapter 5. Art. 3 ECHR, for example, and also Art. 3 of the Convention Against Torture (CAT).

3 Citizenship and Entry into Israel Law – 2003 (as amended 2007). *Adalah (Legal Center for Arab Minority Rights in Israel) v. The Minister of the Interior and others*; judgment of the Israeli Supreme Court of 11 January 2012 HC 830/07 HCJ 466/07, *MK Zahava Galon v. The Attorney General, et al.* (petition dismissed 11 January 2012).

UK undertakes both voluntary and enforced returns to Algeria. The UK Border Agency does not monitor returnees.'[4]

In 1995, the 'Mediterranean 12' (countries) agreed 'appropriate policies to accelerate economic take-off', further agreed to strengthen their cooperation to reduce migratory pressures and illegal immigration, and acknowledged the principle that source countries had 'a responsibility for readmission' of illegal immigrants to Europe.[5]

There are also an increasing number of economic and political regional groupings with their own regional courts and tribunals. These bodies are often the final forum whose decisions bind all member states. Their present judicial activism in the field of human rights impacts on all aspects of migratory control.[6]

The North African countries have been conflated and are dealt with by a single contributor, as they are very similar and cover the geographical area of North Africa. South Africa has the best-developed system and has refugees and IDPs a hundred times more than anywhere in the EU. Canada, to which the UK owes much in the early development of its jurisprudence, training and country information, deals with all immigrants as does the UK and is very comprehensive; Canada is discussed in Chapter 7 simply for convenience. Sweden and Belgium are examples from the EU, but with very different systems; Sweden's approach has radically changed recently and is still seems to be developing and adjusting to this; it will be interesting to see what happens.

The links between all these countries lie in two fields[7] – the administration of a common international set of conventions and a global network of personal cooperation between individual judges and academics built up, largely through the IARLJ over 16 years.

4 24 March 2009 United Kingdom. '*YES. The UK undertakes both voluntary and enforced returns to Algeria. The UK Border Agency does not monitor returnees.*' European Migration Network Ad-Hoc Query on Returns and Readmission Agreements with Algeria 24 March 2009. UK answered YES and it does not monitor returns *emn.ypes.gr/media/16763/returns and readmission agreements with algeria.doc* (accessed: 7 July 2013).

5 Co-operation Project on the Social Integration of Immigrants, Migration and the Movement of Persons. The EC External Migration Policy. The Case of the MENA Countries. Research Reports 2007 European University Institute. http://cadmus.eui.eu/bitstream/handle/1814/7991/CARIM-RR_2007_06.pdf (accessed: 7 July 2013).

6 EU and ECtHR, ECOWAS and ECOWAS Court, AU and ACtHR, SADCC and SADC Court, and OAS Inter America Court.

7 Though this is not quite so in the case of Tunisia.

Refugee Law in Belgium – A Historic Perspective

Anything New in Belgium?[8]

Before independence Until the independence in 1830, the small but prosperous territories of what became the Belgium Kingdom were continuously overrun and occupied.[9] Numerous citizens left during the Middle Ages and the sixteenth and seventeenth centuries, fleeing war, religious persecution and the Spanish Inquisition. Walloon and Flemish Protestants sought shelter in neighbouring countries such as Prussia, England and Sweden. Many went to the Netherlands,[10] joining their religious brothers, the Calvinists.[11] Some of these refugees founded the colony which eventually became New York;[12] others were dispersed by the Dutch rulers throughout their colonies and ended up in Indonesia, South Africa and Latin America.

The nineteenth century The increasingly wealthy elite of the early nineteenth century were sympathetic to those fleeing for political ideals. They were still influenced by the liberal ideas of the time, which had instigated their own uprising against the Dutch and William of Orange. Article 128 of the Belgian Constitution of 7 February 1831 guaranteed that 'All foreigners on the territory of Belgium enjoy

8 Katelijne Declerck speaks entirely in her own name. The text is based on both her research and her own experiences as a former member of the UNHCR and a judge of the Permanent Commission of Refugees and, since 2007, of the Council for Alien Law Litigations.

9 Among others, the Romans, the Spanish, the Austrians, the French, the Dutch and after independence the Germans.

10 About 150,000 Protestants fled to the Northern Netherlands. By the beginning of the seventeenth century, 48 per cent of Haarlem's population and 45 per cent of Gouda's were new immigrants from Belgium, then called the Southern Netherlands.

11 The wife of Calvin, Idelette de Bure, was from Liége, Belgium. This exodus of Protestants was mainly the result of the revocation of the Edict of Nantes by Louis XIV's Edict of Fontainebleau in October 1685, and the response three days later of Frederick William, Duke of Prussia, in the Edict of Potsdam on 29 October 1685. See Bronkhorst, D. (1990), *Een tijd van komen* (Amsterdam: Federatie VON).

12 Although the Portuguese and Spanish had been there earlier, Jessé de Forest, a Belgian refugee in Holland, in 1615 received the permission to settle with other Huguenot families in the New World. In 1624, the vessel *Nieu Nederlandt* chartered by the West-Indian Company (founded by the in Antwerp-born Willem Usselinx) arrived near the island of Manhattan with 30 Belgian refugee families. Many of de Forest's English Puritans contacts were passengers on the *Mayflower*. In 1626, Pierre Minuit, the son of Walloon Huguenot refugees, became the first governor of Nova-Belgica. He later became famous for having purchased the island of Manhattan from the Manhattan Indians for an equivalent of 60 guilders (24 dollars).

the protection given to persons and their belongings, subject to the exceptions prescribed by law.'

It was in this spirit that on 1 October 1833, the rule that political offenders should not be extradited, first found legal expression in the Belgian law on extradition.[13] It was the first legal act that acknowledged the existence of a political refugee.[14] Article 6 of the law stipulated 'that the foreigner shall not be prosecuted or punished for any political offense prior to extradition, nor for any act connected with such an offence'.[15]

The Constitution proclaimed that all persons in the territory were equal but, as well, that the legislator could make exceptions. A major exception came soon into force through the Aliens' Act of 22 September 1835 that gave the executive the power to expel foreigners who disturbed public order, or who were condemned or persecuted for specific crimes abroad.[16] The state security office (Staatsveiligheid/ Sûreté de l'Etat), one of the four departments that had been set up in 1830 by the interim union government, was given authority over the police on persons' entry, sojourn and temporary or indefinite stay in the country. This remained unchanged until 1929 when the Alien Police (Vreemdelingenpolitie/Police des Etrangers) was created as a separate department within the State Security.[17]

The Aliens' Act 1835 introduced three categories of foreigners: non-resident aliens, resident aliens and 'de facto Belgians'. The non-resident aliens were covered by the so-called 'revolutionary legislation', dating from the French rule and the period before the proclamation of the Belgians' independence.[18] No specific definition was given to 'resident alien' and resulted in different interpretations by

13 Law of 1 October 1833 on Extradition, Bull. Off. LXVII, no. 1195.

14 See Grahl-Madsen, A. (1980), *Territorial Asylum* (Stockholm: Almqvist & Wiksell International).

15 See Van den Wijngaert, C. (1994), *Strafrecht en Strafprocesrecht in hoofdlijnen* (Antwerpen: Maklu), pp. 145–6.

16 Loi concernant les étrangers résidant en Belgique, published in the Official Bulletin on 22 September 1835.(Bull. Off.) no. 51. Article 13 of the Civil Code, abrogated by article 93 of the Aliens Act of 15 December 1980, stipulated that the executive power granted the foreigner sojourn that gave him the enjoyment of civil rights as long as he was in Belgium. No political rights were granted as foreigners were excluded this right by the old article 4 of the Constitution.

17 Only in 1 January 1994 did the Office for Alien Affairs (Dienst voor Vreemdelingenzaken/Office des Etrangers) become a separate office within the Ministry of Interior (Sûreté de l'Etat, 2011).

18 Before the law was enacted on 28 March 1952, the status of foreigners in Belgium was governed by the Aliens Law of February 12, 1897, as well as some decrees and laws dating from the French Revolution (Decree of 23 Messidor year III Article 9, Law 28 endémiaire Year VI, article 7), or the beginning of Belgian Independence (Order of the Provisional Government of 6 October 1830, article 3). Article 16 of the Act of March 28, 1952 repeals expressively all earlier dispositions.

the administration and the courts.[19] This continued to create confusion until the Act of 22 September 1835. In practice, however, the differences between foreign citizens, refugees and even Belgians were of little relevance in daily life and only changed when legislation on social welfare and education became significant. Up to the Second World War, Belgium assumed automatic assimilation. Foreigners could integrate, provided they were self-sufficient and not dependent on the state.

During the nineteenth century, Karl Marx, along with other notable writers such as Alexandre Dumas and Charles Baudelaire took refuge in Belgium. Karl Marx resided in Brussels during the key historical period 1845–48, when he founded the international Communist organizations and wrote the Communist Manifesto (which was published later in 1848 in London by a group of German political refugees).

However, wary of the fragility of its new independence, and fearing reprisal from the Dutch and knowing that international recognition was still at order, Belgium was reluctant to admit persons who could jeopardize its future. More specifically, in a panic reaction, unwanted foreigners were expelled after the February revolt in France in 1848 which had ended the Orleans monarchy (1830–48), dethroned King Louis-Philippe (the father-in-law of the Belgian monarch Leopold I) and led to the creation of the French Second Republic. Among those expelled was Karl Marx who had openly supported the French republican Alphonse de Lamartine. Intense diplomacy between Belgium, France and Great Britain was necessary to restore the confidence.[20] The French revolt affected, also in Belgium, the traditional internal relations between the Catholics and the Liberals within the background of a new political reality of monarchies and republics. Furthermore, it became apparent that, regardless of the pressure of its powerful neighbours, Belgium continued to respect the principle of non-*refoulement*. Karl Marx was able to go to Britain and was not returned to the country where he would risk persecution.

Political turmoil in France continued to affect Belgian politics and the treatment of those who had fled from France for their political beliefs. Even though Belgium was one of the first to recognize the Second French Empire and Emperor Napoleon III, the activities of the French immigrants and activists in Belgium remained of concern. The anti-Bonaparte pamphlets that were distributed from Brussels, and the French 'émigré' newspaper printed in Belgium, impelled France to insist on a more stringent penal law on press offences. Belgium followed France's lead,[21] explaining the law was not against the liberty of press (one of the reasons of the revolt against the Dutch in 1830), but also against defamation, more specifically against foreign rulers. Napoleon III was satisfied, at least for the time being, as his attention was diverted to the Crimean War. But it returned when Leopold II, Crown Prince of Belgium was to marry Maria-Hendrika von Habsburg-Lorreinen,

19 The court of Cassation in the case of Jones in 1848 (Cuvelier, 1939)

20 See Luykx, T. (1964), *Politieke geschiedenis van België* (Bruxelles: Elsevier), pp. 95–112.

21 The law Faider of 20 December 1852.

and certainly following the failed attempt to murder Napoleon III by Jules and Célestin Jacquin, two French citizens living in Belgium.[22] The Belgium Court of Appeal refused their extradition on account of the Belgian extradition law interdicting the surrender of political criminals and by doing so, de facto gave them political refuge (1855–56). Neither special refugee status, nor immigration papers were granted at that time, but again in practice, the principle of non-*refoulement* was respected. Yet the attentat clause that was inserted in the Belgian law,[23] redefined the murder of a foreign head of state and his family as an ordinary murder, thus allowing extradition. Gradually, with the exception of England and Switzerland, all European states would adopt this attentat clause.[24]

The Belgian establishment of Catholics and Liberals remained reluctant to accept the revolutionaries who fled France in the 1860s and feared they would strengthen the emerging socialist movement in Belgium. The defeat of the Communes in Paris in May 1871 created a new wave of refugees who were not welcome and seen not as refugees, but as criminals. For a short time, passport requirements were re-introduced but these stringent measures were relaxed some months later.[25] The refugees were allowed to stay legally in the country provided they stayed away from politics and found a way of supporting themselves.

Unwanted foreigners, mainly vagrants, were expelled with an order to leave the country. New bilateral agreements[26] on repatriation changed the expulsion policy. At the same time, the Belgian government reaffirmed it as unacceptable to return political refugees to their home country where they would be persecuted. All those expelled had therefore to be questioned individually.

The First World War The anti-German climate grew with the threat of war. Most Germans left Belgium before the First World War. When in 1914, Germany invaded the then-neutral Belgium, nearly one-third of the Belgian population fled. Most tried to seek refuge in France where 325,000 still had not returned after the end of the war.[27] During the initial stages of the war, 265,000 Belgians went

---

22 See Luykx, T. (1962), 'Napoleon III and the Belgian Press', *International Communication Gazette* 8: 133–44.

23 The so'called 'Nothomb' law came into force on 14 March 1856 after long parliamentary debates as strongly opposed by the opposition who named it 'une loi d'occation' (Luykx, T. (1964), *Politieke geschiedenis van België* (Bruxelles: Elsevier), pp. 95–112).

24 See Oppenheim, L. (2005), *International Law: A Treatise,* vol. 1 (Clark, NJ: The Lawbook Exchange, Ltd), pp. 335–7.

25 See Caestecker, F. (2000), *Alien Policy in Belgium, 1840–1940: the creation of guest workers, refugees and illegal aliens* (New York and Oxford: Berghann Books), p. 330.

26 For instance, with Prussia for the repatriation of the insane (1868) and orphans (1873), with the German Empire for the repatriation of the destitute (1877).

27 See Nivet, P. (2004), 'Les réfugiés de guerre dans la société française (1914–1946)', *Histoire, économie et société*, 23.2: 247–59.

to England and although many returned to Belgium during the war or went to France and the Netherlands, about half of them stayed.[28] The Great War[29] evidently affected the migration system. 'Anti-patriotism' was the measure. In practice, this notion was of little use in administrative decisions on entry and had only some influence through jurisprudence on the rejection of nationality requests.[30] Germans and Austro-Hungarians and even their Belgian spouses who lost their nationality through marriage, were massively expelled if not for (often unproven) military collaboration, than for economic collaboration. Those who did not leave were put in detention centres[31] until their deportation.

Between the World Wars

On the way to a more formal asylum system The liberal culture that had protected Belgians and foreigners in the nineteenth century lost its grip on politics and this led to protectionism. It was the Belgian identity itself that had been under threat during the Great War and this instigated caution. The introduction of the identity card in 1918 would make it easier to detect foreigners who had not entered legally into the country. Most of the people (mainly of German descent) that had been expelled before and after the war for what was considered security measures, were none the less allowed to come back in the 1920s.[32]

The Russian and Armenian refugees of the 1920s The Nansen Bureau, which was connected to the League of Nations, was set up to defend the interests of the refugees. The Russian, Armenian, Assyrian, Chaldean, Syriac and Pontic Greek refugees of the 1920s were not perceived as a threat, as they had had to cross many borders before reaching Belgium, and therefore were not able to arrive in great numbers. Moreover, the Soviet authorities had closed their borders, which excluded pull-factor possibilities. They had also collectively withdrawn the nationality of citizens who left without accord, making the refugees stateless.

In the inter-war period, nationalism and the nation state were seen as stabilizing factors that could deter war. Refugees without a nation(ality) were therefore in need of protection 'of a state' that would accept and integrate them until they could

28 Even Hercule Poirot, a fictional French-speaking Belgian detective, created by Agatha Christie in 1916.

29 Mainly fought on Belgian soil in Flanders fields (immortalized in the poem 'In Flanders Fields', by Lieutenant-Colonel John McCrae, 1872–1918).

30 See Caestecker, F. and Roobrouck, T. (2010), *De jacht of Duitsers in het bevrijde België, 1918–1925* (Ghent: Universiteit Gent), pp. 225–54.

31 There were also practical obstacles to their repatriation or expulsion of German nationals after the First World War. The German Belgian border was closed and the country's transportation system was in total disarray after the war.

32 See Caestecker and Roobrouck, *De jacht of Duitsers in het bevrijde België, 1918–1925*.

return to their own country. Hence no reason was seen to grant them some formal refugee status. Russians could integrate into Belgian society and would, when legitimacy was restored in the Soviet Union (as was thought possible at the time), provide useful connections upon their return.[33] Armenians, who had a recognized country through the Treaty of Sèvres (also signed by Belgium), were neither considered, nor wanted to be considered, stateless,[34] regardless of the fact that they had no registered citizenship or nationality. If the Nansen passport was an attempt to create a legal relationship between the refugee and the host country, economic integration was a major aim. Through the ratification of the Nansen Agreement, these refugees received a more favourable status than other immigrants. They were given work permits much faster and the possibility of expulsion was much more limited (Gousseff, 2008).[35] Automatic assimilation was the bottom line.

Italian anti-fascists The preferential treatment of the Nansen refugees was not extended to the Italian anti-fascists who came in larger numbers to Belgium during the 1920s, notwithstanding that many had become stateless after the withdrawal of their nationality in January 1929. These anarchists, communists, left-wing communists (*bordighistes*), socialists and republicans were, however, well-organized. They had the ear of the Belgian press and received financial aid from the workers' funds.[36] Their political activities in Belgium and protests alongside the Belgian Workers Union became increasingly clandestine after a few Italians workers were expelled.[37] Those expelled, however, were not returned to Italy and were allowed their choice of border.

---

33 Russian immigrants came in several waves to Belgium. The first (after the October Revolution, 1920–1930) were well-educated people, who were followed by a second group of mostly patriotic women and supporters of the Soviet regime, who fled Germany during the Second World War, where they had been imported as labourers. They were followed by war prisoners who were against the Soviet Union and wanted to stay in western Europe. Orthodox Jews who settled after the war and worked in the diamond industry in Antwerp. A third group were Jews who fled after the fall of the Soviet Union and who were followed by the economic immigrants of the recent years. A fourth immigration group are those who fled the war zones of the Russian Federation and those who claim their human rights have been violated (RIC (2009), *De Russischtalige migranten te Brussel* <http://www.foyer.be/article.php3?id_article=7773>).

34 Article 88 of the Treaty of Sevres of 10 August 1920 stipulated that Turkey, in accordance with the action already taken by the Allied Powers, hereby recognizes Armenia as a free and independent State.

35 See Caestecker, *Alien Policy in Belgium, 1840–1940*, pp. 172–4, 192, 211. Gousseff, C. (2008), *L'Exil russe (1920–1939). La fabrique du réfugié apatride* (Paris: CNRS-Editions, coll. «mondes russes»).

36 The Matteotti Fund, which in 1938 became the International Solidarity Fund, later also administered aid for the workers of Germany – that is, refugees from Nazi Germany.

37 It was no secret that the Italian diplomatic services were actively noting out the undesirable, as did the Germans do some years later. Some of these refugees would later

Refugees from Germany and Eastern Europe Persecution in the 1930s hit hard and was not comparable to the circumstances of the nineteenth century. The Italian arrivals and the massive influx of refugees from Germany in the 1930s led to active interventions from the Belgian government. A more formalized attitude towards territorial asylum was bound to impose itself, the emphasis remained on avoiding the granting of entry. After 1933, the Belgian consulate in Germany was swamped with visa requests. Visas were still issued to documented Germans, but it became increasingly more difficult for the (mostly Jewish) Polish community in Germany to obtain Belgian visas, as it was also for the many who were or had become stateless.[38] Increased border controls and strict regulations stopped people without the necessary papers, passport and visa. In practice, it meant that persons who held what were considered 'radical views' (communists), were not admitted at the borders, nor 'the enemy' which were their eastern European neighbours and their allies. However, no political support was found to stop the eastern European Jews at the borders in the 1930s,[39] and especially after 1933, when the NSDAP took power in Germany. Once inside Belgium, refugees were, as had always been the case, allowed to stay unless their political involvement became a problem to Belgian external relations and internal politics.

The massive exodus of destitute refugees that left Nazi Germany by the mid-1930s caused many front-line states to cut back on their protection. The pressure on the Belgian borders became exceptionally heavy. Contrary to the Luxemburg, Danish, Dutch and Swiss authorities, Belgium did not deport Jewish refugees, but instead tried to prevent entry through stringent rules on illegal immigration. This policy failed in practice. Once accepted by one of the Jewish, Socialists and Catholic social services or private organizations such as the Red Cross, the refugees were protected from expulsion. It was, however, understood that the reception of refugees continued to be a matter for civil society and that the state would not take financial responsibility for them. The economic depression of the 1930s could hardly cope with such big influxes of refugees, who were not given a work permit or welfare. They were totally trapped, as they could not return to their own countries, had no future in Belgium nor were they allowed to move on as all the other neighbouring countries had closed their borders.

By 1936, the influx slowed down. The countries neighbouring Germany were again willing to support the refugees. The political situation in Germany and Italy deteriorated. However successful, private initiatives, solidarity campaigns for refugees, and other forms of charity were still not sufficient to cover most of

leave for the Spanish Civil War, while others integrated in the Belgian resistance of the Second World War. See Morelli, A (1984), *Fascisme et antifascisme dans l'immigration italienne en Belgique (1922–1945)*, ULB.

38 See Caestecker, *Alien Policy in Belgium, 1840–1940*.

39 See Caestecker, F. and Morelli, A. (2010), 'Het bewogen ontstaan van een vluchtelingenbeleid (1918–1940)', *Belgisch Tijdschrift voor Nieuwste Geschiedenis – Revue belge d'histoire contemporaine* XL: 383–413.

their needs and could even less provide for a reasonable possibility for integration in the long run. Only well into the 1930s did the public authorities support the reception of refugees, and then only because the large foreign communities living on the sidelines of Belgian society could potentially destabilize society and lead to disorder. The social and private associations were equally wary of infiltration and abuse.

Selection procedures were coming into force to detect impostors and infiltration by Nazi agents. All Germans had to request asylum and were interviewed individually. Moreover, the socialist solidarity organizations only wanted those German workers who could show a serious threat of being arrested upon return to Germany to benefit from the Matteotti Fund. Other socialists were encouraged to go back to Germany. Other social agencies set up similar hearings. From 1936, refugee committees heard all asylum-seekers individually and advised the Minister of Justice on their need of protection. This was in itself important, as it gave all persons fleeing persecution the possibility to claim asylum independently from the government, which at that time was under significant pressure. The State Security (government) remained the sole authority granting entry. However, through changes in immigration policy, border police could no longer refuse undocumented foreigners who asked for asylum.

Initially, the Jewish people were only given temporary protection as, at least in the mid-1930s, it was considered that the state violence (economic boycotts) towards the Jewish was generally less harsh than on political opponents who could face imprisonment and death. The Belgian Jewish community was therefore compelled to organize their emigration and resettlement,[40] which imposed even more on their financial and social responsibilities. The situation remained as such until the Kristallnacht of 9 and 10 November 1938,[41] even if without a doubt anti-Semitism for many years had become a state policy and certainly after the Anschluss of Austria in March 1938.

German pressure on its neighbours increased as well. The German Consulate General in Belgium was not pleased with the reception of German refugees and, in May 1938, started a campaign against 'the benign attitude of some Belgian institutions' to political refugees.[42] The German police pressed their Belgian

40 Einstein was resettled through Belgium in September 1933 and then sailed from Ostend to Dover. In recently discovered documents, he had registered as a Swiss citizen, denying his German nationality (*De Morgen*, 10 May 2011).

41 With the exception of directives imposed for some weeks in the autumn of 1939 which led to the deportation of 150 Jews to Germany. This deportation was contested in court and led to a political crisis. Immigration had thus far been a prerogative of the executive but was now discussed on the street.

42 Waldemar Pötsch, born in Bad Schmiedeberg in 1892, until 1933 led *le socialist seemen syndicat* of Hamburg, and settled as a refugee in Antwerp where he organized political refugees, which is how he eventually became an important figure of the socialist Matteotti Fund.

colleagues for more diligence in the prevention of communist sabotage on German ships in the port of Antwerp; the Belgian attitude was rather averse. It turned completely with the start of the occupation and even more when Germany invaded the Soviet Union on 22 June 1941. The Soviet Union had virtually become an ally of Belgium. The few Belgian police officers who went on working with the Germans in their hunt for communist refugees and resistance fighters were no longer covered by the judiciary and were considered collaborators.[43]

Spanish refugees The Spanish Civil War resulted in another wave of refugees. A special group of refugees were Basque children.[44] After the bombing of Guernica in April 1937, the autonomous Basque government, loyal to the Republic, issued an appeal to save Basque children. Seven countries responded: Belgium, Britain, Denmark, Mexico, the Soviet Union and Switzerland. Most of the children (about 15,000) were taken in by France and its Basque population. About 6,000 came to Belgium, and were taken care by the child care organizations, the Red Cross, and Catholic and socialist organizations.

Refugees continued to occupy part of Belgium's international discussions from the establishment of the Nanssen Bureau. Besides the Arrangements of 12 May 1926 and 30 June 1928, Belgium signed the Conventions of 28 October 1933 and 10 February 1938[45] and the Convention of 10 February 1938, concerning the status of refugees coming from Germany, and acted accordingly.[46]

After the Second World War

When the Second World War broke out in 1939, the Belgian Parliament granted extraordinary powers to the executive and the army entered in a state of war.[47]

---

43 See Van Doorslaer, R. and Verhoeyen, E. (1986), 'L'allemagne Nazie, La Police Belge et L'anticommunisme en Belgique (1936–1944), Un aspect des relations Belgo-Allemandes', *Belgisch Tijdschrift voor Nieuwste Geschiedenis – Revue belge d'histoire contemporaine*, 17.1–2: 61–126 <http://www.flw.ugent.be/btng-rbhc/pdf/BTNG-RBHC,17,1986,201-2, pp 20061-125.pdf>.

44 They were put in the charge of the Belgian Workers Party, while Catholic organizations and other groups (such as *Secours Rouge* and *Croix-Rouge*) took some. The Soviet Union took about 3,000 Basque children, Switzerland 2,500, and Britain almost 4,000.

45 Convention of 28 October 1933 relating to the International Status of Refugees, League of Nations, Treaty Series Vol. CLIX, No. 3663.

46 Conformément à l'arrangement conclu à Genève, le 4 juillet dernier, établissant le statut provisoire des réfugiés provenant 'l'Allemagne, i l a été institué, en faveur de ces étrangers, par arrêté royal du 5 décembre 1936' (Moniteur belge du 1er janvier 1937), 'un certificat d'identité pour les réfugiés provenant d'Allemagne', 'permettant à son titulaire de rentrer en Belgique après avoir effectué un voyage à l'étranger'.

47 The mobilization of the army was proclaimed through the Royal Decree of 27 August 1939.

By the law of 7 September 1939, the King, in view of the 'state security and public peace', was granted extraordinary powers which included a large authority over the presence of foreigners on Belgian soil.[48] This decree-law remained valid in the post-war period and during the legislative process of 1949–52, a period of economic hardship and the most politically tense years of the Cold War. The newly introduced criminalization of the violation of administrative immigration rules were, however, hardly ever applied by the courts.

On the international level, Belgium was active in all forums dealing with refugees. The Act of 5 February 1948 approved the Convention of 28 October 1933 relating to the International Status of Refugees. The International Refugee Organization (IRO), the official agency of the United Nations for the maintenance and resettlement of European refugees established in 1946, was increasingly operative in Belgium determining the refugees' status.[49] The individual refugee status determination was essentially aimed at detecting those who had collaborated with the Nazi regime and granting sojourn to displaced persons who refused to return to the *Eastern Bloc*. The lack of a clear definition of a refugee was criticized by Belgian refugee organizations, as well as the non-recognition of certain groups of refugees (for instance, the Spanish).[50]

Five years of intense debate were necessary to prepare the Aliens Act of 28 March 1952.[51] It was neither political nor public interest that caused the delay, but reluctance on the part of the administration of the Alien Police to adopt a new law. The Minister of Justice[52] stressed public order, the new influx of foreign workers, the difficult political European climate and evidence of a possible new (cold) war, and opted to temporarily prolong the Decree-law of 1939. The outbreak of the Cold War in 1947, with the insertion in 1948 of the Administration of the Alien Police as a department within the State Security Services, emphasized further the importance of public order and national security. The overall aim of the Act of 28 March 1952 continued to be in the interest of the state. The status of 'indefinite sojourn' was no longer absolute and remained the prerogative of the executive. The Alien Act of 28 March 1952 remained a legal framework with unclear juridical definitions and with little control mechanism over the administration, except for the Council of State in a strict annulment procedure. There were, however, some important novelties. For the first time, the Aliens Act explicitly

48 Throught the 'decree-law on the Alien Police' of 28 September 1939 (Besluitwet op de Vreemdelingenpolitie, 28 september 1939 – B.S. 30 September 1939).

49 Previously the UNRRA (United Nations Relief and Rehabilation Agency) alongside the private organizations, provided health and welfare assistance to displaced persons in Belgium.

50 See Caestecker, F. and Luyckx, L. (2009), 'Het individuele vreemdelingendossier: een unieke bron over migratie en migranten', in Tallier, A. (ed.), *Grensgevallen <https://biblio.ugent.be/input/download?func=downloadFile&fileOId=1088613>*.

51 Act on the Alien Police, 28 March 1952 (Staatsblad 30–31 Maart 1952).

52 Minister of Justice Struye, PH Senaat, 26 October 1948, p. 2119.

introduced the notion of 'refugees' as a separate group of aliens who were given the most favourable rights given to aliens, such as the right to sojourn, to work, to assimilation and naturalization. Refugees were also allowed to enter illegally as long as they presented themselves to the authorities within eight days. The status came with a set of rights that were either the same or similar to Belgian citizens (in education, social assistance, intellectual rights, social security and fiscal charges and access to courts for these matters). Refugees were also better protected from expulsion, among others through the creation of a Consultative Commission for Aliens that gave advice to the Minister of Justice on expulsion and extradition.[53] All these measures very much foreshadowed the full bundle of rights in the Refugee Convention of 1951.

For a brief period between the promulgation of the Aliens Act of 28 March 1952 and the ratification of the Refugee Convention in June 1953,[54] the competence to grant refugee status was entrusted to the Minister of Justice who had to consult the Consultative Commission for Aliens.

The UNHCR determines refugee status The law of 1952 did not set up an asylum procedure but declared the representative in Belgium of the UN High Commissioner for Refugees competent to grant, exclude, or withdraw the refugee status for Belgium.[55] Even if more countries involved the UNHCR in their refugee determination system, Belgium set a precedent as at that time, it left the refugee status determination (RSD) entirely in the hands of the UNHCR.

The Aliens Police decided if asylum-seekers could enter the refugee procedure. Asylum-seekers had to lodge their claim upon arrival, within a time frame, and show their documents which proved that they had arrived immediately from the country where they were persecuted. A claim could be declared not receivable if manifestly unfounded. Asylum-seekers were allowed to stay on the Belgian territory until a decision was taken on asylum request by the UNHCR. Decisions

53 It would take more than 20 years to change the Aliens Law. The Aliens Law of 15 December 1980 would grant specific rights and more individual freedom to foreigners.

54 United Nations Convention Relating to the Status of Refugees, Genève, 28 July 1951, adopted by the Act of 26 June 1953, B.S. 4 October 1953, came in force on 22 April 1954. The Protocol relating to the Status of Refugees, New York, 31 January 1967, was adopted by the Act of 27 February 1969, B.S. 3 May 1969, and came into force on 8 April 1969.

55 Article 5 of the Aliens Act of 26 June 1953. The delegation of the competence was formalized in the Royal Decree of 22 February 1954. The trust towards the UNHCR was not surprising as Belgium was one of the 13 countries of the Comité Special de l'Apatridie et des Problèmes Connexes (16 January–16 February 1950) formed by the Economic and Social Council of the United Nations and of the Comité Special pour les Réfugiés et les Apatrides who came together in Genève, 14–25 August 1950, and formalized a new project of the refugee convention. At the same time, Belgian non-governmental refugee support organizations of all political colours were supporting the idea of an international organization to make decisions on refugee claims.

of the UNHCR were not given in a written form. The argument of the UNHCR – that publication might harm their neutrality towards the country of origin of the asylum-seeker as towards Belgium – was often criticized, as the mere fact of granting refugee status implied persecution by a state or its inability to protect. Moreover, asylum-seekers and their legal representatives, upon request, were orally given the decision reasoning for the rejection of the asylum claim and were allowed to submit a written request to review their claim taking into account the reasons for the rejection. In practice, the UNHCR would send a letter notifying that a negative decision would be taken and sent to the Minister of Justice if within three weeks no new elements were submitted.

An administrative appeal to a Belgian court was not possible. The Council of State took a very clear view on this. On many occasions (on appeal against the UNHCR Representative in Belgium alone or on appeal jointly against the Minister of Justice and the Minister of Foreign Affairs), the Council of State decided that it was not competent to see decisions coming from a member of the United Nations who was not under the hierarchal authority of a Belgian minister.[56] Only the order to leave the country, which could follow the rejection of the asylum claim, could be appealed to the Council of State. The Minister of Justice was first obliged to ask the advice of the Advisory Commission for Aliens[57] and could always grant sojourn for other reasons.

In the 1960s and 1970s, refugees came to Belgium mainly from countries in the geographic neighbourhood. After the Hungarian revolution of November 1956, Belgium accepted about 7,000 Hungarians, half of whom were under the age of 21. They were given refugee status and their reception placed in the hands of five non-governmental agencies (Caritas Catholica, Socialist Solidarity, Liberal Solidarity, the Red Cross and Ecumenists organizations).

Although Belgium did not accept extra-territorial asylum granted in embassies or consulates (diplomatic asylum), some sidelines for special categories of foreigners were created who were on an exceptional basis granted protection outside and mostly without the knowledge of the UNHCR. The French 'Organisation de l'Armée Secrète' had to contact directly the Minister of Justice upon arrival (de Diesbach, 1972; Auteurweb, 2011).[58] East European borders remained closed and few people were able to escape. However, refugees fled the Turkish military rule due to its treatment of political opponents, Christian and ethnic minorities, while others fled dictatorships and political upheaval in Latin America, Zaïre (now the *Democratic* Republic of Congo) and Central Africa. Decolonialization, war, insecurity, unstable governments and breaches of human rights led to massive population flows. Belgium would accept the resettlement of Asian minorities from

56 Council of State, 25 September 1970, nr. 14. 264, 21 September, 21 March, nr. 19.151.

57 See Beauthier, G.H. (1984), *Le droit des Etrangers et le Code de la Nationalité* (Bruxelles: Vie Ouvrière), p. 458.

58 Diesbach, 1972; Auteurweb, 2011

Uganda, political prisoners from Latin America, 'boat people' and other political refugees from South East Asia. Ever more people came from other continents. The world had changed, and so did the people arriving in Belgium. At the same time, the foreign population (students, migrant workers) on Belgian territory also wanted to benefit from the social rights and demands that were heard on the barricades of the student revolts of the end of the 1960s. Protection against *refoulement* and the right to appeal were just two of those demands.

The Law of 15 December 1980 Between 1952 and 1980, the Alien Law was modified four times. These modifications were to assure conformity with the international instruments and were further meant to specify the procedure and functioning of the Advisory Commission for Aliens (Adviescommissie voor Vreemdelingen/Commission Consultative des Etrangers). It took almost a decade to finally adopt the Aliens Act of 15 December 1980. Times had changed, so had the notion of the protection of individual rights, even against the state and in the context of public order. By virtue of international treaties, it was necessary to update and assemble the rules applicable to certain categories of foreigners (citizens of member states of the then European Economic Union, refugees, stateless persons, students, and so on) and other measures on expulsion and extradition.

The refugee determination procedures remained unchanged and were expressed in Article 49 of the Aliens Act of 15 December 1980.[59] The UNHCR remained the authority competent for the refugee status determination procedure. As before, the Minister of Justice (the Office for Alien Affairs) still had to declare the asylum claim receivable before the UNHCR could decide on the soundness of it. If, on the one hand, more authorities were competent to register asylum claims (the UNHCR, border authorities, judicial police, gendarmerie, local authorities and the state security), and if when entering the country irregularly, the delay to ask asylum was lengthened from 48 hours to 15 days, there were also strict measures (administrative detention) that could be taken for public order and national security. The notions in the 1952 Act of Belgium being the first country of asylum and the asylum-seeker arriving immediately from the country of persecution, became less stringent as the delay allowed between the country of persecution and the entry into Belgium was three months. The decision that refused to accept an asylum claim had to be reasoned and published and was subject to judicial review.

The Act of 15 December 1980 introduced a new kind of refugee: 'the foreigner assimilated (*assimilé*) to a refugee'. It is ironic to note that this category of refugee was introduced for the same reason the UNHCR did not want to publish its decisions, namely security, diplomacy and protection of interests. According to

59 Article 49: Are considered refugees according to the present law, delegation of power of the Minister of Foreign Affairs, 1 the foreigner who has been granted refugee status by the Minister of Foreign Affairs or by the international authority to whom the Minister has delegated his competence. The competence of the UNHCR had previously been formalized in the Royal Decree of 22 February 1954.

the debate in Parliament, the status of being assimilated to a refugee would give the asylum-seeker the guarantee that their country would not gain any knowledge of their asylum request.[60] This status would be an exception and only those with legitimate reasons would be granted the assimilated status. Fear of targeting or revenge for the family left behind in the country of origin was the principal reason given. However, it was thought that Belgian economic and diplomatic interests would be better served with the additional guarantees of the status of *assimilé*, particularly after some Chinese refugees were granted asylum in the United States and seriously disrupted Sino-American relations. The UNHCR was never officially informed of these asylum requests. The advantage for the asylum-seeker was that they had a right to appeal a rejection and that the rights of the defence against removal were respected. However, the increasing numbers of requests for the status of *assimilé*, and the frustration because of the lack of a proper appeal when refused asylum by the UNHCR, led to the misuse or abuse of this procedure.

A Belgian asylum system The discussions that led to the major amendment of the Aliens Act in 1980 were to some extent similar to those that finally made Belgium opt for a national asylum procedure in 1987, including the establishment of an asylum administration decision-making process and appeal instance. By the 1990s, the UNHCR had changed its policy in Europe, reducing its staff and trying to pull out of the national refugee determination systems. This plus the protests of lawyers and non-governmental agencies pushed the Minister of Justice to accept the radical change in the refugee determination procedure. Certainly, the UNHCR's office was not equipped for the vast influx of asylum-seekers in the 1980s, but financial arrangements with the Belgian government were still possible and procedural difficulties would remain. The UNHCR publicly opted out of the determination processing, referring to their change in priorities, such as stimulating national governments to set up adequate national asylum procedures. The Belgian government accepted, especially after lawyers had, with some success, started to lodge appeals to the ordinary courts. The president of the Court of Liège had prohibited the Minister of Justice from executing an order to leave the country on a claimant after a negative decision from the UNHCR. The main motivation being that the refugee determination procedure before the UNHCR did not respect the guarantees given in the Belgian law on the right of defence, reasoned decision and appeal.[61] The Aliens Act of 15 December 1980 was radically modified by the Act of 14 July 1987, by the Act of 18 July 1991, and again by the Act of 6 May 1993.

60 Parliament, Doc., 1974–75, 653/1, pA6 en ook Kamer, Doc., 1977–78, 144/7, p. 101.

61 It was further decided that as the position of the UNHCR was not motivated according to the law on the motivation of administrative decision, this position could only be an advice or consultation, which cannot constitute a basis for an order to leave the country (Ordonnance de référé Civil-Liège 13/1/1984).

The first Belgian asylum procedure was set up by the Act of 14 July 1987. The Office of the Commissioner General for Refugees and Stateless Persons (CGRS) and the Permanent Appeals Commission for Refugees were created. From the start, it was emphasized that the CGRS was an independent government agency. It examines the content of the asylum application and decides on whether to grant or refuse refugee status or subsidiary protection status. The CGRS also issues certificates and documents to recognized refugees and stateless persons. It has a Documentation and Research Centre (Cedoca), with researchers categorized by geographic region. The Legal Service defends the decisions of the CGRS before the Council of State, and, from 2007, also before the Council for Alien Law Litigations. A Psychological Support Section advises caseworkers on asylum-seekers' mental and psychological state, examines their medical certificates and performs individual psychological examinations.

The Permanent Appeals Commission for Refugees was set up as an independent administrative court that ruled on appeals lodged by the asylum-seeker, or by the Minister of Interior, against the decisions of the CGRS, granting, refusing, or revoking refugee status. The appeal had suspensive effect. The novelty of the law was that all decisions taken in the course of an asylum request could be appealed. The UNHCR was given the option to give advice on asylum claims in writing. The CGRS was obliged, if it did not follow the UNHCR's advice, to expressively reason the decision on this point.

The Office for Alien Affairs remained competent to register the asylum-seekers and to decide on the acceptability of the asylum requests. The emphasis of the new asylum procedure was on the first stage of the procedure. It was hoped that the screening system upon arrival could quickly deal with the fraudulent asylum requests, or those which were manifestly unfounded. Carrier sanctions would avoid undocumented persons entering the country. Accelerated procedures, and at the same time the possibility of putting the asylum-seekers temporarily in administrative detention, were introduced.

The later amendments to the Asylum Act of 18 July 1991 and 6 May 1993 added new receivability criteria. Asylum claims could be unacceptable on pure formal criteria (delay in which an asylum request must be made, length of time between leaving the country of persecution and arrival in Belgium, previous expulsion from Belgium with an order not to return within ten years, being in possession of a travel ticket for another country provided the travel documents permitted continuation of the journey). It also provided criteria that touched the grounds of the case: fraud and manifestly outside the criteria of the Refugee Convention, public order and state security.[62] The decisions on the receivability could be appealed to the CGRS. The role of the CGRS in the first face of the procedure changed with each

62 Some criteria were found unconstitutional because they were specifically directed at certain nationalities, namely those who represented more than 5 per cent of the total of asylum claims and of whom less than 5 per cent were granted refugee status. They were amended in the Act of 6 May 1993.

amendment, from purely advisory in 1987, to decision making in 1993, when the decision could only be appealed by the Minister of Interior to the Council of State.

The emphasis on the entry procedures was common in Europe, leading to the Schengen Agreements (1995) and the later Dublin Regulation (2003), which would prevent an applicant from submitting asylum applications in multiple states and remedy the problem of the orbit refugees. These agreements did not change the number of asylum applications in Belgium. It was a zero-sum operation, but did allow family members to join the applicant.

The status of 'assimilated to the refugee status' was abrogated by the amendment of the Aliens Act in 1996. The reasoning behind this was that the country of persecution could, if it wanted to do so, take negative measures against family members from the moment a person disappeared, whatever the actions they took abroad. Furthermore, as the refugee determination status had been transferred to a national administration, it was considered that the new procedure provided sufficient privacy guarantees, as the decisions were not published, but only notified to applicant and, on appeal, the presiding judge could order that proceedings were held behind closed doors.

The increase of number of asylum requests in the 1990s went out of control. It fluctuated – from 4,510 in 1989 to 14,580 in 1990; 26,882 in 1993; 14,350 in 1994; 35,778 in 1999 and 42,691 in 2000. They decreased slowly to 11,115 in 2007 and then climbed back to 17,186 in 2009 and 19,941 in 2010. The numbers continue to increase in 2011.[63] Political instability and violent conflicts in many countries (Somalia, Congo, Rwanda, Russia, Chechnya, Iraq, Sri Lanka, Nepal, Slovenia, Croatia, Macedonia and Bosnia-Herzegovina, Serbia, Kosovo) continue to create migration flows.

Interventions of the legislator on the asylum procedure, on the reception and *refoulement* of rejected asylum-seekers, led to the introduction of new accelerated procedures, including the application of the LIFO principle ('last in, first out'), whereby civil servants of the asylum services dealt with the receivability of the cases. Other dissuasive measures on reception were considered just as effective (such as longer administrative retention, and material aid in reception centres instead of financial support), and additionally, freeing up the asylum system through periodic massive regularization or amnesty (for instance, in 1999[64]), when people would be given indefinite residence.

New legislation would follow, not only because the new European Directives had to be implemented, but also because the asylum system could not cope with the large influxes that created considerable backlogs at all institutional levels. Indeed, if the receivability procedure had been able to screen out many applicants who did not fit the refugee criteria, an appeal procedure before the Council of State

63 See CGVS (Commissariaat-generaal voor de vluchtelingen en de staatlozen) (2010), *Asielstatistieken, Overzicht 2010* <http://www.cgvs.be/>.

64 Loi du 22 décembre 1999 relative à la régularisation de certaines catégories d'étrangers séjournant dans le royaume.

was still open to them. In practice, they continued to receive social welfare until the outcome of their appeal.[65] The cases that were receivable had the possibility of appeal to the Permanent Commission for Refugees and had a further appeal to the Council of State.

The Aliens Act of 15 September 2006 set up a whole new system that came into force on 1 June 2007. The provisions on subsidiary protection came into force, as required by the European Directive, on 10 October 2006.

The European directives on the procedure and qualification of asylum[66] The entry of the subsidiary protection status, as set out in the qualification directive, certainly filled in an important gap in the Belgian legislation. Up to the introduction of the subsidiary protection status, only the Minister of Justice, and later of the Interior, had the possibility to accept a person on (not always clear) humanitarian grounds. The CGRS, when refusing asylum claims could, in particular cases, draw the attention of the Minister of the Interior to the fact that the person was not removable for reasons independent of their will (war, medical reasons). The minister could also add what became known as a 'non-returnable clause'. These people were not removed, but were not automatically granted the rights attached to the later subsidiary status.

Institutional changes in 2006 Two laws, both enacted 15 September 2006, fundamentally changed the asylum procedure. The first Act of 15 September 2006, 'Reforming the Council of State and establishing a Council for Alien Law Litigations', created an independent administrative court, the Council for Alien Law Litigations (Raad voor Vreemdelingenbetwistingen/Conseil du Contentieux des Etrangers). It became the only court that can rule on appeals submitted against decisions of the government taken in application of the Belgian Aliens Act. The second act amended the Aliens Act of 15 December 1980 and abolished the former first stage (receivability) of the asylum procedure, and more importantly, implemented the European Directives on asylum. The Office for Alien Affairs remained competent to act within the framework of the Dublin Regulations. If Belgium was responsible for the asylum claim, the case is sent to the CGRS.

65 The Council of State controlled the legality of the decision, whether this decision was based on correct facts, if they were correctly assessed and whether the administrative authority could reasonably come to its conclusion.

66 Council Directive 2004/83/EC of 29 April 2004 on minimum standards for the qualification and status of third-country nationals or stateless persons as refugees or as persons who otherwise need international protection and the content of the protection granted, and the Council Directive 2005/85/EC of 1 December 2005 on minimum standards on procedures in Member States for granting or withdrawing refugee status.

The reasons for setting up the Council for Alien Law Litigations were twofold: to remove the judicial backlog that was present at the Council of State, and to aim for a uniform and efficient procedure.

The Council officially started its proceedings on 1 June 2007. The Council currently has 40 judges and 200 employees. There are two different procedures before the Council:[67] full jurisdiction and annulment. The procedure at the Council is written and adversarial. An appeal is brought to the Council by means of a petition. Parties and their legal representatives are allowed to formulate their remarks orally at the hearing. They may not, in principle,[68] advance other arguments than those set out in their procedural documents.

In the full jurisdiction procedure,[69] the Council rules on appeals made against decisions of the CGRS when an alien was given a negative decision on his or her refugee application and/or his or her application for subsidiary protection. The Council provides its ruling in last instance on the grounds of the dispute. The Council can reform, confirm, or quash the challenged decision and also can remit it to the CGRS for further examination. The procedure has suspensive effect until the Council promulgates the ruling. The judges, in full jurisdiction procedures, *consider all facts as applicable at the time of the conclusion of the debates*.

In the annulment procedure,[70] the Council rules on the legality of the challenged administrative act. The majority of these decisions are taken by the Office for Alien Affairs, but may also be taken by a municipal official. Examples of decisions are refusal for visa applications, residence permits, or removal decisions. If the Council annuls a decision, the Office for Alien Affairs will be responsible for taking a new decision. The decision not to allow a consecutive asylum application on the basis that no change of circumstances are forwarded, as well as the rejection of the CGRS of the asylum application of a person from the European Union, are dealt with according to the annulment procedure.

Afterword

When it comes to asylum, it seems that there is always an emergency situation allowing for special laws and regulations. Rapid changes, overwhelming influxes of people, compelling pressures on asylum systems seem to prevent long-term thinking. Since the beginning of the twentieth century, Belgium has constantly

67 Each of these procedures have additional accelerated procedures. In full jurisdiction, there are fast-track procedures for asylum-seekers who are in (administrative) detention and for certain nationalities.

68 New elements can be advanced in full jurisdiction, even orally during the court session, provided they fall within the criteria set out in the law on the matter.

69 Formally the competence of the Permanent Appeals Commission for Refugees that had investigation and therefore no annulment possibilities.

70 Formally the competence of the Council of State.

been trying to come to terms with large influxes of people, asylum-seekers and migrants.

The overview makes it evident that the Belgian policy making on refugees before and since the First World War, and certainly in the 1930s, was just as challenging as today. The balance between the protection of the state itself and the protection of foreigners on Belgian territory has at times been very tense and maybe even necessarily ambiguous. Certainly, if the ancient claim that *necessitas legem non habet* (necessity has no law) is without doubt foreign to the basis of the Belgian system of responsibility and accountability, it does come to mind when noting the post-war seeming unwillingness of the State Security to establish basic laws on the administration of aliens and asylum-seekers.

Nevertheless, the virtue of the practice can be seen in what has been done. Belgium, through its extradition law, was the first country to acknowledge the existence of a political refugee. The attentat clause, taken under pressure from France, caused much debate in the Belgian Parliament. Seen from today's exclusion clauses of the Refugee Convention on the one hand, and the absolute application of Article 3 of the European Convention for the Protection of Human Rights and Fundamental Freedoms on the other, this is hardly surprising. Belgium respected non-*refoulement* in the turbulent years of the nineteenth and twentieth centuries, allowed acceptance of Italian refugees against the political discourse of the establishment, and in the mid-1930s, contrary to neighbouring countries, refrained from the deportation of the Jews.[71] The pressure and deep involvement of civil society of all sides and colours was a constant security for those in need of protection. Civil society groups were, up to the 1950s, solely responsible for the screening, reception and social welfare of the new arrivals. These tasks would only gradually be taken over by the state. Remarkably enough, the last task to be accepted by the Belgian authorities, was the screening itself of refugees and the determination of the status of refugee.

Refugee law, based on international law, has its roots in the fundamental and common understanding of protection. The post-First and Second World War treaties were in many ways well embedded in long-held practices. The thinking was not new, but expressing it in treaties and conventions was in many ways revolutionary. The development of regional instruments became predominant in Europe. Yet it remains unclear where European legislation on asylum will eventually take us. Unless the member states want to protect themselves against each other and perhaps from themselves, the benefits that derive from common legislation will determine its progress.

The modifications of the Belgian Aliens Act have been equally stimulated by the jurisprudence of courts on national and European levels. The jurisprudence of the Constitutional Court of Belgium showed its concern for procedural equality

71 This might be some of the reasons which explain why more than 50 per cent of Belgian Jews from before the Second World War survived the war. As was explained above, a far larger number survived there than any other neighbouring occupied country.

in administrative and judicial procedures. The Constitutional Court did accept specific asylum procedures,[72] but not the difference in legal protection between certain categories of foreigners (asylum-seekers) in Belgium.[73] The Constitutional Court also obliged the legislator to organize shelter for the applicant during the entire asylum procedure, including any appeal.

The importance of the jurisprudence of the European Court of Human Rights can scarcely be over-estimated. Whether on removal[74] or detention,[75] it sets a path to be followed and stimulates a coherent approach in larger Europe. The Court of Justice of the European Union in Luxembourg is now the last arrival on the jurisprudential scene. The Court of Justice of the European Union is becoming progressively more important with the increasing number of asylum cases relating to the interpretation of the Qualification Directive.[76]

If the UNHCR rightly claims that the Refugee Convention is a living instrument as such, then it is to be expected that, alongside juridical technicalities, the nature of asylum claims will continue to cause debate on a wide variety of issues such as gender, unaccompanied minors, medical matters, multiple asylum requests, cessation clauses and exclusion clauses. Some of these will be sent for preliminary rulings to the European Court of Justice and no doubt have a major impact on future Belgian asylum and protection law.

---

72 Arbitragehof nr. 14/97, 18 March 1997; Grondwettelijk Hof nr. 81/2008, 27 May 2008.

73 Arbitragehof nr. 20/93, 4 March 1993; Arbitragehof nr. 61/94, 14 July 1994, Arbitragehof nr. 43/98, 22 April 1998; Arbitragehof nr. 77/2002, 8 May 2002 <http://www.constcourt.be>.

74 ECHR, *Moustaquim v. België*, 18 February 1991; ECHR, *Conka v. België*, 5 February 2002; ECHR, *Mubilanzila Mayeka& Kaniki Mitunga v. België*, 12 October 2006; ECHR, *MSS v. Belgium & Greece*, ECHR 21 January 2011.

75 ECHR, *Conka v. België*, 5 February 2002; ECHR, *Riad en Idiab v. België*, 24 January 2008; ECHR, *Muskhadzhiyeva e.a. v. België*, 19 January 2010.

76 For instance: C-133/06 *European Parliament v Council*, 6 May 2008 (on respective powers of European Parliament and Council on the procedure of adoption of the common list of safe countries of origin); C-19/08 *Migrtionssverket v Petrosian*, 29 January 2009 (implementation of the Dublin Regulation); C-465/07 Elgafaji (Grand Chamber) (Article 15(c) Qualification Directive) (Grand Chamber) 17 February 2009; C-175/08 and 179/08 Abdullah (Grand Chamber) (cessation and Articles 11 and 7 of Qualification Directive), 2 March 2010; C-31/09 *Bolbol Nawras v Bevandorlasi es Allampolgarsagi Hivatal* (Grand Chamber) 17 June 2010 (Article 1D of Refugee Convention; Article 12 of Qualification Directive).

The North African Asylum Systems and the Geneva Convention[77]

Introduction

Asylum is rooted in the history of North Africa, where refugees have always escaped persecution and sought refuge. In fact, the asylum phenomenon in the region dates back thousands of years. Its first traces can be found in the time of the Pharaohs in Egypt when refugees were afforded religious asylum.[78] In modern times, North Africa has remained a preferred destination for asylum-seekers. North African people have, indeed, afforded generous asylum to persecuted persons regardless to their ethnic origin or their religion. Besides, the main features of asylum had been generality and openness, in so far as refugees secured asylum without restriction or exception. Furthermore, asylum was mainly a humanitarian act that gave full rights to refugees who usually ended up becoming part of the local societies.

In regard to present times, asylum has become a act of solidarity between North African people; asylum was offered during the struggle for independence against foreign occupation. The massive influx of Algerian refugees into Morocco and Tunisia during the Algerian War of Liberation (1954–62) was at the origin of the first operations carried out outside Europe by the United Nations High Commissioner for Refugees (UNHCR). After North African countries gained their independence, asylum definitely changed in the North African countries. Thus, the traditional asylum regime was abolished in favour of a modern regime composed of new national legislations through which North African countries were aiming to confirm their sovereignty towards foreigners in general. As a result, asylum became limited and subject to some restrictions that, unfortunately, hinder refugees in their search for safe refuge. Currently, refugees are likely to be unwelcome in the region since barriers have been raised to avoid flows of refugees and to dissuade asylum-seekers. The number of the refugee population in North Africa perfectly illustrates this situation. In fact, a country like Tunisia, for example, was hosting only 92 refugees as of January 2010.[79]

The situation of refugees in North Africa has worsened during the last few years, when migration flows have increased mainly as refugees pass through the region while attempting to reach Europe.[80] The fight against illegal migration has, indeed, sacrificed the refugees' rights which had guaranteed by the international

---

77 Amor Boubakri, Associate Professor in Public Law, Faculty of Law, University of Sfax, Tunisia; email: amor.boubakri@fdseps.rnu.tn.

78 Elmadmad, K. (2002), *Asile et réfugiés dans les pays afro-arabes* (Rabat: éd. Eliff), p. 170.

79 UNHCR (2010), *UNHCR Country operations profile: Tunisia*, available at <www.unhcr.org>.

80 Coluccello, S. and Massey, S. (2007), 'Out of Africa: The human trade between Libya and Lampedusa', *Trends in Organized Crime* 10.4 (December): 77–90.

law principles that bind North African countries. In this context, it is worth studying the North African asylum systems and assessing their compatibility with the Geneva Convention's principles. This study should include different legislations related to asylum that have been adopted by the four North African countries. In this respect, North Africa displays deficient asylum systems with a paradoxical legal framework.

A Paradoxical Legal Framework

The paradoxes of the legal framework of the North African asylum systems result from adherence to the international instruments which contrasts with the deficiency of the national legislations.

Adherence to the International Instruments

The 1951 Geneva Convention and the 1967 Protocol of New York All North African countries, except Libya, are bound by the 1951 Convention relating to the Status of Refugees. Egypt was the only North African country to participate in the UN Conference on the status of refugees held in Geneva which adopted this Convention on 28 July 1951. However, although it was a signing country, Egypt had hesitated for a long time before ratifying the Geneva Convention on 15 May 1984. The other North African countries were under French rule (Algeria, Morocco and Tunisia) or British occupation (Libya) when the Convention was adopted in 1951. Unlike Britain, France extended the Geneva Convention to the three North African countries that were under its authority at that time. Thus, the Convention has had legal force in Algeria, Morocco and Tunisia since it entered into force on 22 April 1954.

After gaining independence, Algeria, Morocco and Tunisia have formally expressed their intention to continue to be bound by the Geneva Convention without confirming the reservation made by the French government towards Article 17.[81] Thus, the three countries are logically bound by the Convention without any reservation, although they sometimes argue the opposite. As regard Egypt, reservations were made about articles 12(1), 20, 22, 23 and 24.[82]

As regarding the Protocol relating to the Status of Refugees, signed in New York on 31 January 1967 (the 1967 Protocol of New York), all North African countries, except Libya, are signatory states and have already ratified this text.

81 Flory, M. (1966) 'La succession aux Traités lors de la décolonisation de l'Afrique du Nord', *Annuaire de l'Afrique du Nord*, pp. 11–24. Cf. also Zemanek, K. (1965), 'State Succession after Decolonization', *Collected Courses of the Hague Academy of International Law* 116.3: 213–15.

82 See Amor Boubakri, A. (2007), 'L'adhésion de la Tunisie aux instruments internationaux relatifs aux réfugiés', *Etudes Internationales (Tunis)* 105 (December): 93–118; Elmadmad, *Asile et réfugiés dans les pays afro-arabes*, pp. 102–103.

Hence, the scope of the 1951 Geneva Convention provisions has been legally extended to these countries when they were originally confined to the European territories in relation to events which had occurred before the Second World War. This extension had been made, however for North African countries even before the adoption of the 1967 Protocol of New York as mentioned previously.

International humanitarian and human rights instruments The international humanitarian instruments already have a legal force since the French occupation in Algeria, Morocco and Tunisia.[83] After gaining independence, these three countries expressed their intention to continue to be bound by the 1949 Geneva Conventions. Egypt and Libya have acceded to these Conventions, respectively, on 11 November 1952 and 22 May 1956.

Concerning international human rights instruments, all North African countries have, indeed, ratified or acceded to the most important ones that provide a partial protection for refugees. Thus, the 1966 International Covenant on Civil and Political Rights, the 1966 International Covenant on Economic, Social and Cultural Rights, the 1984 Convention against Torture are, among other instruments, binding the five North African countries.

Regional instruments The North African countries have three main membership circles: the African Union (AU), except for Morocco which is not a member, the League of Arab States (LAS) and the Organisation of Islamic Cooperation (OIC). However, only the AU has a regional legal framework to deal with asylum issues, while Arab and Islamic countries have failed to reach a common instrument in this respect.

The main African instrument regarding refugee status is the Organisation of African Unity Convention, governing the specific aspects of refugee problems in Africa and signed in Addis Ababa on 10 September 1969 (the 1969 Addis Ababa Convention).[84] Aware of the narrowness of the definition of the term 'refugee' adopted in the 1951 Geneva Convention and its inadequacy in an African context, the African countries agreed in the 1969 Addis Ababa Convention about a wider definition which aimed to provide African people with a suitable regional legal framework for their struggle for liberalization from European colonization.[85]

83 Flory, 'La succession aux Traités lors de la décolonisation de l'Afrique du Nord', pp. 15–17.

84 Awuku, E.O., (1995), 'Refugee Movements in Africa and the OAU Convention on Refugees', *Journal of African Law* 39.1: 79–86; Okoth-Obbo, G. (2001), 'Thirty Years on: A Legal Review of the 1969 OAU Refugee Convention Governing the Specific Aspects of Refugee Problems in Africa', *Refugee Survey Quarterly* 20.1 (January): 79–138.

85 It should be mentioned, in this respect, that the definition of a refugee adopted in the 1951 Geneva Convention is now questionable in the light of the recent developments and challenges faced by the refugees' protection in the world as a result of the emergence of new forms of asylum not covered by this Convention. See Fombeno, H.J.T. (2004),

The 1969 Addis Ababa Convention has been ratified by Algeria, Egypt, Libya and Tunisia. These countries have also ratified the African Charter of Human and People's Rights adopted in Nairobi on 22 June 1981. However, none of the North African countries has signed the African Union Convention for Protection and Assistance of Internally Displaced Persons in Africa, adopted in Kampala on 23 October 2009.

Deficient National Legislation

A main feature of the North African countries' asylum systems consists in the absence of national legislations on asylum.

The lack of national legislation on asylum Special asylum legislation has a major importance for those with refugee status in so far as it determines the procedural aspects of asylum and refugees' rights and duties. The North African countries have chosen to keep a harmful silence in this respect and, by doing so, displaying a certain disrespect towards the international standards which protect refugees. Indeed, the adherence both to the 1951 Geneva Convention and the 1969 Addis Ababa Convention pre-supposes that national legislation should be enacted in order to insure the implementation of the rules resultant from those instruments and their effectiveness in the national legal system; otherwise, the international commitment to refugee protection becomes questionable and reveals a kind of hypocrisy.

Scholars have argued, indeed, that states bounded by the 1951 Geneva Convention do not have the liberty of refusing to issue a national legislation on asylum. Such legislation is necessary to allow refugees to benefit from the protection provided by this Convention.[86] The absence of such legislation should be considered, therefore, as an infraction of the principles of this Convention. The imperative international customary rule *pacta sunt servanda* requires, indeed, that states should observe with good will the rules resulting from an international Convention.[87]

It should be mentioned, however, that some internal legal texts with a limited importance for refugee status do exist in Algeria, Egypt and Morocco. The first is Moroccan Decree No. 2-57-1256, issued on 29 August 1957, which determined how to implement the Geneva Convention. This Decree was amended by the

'Réflexions sur la question des réfugiés en Afrique', *Revue Trimestrielle des Droits de l'Homme* 57 (January): 245–74.

86 Elmadmad, *Asile et réfugiés dans les pays afro-arabes*, pp. 157–9.

87 The rule of *pacta sunt servanda* is, expressly, provided in the Vienna Convention on the Law of Treaties adopted on 23 May 1969 (art. 26). Still, this rule remains, fundamentally, a *jus congens* customary rule. See Lukashuk, I.I. (1989), 'The Principle Pacta Sunt Servanda and the nature of obligation under international law', *American Journal of International Law* 83.3 (July): 513–18.

Decree of 8 October 1970 and Decree No. 2-84-836, issued on 28 December 1984.[88] Algeria has a similar text, which is Decree No. 63-274, issued on 25 July 1963, with the same subject as the Moroccan Decree.[89] Egypt issued the Decree of 15 May 1984, creating the Permanent Commission of Refugees' Affairs.

Still, the importance of these texts remains limited, in so far as they emanate from the executive branch of government and have no legislative nature. Therefore, refugees are not secured sufficient protection because executive texts, in general, offer only a low legal security for stakeholders. However, one can say that the texts, though with limited importance, are more than a complete absence of legal texts that would implement the international refugee rules in the national legal system.

Asylum in the general legislation The norms of asylum legislation system in the North African countries are spread out through different categories of legal texts. The first ones to be mentioned in this respect are Constitutions, which provide protection against extradition. Indeed, all North African constitutional texts are unanimous in forbidding extradition of political refugees. Such protection is clearly stated in the 1998 Algerian (art. 69), the 1971 Egyptian (art. 53), and the 1959 Tunisian (art. 17) Constitutions. Unlike the other North African countries, Libya does not have a written constitution. However, some texts have a constitutional value in this country, among them the 1969 Revolutionary Declaration which provided the same protection for political refugees (art. 11).[90]

Besides, the North African asylum norms exist in the laws that determine foreigners' status. Some aspects of asylum regime are, thus, lined up with this status, which address mainly social and economic rights. Other aspects of asylum regime have even been included in the new legislations intended to fight against illegal migration. Thus, there is intentional confusion in the distinctions between asylum-seekers and illegal migrants in, inter alia, the Libyan Law No. 2 (2004) governing the entry, sojourn and departure of foreigners, and the Tunisian Law No. 68-7 about foreigners' status as amended by the Law No. 2004.[91]

Unfavourable Asylum Systems

The analysis of the different elements of the asylum legal framework leads us to conclude that North African countries do not offer favourable asylum systems

88 Bulletin officiel, 6 September 1957, p. 1161; 28 April 1971, p. 469; 2 January 1985, p. 47. Cf. also Elmadmad, *Asile et réfugiés dans les pays afro-arabes*, pp. 175–9.

89 *Journal Officiel de la République Algérienne*, No. 52, 30 July 1963, p. 763. Cf. Elmadmad, ibid., pp. 165–8.

90 All these texts are available in the UNDP's legal database for the Arab countries <www.undp.org>.

91 See Boubakri, A. (2005), 'Protection of Refugees and Asylum Seekers in the Migration Flows', *International Studies (Tunis)*, 94 (March): 81–9 (in Arabic).

because refugee status determination (RSD) procedures are inadequate. Besides, refugees and asylum-seekers do not have sufficient guarantees.

Inadequate RSD procedures The RSD procedures are at the core of the asylum system, in general, and have a vital importance for asylum-seekers since it is an unavoidable way to have access to the needed protection. This is why RSD procedures are usually considered as a key indicator for showing how serious is the state's commitment to protect refugees. Consequently, the more adequate the RSD, the more serious this commitment will be, and vice versa.

Unfortunately, the North African RSD procedures do not display a genuine willingness to provide refugees with the protection in accordance with the international standards. The RSD procedures' deficiencies reveal that refugees are, somehow, unwelcome and even undesirable in the North African countries, since they do not have set up RSD procedures which are an evident consequence of their adherence to the 1951 Geneva Convention.

The North African countries can be divided into groups with regard to their RSD procedures. The first group includes countries where RSD procedures are totally non-existent, that is, Libya and Tunisia. In these two countries, asylum-seekers have no possibility to present an asylum claim to the authorities. However, the Tunisian government has allowed the UNHCR to carry out RSD procedures and examine, therefore, asylum claims according to the Agreement of 16 January 1992. The UNHCR uses its own standards to determine the applicant's refugee status, which figures in the guidelines elaborated for this purpose.[92] People recognized as refugees by the UNHCR delegation obtain, therefore, a document from the Tunisian authorities legalizing their stay in the country. Asylum-seekers who not attain refugee status can only make an internal appeal before the UNHCR delegation.

As far as Libya is concerned, the situation is worse since the UNHCR is not formally allowed to carry out RSD procedures. However, the UNHCR has had a presence in the country since 1999, and this country registers refugees and asylum-seekers and provides them with material assistance, despite the absence of a memorandum of understanding with the Libyan government. Still, the UNHCR's situation was not comfortable at all since it depended on the political situation of the Libyan government, especially in the last few years. On 8 June 2010, unrest in Libya led to the Libyan government to order the UNHCR's officials to end their activities and close their offices in Tripoli. As of May 2013, the offices were still closed.

The second group is composed of countries that have their own RSD procedures. Indeed, Algeria, Egypt and Morocco have each set up a national committee to assess asylum claims. These committees belong to the Ministries

92 UN High Commissioner for Refugees (January 1992), *Handbook on Procedures and Criteria for Determining Refugee Status under the 1951 Convention and the 1967 Protocol relating to the Status of Refugees* (Geneva: UNHCR).

of Foreign Affairs and they are composed of representatives of the Interior and Justice Ministries; the UNHCR is represented as well.

The decisions made by these ad hoc committees are definitive and cannot be reviewed. Thus, refugees are deprived of the right to a fair trial, as required by the international instruments binding the North African countries. Even if appeal was possible in theory, refugees are not provided with sufficient legal aid to present their appeal.

Lack of Guarantees

The most important guarantee that refugees need is definitely protection against expulsion and extradition. In the international asylum system, non-*refoulement* is considered a part of international customary standards and has the value of a *jus cogens* rule. Every country has, therefore, the duty to respect the non-*refoulement* principle, whether it is bound by the 1951 Geneva Convention or not. Hence, the North African countries, as members of the international community, have to ensure respect for this fundamental rule of international refugee law.

Furthermore, non-*refoulement* has a large scope in international refugee law, since it covers situations such as non-admission, expulsion and extradition. Thus, states should not, under any case, send an asylum-seeker or refugee to the country or territories in which they fear persecution.[93]

The question which is worth being asked is: how far the North African countries have been respectful of these provisions?

In fact, the answer can be summarized as follows: like asylum systems, like refugees' guarantees. The North African states have not proved, in reality, to have any scruples regarding the non-*refoulement* principle and other fundamental standards which aim to protect refugees and asylum-seekers mainly against arbitrary and harmful measures such as non-admission, expulsion and extradition.

Sub-Saharan refugees and asylum-seekers have become, during recent years, the main victims of illegal and unfair measures taken by the North African authorities. Cooperation with European states to fight against illegal migration has worsened the situation in so far as North African countries have received a green light to use all means of deterrence in this respect. Mainly Eritrean and Somali refugees are among the most injured refugee populations in the region. Asylum-seekers report that they have been forcibly returned to their countries where they faced torture and other ill treatments.[94]

---

93 See Durieux, J.F. and McAdam, J. (2004), 'Non-*refoulement* through time: The case for a derogation clause to the refugee convention in mass influx emergencies', *International Journal of Refugee Law* 16.1: 4–24.

94 Amnesty International (June 2010), '"Libya of tomorrow" What hope for human rights?' (London: AI), pp. 96–7; Human Rights Watch (September 2006), 'Stemming the flow: Abuses against migrants, asylum seekers and refugees' (New York: HRW); HRW

In Lieu of a Conclusion

North African countries' asylum systems are far from fulfilling the requirements of protection for refugees and asylum-seekers. Thus, the countries of the region need to make much more effort in order to follow the international trend in field of legal protection for refugees. The implementation of the 1951 Geneva Convention in the national legal systems is definitely a key measure to achieve this goal; otherwise, asylum will remain an unattainable right for refugees in North African countries. The values of hospitality and shelter, which are deeply rooted in the region, require a courageous attitude to reconcile reality with tradition.

The South African Refugee Status Determination System, by Ahmed Arbee[95]

Acknowledgement

I am indeed humbled and profoundly honoured to respond to Geoffrey Care's invitation to include a chapter on the South African refugee status determination (RSD) system in his book.

Soon after I was appointed as the first full-time chairperson of the South African Refugee Appeal Board in April 1998, I was invited to address a Judicial Symposium in Delhi, India, in October 1998. During this symposium, I had the pleasant opportunity to meet Geoffrey Care, then president of the IARLJ, as well as Erika Feller, from the UNHCR.

The support given to me by Geoffrey Care and Erika Feller provided me with a window of opportunity to interact with the IARLJ/UNHCR fraternity, and study RSD systems in Canada, the United Kingdom and New Zealand, including participation in the 'Train the Trainers' seminars facilitated by the UNHCR.

I will indeed always remain indebted to Geoffrey Care by virtue of our long association in the IARLJ. In fact, Africa will always remain deeply indebted to Geoffrey for his unstinting commitment towards the development of refugee law in Africa.

Background

The development and importance given to South African refugee law is intricately intertwined with the political history of the country. The progressive nature of the current legislation is indicative of the theoretical utopia envisioned in the 'New

(November 2008), 'Sinai perils: Risks to migrants, refugees and asylum seekers in Egypt and Israel' (New York: HRW).

95 Ahmed Arbee, former Chairperson of the South African Refugee Appeal Board, Associate Executive Member and Head of the Africa Chapter of the International Association of Refugee Law Judges (IARLJ).

South Africa', a model aimed at redressing racial, social, political and cultural injustices manufactured in an era that bred an accepted culture which categorically ignored fundamental human rights, including the right to equality, dignity and the rule of law.

In tracing the development of the South African refugee legislation, an overview of past legislation will be considered in relation to the political climate of the time. The motivating factors leading to the development of the Refugees Act will outline some of the distinctive characteristics implicit in the current legislation which represent arguably the most progressive piece of refugee protection in the world.

Precursory Legislation Leading to the Refugees Act

Before the implementation of the South African Refugees Act, the Aliens Control Act (Act 96 of 1991) was the guiding legislation, which effectively regulated all categories of people who entered or even attempted to enter the country. The Aliens Control Act defined an 'alien' as an individual who is not a South African citizen; hence, a refugee would be deemed to be a foreign national under the Aliens Control Act. There are two categories of foreign nationals, namely 'legal foreign nationals' and 'illegal foreign nationals'. A legal foreign national includes individuals who have obtained permanent residence or visiting status by legal means. An illegal foreign national would include those individuals who have entered the country in the absence of proper documentation, or are admitted to the country on a temporary basis and, by continuing to reside thereafter, are deemed illegal. In fact, there was no reference to convention refugees under the Act. The legislation did not specifically address the rights of asylum-,seekers and refugees but instead included them under a broad classification of prohibited persons. By simply categorizing such individuals in this fashion there was a marked absence of legislative provisions addressing the special status entitled to those people compelled to flee their country of origin seeking surrogate protection elsewhere, based on the occurrence or risk of serious human rights violations and the absence of state protection. As a result, the public could not distinguish between illegal/ foreign nationals and asylum-seekers. The depiction of asylum-seekers as reflected in the Aliens Control Act has resulted in xenophobic attitudes, a legacy hampering legitimate claimants to this day.

Emergence of the South African Refugees Act

Following fair and democratic elections resulting in the ousting of the apartheid regime by the African National Congress (ANC) in 1994, significant legislative initiatives were undertaken in order to attempt to redress injustices lingering from the previous government. The limited scope of human rights and archaic provisions inherent in the Aliens Control Act, in conjunction with the rapidly increasing volume of asylum-seekers pouring into the 'New South Africa', provided the platform for the initiation of specialized refugee legislation. The Aliens Control Act was abolished and replaced by the Immigration Act.

The Refugees Act was introduced in the context of South Africa's transition into a leading democratic State in the African continent. The South African Refugees Act No. 130 of 1998 was enacted in 1998 and promulgated on 1 April 2000. The Act was signed by then President Nelson Mandela, culminating in South Africa's transition from a refugee-producing country to a refugee-receiving country. Not only was the legislation significant from a human rights perspective, but it was also monumental from a political point of view, as the legislation was introduced by former refugees who now graced the corridors of Parliament. Effectively, the legislation represents an initiative by the sons and daughters raised on African soil, seeking to enshrine a human rights perspective to protect individuals and groups from persecution and other human rights violations.

The Act outlines the rights, principles and standards relating to refugee status. The Act makes provision for asylum-seekers to report to one of the five Refugee Reception Centres in various provinces who are dealt with in the first instance by Refugee Status Determination Offices (RSDOs) after eligibility forms are completed and facilitated by Refugee Reception Officers (RROs) from the Department of Home Affairs (DHA).

It also specifies the authority of the Refugee Appeal Board (RAB), which is an independent Statutory Board with quasi-judicial functions and is the body created to deal with refugee appeal matters. The RAB conducts non-adversarial hearings entitling appellants to legal representation. The state does not provide legal aid, although Lawyers for Human Rights and other non-governmental organizations (NGOs) legal clinics attached to the universities do provide legal representation.

The Act is remarkably progressive. In addition to including the definition of a refugee as outlined in the Geneva Convention, it also implements an extended definition of a refugee as reflected in the Organisation of African Unity's 1969 OAU Convention Governing the Specific Aspects of Refugee Problems in Africa. This effectively expands the scope of admission on the grounds justifying refugee status to include serious violations of human rights, victims of civil war, generalised conflict and the breakdown of public order.

A 'refugee' means any person granted asylum in terms of the Act and an 'asylum-seeker' means a person seeking recognition as a refugee in the Republic. Unlike the Aliens Control Act, the Refugees Act clearly stipulates the rights of refugees. Specifically, a refugee is entitled to: formal written recognition of refugee status; legal and constitutional protection (Chapter 2) including the right to remain in the Republic; identity documents and a South African travel document; the right to apply for an immigration permit after five years of continuous residence under particular conditions; the right to seek employment, and to the same basic health services and basic primary education which inhabitants of the Republic receive from time to time. The rights accorded under the provisions of the Refugees Act demonstrate the legislature's commitment to distinguishing refugees from the stigma-charged depiction of an 'alien' and instead endorses clear rights designed to ensure that their basic human rights are met.

The Refugees Act endorses its commitment to a human rights perspective by interpreting and applying its provisions with due regard to the following instruments:

1. The 1951 Convention Relating to the Status of Refugees
2. The 1967 Protocol relating to the Status of Refugees
3. The OAU Convention Governing the Specific Aspects of Refugee Problems in Africa (OAU 1969)
4. Universal Declaration of Human Rights (1948)
5. Any other relevant convention or international agreement to which the Republic becomes a member.

Global and Regional Events Impacting on South Africa

As we project our vision into the future, we must acknowledge that the political landscape of the African continent will continue to beam conflicting signals of hope and despair. The ongoing conflicts in the Central African Region and the sudden upsurge in the Arab world clamouring for democracy and human rights, has changed the political landscape, ousting despotic leaders who ruled with an iron fist for almost three to four decades. The prevailing conditions in Côte d'Ivoire (Ivory Coast), where the incumbent president simply refused to acknowledge the will of the people by clinging to his position, has resulted in disarray and mayhem, with thousands fleeing the violence and hundreds killed in the process. The large-scale movement of people in a global and regional context has become a defining characteristic in the contemporary world. Factors such as the global economic meltdown, the events of 9/11 in the United States and the ensuing security threat and terrorist attacks have forced the so-called 'developed' states to tighten legislation, deflecting the movement of asylum-seekers through interdictions, detentions and other blatantly restrictive practices.

The net result of this 'fortress mentality' is that South Africa in particular, with its porous borders, has attracted a flood of all categories of immigrants, asylum-seekers and other irregular movers who are allowed to apply for asylum. This massive influx has congested the administrative procedures already in place, resulting in huge backlogs which have enabled the predominantly economic migrants and manifestly abusive claimants residing for many years in the country, taking advantage of the time taken by the DHA in processing and finalizing asylum applications. The delay in finalizing applications also impacts on those asylum-seekers in need of genuine protection who linger frustratingly under the same conditions. It may be mentioned that many asylum-seekers in the DHA system for over ten years still await the outcome of their applications.

The DHA is presently amending legislation to introduce a fast-track system that would be structured to finalize the manifestly unfounded claims in terms of accelerated procedures in order to deal decisively with those requiring genuine surrogate protection.

Although the DHA has increased the number of frontline decision makers (RSDOs) to cope with the huge inventory of applications, the institutional guidelines given to each RSDO to complete approximately ten cases per day has clearly compromised the quality of first-instance decisions. The lack of a professionally structured research and documentation support service on updated country information also compromises the qualitative decision-making ability of the RSDOs.

Whereas the DHA increased the numbers of RSDOs, the Refugee Appeal Board comprises only five members to deal with the pending inventory of appeals nationally. It took the DHA five years to fill the vacancy of the chairperson's position. With the package of amendments contemplated in the Refugees Act, the DHA hopes to increase the membership of the RAB and to possibly decentralize the hearings to the five RROs to comply with the service-delivery targets of the DHA. Currently, only three members have been deployed to the three reception offices to deal with the volume of appeals, with the chairperson based in Pretoria. Against the backdrop of scarce government resources in addressing the legitimate aspirations of the previously disadvantaged communities from the apartheid era in terms of the provision of adequate health, housing education and social welfare grants for its citizens, the government of South Africa remains committed to addressing the challenges confronting genuine asylum-seekers. However, asylum-seekers countrywide are generally dissatisfied with the government's service-delivery standards and other assistance, as they often experience insurmountable barriers seeking medical assistance or enrolling their children in school.

The influx of all types of immigrants clearly fuels xenophobic attitudes and outbursts. These erupt periodically against foreigners, such as the Somalian traders who operate their businesses in informal townships and are being targeted by protesters and criminal elements who seek to take advantage of the public disorder by ransacking their stores and or killing such foreigners. The government of South Africa and the UNHCR have worked together to counter this disturbing tendency. From the perspective of an asylum-seeker, the road to recognition of refugee status in South Africa appears to be very long and unpredictable.

Fortunately, for asylum claimants and other categories of Immigrants, the South African judicial system is independent and provides protection to those who challenge the DHA or the RAB on any arbitrary or restrictive administrative practices and decisions.

The challenges of seeking humane or surrogate protection in a self-interested world has indeed become a sensitive topic both locally and internationally. The collision of interest between persons seeking genuine protection and those countries who wish to regulate the scope of entry will remain an ongoing crusade in the foreseeable future.

It would be the arduous task of an independent judiciary to balance this very sensitive equation within the spirit of what Jawaharlal Nehru once said: 'The rule of law must strengthen the rule of life.'

The Asylum Procedure in Sweden: From the Cabinet to the Courts of Law[96]

The Aliens Appeals Board, which until 2006 considered appeals against decisions by the Migration Board and was the appeal of last instance, was abolished in that year and a new system for appeal in immigration cases was introduced in Sweden.[97] If an application for asylum or a residence permit is rejected by the first instance – that is, the Swedish Migration Board – the decision can be appealed to a Migration Court at one of three administrative courts, depending on in which region the decision has been taken. The decision by the Migration Court can be appealed to the Migration Court of Appeal at the Administrative Court of Appeal in Stockholm. The decision by the Migration Court will only be reconsidered if the Migration Court of Appeal grants leave to appeal. In the Migration Court, the case is decided by a judge alone or with three lay judges. In the Migration Court of Appeal, three judges take the decision. The rulings by the Migration Court of Appeal, which is the last instance, are binding as precedents. The introduction of the new system might be said to mark the end of a long and tortuous road towards a system for handling immigration cases which could be met with consensus in most parts of Swedish society.

Having been preceded by consecutive laws since 1914, on the rights of aliens to reside in Sweden, a more modern and all-encompassing law on aliens, taking into account the 1951 Geneva Convention on Refugees, was introduced in 1954. This law was replaced by a new law in 1980. The present Aliens Act was enacted in 2005.[98]The Act regulates all kinds of immigration, by asylum-seekers, relatives seeking residence permits because of affiliation and also persons applying for a work permit. These cases are all handled by the Migration Board and the Migration Courts.

In 1968, the Swedish Parliament decided on guidelines for immigration into the Swedish labour market. It was decided that Sweden, in principle, was in no need of labour immigration: Only if it was not possible to find a person in Sweden with the required skills could an alien with this skill be granted a residence permit. This principle was radically altered in 2008, so that thenceforth a person who shows that he or she is in possession of a serious job offer in Sweden may now obtain a residence permit.[99] Integration into the Swedish labour market may also

---

96 Göran Hakansson, Director General of the Swedish Aliens Appeals Board, later Ambassador of Sweden to Latvia.

97 Prop. 2004/05: 170, 2004/05: SfU17, SFS 2005: 716.

98 SFS 2005: 716.

99 Prop. 2007/08: 147, 2008/09: SfU31.

be a ground for granting a person a residence permit if his or her application for asylum or right to stay in Sweden on protection grounds has been rejected.

As first instance in immigration matters, a central governmental agency was created in 1969 called the Swedish Immigration Board, later renamed the Swedish Migration Board. Following Swedish legal tradition for appeals against a decision by a central agency, the decisions by the Board could be appealed to the responsible ministry. However, due to the Swedish Constitution, the appeal could not be decided upon by the minister alone, but by the whole Cabinet (all decisions at ministerial level must in principle be taken collectively by the Cabinet).

However, the decision making in asylum and immigration cases became more and more burdensome for the Cabinet, not least because of the refugee movements caused by the collapse of Yugoslavia. The agenda for the weekly Cabinet meetings grew to be more and more occupied with appeal cases from the Immigration Board.

Swedish public opinion – perhaps to a larger extent than at present – has traditionally shared and upheld the self-image of Sweden as a power for humanity and solidarity with those who are less fortunate, both nationally and internationally. Negative decisions by the Cabinet applying the law in appeal cases, therefore, caused more and more uproar among the general public, mass media and politicians, and it became increasingly difficult for the minister responsible for immigration to handle the issues, not least from a political viewpoint.

In 1992, the Aliens Appeals Board created a purely judicial framework for asylum and immigration appeals and the Board should, except for some procedural matters, function as a court of law; the only basis for its work being the law. Although, being a court of last instance, the Board could hand over to the Cabinet cases concerning mass immigration or cases where the law did not give an answer.

The decision makers at the Board were almost all judges, seconded from their courts. In around 70 per cent of the cases, judges reached a decision on their own after hearing the case, presented by a case officer. In more complicated cases, the decision was taken by a judge and two lay persons, representing the political parties in Parliament.

The decisions were made on the documentary material in the case. In 5–10 per cent of the cases, the file with the hearing of the claimant at the Migration Board was complemented by an oral hearing at the Board, especially when questions of credibility were involved. In practically all appeal cases, the claimant was assisted by a legal counsel, paid for by the state.

Until 1995, the Board was not much debated. However, from 1995 on, due to the tragic suicide of an appellant in an appeal case, the Board attracted growing criticism, as public opinion became aware of the frequent tragic circumstances in asylum cases and could not accept that, according to the law, these circumstances were not grounds for asylum or protection in Sweden.

A special problem was created by the wording in the law, which allowed the possibility of granting a residence permit on humanitarian grounds. When the law on aliens was decided in Parliament, it was underlined in the *travaux préparatoires* that this possibility should in principle only be used in cases where a deportation would carry with it a high risk for the claimant's life. The heavy criticism of the Board by Members of Parliament, when an appeal was rejected, seemed to show that the honourable Members were not aware of the content of the law. They also did not seem to be aware of the constitutional[100] independence of the tribunal, as was demonstrated when the leaders of the parties in Parliament (with the exception of one party) wrote to the head of the Board, ordering him to decide in an individual case in a certain way, referring to the fact that there was a majority in Parliament for a positive decision in the case. That the Board in around 30–40 per cent of appealed cases changed the decisions by the Migration Board did not seem to be enough in the opinion of the public.

The possibility of applying anew directly to the Board after its final decision for an asylum or residence permit, claiming fresh circumstances, had the effect the Board using its resources as much for already decided cases as for new appeals. Thus, through this practically unlimited possibility to apply anew, many cases were never really completed and the consequent human suffering often worsened, with consecutive suicide attempts or children becoming apathetic, until the high threshold for human suffering as a condition for a residence permit on humanitarian grounds had been reached.

As a result, since 2004 the Migration Board has handled a reformed and more restricted version of new applications.

The Appeals Board had also to fight with inadequate resources (except during its later years when the Board was allocated sufficient resources to present an almost clean sheet to the succeeding courts), which created backlogs, which in their turn created more suffering and frustration amongst the claimants.

However, even as the Board tried to work as much as possible as a court of law, it had in some aspects to follow rules adapted for a purely administrative procedure, which influenced the legitimacy of the decisions and the will to accept those decisions.

The procedure was inquisitorial and not adversarial; the Migration Board was only present in the proceedings at the Appeals Board by its decision. Even if the Appeals Board had to weigh the pros and cons for a change of the decision by

100 There seems to be a difference between the British and the Swedish administration. In Sweden, even if an individual case is handled by administrative authorities, these authorities have, according to the constitution, the same independence as a court of law in relation to the minister and the ministries (as well as Parliament). The ministry or the cabinet cannot intervene in any way in an administrative authority's handling of an individual case. The difference between the administration and the courts of law is the way cases are handled and the standing of the judges in the courts of law. At an administrative authority, there is no adversial procedure and usually no oral hearings, which influences the transparency and credibility in general of the administrative procedure. The judges of course are in the constitution assured a strong independent status and in a way a lifelong tenure which differentiates them from civil servants in general.

the Migration Board objectively, the proceeding could give the impression to the claimant that it was he or she against the Appeals Board.

Oral hearings were only supposed to take place in exceptional circumstances and therefore most cases were decided on the documents in the case. This did not create any possibility for a real dialogue between the Board and the claimant – even if the Board tried to solve this dilemma by letting the claimant meet the presenting officer (as it did in many cases) before the case was presented before the judge. Even if the absence of an oral hearing did not influence the quality of the decision, it did not strengthen the confidence of the claimant in the decision nor their impression that the decision was based on all relevant facts. Sometimes, the claimants were of the view that the Board did not read the submitted papers.

Added to this impression was the fact that the Board, in times of overwhelming numbers of asylum-seekers coming to Sweden and appealing, was forced to write rather standardized decisions, making summaries of what the claimant had referred to and giving rather short reasons for the actual decision, in order to prevent the build-up of a tremendous backlog. Even if this did not mean that the Board had not thoroughly analysed the case, it could also influence confidence in the decisions.

In contrast with what the courts now can do, the Board provided itself with direct information about the situation in countries from where the asylum-seekers came, through investigative visits to these countries, reports of which it published. The Board had access to one source which created problems in relation to the claimant. This source was the reports by the Swedish embassies on the human rights situation in their respective countries. These reports were only used as general background material in the working by the Board, but were classified (at that time, they have now become public) by the Ministry of Foreign Affairs and the claimant was not allowed access to them. If some special information pertaining to an appealed case had been gathered through an embassy, this of course had to be divulged to the claimant. That the Board had access to general information of which the claimant did not have the possibility to know the content, was disturbing even for the Board, even if the information was not used in any decisive way in the individual cases.

As the decisions by the Board and its way of handling the issues – and even the personnel – were looked upon as the main problem in Swedish immigration policy, a governmental committee in 1999 proposed the abolition of the Board. The committee proposed that the appeal cases instead should be handled by the Administrative Court of Appeal in Stockholm. From then on, the Board was more or less doomed. In spite of this, the Board succeeded in its remaining years – thanks to a loyal and engaged personnel – to raise the quality of its decision making and even to shorten the procedural time from appeal to decision.

When the proposal by the Committee was sent out for consultation, it was met with resistance from some heavy legal bodies, among them the courts. A period of political wrangling started where the Ministry presented (inter alia) a solution which consisted of transforming the Board into a regular court of law with the task of handling appeal cases.

Due to the negative attitude in Parliament regarding the Board, this solution was never presented before Parliament. In the meantime, Parliament instead decided on its own in a decision of principle, that the appeal cases should be handled by the administrative courts.

In 2002, the government submitted a draft bill, proposing the abolition of the Board and a somewhat revised version of the present regulations concerning aliens to the Council on Legislation (this is an independent judicial body, consisting of Supreme Court judges, which according to the Constitution must examine governmental bills before they are presented for Parliament). The Council however advised the government not to present the bill to Parliament as it found that the current problems in the immigration field were connected more with the substantive regulations in the law than with the workings of the Board. In any case, the Council found that the substantive law on aliens was not in its current substance of a nature which made it feasible for a court of law to implement it.

A further rewriting of the law took place and the government finally presented a new bill, which led to the introduction of the present system in 2006 and 60 new judges were appointed to the administrative courts.[101] It might be added that the new system was preceded in 2005 by a provisional law regarding the 30,000 persons staying in Sweden illegally after having received a final decision of rejection of their application to stay. This provisional law made it possible for them to obtain a new examination of their case by the Migration Board.

A Governmental Committee[102] has evaluated the reform and found that mainly the goals of the reform have been achieved. Still – according to the law regulating the procedure in the administrative courts – the procedure before the courts is in principle based on the documents. However, oral hearings took place in 19 per cent of the cases in general and in 35 per cent of the asylum cases in 2008. The transparency of the process has thus increased, as has also the confidence of the claimant in the procedure.

The adversarial procedure has also increased the transparency and also made more evident the standpoints of the claimant and the Migration Board, also in relation to each other. The Migration Board and also the claimant and their counsel are now required to be clearer in their arguments than before. The quality of the decisions may therefore be assumed to have improved.

Even if 90 per cent of all decisions by the Migration Board leading to deportation or rejection are appealed, only 10 per cent of the decisions by the Board are changed by the court. The low rate of changes made by the court is said to show that the main point of substance of a case lies in the proceedings before the Migration Board, it being one of the aims of the reform to strengthen this principle.

In general, all relevant facts in a case are presented and tried and taken into account in the decision by the Migration Board. However, the Board could,

101 Prop. 2004/05:170, 2004/05: SfU17, SFS 2005:715.

102 SOU 2009:56.

according to the Committee, make the disputes in a case clearer and also more thoroughly present the country information which has been of importance for the decision. It may also happen that the Board has another standpoint or presents new facts when the case comes to the court, this being most frequent when the Board in its decision has not evaluated the credibility of the applicant but rejected the application on the ground that their arguments are not sufficient for asylum or residence permit. This creates the risk of the main point of the evaluation of the case being moved to the court and thus that a complete evaluation of the case in all aspects is first argued and deliberated at the court.

Leave to appeal may be granted if the case may create a precedent, meaning that a case can provide future guidance for future decisions. Leave to appeal may also be granted if there exist some extraordinary reasons for considering an appeal.[103] The decisions of the Migration Court of Appeal have mainly concerned the legal interpretation of the requisites of the law and not the importance in a case of such factors as, for example, from which country a person is fleeing or his or her belonging to a certain group. The lack of precedents in these areas has, according to the Committee, led to differing decisions by the three migration courts.[104]

The humanitarian aspect in granting a residence permit still creates problems. In the Act of 2005, a new formulation was introduced which aimed to better cover the cases the legislator was aiming for and also to make it more evident that this condition was meant to be applicable only in exceptional cases. The impression of the Committee was, however, that on the one hand, humanitarian grounds were applied more widely than was intended, but on the other hand, in certain concerned quarters, it was said that the application had become more strictly applied than before. Generally, the Committee, having evaluated the situation, recommended that the wording of the law should be made more precise in order to create greater consistency in similar cases between the courts.

The public interest in immigration matters seems to have waned with the introduction of the new system. The politicians, the mass media, the opinion makers have moved on to other areas suitable for public outcry. However, in the parliamentary elections of 2010, the Swedish Democrats, a small anti-immigration party, got a pivotal role in the voting of Parliament as neither the reigning alliance of the parties in government nor the other parties creating the opposition constitute a majority. In order to quell the influence of the Swedish Democrats on immigration policy, the parties in Government and the opposition Green Party in March 2011 made an agreement on future migration policy.

Among other things, it has been agreed to create a fourth migration court in order to speed up the time it takes from appeal to decision. It has also been agreed

103 This is a safety clause, which is very seldom used. What is lacking is the ground used by other courts of last instance, that there is reason for changing the decision. It has, however, been said that this ground is not suitable in migration cases.

104 A proposal to widen the scope for granting leave to appeal in order to get a wider field of precedents has so far been dismissed (SOU 2010: 44).

to investigate how decisions are formulated and how they are understood by the parties concerned.[105] The investigation must lead to conclusions about how to develop the formulation of decisions and give the courts a basis for their work on these issues. If the ongoing investigation on the application on humanitarian grounds shows that some categories have not been granted residence permits, in spite of the intention of the legislator, the parties to the agreement will find a sustainable solution in order for these categories to be covered by the regulation.[106] As the question of identity has shown to be an obstacle[107] in the granting of a residence permit on family reunification grounds, a solution shall be found to the present claim for passport and proven identity.[108]

In the agreement the parties state their adherence to the principle of a humane asylum policy and also to the principle that a person who wants to come to Sweden to work shall have that possibility. Against a background of regulated migration, the free cross-border movement of people shall be facilitated. In this context, some figures can be mentioned.

During the period 1980–2010, 1.3 million asylum and residence permits were granted.[109] In 2010–2011, Sweden was ranked first in Europe in terms of receiving unaccompanied children as asylum-seekers, the number being 5,050. Of these, 82 per cent were granted asylum. In 2011, 93,134 persons were granted asylum or residence permits. The number of people seeking asylum was around 30,000, slightly less than in 2010. During the first half of 2012, 16,335 asylum-seekers arrived in Sweden, 30 per cent more than during the same period in 2011.

105 Dir. 2012: 17.

106 The investigation is now completed (Ds 2011: 14) and shows that no category has been excluded from residence permits.

107 By a decision by the Migration Court of Appeal, cf. UM 9536-10, UM 3325-10.

108 The Migration Court of Appeal has in a later decision, MIG 2012: 1, opened up for reunification of families with children in certain cases (for example, Somalia), where it is not possible to obtain satisfactory identification documents. In those cases, a DNA-analysis is necessary and the identity should in any case be deemed likely.

109 Including work permits, *c.* 11,000, and citizens from EES countries, *c.* 192,000.

Chapter 7
How Other Countries Do It – Canada The Evolution and Development of the Refugee Status Determination System in Canada and the Balanced Refugee Reform Act

With James C. Simeon[1]

Introduction

The historic record clearly demonstrates that Canada's refugee and immigration policies were far from unblemished, let alone ideal or just.[2] In the nineteenth and early part of the twentieth centuries, they were, in fact, blatantly racist. Indeed, this was duly acknowledged by the Canadian government when it made a formal apology to the Canadian Chinese community, on 22 June 2006, for the use of the

1 James C. Simeon, PhD, Associate Professor, Director, School of Public Policy and Administration, Faculty of Liberal Arts and Professional Studies, York University, Toronto, Canada; email: jcsimeon@yorku.ca.

2 Knowles, V. (2000), *Forging Our Legacy: Canadian Citizenship and Immigration, 1900–1977* (Ottawa: Public Works and Government Services). Valerie Knowles points out that under Clifford Sifton's stewardship the Immigration Branch of the Ministry of Interior did not welcome black settlers. She notes that even though 'no law was passed to exclude them, although administrators devised careful procedures to ensure that most applications submitted by black people were rejected' (p. 10). When Frank Oliver succeeded Sifton as the Minister of the Interior, he introduced legislation that was blatantly racist, that is, the 1906 Immigration Act and the 1910 Immigration Act. Knowles notes that these Acts 'barred a broad spectrum of individuals and increased the government's power to deport certain classes of immigrants' (p. 32). Following the passage of the 1910 Immigration Act, a $500 head tax was imposed on Asiatic immigrants (p. 34). The *Komagata Maru* incident was another disparaging mark on Canadian history when, in May 1914, some 376 East Indians on the ship *Komagata Maru* were refused entry into Canada (p. 38). It was not until 1962 that Canada eliminated its racist immigration policy. Valerie Knowles states, 'The reform was introduced to the public on 19 January 1962 when Ellen Fairclough [Minister of Citizenship and Immigration at the time] tabled new regulations in the House that virtually eliminated racial discrimination as a major feature of Canada's immigration policy' (p. 81).

head tax and the exclusion of Chinese immigrants to Canada.[3] On 20 January 2011, the Canadian government participated in a ceremony unveiling a permanent memorial, *The Wheel of Conscience*, that remembers the *MS St. Louis* and its 900 Jewish passengers who were escaping Nazi Germany in 1939 and who were not given refuge in Canada when it was sought.[4] Despite Canada's shameful past record of injustices in this policy field, not to mention many others, there is still the often frequent reference to Canada's 'humanitarian tradition'. Indeed, the 1976 Immigration Act makes specific reference to this by 'provide for an admissible refugee class "to fulfil Canada's international legal obligations concerning refugees and to uphold its *humanitarian tradition* with respect to the displaced

3 Munroe, S. (2006) 'Canada Gives Formal Apology for the Chinese Head Tax', *Canada Online*, 25 June http://canadaonline.about.com/b/2006/06/25/canada-gives-formal-apology-for-chinese-head-tax.htm (accessed on 22 March 2011). In 1923, the Canadian Government passed the Chinese Exclusion Act which effectively stopped Chinese immigration into Canada for the next 25 years. The date on which the Chinese Exclusion Act came into effect, 1 July 1923, is known as 'humiliation day': Munroe, S. (n.d.), 'Chinese Head Tax and the Chinese Exclusion Act in Canada: Discrimination in Chinese Immigration in Canada 1885–1947', *Canada Online* http://canadaonline.about.com/od/historyofimmigration/a/chineseheadtax.htm (accessed on 22 March 2011). See also 'Harper makes long-anticipated apology for Chinese Head Tax': 'On behalf of the people of Canada, we offer a full apology to Chinese-Canadians for the head tax and express our deepest sorrow for the exclusion of Chinese immigrants', *CanWest News Service*, 22 June 2006 <http://www.canada.com/nationalpost/news/story.html?id=b902615e-3dfc-4fda-b843-feed3f45514f&k=37539> (accessed on 22 March 2011) It should perhaps be noted that the Canadian Government also made a formal apology on 22 September 1988, to Japanese Canadians for their internment during the Second World War. Citizenship and Immigration Canada, '20th Anniversary of the Canadian Government's Formal Apology for the Japanese Internment in World War II', Prime Minister Brian Mulroney made the following remarks in the House of Commons on 22 September 1988: 'I know that I speak for Members on all sides of the House today in offering to Japanese Canadians the formal and sincere apology of this Parliament for those past injustices against them, against their families, and against their heritage, and our solemn commitment and undertaking to Canadians of every origin that such violations will never again in this country be countenanced or repeated' <http://www.cic.gc.ca/english/multiculturalism/asian/20years-jap.asp> (accessed on 22 March 2011).

4 Citizenship and Immigration Canada, 'Speaking Notes of the Hon. Jason Kenny, PC, MP, Minister of Citizenship, Immigration and Multiculturalism at the unveiling, at Pier 21, of The Wheel of Conscience, a monument to commemorate the MS St. Louis', Halifax, Nova Scotia, 20 January 2011 <http://www.cic.gc.ca/English/department/media/speeches/2011/2011-01-20.asp#cont> (accessed on 22 March 2011). See also Abella, I. and Troper, H. (1982), *None is too Many: Canada and the Jews of Europe, 1933–1948* (Toronto: Lester & Orpen Dennys).

and persecuted"'.[5] Humanitarianism,[6] of course, is associated closely with and identified as the basis of refugee law and refugee policy.[7]

Is it reasonable to argue that Canadian refugee laws and policies are ingrained and rooted deeply in Canada's 'humanitarian tradition'? Can Canada's 'humanitarian tradition' be traced back to the first European settlers who came to the New World to escape religious persecution?[8] Can it be traced back to those who were forcibly displaced and expelled from the Thirteen American Colonies during the American Revolution for their loyalty to the British Crown?[9] Can it also be traced to the British North America Colonies providing asylum to those who were escaping the abomination of slavery in the United States in serving as the last stop on the Underground Railroad in the mid-nineteenth century?[10]

---

5 Canada, Immigration Act, s. 3(g). R.S.C. 1985, c. I-2. As quoted in Dirks, G.E. (1995), *Controversy and Complexity: Canadian Immigration Policy during the 1980s* (Montreal and Kingston: McGill-Queen's University Press), p. 24, emphasis added.

6 The *Oxford Paperback Dictionary* defines 'humanitarian' as 'concerned with human welfare and the reduction of suffering', Pollard, E. and Liebeck, H. (eds) (1994), *Oxford Paperback Dictionary*, 4th edn (Oxford: Oxford University Press), p. 388. Humanitarianism is defined as '1. Concern for human welfare, especially as manifested through philanthropy. 2. The belief that the sole moral obligation of humankind is the improvement of human welfare': *The Free Dictionary*, by Farlex <http://www.thefreedictionary.com/humanitarianism> (accessed on 23 March 2011) For a scholarly treatment of humanitarianism and migration from a comparative perspective, see Jonathan Klaaren's review of Dauvergne, C. (2005), *Humanitarianism, Identity and Nation: Migration Laws of Canada and Australia* (Vancouver: UBC Press), in *Law and Politics Book Review* 15. 8 (August 2005): 746–8 <http://www.bsos.umd.edu/gvpt/lpbr/subpages/reviews/dauvergne805.htm>.(accessed on 23 March 2011)

7 See, for instance, Garvey, J.I. (1985), 'Toward a Reformulation of International Refugee Law', *Harvard International Law Journal* 26.2 (Spring 1985): 483, where he states, 'International refugee law rests on a humanitarian premise. It is a premise tragically inadequate for our time, but one which remains unexamined despite the frequency and enormity of contemporary refugee crises.'

8 *Religion and the Founding of the American Republic*, 1. 'America as a Religious Refuge: The Seventeenth Century' <http://www.loc.gov/exhibits/religion/rel01.html> (accessed 21 March 2011).

9 Wilson, B.G. (n.d.), 'Loyalists', *The Canadian Encyclopedia* <http://www.thecanadianencyclopedia.com/index.cfm?PgNm=TCE&Params=A1ARTA0004796> (accessed on 21 March 2011) See also Knowles, V. (1997), *Strangers at Our Gates: Canadian Immigration and Immigration Policy, 1540–1997* (Toronto: Dundurn Press Limited), Chapter 2, 'Canada's First Large Influx of Refugees'.

10 Winks, R.W. (n.d.), 'The Underground Railroad', *The Canadian Encyclopedia* <http://www.thecanadianencyclopedia.com/index.cfm?PgNm=TCE&Params=A1ARTA0008199>, and *idem* (n.d.), 'Slavery', *The Canadian Encyclopedia* <http://www.thecanadianencyclopedia.com/index.cfm?PgNm=TCE&Params=A1ARTA0007449> (accessed on 21 March 2011)

In spite of Canada's shameful past racist immigration policies, Canada has accepted successive waves of asylum-seekers or refugees and, most notably, in the second half of the twentieth century when it became a place of refuge for those who suffered political, social and economic oppression and gross human rights violations amounting to persecution; for example, when the 1956 Hungarian Revolution was crushed by the Soviet Union, when the 1968 'Prague Spring' was abruptly ended by the Warsaw Pact, and those who were escaping repressive military dictatorships and totalitarian regimes in Africa, South America and South East Asia.[11] Has Canada's deeply ingrained and rooted 'humanitarian tradition', as noted in the 1976 Immigration Act, come to the fore on these and other occasions and has it helped to shape its human rights and refugee policies throughout its history, and, more specifically, has it shaped the evolution and development of its refugee status determination (RSD) systems since it was first formalized with its 1976 Immigration Act? Does Canada's 'humanitarian tradition' continue to shape the evolution and development of Canada's RSD system up to the present with the latest iteration of RSD system reforms under the Balanced Refugee Reform Act? Throughout this process, it is asserted here, that the courts and, ultimately, the Supreme Court of Canada, have decided the essential nature and composition of the RSD system in Canada.

This chapter takes a broad historical perspective and overview of the nature of Canada's 'humanitarian tradition', with respect to providing a sanctuary or refuge for those who have suffered severe and sustained human rights abuses that have resulted in their forcible displacement from their homes and/or their previous lives. While acknowledging Canada's shameful past injustices with respect to its treatment of those seeking asylum, it explores the notion that Canada's 'humanitarian tradition' can be traced to its very foundations.

The chapter begins by addressing the apparently anomalous fact that Canada was *not* one of the initial signatories to the 1951 Convention relating to the Status of Refugees or its 1967 Protocol.[12] Canada only became a State Party to these seminal international refugee rights instruments in 1969. Nevertheless, Canada still supported the UNHCR and accepted mass influxes of refugees during the first two decades of the nascent international refugee protection regime.

The chapter further notes that it was the patriation of the 1867 British North America Act and the proclamation of the 1982 Constitution Act, with its entrenched

11 Dirks, *Controversy and Complexity: Canadian Immigration Policy during the 1980s*, p. 61. A full citation for all of these successive waves of refugees coming to Canada are found in the footnotes below.

12 Convention relating to the Status of Refugees, Geneva, adopted 28 July 1951, entry into force 22 April 1954, 189 UNTS 150, http://treaties.un.org/pages/ViewDetailsII.aspx?&src=TREATY&mtdsg_no=V~2&chapter=5&Temp=mtdsg2&lang=en and Protocol relating to the Status of Refugees, New York, adopted 31 January 1967, entry into force 4 October 1967, 606 UNTS 267, http://treaties.un.org/pages/ViewDetails.aspx?src=UNTSONLINE&tabid=2&mtdsg_no=V-5&chapter=5&lang=en (accessed on 13 February 2011)

Canadian Charter of Rights and Freedoms, that laid the basis for today's RSD system and the famous 1985 Supreme Court of Canada decision in the *Singh*[13] case upon which it rests. This then led to the establishment of the Immigration and Refugee Board of Canada in 1989, which is charged with administering the present 2001 Immigration and Refugee Protection Act that came into force in 2002.

It is from this broader historical overview and contextualized analysis that the most recent legislative amendments in the Balanced Refugee Reform Act are considered and examined. The Balanced Refugee Reform Act seeks to achieve particular policy objectives that seek to reduce significantly the processing times for refugee protection claims and by doing so reduce substantially, most importantly, the number of fraudulent refugee claims thereby reducing additionally the overall costs of the RSD system in Canada. The mechanisms and administrative means selected to undertake these significant changes have been the subject of great controversy within the refugee policy community within Canada. The chapter considers the most salient changes, that are being implemented currently to the RSD system in Canada, in some detail.

The chapter concludes by noting that the differences at issue with respect to the Balanced Refugee Reform Act between the policy-makers and stakeholders will eventually be resolved by the Canadian courts and ultimately, of course, the Supreme Court of Canada. The RSD system will continue to evolve, accordingly, in Canada, but most probably in congruity with its deeply ingrained and rooted 'humanitarian tradition' of providing asylum to those who have been forcibly divested of their most fundamental human rights and dignity as persons.

The Historical Roots: The Evolution of Canada's Refugee Status Determination System

Canada ratified and acceded to the 1951 Convention relating to the Status of Refugees and its 1967 Protocol on 9 June 1969.[14] This was some 18 years after the 1951 Convention was first adopted on 28 July 1951, and nearly two years after the 1967 Protocol was adopted on 31 January 1967, and came into force on 4 October of that same year. Even though Canada played a significant, if not pivotal, role in the formation of the United Nations and its international human

13 *Singh v. Minister of Employment and Immigration* [1985] 1 S.C.R. 177.

14 Convention relating to the Status of Refugees, Geneva, adopted 28 July 1951, entry into force 22 April 1954, 189 UNTS 150, <http://treaties.un.org/pages/ViewDetailsII.aspx?&src=TREATY&mtdsg_no=V~2&chapter=5&Temp=mtdsg2&lang=en> and Protocol relating to the Status of Refugees, New York, adopted 31 January 1967, entry into force 4 October 1967, 606 UNTS 267 <http://treaties.un.org/pages/ViewDetails.aspx?src=UNTSONLINE&tabid=2&mtdsg_no=V-5&chapter=5&lang=en> (accessed on 13 February 2011).

rights legal system,[15] it did not become a State Party to these seminal international refugee rights instruments until a number of years after they were first adopted. It is interesting to note, then, that Canada was not one of the original States Parties to either the 1951 Convention or its 1967 Protocol.

New States Parties Ratify and Accede to the 1951 Convention in the Decades of the 1960s and the 1990s

There are presently 148 States Parties to either one or both the 1951 Convention or its 1967 Protocol, about three-quarters of all of the member States of the United Nations.[16] It is interesting to consider when these States Parties ratified and acceded to these human rights treaties (See Table 7.1).

15 John W. Holmes and Don Page have stated: For Canada, which was so active in the founding of most of the UN's organs, the UN remains its best hope for influencing the decisions of other nations through consensus building. It has been at the forefront in promoting universality of membership in the UN. While it may no longer be in a position to play the mediatory role that it did in resolving the Suez Crisis of 1956, it is no less committed to peacemaking and has moved with the times to make its unique contribution of constructive internationalism through such means as verification procedures. By population Canada ranks about fortieth in the world and among the Western industrialized nations it ranks seventh, but it is the fourth largest financial contributor to the UN system. Canada believes that in combination with other nations lies the best hope for dealing with global problems such as pollution, racial discrimination, hunger, sexual discrimination, and others that trouble and ultimately affect Canadians. However frustrating the UN system may at times appear, its essential purpose is being served as long as it provides the principal forum for discussing these issues and avoids the centuries-old effort to create a world order. See 'United Nations', *The Canadian Encyclopedia* <http://www.thecanadianencyclopedia.com/index.cfm?PgNm=TCE&Params=A1ARTA0008231> (accessed on 14 February 2011). The principal drafter of the Universal Declaration of Human Rights (UDHR) was Professor John Humphrey. The blueprint for the UDHR was written by a Canadian – John Humphrey, who worked with the United Nations as the Director of the Human Rights Division in the Secretariat's Department of Social Affairs. His 400-page draft outline is the foundation for the UDHR's 30 articles, including a bill of rights which he had drawn up. Moreover, John was also a talented mediator who often served to bridge the chasms between different philosophical viewpoints around the negotiating table. See Canadian Human Rights Commission, 'Human Rights in Canada: A Historical Perspective', 'The Universal Declaration of Human Rights' <http://www.chrc-ccdp.ca/en/timePortals/milestones/53mile.asp> (accessed on 14 February 2011).

16 UNHCR, United Nations High Commissioner for Refugees, *States Parties to the 1951 Convention Relating to the Status of Refugees and its 1967 Protocol, As of the 1 October 2008* <http://www.unhcr.org/3b73b0d63.pdf> (accessed on 13 February 2011) There are currently 192 member states of the United Nations: United Nations Press Release ORG/1469, United Nations Member States, 3 July 2006 <http://www.un.org/News/Press/docs/2006/org1469.doc.htm> (accessed on 13 February 2011)

Table 7.1 Number of states parties and their ratification of the 1951 Convention by decade*

Decade	Number of States Parties
1950s	22
1960s	35
1970s	18
1980s	26
1990s	32
2000s	12
	145

* *Note* See Appendix 7, which list the States Parties by the decade of their accession to the 1951 Convention Relating to the Status of Refugees.

Source: UNHCR, United Nations High Commissioner for Refugees, *States Parties to the 1951 Convention Relating to the Status of Refugees and its 1967 Protocol, As of the 1 October 2008*

From Table 7.1, it appears that the 1960s saw the largest number of States Parties, Canada included, ratify and accede to the 1951 Convention. It is noteworthy that the vast majority of States to ratify and accede to the 1951 Convention during the decade of the 1960s were African States. Out of the 35 States to ratify the 1951 Convention in this decade, 23 of these States, about 66 per cent or two-thirds, were from Africa.[17] And, out of the 32 States that ratified the 1951 Convention in the 1990s, many of these States were former Eastern Bloc Communist States. The collapse of the Soviet Union, followed by the disintegration of the Socialist Federal Republic of Yugoslavia, with the death of Marshall Tito and as a consequence of the Yugoslav Wars, as well as the division of Czechoslovakia, all contributed to a number of new independent States ratifying the 1951 Convention during the decade of the 1990s.[18] Thus, out of the 32 States to ratify the 1951 Convention in

17 Loescher, G. (1993), *Beyond Charity: International Cooperation and the Global Refugee Crisis* (Oxford: Oxford University Press), pp. 77–84.

18 Ibid., pp. vii and 13. Indeed, at p. 11, Loescher states, 'It is now clear that we are living in an era in which fundamental political and economic changes in the international system result in large-scale movements of people. It is also a time when mass migrations themselves affect political, economic, and strategic developments worldwide. Indeed, it was the outpouring of refugees from East to West Germany in late 1989 that brought down the Berlin Wall, led to the unification of the two Germanys, and generated the most significant transformation in international relations since World War II.' See also Kushner,

the 1990s, eleven were previously a part of the Union of Soviet Socialist Republics (USSR),[19] six were former Warsaw Pact or Eastern Bloc states,[20] and four were a part of the former Socialist Federal Republic of Yugoslavia.[21] Hence, some 20 of the 32 States that ratified and acceded to the 1951 Convention in the decade of the 1990s, about 63 per cent were former Warsaw Pact States or formerly members of the Socialist Federal Republic of Yugoslavia.[22]

It is interesting to point out that the average number of States per decade to adopt the 1951 Convention, over the last 60 years, is 24 States. The three decades in which this average was exceeded were the 1960s, 1980s and the 1990s. The two decades where this average was exceeded the most were clearly the 1960s and the 1990s.

In the 1960s, one of the central concerns internationally was, indubitably, the decolonization of Africa and, in the 1990s, the international community was transformed by the fall of the Berlin Wall, the collapse of the Soviet Union and the emergence of newly liberated former Warsaw Pact States, and the disintegration of the Socialist Federal Republic of Yugoslavia. These significant liberating and profound transformative world events, during these two different decades, coming

---

T. and Knox, K. (1999), *Refugees in an Age of Genocide*, Chapter 13, 'Refugees from Former Yugoslavia: The Last "Programme" Refugees?' (London: Frank Cass), pp. 355–60. See 'Josip Broz Tito', in Cavanagh, D. (ed.) (1998, 2003), *A Dictionary of Political Biography* (Oxford: Oxford University Press <http://www.answers.com/topic/josip-broz-tito> (accessed on 21 February 2011). The six constituent republics of Socialist Federal Republic of Yugoslavia were Slovenia, Croatia, Bosnia and Herzegovina, Macedonia (which declared independence in 1991), Serbia and Montenegro (which abandoned the name Yugoslavia in 2003). The federation dissolved in its entirety in 2006: 'Yugoslavia', *The American Heritage® Dictionary of the English Language*, 4th edn (Houghton Mifflin Company, 2004) <http://www.answers.com/topic/yugoslavia>. 'Yugoslavia', *The Columbia Electronic Encyclopedia*, 6th edn (Columbia University Press, 2008) <http://www.answers.com/topic/yugoslavia> (accessed on 19–20 March 2011)

19 Palmowski J. (2004), 'Soviet Union', *A Dictionary of Contemporary World History* <http://www.encyclopedia.com/doc/1O46-SovietUnion.html> (accessed on 18 February 18 2011).

20 The Eastern Bloc or the Warsaw Treaty Organization (WTO), or simply the Warsaw Pact, consisted of Albania, Bulgaria, Czechoslovakia, East Germany, Hungary, Poland, Romania and the USSR or Soviet Union: Michta, A.A. (2004), 'Warsaw Treaty Organization', *Encyclopedia of Russian History* <http://www.encyclopedia.com/doc/1G2-3404101476.html> (accessed on 18 February 2011). Czechoslovakia peacefully split into the Czech Republic and Slovakia on 1 January 1993: 'Czechoslovakia', *The Columbia Encyclopedia*, 6th edn, 2008 http://www.encyclopedia.com/doc/1E1-Czechosl.html (accessed on 18 February 2011).

21 'Yugoslavia' *The Columbia Encyclopedia*, 6th edn, 2008 http://www.encyclopedia.com/doc/1E1-Yugoslav.html (accessed on 18 February 18 2011).

22 In fact, five more of the former Warsaw Pact and Yugoslavia states ratified the 1951 Convention in the first decade of the new millennium: Belarus, Moldova, Montenegro, Serbia and Ukraine.

some 30 years apart, helps to account for the large increases in the number of States Parties that ratified and acceded to the 1951 Convention. Indeed, the increase in the number of States Parties to the 1951 Convention over these two decades was, it can be argued, part and parcel of the process of the emergence of new independent States in Africa, Europe and in Asia. Some 43 newly independent States, nearly one-third of the present States Parties to the 1951 Convention, were a consequence of the disintegration of the old nineteenth-century colonial and twentieth-century communist empires.

These profoundly liberating and transformative world events, typically the result of social and economic unrest, mass public protests, if not violent intra-state conflicts and international wars, produced massive internal and external displacements of people and the creation, in turn, of refugees.

By the end of the 1960s, there were 57 States Parties to the 1951 Convention and 35 States Parties to the 1967 Protocol. In 1969, the Organization for African Unity (OAU), the predecessor to the African Union (AU), had negotiated the Convention Governing Specific Aspects of the Refugee Problems in Africa.[23] It is evident that at the end of the first two decades following the negotiation of the 1951 Convention, the international refugee rights instruments were far from being accepted universally or even by the majority of the world's States. In fact, most of the State Parties to these international instruments were from Western Europe and Africa, with a smattering of States in the Americas and the Middle East, along with Australia and New Zealand. Indeed, it was not until the end of the decade of the 1980s that there were 100 or more States Parties to the 1951 Convention and its 1967 Protocol. Thus, it took approximately four decades before these international instruments were accepted by about half the world's States.

Canada's 'Humanitarian Tradition' in the 1950s, 1960s and 1970s

As noted, Canada ratified and acceded to the 1951 Convention and its 1967 Protocol in 1969, in the last year of the decade of the 1960s, but not until after the United States ratified the 1967 Protocol on 1 November 1968.[24] Moreover, it was not until the 1967 Protocol had lifted the geographic and temporal limitations of the 1951 Convention that Canada, the United States, and other countries chose to become signatories to these international refugee rights instruments. None the

23 Organization for African Unity, Convention Governing Specific Aspects of Refugee Problems in Africa, Heads of the African State and Government, 10 September 1969 http://www.africa-union.org/Official_documents/Treaties_%20Conventions_%20Protocols/Refugee_Convention.pdf (accessed on 22 March 2011).

24 UNHCR, United Nations High Commissioner for Refugees, States Parties to the 1951 Convention Relating to the Status of Refugees and its 1967 Protocol, As of the 1 October 2008 http://www.unhcr.org/3b73b0d63.pdf (accessed on 13 February 2011). The United States is not a State Party to the 1951 Convention.

less, the fact that Canada was not a State Party to the 1951 Convention did not mean that it did not provide asylum to those in need of international protection.[25]

The Ministry of Citizenship and Immigration Canada (CIC) points to Canada's 'humanitarian tradition'[26] as one of the driving forces in its refugee policies and

25 Ninette Kelley and Michael Trebilcock note the following: 'In June 1969, Canada finally acceded to the 1951 U.N. Convention Relating to Refugees and the 1967 Protocol. Prior to 1969, Canada adhered in practice to the terms of the convention and also was a member of the UNHCR's executive committee. Canada did not sign the convention earlier, primarily because of the RCMP's [Royal Canadian Mounted Police] belief that it would constrain Canada's ability to deport refugees on security grounds': Kelley, N. and Trebilcock, M. (1998), *The Making of the Mosaic: A History of Canadian Immigration Policy* (Toronto: University of Toronto Press), p. 363.

26 It can be reasonably argued that Canada's 'humanitarian tradition' actually predates Confederation, 1 July 1867, when the British North American colonies were the state authorities in the northern part of the North American continent, and earlier. (The New World/Americas were settled initially by those who were escaping religious persecution in the Old World/Europe. For instance, see *Religion and the Founding of the American Republic*, 1. 'America as a Religious Refuge: The Seventeenth Century' (see n. 8 above). In the famous judgement *R v Knowles, ex parte Somersett* (1772) 20 State Tr. 1, Lord Chief Justice Mansfield of the English Court of King's Bench held that slavery was unlawful in England <http://downloads.members.tripod.com/medicolegal/somersetvstewart.htm> (accessed on 22 February 2011) On 9 July 1793, the Legislature of Upper Canada passed a bill, An Act to Prevent the further Introduction of Slaves and to limit the Term of Contracts for Servitude within this Province, under the leadership of Lieutenant Governor John Grave Simcoe, an abolitionist; the Act made it illegal to bring a person into the colony to be enslaved. Upper Canada was the first jurisdiction in the British Empire to pass a law freeing slaves. It should also be noted that thousands of Black Africans volunteered to serve in the War of 1812, and in 1819, Attorney General John Robinson declared that by residing in Upper Canada, black residents were set free, and that the courts would protect their freedom. The Historica Dominion Institute, 'Black History Canada, Enslavement' <http://blackhistorycanada.ca/topic.php?id=112&themeid=1> (accessed 26 February 2011) Her Excellency the Right Honourable Michaëlle Jean, Speech on the Occasion of the Student Forum: 'From the Abolition of the Slave Trade to the Elimination of Racial Discrimination', Rideau Hall, 21 March 2007 <http://www.gg.ca/document.aspx?id=12400>. However, slavery was not ended formerly in the British North American colonies until 1834, following the Slavery Abolition Act 1833, that was passed by the United Kingdom Parliament: Library and Archives of Canada, 'The Anti-Slavery Movement in Canada, Introduction' <http://www.collectionscanada.gc.ca/anti-slavery/index-e.html> (accessed on 26 February 2011) *The Canadian Encyclopedia*, 'Slavery' <http://www.thecanadianencyclopedia.com/index.cfm?PgNm=TCE&Params=A1ARTA0007449> (accessed on February 26, 2011) The National Archives, 'Slavery, How did the Abolition Acts of 1807 and 1833 affect the slave trade?' <http://www.nationalarchives.gov.uk/education/lessons/lesson27.htm> (accessed on February 26, 2011) On 25 March 1807, the House of Lords passed An Act for the Abolition of the Slave Trade. It was this Act, the Slavery Abolition Act of 1833, the 1793 legislation in Upper Canada limiting the further introduction of slavery, and the 1772 Somersett case that made the British North American colonies the last stop on the

'Underground Railroad', the informal network of safe houses and stops from the southern United States to Canada. The British North American colonies became the safe haven for runaway slaves seeking freedom in Canada. See the Harriet Tubman Institute for Research on the Global Migrations of African Peoples at <http://tubman.apps01.yorku.ca/about_us> (accessed on 22 February 2011) See also the Library and Archives of Canada, 'The Anti-Slavery Movement in Canada, Refugees'; in particular, see 'Map of the 'Underground Railroad', circa 1850s,' and 'Benjamin Drew, The Refugee, or, The Narratives of Fugitive Slaves in Canada, 1856' <http://www.collectionscanada.gc.ca/anti-slavery/033004-3000-e.html> (accessed on 26 February 2011)

Although it can be argued that Canada has a strong 'humanitarian tradition', others have noted rightly that it is a pervasive Canadian myth that 'Canada has a long history of welcoming refugees and dissidents and has always been available to the proverbial huddled masses yearning to breathe free. In fact, for most of its history, Canada's immigration practices have been racist and exclusionary. As Granatstein et al. note, Canada's immigration policies since before Confederation established a clear order of preference (rendered explicit, for example, in the Canada Year Book, 1930) as to who would be allowed into the country: 'At the top of the list were British and white Americans who were always acceptable … .': Kelley and Trebilcock, *The Making of the Mosaic*, pp. 441–2. Nevertheless, one ought not to forget that the largest influx of forcibly displaced people to the British North American colonies took place during the time of the American Revolution or the American Revolutionary War, 1775–83. The American Revolution, <http://www.myrevolutionarywar.com/> (accessed on 19 March 2011) It is estimated that about 70,000 Loyalists fled the 13 American colonies and that approximately 50,000 came to the British North American colonies of Quebec and Nova Scotia. See Mackenzie, A. (n.d.), 'A Short History of the United Empire Loyalists' <http://www.uelac.org/PDF/loyalist.pdf> (accessed on 19 March 2011) Ann Mackenzie writes:

The signing of the Treaty of Paris (1783), which recognized the independence of the United States, was the final blow for the Loyalists. Faced with further mistreatment and the hostility of their countrymen, and wishing to live as British subjects, Loyalists who had remained in the Thirteen Colonies during the war now were faced with exile. Those who wished to live in North America had two choices; Nova Scotia (Maritimes) or Quebec (Ontario-Quebec). (p. 2)

The United Empire Loyalists were undoubtedly facing severely harsh and hostile conditions in the former 13 American colonies. There were incidents of tarring and feathering and, as Ann Mackenzie has noted, :

Patriot authorities punished Loyalists who spoke their views too loudly by stripping them of their property and goods and banishing them on pain of death should they ever return. They coerced others into silence with threats. Throughout the Thirteen Colonies that were under Patriot control, Loyalists could not vote, sell land, sue debtors, or work as lawyers, doctors, or schoolteachers. To be fair, in Loyalist controlled areas, supporters of the Revolution met with similar treatment at the hands of British authorities. (p. 2)

For a more detailed treatment of the United Empire Loyalists in the British North American colonies, that includes additional sources of information, see Wilson, B.G. (n.d.), 'Loyalists', *The Canadian Encyclopedia* <http://www.thecanadianencyclopedia.com/index.cfm?PgNm=TCE&Params=A1ARTA0004796> (accessed on March 19, 2011) Bruce G. Wilson states that:

in fulfilling its obligations to provide protection to refugees, whether they are seeking refugee protection within Canada or through its resettlement programmes for those refugees who are located in refugee camps.

Canada's refugee protection program is an expression of Canada's humanitarian tradition. The Canadian government made refugee protection a priority following the Second World War in response to global efforts to share responsibility for those displaced by war. By protecting refugees, Canada asserts the need to uphold international agreements and obligations and to share responsibility internationally for the displaced and persecuted.

Canada partners with many other countries and international organizations to come to the aid of refugees. Every year, Canada resettles 10,600–12,000 – or one out of every ten – of the refugees resettled globally. Indeed, Canada has one of the largest refugee resettlement programs in the world with more than 780,000 refugees and persons in similar circumstances resettled here since the Second World War.[27]

It is important to stress that even before Canada became a signatory to the 1951 Convention and its 1967 Protocol, it was accepting large groups of refugees. Perhaps the six most prominent waves of refugees to enter Canada throughout the decades of the 1950s, 1960s and 1970s were the 37,000 Hungarian refugees who were admitted in to Canada following the 1956 Hungarian Revolution that was crushed by the Soviet Union;[28] throughout the Vietnam War, 1955–75, Canada took in US draft evaders who did not want to serve in the US military and fight

> During the Revolution, over 19,000 Loyalists served Britain in specially created provincial corps, accompanied by several thousand Indians. Others spent the war in such strongholds as New York City or in refugee camps such as those at Sorel and Machiche, Qué[bec]. Between 80,000 and 100,000 eventually fled, about half of them to Canada.

See also Troper, H. (n.d.), 'Immigration', *The Canadian Encyclopedia* <http://www.thecanadianencyclopedia.com/index.cfm?PgNm=TCE&Params=A1ARTA0003960> (accessed on 23 March 2011)

Perhaps it would be trite to point out that refugeehood or the refugee experience is rooted deeply in the very foundations of Canada's history, from those fleeing persecution from the Old World/Europe in the sixteenth century to those fleeing persecution from the American Revolutionary Patriots in the seventeenth century.

27 'Strategic Outcomes and Program Activity Architecture, Program Activity 4 – Refugee Program', Citizenship and Immigration Canada <www.cic.gc.ca>, http://www.cic.gc.ca/english/department/paa/activity-04.asp (accessed on 21 February 2011).

28 Institute for 1956 <http://www.rev.hu/history_of_56/naviga/index.htm> (accessed on 21 February 2011). See also Keyserlingk, R.H. (1993), *Breaking Ground: The 1956 Hungarian Refugee Movement to Canada* (Toronto: York Lanes Press). In particular, see The Honourable J.W. Pickersgill, Minister of Citizenship and Immigration in 1956, 'The Minister and the Hungarian Refugees', pp. 47–51.

in Vietnam,[29] and the 1968 invasion of Czechoslovakia that ended the 'Prague Spring', which led to some 11,000 Czech and Slovak refugees coming to Canada.[30] In 1972, Canada also accepted some 7,000 highly trained and educated Ugandan Asians that were expelled by dictator Idi Amin under his racist policies.[31] This was followed in 1973 by about 7,000 Chileans, who fled to Canada after the democratically elected Marxist government of Salvador Allende was disposed by a military coup by General Augusto Pinochet.[32] However, the largest group of refugees who were accepted in Canada during this period was the 'boat people' – Vietnamese, Laotians and Kampucheans who fled Communist regimes after the fall of Saigon in 1975.[33] From 1975 to 1981, Canada, in fact, admitted some 77,000 Indo-Chinese refugees.[34]

---

29 'Vietnam War', *GlobalSecurity.org* <http://www.globalsecurity.org/military/ops/vietnam2.htm> (accessed on 21 February 2011) See Kelley and Trebilcock, *The Making of the Mosaic*, pp. 363–4. The estimates of the number of draft evaders that came to Canada varies widely. Some reports indicated by 1969, there were 60,000 draft evaders in Canada. The Canadian Department of Manpower and Immigration put the number of draft-age male immigrants to Canada from the United States at 17,000, over the five-year period from 1965 to 1969.

30 Velinger, J. (n.d.), 'The Soviet Invasion of Czechoslovakia and the crushing of the Prague Spring', *Radio Praha* Ceskey Rozhlas, 20-082003 <http://www.radio.cz/en/section/czechs/the-soviet-invasion-of-czechoslovakia-and-the-crushing-of-the-prague-spring> (accessed on 21 February 2011) For further information on these three waves of refugees, see Kelley and Trebilcock, *The Making of the Mosaic*, pp. 363–7.

31 Abella, I. (n.d.), 'Refugees', *The Canadian Encyclopedia* <http://www.thecanadianencyclopedia.com/index.cfm?PgNm=TCE&Params=A1ARTA0006738> (accessed on 6 March 2011). See also 'Idi Amin', *A Dictionary of Political Biography* (Oxford University Press, 1998, 2003) <http://www.answers.com/topic/idi-amin>; 'Idi Amin Dada' *Gale Encyclopedia of Biography*, 2006 <http://www.answers.com/topic/idi-amin>; 'Idi Amin', *Dictators of the Twentieth Century* <http://www.cbv.ns.ca/dictator/Amin.html> (accessed on 6 March 2011)

32 Kelley and Trebilcock, T*he Making of the Mosaic*, pp. 365–6. In 1998, General Augusto Pinochet was arrested in London, and extradited in 2000 to Chile to be prosecuted for crimes against humanity. See 'Criminal Proceedings Against Pinochet in Spain, Will There Be Justice?', *Derechos, Human Rights, Equipo Nizkor* <http://www.derechos.org/nizkor/chile/juicio/eng.html> (accessed on 19 March 2011).

33 Citizenship and Immigration Canada, 'Forging Our Legacy: Canadian Citizenship and Immigration, 1900–1977' <http://www.cic.gc.ca/english/resources/publications/legacy/chap-6a.asp#chap6-15> (accessed on 6 March 2011) Lam, L. (1996), *From Being Uprooted to Surviving: Resettlement of Vietnamese-Chinese 'Boat People' in Montreal, 1980–1990* (Toronto: York Lanes Press), Chapter 1, 'The Boat People Phenomenon', pp. 1–20.

34 Ibid. Lam notes that in July 1979, the Canadian government at the time stated that 'it would admit 50,000 refugees to Canada by the end of 1980. The decision provided for both privately sponsored and government-sponsored refugees, the government initially agreeing to match each refugee that individuals and churches and other voluntary groups

Ninette Kelly and Michael Trebilcock have pointed out that for the 14-year period, from 1963 to 1976, Canada averaged about 3,600 refugees per year, for a total of fewer than 60,000.[35] However, they go on to note the following:

> In 1968–9, 12,000 Czechoslovakian refugees were admitted after the Soviet suppression of the Czech uprising in 1968; slightly more than 200 Tibetans were admitted in 1970–71 following China's occupation of Tibet; 7,000 Asians, primarily East Indian, were admitted from Uganda in 1972, following Idi Amin's expulsion of the Asian population of Uganda; and, in 1973–4, about 7,000 refugees were admitted from Chile, after a military coup ousted the democratically elected socialist government of Salvador Allende.[36]

The 1976 Immigration Act, that was enacted in 1978, established, for the first time, the objectives of Canada's immigration policy, which included

> … the promotion of Canada's demographic, economic, social and cultural goals; family reunion; nondiscrimination; the fulfillment of Canada's international obligations in relation to refugees: and co-operation among all levels of government, as well as with the voluntary sector, in promoting the adaptation of newcomers to Canadian society.[37]

The 1976 Immigration Act also sanctioned an open and broad-based consultation process with Canadians to set annual immigration targets and, since 1980, the federal government has tabled in Parliament one to three-year annual projections for the desired immigration and refugee levels for Canada.[38] The statute also established an Immigration Board, a fully independent body from government that was first put in place in 1967, and which could only be overruled by the government on national security matters.[39]

The 1976 Immigration Act created the first refugee determination process in Canada and entrenched the definition of refugee found in the 1951 Convention in Canadian law. The new Act also created the Refugee Status Advisory Committee

---

supported.' See also W. Gunther Plaut (1995), *Asylum: A Moral Dilemma* (Toronto: York Lanes Press), Chapter 12, 'The North American Experience'.

35 Kelley and Trebilcock, *The Making of the Mosaic*, p. 347.

36 Ibid., pp. 347–8.

37 Dirks, *Controversy and Complexity*, Chapter 7, 'Determining Refugee Status Within Canada', pp. 77–96, and *idem*, 'Immigration Policy', Institut Historica-Dominion Institute, *The Canadian Encyclopedia* <http://www.thecanadianencyclopedia.com/index.cfm?PgNm=TCE&Params=A1ARTA0003961> (accessed on March 6, 2011)

38 Dirks, 'Immigration Policy'.

39 Ibid.

(RSAC) and also allowed for the admission to Canada of designated classes of persons on humanitarian grounds and enable the private sponsorship of refugees.[40]

In 1982, Canada's Constitution, the British North America Act, was patriated from the United Kingdom Parliament. The new Constitution Act, 1982, incorporated an entrenched Canadian Charter of Rights and Freedoms. It is important to note that Section 27 of the Canadian Charter of Rights and Freedoms states, 'This Charter shall be interpreted in a manner consistent with the preservation and enhancement of the multicultural heritage of Canadians.'[41] Canada has an official policy of multiculturalism.[42] The 1985 Canadian Multiculturalism Act states, in part:

> The Government of Canada recognizes the diversity of Canadians as regards race, national or ethnic origin, colour and religion as a fundamental characteristic of Canadian society and is committed to a policy of multiculturalism designed to preserve and enhance the multicultural heritage of Canadians while working to achieve the equality of all Canadians in the economic, social, cultural and political life of Canada.[43]

Indeed, multiculturalism is deemed to be one of the rights and responsibilities of Canadian citizenship.[44]

Perhaps it is overly trite to note that both the Canadian Charter of Rights and Freedoms, an integral part of the Canadian Constitution, and Canada's official policy of multiculturalism reinforce, or perhaps manifest distinctively, Canada's humanitarian values, premises, traditions and heritage. Indeed, this came fully and

---

40 Citizenship and Immigration Canada, 'Forging Our Legacy: Canadian Citizenship and Immigration, 1900–1977, The Immigration Act 1976' <http://www.cic.gc.ca/english/resources/publications/legacy/chap-6.asp#chap6-8> (accessed on 15 March 2011); Dirks, *Controversy and Complexity*, Chapter 7, 'Determining Refugee Status within Canada', pp. 77–96.

41 Canadian Charter of Rights and Freedoms, Part I of the Constitution Act 1982, Assented to 29 March 1982, Department of Justice Canada <http://laws.justice.gc.ca/en/charter/1.html#anchorbo-ga:l_I-gb:s_1> (accessed on 6 March 2011)

42 Canadian Multiculturalism Act, 1985, c. 24 (4th Supp.), An Act for the preservation and enhancement of multiculturalism in Canada, assented to 21 July 1988. Department of Justice Canada <http://laws.justice.gc.ca/eng/C-18.7/page-3.html> (accessed on 6 March 2011)

43 Ibid., Preamble.

44 Citizenship and Immigration Canada, Study Guide, 2010 edn, 'Discover Canada: The Rights and Responsibilities of Citizenship' <http://www.cic.gc.ca/English/pdf/pub/discover.pdf> (accessed on 6 March 2011), where it states at p. 8 the following: 'Multiculturalism – A fundamental characteristic of the Canadian heritage and identity. Canadians celebrate the gift of one another's presence and work hard to respect pluralism and live in harmony.'

officially to the fore and to the international public's attention when the UNHCR awarded the people of Canada with the Nansen Medal in 1986.[45]

None the less, the roots of the present refugee status determination (RSD) system in Canada can be traced to the historic 1985 Supreme Court of Canada decisions in *Singh*.[46] What is especially noteworthy is that the *Singh* decision was one of the first cases to be rendered by the Supreme Court of Canada on the Canadian Charter of Rights and Freedoms.[47] Indeed, this Supreme Court of Canada decision led directly to the establishment of the Immigration and Refugee Board of Canada in 1989. It is also pertinent to underscore that the Supreme Court of Canada issued its decision in the famous *Singh* case on 4 April 1985. And, to this day in Canada, 'Refugee Rights Day', is held on 4 April to commemorate the *Singh* decision and its impact on refugee rights within Canada.[48]

In the 1985 *Singh* decision, the Supreme Court of Canada ruled that the word 'everyone' in Section 7 of the Canadian Charter of Rights and Freedoms, which states, 'Everyone has the right to life, liberty and security of the person and the right not to be deprived thereof except in accordance with the principles of fundamental justice',[49] includes 'everyone' on Canadian soil and not just Canadian citizens, and hence, refugee claimants. The Supreme Court of Canada also ruled in the *Singh* decision that refugee claimants were entitled to an oral hearing in accordance with the principles of fundamental justice and international law. The Supreme Court of Canada ruled, furthermore, that the refugee determination system that existed under the 1976 Immigration Act also violated the Canadian Bill of Rights, Section 2(e), which states, '... *no law of Canada shall be construed or applied so as to ...*

45 UNHCR, The UN Refugee Agency, 'Archive of Past Nansen Winners' <http://www.unhcr.org/pages/49c3646c467-page5.html> (accessed on 6 March 2011). The citation for the award recipient states, 'In 1986, the Nansen went to the people of Canada – the only country to have received the award as a nation.' It further states that the people of Canada received the Nansen medal, 'in recognition of their essential and constant contribution to the cause of refugees within their country and around the world. Canada is a leading contributor to international humanitarian and refugee aid programmes. Canada has, from the beginning, supported international efforts on behalf of refugees. It has one of the best records for resettlement of refugees and is a leading UNHCR donor.' See also Immigration and Refugee Board of Canada, 'Nansen Medal Awarded to the People of Canada' <http://www.irb-cisr.gc.ca/eng/media/newsnouv/2009/pages/nansen.aspx> (accessed on 13 March 2011)

46 *Singh v. Minister of Employment and Immigration* [1985] 1 S.C.R. 177.

47 Immigration and Refugee Board of Canada, 'IRB's 20th Anniversary: The Landmark Singh Decision' <http://www.irb-cisr.gc.ca/eng/media/newsnouv/2009/pages/singh.aspx> (accessed on 6 March 2011)

48 Canadian Council for Refugees, Refugees Rights Day, 'Guaranteeing life, liberty, security and humanity for refugees in Canada – 25 years after Singh, Celebrate refugee rights in Canada this April 4th!' <http://ccrweb.ca/RRDay.htm> (accessed on 6 March 2011)

49 Canadian Charter of Rights and Freedoms, Part I of the Constitution Act 1982, Assented to 29 March 1982, Department of Justice Canada <http://laws.justice.gc.ca/en/charter/1.html#anchorbo-ga:l_I-gb:s_1> (accessed on 6 March 2011).

(e) deprive a person of the right to a fair hearing in accordance with the principles of fundamental justice for the determination of his rights and obligations.'[50]

One of the more enduring portions of the *Singh* decision, the majority opinion, was written by Justice Bertha Wilson, Canada's first female Supreme Court Justice, which states as follows:

> Certainly the guarantees of the *Charter* would be illusory if they could be ignored because it was administratively convenient to do so. No doubt considerable time and money can be saved by adopting administrative procedures which ignore the principles of fundamental justice but such an argument, in my view, misses the point of the exercise of s. 1. The principles of natural justice and procedural fairness which have long been espoused by our courts, and the constitutional entrenchment of the principles of fundamental justice in s. 7 implicitly recognize that a balance of administrative convenience does not override the need to adhere to these principles.[51]

In essence, governments could never use administrative convenience to trump the principles of natural justice and procedural fairness, along with the constitutionally entrenched principles of fundamental justice.[52]

The Supreme Court of Canada ruled that, as a minimum, the refugee claimant was entitled to a procedural scheme that provides 'an adequate opportunity to state his case and to know the case he has to meet'.[53] Justice Bertha Wilson also

---

50 Canadian Bill of Rights, 1960, c. 44, [Assented to 10 August 1960], Department of Justice, Canada, <http://laws.justice.gc.ca/en/showdoc/cs/C-12.3///en?page=1> (accessed on 6 March 2011)

51 *Singh v. Minister of Employment and Immigration* [1985] 1 S.C.R. 177. As quoted in Evans, J.M., Janisch, H.N. and Mullan, D.J. (1995), *Administrative Law: Cases, Text, and Materials*, 4th edn (Toronto: Edmond Montgomery Publications Limited), p. 172.

52 It is interesting to note on point that Canadian constitutional law scholars have stated that:

The most activist aspect of Justice Wilson's opinion is her response to the government's attempt to save its legislation by arguing that the cost of providing a hearing to determine refugee status constitutes a reasonable justification under section 1 of limiting the Charter right. In Justice Wilson's and her concurring colleagues' view, administrative convenience cannot justify overriding a Charter right. In support of this view she points to statements of a senior immigration official and a ministerial task [force] calling for reform of refugee procedures

Russell, P.H., Knopff, R. and Morton, T. (1990), *Federalism and the Charter: Leading Constitutional Decisions, A New Edition* (Ottawa: Carleton University Press), p. 393. Indeed, in its most meaningful sense, it is reasonable to ask whether it is possible to put a market price, like any commodity, on our most fundamental rights or on the administration of justice itself?

53 *Singh v. Minister of Employment and Immigration* [1985] 1 S.C.R. 177, para. 58 (emphasis added).

stated at paragraph 57 of her judgement that Section 2(e) of the Canadian Bill of Rights means that no law in Canada shall be construed or applied so as to deprive the person of 'a fair hearing in accordance with the principles of fundamental justice'.[54] She went on to state that:

> Without attempting to formulate any final definition of those words, I would take them to mean, generally, that the tribunal which adjudicates upon his rights must act fairly, in good faith, without bias and in a judicial temper, and must give to him the opportunity adequately to state his case.[55]

The Immigration and Refugee Board of Canada

In 1987, a ship arrived on Canada's east coast carrying 174 Sikh refugee claimants; the resulting public furore led to the government introducing new legislation that restructured the Canadian refugee determination system, replacing the Immigration Appeal Board with the Immigration and Refugee Board of Canada (IRB).[56] The IRB was established with two divisions: the Convention Refugee Determination Division (CRDD) and the Immigration Appeal Division (IAD). The CRDD

54 Ibid., para. 57

55 Ibid. Gary Yee has noted that 'A party's right to natural justice and procedural fairness before a public decision-maker is one of the key components of administrative law.' He goes on to note in Yee. G. (2010), 'The Intersection of Human Rights and Procedural Fairness in Tribunals', *Canadian Diversity* 8.3 (Summer): 42.

Natural justice basically involves the right to be heard and the right to an impartial decision maker. The right to be heard includes the right to know the case against you and the opportunity to respond to that case by presenting evidence and making arguments. This is very flexible and it depends upon such factors as the nature of the tribunal or government department, the governing legislation, the decision that is being made and the impact on the party, and so forth … The second branch of natural justice is the right to an impartial decision maker, which is basically the rule against bias. An adjudicator is disqualified if there is actual bias or a reasonable apprehension of bias

56 Kelley and Trebilcock, *The Making of the Mosaic*, pp. 386, 417. The Immigration and Refugee Board of Canada (IRB) was inaugurated formally on 1 January 1989. Kelley and Trebilcock further note that when a ship carrying 155 Sri Lankan Tamil refugee claimants arrived off the east coast of Canada the previous summer, it did not create the same furore as the arrival of the 174 Sikh refugee claimants. See also Showler, P. (2010), 'Tough talk on boats and refugees', *The Ottawa Citizen*, 20 August, University of Ottawa, Human Rights Research and Education Centre, Refugee Forum, Op-ed. <http://www.cdp-hrc.uottawa.ca/projects/refugee-forum/index.php> (accessed on 23 March 2011); Waldman, L. and Macklin, A. (2010), 'We can't turn away the Tamil ships', *Globe & Mail*, 17 August, University of Ottawa, Human Rights Research and Education Centre, Refugee Forum, Opinion Piece <http://www.cdp-hrc.uottawa.ca/projects/refugee-forum/index.php> (accessed on 23 August 2011)

adjudicated claims for Convention refugee status.[57] A Special Backlog Clearance Program was also put into place to help determine some 115,000 refugee claims that had accumulated under the previous RSD system.[58]

In 1993, the Canadian government introduced Bill-C-86 that transferred the Adjudication Branch, which conducted admissibility inquiries and detention reviews, from Citizenship and Immigration Canada (CIC) to the IRB. This established a separate third division at the IRB, the Adjudication Division.[59] In addition, the IRB issued two sets of Guidelines for its refugee law decision-makers to apply in relevant cases: the Chairperson's Guidelines on Woman Fearing Gender-Related Persecution and the Guidelines on Child Refugee Claimants.[60]

An extensive initiative, that involved an intensive exercise of organizational renewal, took place at the IRB in the mid-1990s, which led to the adoption of a mission statement, a vision statement and guiding set of values.[61] The mission statement of the IRB is 'The Immigration and Refugee Board of Canada is an independent tribunal established by the Parliament of Canada. Our mission, on behalf of Canadians, is to resolve immigration and refugee cases efficiently, fairly and in accordance with the law.'[62]

The IRB also adopted a vision statement that states, 'We will excel in everything we do and will deal simply, quickly and fairly with everyone. Through innovation, we will be a leading edge administrative tribunal and a creative partner in building the future of the Canadian immigration system.'[63]

57 Immigration and Refugee Board of Canada, 'Events that Shaped the Immigration and Refugee Board of Canada' <http://www.irb-cisr.gc.ca/Eng/media/newsnouv/2009/Pages/20.aspx> (accessed on 13 March 2011)

58 Ibid.

59 Ibid.

60 Ibid.

61 Simeon, J.C. (1998), 'Organizational and Administrative Renewal at the Immigration and Refugee Board', in Hoffman, R. et al. (eds), *Public Administration: Canadian Materials*, 3rd edn (North York, Ontario: Captus Press Inc.), pp. 285–99.

62 Immigration and Refugee Board of Canada, 'About the Board', Mission Statement <http://www.irb-cisr.gc.ca/Eng/brdcom/abau/Pages/Index.aspx> (accessed on 12 March 2011) It is perhaps worth noting that initially the Mission Statement of the IRB was 'The Immigration and Refugee Board is an independent tribunal established by the Parliament of Canada. Our mission, on behalf of Canadians, is to make well-reasoned decisions on immigration and refugee matters, efficiently, fairly and in accordance with the law.' See Simeon, 'Organizational and Administrative Renewal at the Immigration and Refugee Board', pp. 286.

63 Immigration and Refugee Board of Canada, 'About the Board', Vision Statement. The organizational renewal exercise undertaken in the mid-1990s also identified five value clusters, including: (1) relevant, responsive and accountable management; (2) open, honest, timely communication; (3) valuing people; (4) working together effectively; (5) excellence in delivery. See Simeon, 'Organizational and Administrative Renewal at the Immigration and Refugee Board', pp. 296.

The values that were articulated in the extensive consultation exercise that was undertaken at the IRB with its staff and management across the country were as follows:

- Excellence in delivery
- Valuing people
- Open, honest, timely communication
- Relevant, responsive and accountable management
- Working together effectively.[64]

The mission, vision and value statements are intended to provide everyone who is employed at the IRB with guidance and direction on how to conduct their work but, in particular, it provides refugee law decision-makers at the Refugee Protection Division with guidance on how to implement refugee determination procedures as described in the *CRDD Handbook*.[65]

On 21 February 2001, the Bill C-11, the Immigration and Refugee Protection Act (IRPA) was introduced in the House of Commons and it received Royal Assent on 1 November 2001 and came into force on 28 June 2002.[66] The Immigration and Refugee Protection Act replaced the 1976 Immigration Act. Under the new Act, the Adjudication Division became the Immigration Division (ID) and the Convention Refugee Determination Division became the Refugee Protection Division (RPD). In addition, the new Act called for the establishment of a Refugee Appeal Division (RAD).[67]

There were a number of important changes to the Canadian refugee determination process under IRPA. Chief among these was the expanded definition of who qualified for refugee protection under IRPA. 'Refugee protection' is conferred on a person when the IRB determines the person to be either a Convention refugee or

64 Immigration and Refugee Board of Canada, 'Mission, Vision and Values of the Immigration and Refugee Board' <http://www.irb-cisr.gc.ca/Eng/brdcom/references/legjur/rpdspr/guide/Pages/hbmission.aspx> (accessed on 13 March 2011)

65 Ibid.; *The CRDD Handbook*, 31 March 1999, is found at Immigration and Refugee Board of Canada <http://www.irb-cisr.gc.ca/eng/brdcom/references/legjur/rpdspr/guide/Pages/index.aspx> (accessed on 13 March 2011)

66 Immigration and Refugee Board of Canada, 'Events that Shaped the Immigration and Refugee Board of Canada' <http://www.irb-cisr.gc.ca/Eng/media/newsnouv/2009/Pages/20.aspx> (accessed on 13 March 2011) It is important to note that the Immigration and Refugee Protection Act was passed after the horrific terrorist attacks that took place in the United States on 11 September 2001. In fact, Bill C-11, IRPA, received a rather quick approval in both the House of Commons and the Senate in response to the global threat of terrorism that was widely perceived as a threat to international peace and security.

67 Ibid. The Sections of the IRPA that dealt with the RAD were never proclaimed by the Canadian Government and, consequently, the RAD was never put into effect at the IRB. It has, however, been reintroduced in a revised format under the Balanced Refugee Reform Act.

a 'person in need of protection'.[68] Section 96 of IRPA defines who is a Convention refugee, in essence, the refugee definition as found in the 1951 Convention relating to the Status of Refugee, Article 1A.[69] A 'person in need of protection' is defined in Section 97 of IRPA as:

> a person in Canada whose removal to their country or countries of nationality or, if they do not have a country of nationality, their country of former habitual residence, would subject them personally
> (a) to a danger, believed on substantial grounds to exist, of torture within the meaning of Article I of the Convention Against Torture, or
> (b) to a risk to their life or to a risk of cruel and unusual treatment or punishment.[70]

There were many other changes to the RSD system that were introduced under IRPA, such as single-member panels for refugee hearings, and the RPD having the authority to refuse a refugee claimant from withdrawing their claim for refugee protection, if in the IRB's opinion the withdrawal of the application for refugee protection would be an 'abuse of process' under its rules.[71]

The Balanced Refugee Reform Act

Bill C-11, An Act to amend the Immigration and Refugee Protection Act. and the Federal Courts Act (Balanced Refugee Reform Act) received Royal Assent on 29 June 2010.[72] This legislation introduced substantial and significant changes to Canada's RSD system and included the following:

- *Members of the Refugee Protection Division* (RPD): Under the Balanced Refugee Reform Act, members of this Division will be public servants hired under the Public Service Employment Act. They will no longer be Governor-in-Council appointees with fixed terms of office.[73]
- *Interview*: Refugee claimants will be required to attend an interview within 15 days of their referral to the IRB with a member of the RPD prior to their

68 Immigration and Refugee Protection Act, S.C. 2001, c. 27, Section 95(1)(b).

69 Ibid., S. 96.

70 Ibid., S. 97(1).

71 Ibid., S. 168(2).

72 Citizenship and Immigration Canada, Backgrounder, 'Bill C-11: The Balanced Refugee Reform Act' <http://www.cic.gc.ca/english/department/media/backgrounders/2010/2010-06-29.asp> (accessed on 5 February 2011)

73 Canadian Council for Refugees (September 2010), 'Changes to the Refugee System – What Bill C-11 Means', p. 2 <http://ccrweb.ca/files/c11_summary.pdf> (accessed on 5 February 2011)

refugee hearing. The refugee claimant will have a right to be represented by counsel at the interview and the date of their refugee hearing will be set at this interview.[74]

- *Appeal*: The Balanced Refugee Reform Act will establish the Refugee Appeal Division (RAD). Some refugee claimants, who are not from a country on a 'designated area or group' safe list, will be allowed to appeal their negative determinations. The minister will also have the right to appeal positive determinations to the RAD.[75]
- *Designated Country of Origin*: Refugee claimants who come from certain designated areas or groups, as identified by the minister under the regulations, will have shorter timelines for their refugee hearings and will not have a right to appeal to the RAD.[76]
- *Manifestly Unfounded*: If the RPD determines that the refugee claim is clearly 'fraudulent', it may declare it 'manifestly unfounded'. These refugee claimants will have the same shorter timelines of those from the designated country of origin list.[77]

These changes to the RSD system in Canada will be implemented over a two-year period, following the Royal Assent to the Balanced Refugee Reform Act, which took place, as noted, on 29 June 2010.[78]

The minority Conservative government that introduced this new legislation asserted that Canada's refugee determination system was broken and that it is 'crippled by an ever-increasing number of new unfounded claims and it can take years to deal with them … [and that this] reduces our ability to help those

74 Ibid.

75 Ibid.

76 Ibid. The Canadian government has changed its position on whether failed refugee claimants from designated countries of origin can seek an appeal at the RAD. None the less, refugee claimants from designated countries of origin, like those determined to be manifestly unfounded, will have shorter timelines for their RAD appeals.

77 Ibid. Refugee claims under the Balanced Refugee Reform Act will take 120 days to complete and those from a designated country of origin will take 30 days to complete ('Timelines', at p. 3).

78 Citizenship and Immigration Canada, Backgrounder, 'Bill C-11: The Balanced Refugee Reform Act' <http://www.cic.gc.ca/english/department/media/backgrounders/2010/2010-06-29.asp> (accessed on 5 February 2011) where it states, 'The new asylum system would come into effect in the next 12 to 18 months, following royal assent.' For further analysis and commentary on Bill C-11, see Showler, P. (2010), 'Proposed Refugee Reforms may be a step towards a Faster, Fairer System', press release, 30 March http://www.maytree.com/wp-content/uploads/2010/03/REFUGEE-FORUM-__Press-Release.pdf (accessed on 20 March 2011). Peter Showler is director of the Refugee Forum, Human Rights Education Centre, University of Ottawa.

who truly need our protection'.[79] The minority Conservative government further contends that it is taking far too long for failed refugee claimants to be removed from Canada. Indeed, they assert that 'On average, this process takes 4.5 years with the removal of some failed claimants taking more than 10 years.'[80]

Daphne Keevil Harrold and Sandra Elgersma, who are with the Social Affairs Division, Parliamentary Information and Research Service, Library of Parliament, in their Legislative Summary of Bill C-11, have noted that 'governments strive to operate a refugee determination system that is fair and that upholds Canada's legal obligations, while at the same time minimizing the risk of abuse and is reasonably efficient and cost-effective to administer.'[81]

They further note that the IRB, the largest administrative tribunal in Canada, faces a number of challenges in handling its high volume of refugee claims. These challenges include the growing number of asylum claims that are being made in industrialized countries around the world, while including at the same time, the increasing complex mixed migratory flows, the resources that are available to the IRB to address its case load, and the minority Conservative government's delay in making appointments and reappointments at the IRB between 2004 and 2008. They point out that all of these factors have contributed to the IRB's backlog of some 63,000 refugee claims.[82]

The refugee advocacy community have raised some significant concerns regarding the Balanced Refugee Reform Act. For instance, one question that has been raised is will the new public servants who will be hired to work in the RPD, to conduct the interviews and refugee hearings, be at a position grade sufficiently high enough to be able to perform these functions properly? Moreover, will these public servants be sufficiently independent from their supervisors to be able to conduct fair hearings?

Another similar concern that has been raised is with the new Governor-in-Council appointees who serve on the RAD. Will the people hired to fill these positions on the RAD be not only independent, but also sufficiently qualified to be able to decide refugee appeals from the RPD? The Canadian Council for Refugees

79 Citizenship and Immigration Canada, 'Frequently Asked Questions: The refugee system, Balanced Refugee Reform, "Why are these changes necessary?"' <http://www.cic.gc.ca/english/information/faq/refugees/ref-reform-faq.asp#changes> (accessed on 5 February 2011)

80 Ibid.

81 Harrold, D.K. and Elgersma, S. (2010), 'Bill C-11: An Act to amend the Immigration and Refugee Protection Act and the Federal Courts Act (Balanced Refugee Reform Act)', Library of Parliament, Legislative Summary, Publication No. 40-3-C11-E, 12 May, p. 1 <http://www2.parl.gc.ca/Content/LOP/LegislativeSummaries/40/3/40-3-c11-e.pdf> (accessed on 5 February 2011)

82 Ibid., p. 2.

(CCR) makes the point that 'RAD members must be adequately qualified to review and correct RPD decisions.'[83]

The CCR has also raised concerns about the timelines that have been set for the RAD, both in filing and perfecting an application before the RAD and whether this would have a detrimental effect on the quality of the decision-making at the RAD.[84]

Concerns have also been raised about the new, shorter, timelines for processing refugee claims under the Balanced Refugee Reform Act. Will the new timelines make it extremely difficult for vulnerable refugee claimants, those who are torture victims, separated minors, women fearing gender-related persecution, including the members of the LGBT (lesbian, gay, bisexual, transgender/transsexual) community, be able to meet the new shorter timelines?

One of the most contentious aspects of the reforms in the Balanced Refugee Reform Act is the designated country of origin. Many advocacy groups, including the CCR, have come out against the designated country-of-origin, or safe country-of-origin, list in principle. They note that any discriminatory treatment of refugee claimants on the basis of their country of origin is patently unfair, such as prohibiting, for instance, refugee claimants from 'designated countries', the so-called 'non-refugee-producing' countries, from a right to appeal to the RAD.[85]

Assessing the Changes to the Refugee Status Determination System in Canada Under the Balanced Refugee Reform Act

The RSD system in Canada, along with the Immigration and Refugee Board of Canada (IRB), are being changed dramatically by the *Balanced Refugee Reform Act*. The current Chairperson of the Immigration and Refugee Board of Canada, Brian Goodman, makes the point that 'As required by the new legislation, the IRB will implement two new divisions: a new Refugee Protection Division and a new Refugee Appeal Division, as well as various new processes in support of these new divisions.'[86]

---

83 Canadian Council for Refugees (2010), 'Changes to the Refugee System – What Bill C-11 Means', September, p. 5 <http://ccrweb.ca/files/c11_summary.pdf> (accessed on 5 February 2011)

84 Ibid.

85 Ibid.

86 Immigration and Refugee Board of Canada, 'Balanced Refugee Reform Act Receives Royal Assent,' Brian Goodman, Chairperson, Immigration and Refugee Board of Canada <http://www.irb-cisr.gc.ca/Eng/media/newsnouv/2010/Pages/royal.aspx> (accessed on 17 March 2011) As noted previously, the Canadian government has changed this to allow refugee claimants from a designated country of origin to file an appeal to the RAD. Sadly, Brian Goodman passed away suddenly on 18 June 2013, one day before his formal retirement as the IRB Chairperson. See Immigration and Refugee Board of Canada, 'Chairperson's Passing,' http://www.irb-cisr.gc.ca/Eng/media/newsnouv/Pages/

As noted above, the members of the new Refugee Protection Division (RPD) will be permanent civil servants as opposed to Governor-in-Council appointees. The members of the Refugee Appeal Division (RAD) will remain Governor-in-Council appointees with fixed terms of office. In essence, then, the first-instance decision maker at the IRB will be an indeterminate public servant, while the second-instance decision maker at the IRB will be a Governor-in-Council determinate appointee whose selection is not necessarily based exclusively on merit or the fitness to do the job. Partisan considerations will inevitably be factored in to the selection process for these Governor-in-Council positions.

On the question of whether the RPD public-service decision makers will be truly independent, the Canadian government has responded by stating the following:

> Yes. These decision makers will be hired by the IRB, which is an independent organization. Both the institution of the IRB and individual decision makers are fully independent.
>
> In addition, any IRB research used to assist its decision makers is not affected or influenced by immigration or visa policies, which are CIC's responsibility.[87]

However, the answer to this question does not fully address the concerns that have been raised with respect to the independence of the new public-service RPD decision makers. The concerns expressed are whether the new RPD public-servant positions will be at the appropriate position grade, so that the persons filling these refugee law decision-making positions will have the appropriate educational attainment and skill sets necessary to be able to make sound refugee law decisions on claims to refugee protection. The institutional independence of the IRB as a quasi-judicial administrative tribunal is not at issue here. It is, rather, whether the new public-service positions at the RPD are at the appropriate position grade to perform the job function required.

A related concern is whether these new RPD public-service decision-makers' positions are truly independent, in spite of the fact they will be reporting directly to their public-service supervisors? Indeed, can public servants ever be truly independent in their job functions, when they are bound by the dictates of a chain of command, with superior and subordinate relationships, within a bureaucratic hierarchy? This will be contingent undoubtedly on the character and abilities of

---

bg.aspx. (accessed on 1 July 2013). For the Minister of Citizenship, Immigration and Multiculturalism, Jason Kenny's statement on the passing of Brian Goodman, Chairperson of the Immigration and Refugee Board of Canada on 19 June 2013, see http://www.cic.gc.ca/english/department/media/statements/2013/2013-06-19.asp. (accessed on 1 July 2013). As of the publication of this chapter, the Acting Chairperson of the IRB was Ken Sandhu, Deputy Chairperson of the Refugee Appeal Division.

87 Citizenship and Immigration Canada, 'Frequently asked questions, The refugee system, Balanced Refugee Reform'.

the persons selected to fill these key first-instance RPD decision-making roles. Moreover, it will also be contingent on the degree of discretion that these RPD decision makers will have in being able to render their decisions. In fairness, there does not appear to be anything in the Balanced Refugee Reform Act that would preclude the RPD decision makers from being independent decision makers in the true 'judicial' sense of the term.[88]

One of the main objectives of the Balanced Refugee Reform Act is to reduce the processing times for refugee claimants, especially for those who are truly in need of international protection. The minority Conservative government has identified this as the most salient issue of concern.

Currently, a large number of asylum claims, including those from major source countries, are determined to be unfounded at the Immigration and Refugee Board (IRB). This has placed pressures on Canada's asylum system, leading to long wait-times and contributing to a significant backlog of claims. As a result, individuals in genuine need of protection currently wait about 20 months or more for a protection decision and individuals not in need of protection end up staying in Canada for long periods of time. In fact, failed claimants have access to multiple layers of recourse, resulting in delays in removal from Canada. It takes, on average, four-and-a-half years from the initial claim until the removal of a failed asylum claimant, and in some cases ten years or longer. The result is that long wait-times, with access to work permits, social services and welfare, may attract persons who are not in need of protection to make asylum claims in order to live and work in Canada for years.[89]

The manner in which this was addressed in the *Balanced Refugee Reform Act* was to give the Minister of Citizenship, Immigration and Multiculturalism 'the authority to set processing time limits in the Regulations and to designate countries, parts of countries or classes of nationals of countries that do not normally produce refugees, for the purposes of further expediting the processing of claims'.[90] With

---

88 Peter Showler has taken the view that 'It is not necessarily a bad thing to have the Public Service making the first-level decision. There is a danger that they will import departmental biases into their decision making. But, they will be under the management of the IRB, an independent body': Showler, 'Proposed Refugee Reforms may be a step towards a Faster, Fairer System'. It is important to point that Peter Showler is, however, strongly opposed to the Governor-in-Council appointment process that he considers to be 'secretive and susceptible to political interference'. He also considers it to be inefficient.

89 'Regulations Amending the Immigration and Refugee Protection Regulations, Statutory authority, Immigration and Refugee Protection Act, Sponsoring department', Department of Citizenship and Immigration, Regulatory Impact Analysis Statement, *Canada Gazette* 145.12 <http://www.gazette.gc.ca/rp-pr/p1/2011/2011-03-19/html/reg1-eng.html (accessed on 18 March 2011)

90 Ibid. The rationale for a designated countries of origin list, according to the Minority Conservative Government, is as follows:

The purpose of the Designated Countries of Origin (DCO) policy, the faster processing timelines and the identification of manifestly unfounded claims is to reduce pressure on

respect to setting processing times, the minister will have the authority to regulate time limits. These time limits have been set as follows:

> No earlier than 15 days after having their asylum claim referred to the IRB, claimants will be interviewed by a public servant. Interviews will occur sooner only if the claimant agrees;
> During this interview, information on claims will be gathered and hearings scheduled;
> A different public servant at the IRB will conduct the hearing within 90 days in most cases;
> For claimants from designated countries of origin hearings will occur within 60 days.[91]

It is evident that these new time limits should reduce the overall processing times of the refugee status determination system within the Refugee Protection Division of the IRB. However, it is reasonable to expect that most failed refugee claimants will appeal their failed claims to the RAD. This will require additional processing time to conclude. Accordingly, it remains to be seen whether the total processing time for refugee claimants will be reduced significantly given this two-tiered decision-making process with multiple interviews/hearings, potentially three-tiered if an interview is also conducted at the RAD.

The designated countries-of-origin list or the safe country-of-origin list is perhaps one of the most controversial reform measures under the Balanced Refugee Reform Act. Essentially, what it seeks to do is to establish which countries in the world are non-refugee-producing countries. As already noted above, the Canadian Council for Refugees has come out strongly against a designated countries-of-origin policy. The CCR's position is quite clear, 'the CCR is completely opposed on principle to discriminatory treatment based on country of origin.'[92] The minority Conservative government, on the other hand, has taken the following position with respect to the designated countries of origin:

> Designated countries of origin will include countries that do not normally produce refugees, that have a robust human rights record and offer strong state

---

Canada's asylum system by deterring unfounded claims, thus contributing to a system that is able to provide faster decisions to those who are in need of protection.

91 Citizenship and Immigration Canada, 'Changes to the Immigration and Refugee Board of Canada (IRB)' http://www.cic.gc.ca/english/refugees/reform-irb.asp (accessed on 18 March 2011)

92 Canadian Council for Refugees (2011), 'Changes to the Refugee System – What C-11 Means' (September) <http://ccrweb.ca/files/c11_summary.pdf>, p. 5 (accessed on 18 March 2011)

> protection. States with strong democratic, judicial and accountability systems are likely to provide the necessary protection to their citizens.[93]

If a refugee claimant, from a designated country of origin, receives a negative decision or their claim for refugee protection is denied, then, they will have an opportunity for an expedited appeal process before the Refugee Appeal Division.[94] This is a major change from the minority Conservative government's original position with respect as to whether rejected refugee claimants from designated countries of origin should be denied an appeal to the new Refugee Appeal Division.[95] The minority Conservative government has calculated that there would be substantial savings through the application of a designated country-of-origin policy not unlike that of the United Kingdom.

For the purposes of the cost-benefit analysis, it has been assumed that designations would result in a 57 per cent decline in the number of claims received from designated countries, over the 12 months following a designation. This assumption is based on the experience of the UK, following designations made under their non-suspensive appeal (NSA) policy. While recognizing the imperfect nature of any international asylum trend comparisons, the UK's experience provides a useful and reasonable proxy.[96]

Another major criticism is that the timelines planned for completing the RSD process is really difficult and unfair for particular types of refugee claimants. The overall objective in processing refugee-status determination claims in the Balanced Refugee Reform Act is to have them completed within one year.[97] Clearly, this

93 Citizenship and Immigration Canada, 'Designated Countries' <http://www.cic.gc.ca/english/refugees/reform-safe.asp> (accessed on 18 March 2011)

94 Ibid.

95 Ibid. In fact, the Canadian government asserts that during its consultation process with stakeholders on the Regulations attendant to the Balanced Refugee Reform Act, it has affected the following changes. Criticism focused notably on the lack of clarity regarding the criteria for designation, the extent of ministerial discretion to select countries for designation, and the creation of a 'two-tiered' system under the original proposal, which would have denied access to the RAD for DCO claimants. Amendments to Bill C-11 addressed both of these concerns by introducing criteria into the legislation and by providing access to the RAD for all claimants. See, 'Regulations Amending the Immigration and Refugee Protection Regulations …', *Canada Gazette* 145.12 (19 March 2011) – see n. 90 above.

96 Ibid. Indeed, the government has calculated the following savings over a ten-year period: 'A full cost-benefit analysis has been completed, and indicates that the proposed regulatory amendments are expected to have a positive net impact on each affected party and would result in a net, quantifiable and monetizable benefit for all parties of $91.4M over the 10-year study horizon (2011–2020).'

97 Canadian Council for Refugees (2011), 'Changes to the Refugee System – What C-11 Means' (September) <http://ccrweb.ca/files/c11_summary.pdf>, p. 3 (accessed on 19 March 2011)

would be a substantial change over the current average RSD processing time at the IRB of 20 months. However, it is anticipated that with this new RSD process and timelines, the average processing time at the IRB would drop to six months.[98] None the less, the CCR has taken the position that the timelines outlined for the Refugee Appeal Division of 15 days to file and perfect an application is totally unworkable.[99] In fact, the CCR states:

> This timeline is completely unworkable. In most cases, it would be impossible to complete a meaningful application within 15 days, especially for vulnerable claimants. Timelines must be at least those for judicial review: 15 days to file the application, 30 days to perfect (complete) it.[100]

The timetable of 120 days that has been presented for the RAD to make its decision on a non-designated country-of-origin claim, and 30 days for a designated country-of-origin claim and manifestly unfounded claims is seen by the CCR to be a positive development and something that ought to be considered for immigration decisions such as family reunification and humanitarian and compassionate applications.[101] However, the general note of caution here is that it would be contingent on the Canadian government appointing sufficient RAD decision makers to be able to deal with the volume of appeals that it will be bound to get.[102]

Establishing realistic timelines based on the nature of the claim to refugee protection and its appeal within the IRB is undoubtedly a sensible step forward. However, the timelines must be realistic and practicably attainable, from both the perspective of the key institutional actors in the process, as well as the refugee law practitioners who practice before the IRB and the courts and refugee claimants themselves. As the CCR has noted, if the Canadian government is not going to appoint a sufficient number of qualified members to the RAD then it will never be able to achieve its own time limits. Equally, if there are an insufficient number of qualified legal counsels, lawyers and/or immigration consultants, available to represent refugee claimants then it would be difficult, if not impossible to meet these timelines. Likewise, if refugee claimants are not able to comply, despite their 'good faith' intentions, with these timelines then they will not likely be met. Ensuring that all the institutional actors and their participants are properly resourced and creating the appropriate conditions to ensure that everyone is

98 'Regulations Amending the Immigration and Refugee Protection Regulations …', *Canada Gazette* 145.12 (19 March 2011) – see n. 90 above.

99 Ibid., p. 5.

100 Ibid.

101 Ibid.

102 Ibid. On the concern of the provision of adequate resources for the RSD system, see Creskey, J. (2010), 'Too early for congratulations on refugee reforms', *Embassy*, 16 June <http://www.embassymag.ca/page/view/creskey-06-16-2010> (accessed 20 March 2011)

working in unison to try to achieve these timelines is absolutely essential. Whether this will likely come about is an open question.

The pressure for the Canadian government to change the timelines, for justifiable reasons, will inevitably lead to the Canadian government extending the timelines as recommended by the CCR. The extension of the proposed timelines for processing refugee claims at the RPD and refugee appeals at the RAD will inevitably increase the projected processing times under the Balanced Refugee Reform Act. Again, this does not appear to augur well for the Canadian government's ambitions to reducing refugee claim-processing times significantly.

The minority Conservative government has argued that the Balanced Refugee Reform Act will not limit the access to Canada's RSD system and points out that 'all eligible asylum claimants continue to be entitled to a fair hearing before an independent decision maker.'[103] Moreover, they also go on to state that 'These new measures will strengthen our system and our humanitarian tradition of helping those in need of protection while continuing to exceed international and legal domestic obligations.'[104]

It is also important to indicate that three years after the Balanced Refugee Reform Act is implemented, there will be a full review of how the new RSD system is operating, including the new Regulations, and its impact on achieving its stated objectives.[105]

Conclusions

Although Canada is perhaps one of the staunchest supporters of the United Nations and its international treaty system of human rights instruments, it did not accede to the 1951 Convention and its 1967 Protocol until 1969 and only after the United

103 Citizenship and Immigration Canada, 'Frequently asked questions, The refugee system, Balanced Refugee Reform' (accessed on 19 March 2011)

104 Ibid. In addition, the Canadian government estimates that it will achieve a substantial overall savings from implementing the Balanced Refugee Reform Act. Overall, the Balanced Refugee Reform Act will result in savings estimated at $1.2B (present value [PV]) [or $310M (PV) in net savings] over 10 years, largely as a result of failed claimants spending less time in Canada with access to welfare and social services, due to faster processing and faster removals. The proposed regulatory amendments would contribute to the Balanced Refugee Reform Act objective of creating a faster and fairer asylum system that is less open to abuse: 'Regulations Amending the Immigration and Refugee Protection Regulations …', *Canada Gazette* 145.12 (19 March 2011) – see n. 90 above.

105 Ibid. The overall objectives of the Balanced Refugee Reform Act include: faster decisions on asylum claims, faster removals for failed claimants, and reduced abuse of Canada's asylum system. Citizenship and Immigration Canada, 'Designated Countries' – see n. 94 above.

States had acceded to the 1967 Protocol.[106] A historical overview and analysis of the accession of States Parties to these seminal international refugee rights instruments reveals that it took more than 40 years before half the current members of the United Nations ratified these international instruments. Indeed, the bulk of the States Parties that acceded to these international instruments did so during the 1960s, with the decolonization of Africa, the liberation of former European colonies and the emergence of new African States, and during the 1990s, with the fall of the Soviet Union and the Warsaw Pact and the collapse of the Socialist Federal Republic of Yugoslavia and Czechoslovakia. The disintegration of the European colonial empire in Africa and the Communist empire in Eastern Europe and Asia gave an impetus to new States not only to become members of the United Nations, but States Parties to the 1951 Convention and its 1967 Protocol.

Canada has deep 'humanitarian' roots, traditions and instincts that pre-date Confederation and the founding of the 'Dominion of Canada' in 1867. Indeed, it was the first British colony to abolish the slave trade and slavery, when it was constituted as Upper Canada, formed largely by United Empire Loyalists or those who were expelled or otherwise forcibly displaced from the American Colonies for their loyalty and support of the British Crown rather than the American Revolution.[107] However, this is not to say that after Confederation it did not adopt racist and exclusionary immigration policies that were in place from the mid-nineteenth century to the mid-twentieth century. Fortunately, the Canadian government has acknowledged as much and has undertaken some measures of redress and efforts to ensure that these offensive and atrocious injustices are never forgotten or repeated.

In the second half of the twentieth century, Canada accepted successive waves of refugees from all parts of the world. The six most prominent and perhaps well-known included: 37,000 Hungarian refugees who fled Hungary in 1956 due to the Soviet Union's suppression of the Hungarian Revolution; the American 'draft evaders' who came to Canada to avoid serving in the US military during the Vietnam War from 1955 to 1975; the 11,000 Czech refugees who fled Czechoslovakia in 1968 when the 'Prague Spring' was crushed by the Warsaw Pact; 7,000 Ugandan Asians who were forced into exile by dictator Idi Amin's racists policies; 7,000 Chileans fleeing the oppressive post-military coup regime of General Augusto Pinochet, and, the 77,000 Indo-Chinese 'boat people' who fled the Communist-dominated countries of South East Asia from 1975 to 1981. There were many

---

106 The United States acceded to the 1967 Protocol Relating to the Status of Refugees on 1 November 1968. See UNHCR RefWorld, 'International Instruments, Asylum, Protocol relating to the Status of Refugees of 31st January 1967' <http://www.asylumlaw.org/docs/international/NewYork1967.pdf> (accessed on 19 March 2011).

107 Wilson, 'Loyalists', *The Canadian Encyclopedia* – see n. 27 above; Winks, 'The Underground Railroad' – see n. 10 above. See also n. 27 about on the Legislature of Upper Canada's 1793 Act to Prevent the further Introduction of Slaves and to limit the Term of Contracts for Servitude within this Province.

other groups as well, such as the 200 Tibetans admitted after China's occupation of Tibet in 1970–71.[108]

Canada's first formal RSD system was implemented under the 1976 Immigration Act. However, the basis of Canada's present RSD system is the Supreme Court of Canada's decision of April 4, 1985, the *Singh* decision.[109] The Supreme Court found that the word 'everyone' in Section 7 of the Canadian Charter of Rights and Freedoms means every person on Canadian soil, including, of course, refugee claimants. It followed then that refugee claimants were entitled to an oral hearing, in accordance with the principles of fundamental justice and international law, to adjudicate their claims to refugee protection. Hence, the *Singh* decision stands for the principle that refugee claimants are entitled to an RSD process that provides 'an adequate opportunity to state his[/her] case and to know the case he[/she] has to meet.'[110]

Refugee Rights Day is celebrated each year in Canada on 4 April, in commemoration of the Supreme Court of Canada's ruling in the famous *Singh* case.[111]

The Immigration and Refugee Board of Canada was established in 1989.[112] It is the largest independent administrative or quasi-judicial tribunal in Canada.[113] The IRB has evolved over time and is governed by the Immigration and Refugee Protection Act since it came into force in 2002. One of the major challenges confronting the IRB, at present, is the implementation of the Balanced Refugee Reform Act that came into force in 2010. The IRB is in the midst of establishing a new Refugee Appeal Division and revamping its Refugee Protection Division. Another major reform to the RSD process that will have a major impact on the work of the IRB and its case management system is the designated countries-of-origin or safe countries-of-origin policy. Refugee claimants who come from a designated country, parts of countries, or classes of nationals of countries that are designated as safe will be put on a different timeline for rendering a decision than refugee claimants who do not come from one of these designated countries

108 Kelley and Trebilcock, *The Making of the Mosaic*, p. 347.

109 *Singh v. Minister of Employment and Immigration* [1985] 1 S.C.R. 177.

110 Ibid., para. 58. (emphasis added)

111 Beaudoin, G.A., 'Singh Case', *The Canadian Encyclopedia* <http://www.thecanadianencyclopedia.com/index.cfm?PgNm=TCE&Params=A1ARTA0007420>' (accessed on 20 March 2011) The Canadian Council of Refugees, Refugee Rights Day, 'The 25th Anniversary of the Singh Decision' <http://ccrweb.ca/RRDay.htm> (accessed on 20 March 2011)

112 Kelley and Trebilcock, *The Making of the Mosaic*, pp. 415–16. Bill C-55, the Refugee Reform Bill, that amended the 1976 Immigration Act was passed in June 1988 and came into force in January 1989, replacing the Immigration Appeal Board with the Immigration and Refugee Board of Canada.

113 Immigration and Refugee Board of Canada, 'About the Board' – see n.63 above.

of origin or safe countries of origin, parts of countries, or classes of nationals of countries.[114]

Although the Balanced Refugee Reform Act has been praised as an important step forward, the foremost concerns remain with the designated countries-of-origin policy and the timelines that have been suggested for the completion of applications for refugee protection. Indeed, two well-known legal counsels and refugee law advocates have already predicted that some of the provisions of the Balanced Refugee Reform Act will be challenged in the courts.

The timeframes proposed by the Minister are unrealistic and will place immense pressure on the administrative structures of the IRB. In its current form, the Bill (C-11, Balanced Refugee Reform Act) will lead to many legal challenges under the Charter.[115]

Legal challenges on the designated countries-of-origin policy and the timelines set out in the new RSD process under the Balanced Refugee Reform Act are undoubtedly inevitable. But, as the 1985 decision of the Supreme Court of Canada in *Singh* affirmed, no government will ever be able to justify a refugee determination system that seeks to process refugee claims faster and more efficiently that neglects the rights of refugees under the Canadian Charter of Rights and Freedoms and is not premised on the principles of natural justice, procedural fairness and the constitutional principles of fundamental justice. Our universal and essential human rights and freedoms are not subject to the whims of administrative convenience. Whether the balance that the Balanced Refugee Reform Act seeks to achieve between constitutional principle of 'fundamental justice' and a 'faster,' 'fairer' and more 'efficient' and 'effective' RSD system will be determined, in the end and as always, by Canadian courts, and ultimately the Supreme Court of Canada.

Postscript

Canada held its 41st general federal election on 2 May 2011, and the Conservative Party won a clear majority of the seats in the House of Commons and, consequently, formed a majority government under Prime Minister, Stephen Harper.[116] One of the first actions of the new majority Conservative government was to introduce

---

114 'Regulations Amending the Immigration and Refugee Protection Regulations …', *Canada Gazette* 145.12 (19 March 2011) – see n.90 above.

115 Waldman, L. and Showler, P. (2010), 'Joint Statement by Lorne Waldman and Peter Showler', 5 May, Publications, Op-Eds <http://www.cdp-hrc.uottawa.ca/projects/refugee-forum/publications/index.php> (accessed on 20 March 2011)

116 See 'Elections, 2011: Canadian Election Results' <http://www.sfu.ca/~aheard/elections/results.html> (accessed on 9 August 2012). The last majority government elected to the Parliament of Canada was in 2000 when then Prime Minister Jean Chrétien, leader of the Liberal Party, won his third majority government in a row.

new legislation, Bill C-31, Protecting Canada's Immigration System Act.[117] The Minister of Citizenship, Immigration and Multiculturalism, Jason Kenny, justified this new legislation in the following terms:

> To be blunt: Canada's asylum system is broken. That's why Parliament passed the *Balanced Refugee Reform Act* in 2010. The *Act* contains long-needed improvements that will result in faster protection for real refugees and quicker removal of bogus refugee claimants. That *Act* went a long way toward addressing problems in our system. But it's become clear that there are still some gaps, and that further reforms are needed. We need stronger measures that are closer to the original bill that we tabled back in March of 2010.[118]

Citizenship, Immigration and Multiculturalism Minister Kenny went on to assert that

> We will speed up processing of refugee claims. In particular, the refugee claimants from democratic rights-respecting countries, such as those in the EU, will be processed in about 45 days, compared to more than 1,000 days under the current system, or about 171 days under the reforms adopted in 2010. Claimants from designated countries of origin will also have their claims heard sooner and will not have access to the new Refugee Appeal Division that we are creating.[119]

Minister Kenny also pointed out that Bill C-31 would allow for the implementation of biometric screening that would begin sometime in 2013 and went on to note:

> And I should just highlight that we have seen many cases of foreign criminals arrested, convicted and deported, who came back to Canada using fake papers. Under the biometric visa system, this will effectively be virtually impossible. We'll be able to identify them when they come back using fake papers. It will substantially improve immigration security and ensure as well that deported failed refugee claimants don't return on fake papers.[120]

However, Bill C-31 was immediately denounced by its critics. Indeed, a new coalition was formed that strongly opposed and spoke out against the new majority Conservative government's reintroduction of legislation that had lapsed

---

117 Speaking Notes for the Honorable Jason Kenny, PC, MP, Minister of Citizenship, Immigration and Multiculturalism, at a news conference following the tabling of Bill C-31, Protecting Canada's Immigration System Act, Ottawa, 16 February 2012 <http://www.cic.gc.ca/english/department/media/speeches/2012/2012-02-16.asp> (accessed on 9 August 2012)

118 Ibid.

119 Ibid.

120 Ibid.

under the previous Parliament as Bill C-4 and C-49, Preventing Human Smugglers From Abusing Canada's Immigration Systems Act. The new coalition that formed opposing Bill C-31 was called the Justice for Refugees and Immigrants Coalition, and it comprised Amnesty International (AI), the Canadian Association of Refugee Lawyers (CARL), the Canadian Civil Liberties Association (CCLA), and the Canadian Council for Refugees (CCR). This new coalition of powerful NGOs stated that Bill C-31 was not only bad policy but that it was 'unconstitutional, undermines our humanitarian traditions, and violates our international obligations'.[121]

The Justice for Refugees and Immigrants Coalition denounced Bill C-31 on the following six grounds.

1. Hasty timelines deny refugees a fair chance to prove their claims.
2. The revised process for designating certain countries as 'safe' eliminates an expert, independent advisory body that would have guarded against countries being designated on the basis of erroneous or irrelevant political, trade and other considerations.
3. The Bill gives the Ministers of Citizenship and Immigration, and Public Safety and Emergency Preparedness, extensive powers to imprison refugee claimants, to deny refugees the ability to reunite with family members and to strip refugees of secure legal status. Bill C-31 also minimizes the opportunity for judicial oversight of the exercise of these extraordinary powers.
4. The Bill makes permanent residence status for resettled and in-land refugees precarious and insecure, placing hundreds of thousands of refugees who have resettled in Canada at risk of deportation.
5. The Minister's references to 'bogus' claims are an egregious misrepresentation.
6. Canada's humanitarian safety net is gravely weakened.[122]

Accordingly, the Justice for Refugees and Immigrants Coalition called for nothing less than the withdrawal of Bill C-31.[123]

The new coalition and other critics undertook a vigorous public campaign against Bill C-31. This did produce some movement on the majority Conservative government's part when it announced on 9 May 2012, that it was prepared to accept a series of amendments to Bill C-31 that included: limiting the application of the cessation of permanent residence status; the 12-month bar of failed refugee claimants applying for Pre-Removal Risk Assessment (PRRA) would be implemented immediately after Bill C-31 receives Royal Assent; the bar to

121 Canadian Council for Refugees, 'Protect Refugees from Bill C-31: Joint Statement' <http://ccrweb.ca/en/protect-refugees-c31-statement> (accessed on 9 August 2012).

122 Ibid.

123 Ibid.

a PRRA for those who receive a negative decision from the Immigration and Refugee Board of Canada, or who withdrew or abandoned their refugee claim or who received a negative decision on their PRRA and who come from a designated country of origin would increase from 12 to 36 months; and, for those who arrive in Canada as part of a designated irregular arrival and subject to mandatory detention, they will now receive a first detention review within 14 days and subsequent detention reviews every 180 days thereafter.[124] However, this did not placate the new coalition and other critics of Bill C-31.[125]

Despite intense opposition both inside and outside Parliament, the new majority Conservative government passed the Bill C-31 and it received Royal Assent on 28 June 2012.[126] The Protecting Canada's Immigration System Act will have a significant impact on Canada's refugee status determination system. However, it will not go unchallenged in Canada's courts and most probably through each instance of the judiciary to the Supreme Court of Canada.

124 Press release: 'Amendments to the Protecting of Canada's Immigration Act, Ottawa, May 9, 2012 – Minister of Citizenship, Immigration, and Multiculturalism Jason Kenney today announced that the Government is proposing amendments to Bill C-31, the Protecting Canada's Immigration System Act' <http://www.cic.gc.ca/english/department/media/releases/2012/2012-05-09.asp> (accessed on 9 August 2012).

125 Levitz, S. (2012), 'Bill C-31: Refugee Legislation Amended As Conservatives Bow to Pressure', *Huffington Post*, 'Politics', 'Canada', posted 9 April 2012 <http://www.huffingtonpost.ca/2012/05/09/bill-c31-refugee-canada-jason-kenney_n_1503262.html> (accessed on 9 August 2012).

126 Citizenship and Immigration Canada, 'Protecting Canada's Immigration System' <http://www.cic.gc.ca/english/refugees/reform.asp> (accessed on 9 August 2012).

Chapter 8
Afterword

When Worship ends tyranny begins.[1]

New institutional architecture is needed at international level for *enlightened policies*. (original emphasis)

Jagdish Bhagwati[2]

If we liken the movement by humans since they were first on earth to the tides of the oceans, we can see that governments can no more arrest that human movement than Cnut could turn back the tide. Perhaps on this all are agreed: but that is perhaps all we can agree upon when it comes to deciding when and how to control such movement[3]. In this final chapter, we try to draw together the attempts at control in one area – the appeal against decisions by the executive, which have been made to exercise such control.

Readers who are either still involved with immigration, or more recently retired than the author, will be able to see the changes and reflect on whether those changes have been for the better, but overall things seem not to have improved if the report in *The Times* on 22 November 2012 is anything to go by: 'Border Agency sinking under a backlog as 100,000 letters are left unopened!' If things have not changed, perhaps some of what is gathered together in what follows may indicate where something is yet to be tackled[4].

History up to the end of the nineteenth century gives some idea of how and why people move and reveals the beginnings of methods of control. The twentieth and the present centuries have seen how methods of control have developed and a quasi-judicial administrative tribunal emerged to review decisions by the executive in the UK, together with the interrelationship between the migrant and society. This chapter looks at six particular aspects of those workings on which an assessment of the effectiveness of the present method of review of an adverse immigration decision depends in the UK. Suggestions have varied from scrapping the review

1 Introduction in The Message to Revelation Peterson EH '*If Worship is neglected or perverted our communities fall into chaos or under tyranny.*' 2002 Navpress USA

2 Bhagwati, J. (2004), *In Defense of Globalisation* (Oxford: Oxford University Press).

3 A clear lesson from the Blair decade would seem to be that migration cannot be managed solely through tighter controls and tougher enforcement.

4 2013 seems yet worse. *Immigration backlog of 500,000 cases will take 37 years to clear, say MP.s* Parliamentary watchdog warns Home Office that axed UK Border Agency needs more than just rebranding http://www.guardian.co.uk/uk-news/2013/jul/13/immigration-backlog-37-years-clear#start-of-comments.

method to modifying what is there already: hopefully enough is described here to allow the readers to judge themselves.

These six issues or threads have been broken down into two main groups, the first group comprises matters which affect how the immigration judges do their job. Matters such as, first, government policies and legislation, as well as ministerial management of the tribunal and media activities, all of which judges must live with, and secondly, those matters upon which the judges have it in their own hands to make changes where they think necessary. Examples of these are the judges' own approach and attitudes, the nature of the hearing process itself, and the manner in which the tribunal handles its own internal administration.

Since law and politics are intertwined, the independence of the immigration judge is less than absolute. Government will inevitably try to attain the outcome it desires by any direct or indirect means, as we have seen.[5] Even though the judge has no direct influence on such extraneous forces, the manner in which he or she fulfils the role of judge may have some opposing or confirming influence. There is a constant call for critical self-examination of the response to be adopted in each case.

The Countess of Mar spent about 20 years as a lay member of the IAT, and later the AIT. Her speech in a debate in the House of Lords on the Immigration Asylum and Nationality Bill 2006 (during which she announced her resignation from the Tribunal), which followed closely on the heels of the last Act in 2004 (and the one before in 2002) was brutally frank; she condemned the Home Office's approach on the manner in which it handled the appellate system, in particular, and immigration as a whole.[6]

What she said is a comprehensive survey of both some of the major issues to be addressed in a fair and economically run system and a condemnation of the system which existed when she resigned, and is worth quoting in full:

> This Government have done much to weed out the solicitors' firms and other advisory agencies that were obviously exploiting asylum seekers, other would-be immigrants and the British taxpayer. Most of those who remain try to provide an acceptable service given the financial and time constraints imposed on them by the law and the handicaps that are the hallmarks of an inefficient bureaucracy. The usually excellent Home Office presenting officers are also handicapped—by the late service of papers, lost files, incomplete bundles and insufficient time in which to absorb the details of a case. This is no way to administer justice fairly. It is not fair to the appellant or to the British citizen who must foot the bill. It leads to appeals, which clog up the courts and create further delays. The longer an asylum seeker or other immigrant remains in the appeal pipeline, the more embedded they get into the British way of life and, strangely enough, the

5 Recall the attempts to remove or emasculate the remedy of judicial review in 2004: Rawlings, R. (2005), 'Review, Revenge and Retreat', *Modern Law Review* 68.3: 378.

6 HL Deb 19.7.06 col 1306 http://www.publications.parliament.uk/pa/ld199697/ldhansrd/pdvn/lds06/text/60719-0005.htm (last accessed on 3 July 2013). See Appendix 6.

> more right they think that they have to stay here. Whatever happened to firm, fast and fair?

Ideally, perhaps, we should put the whole of the current system in the bin and start again, with a totally new, streamlined department using experienced personnel. This, however, is extremely unlikely, although there is no reason why discussion with the experienced people cannot be carried out and – who knows? – solutions may surface. An independent review is long overdue.[7] There is constant frustration at the lack of both efficiency and transparency in case management, felt deeply by immigration lawyers, judges and the public. However, one suspects it was not this element of concern which was in Mr Reid's mind when he told the Home Affairs Select Committee in 2006 that his department was 'not fit for purpose', and then instigating a review of the IND which finally led to its separation in April 2007 into the Border and Immigration Agency.

Notwithstanding that there are many calls on governments for priority for action in immigration, none seems ever to have had the hoped-for result. Where a country experiences a reduction in asylum-seekers it must be remembered that whilst global figures suggest a downward trend in refugees they show rise in the numbers of IDPs, who provide a large potential pool for continued flows of those seeking asylum – when they can leave their own countries[8]. Despite this, government's view seems very clear, that the UK system maintains the right balance between the legitimate demands of the immigrant and the state. If that is the case, then one wonders why it needs to be changed so often.

There is room for debate about what is the most ideal appeal structure, but there is none about time, effort and money which has been spent on the issue. Not everyone will agree, however, that it has been spent on the right things, at the right times, nor that the results have been worth the expenditure. Some examples have emerged in the course of earlier pages where it is clear that the money might have been spent more wisely and effectively, by, for example, achieving a reliable first decision by the Home Office or being less lavish with appeals when it lost – especially when the Home Office did not appear at the first hearing. Financial costs of refugee determination systems are high, so high that the cost must be justified by results. This is what the Forced Migration Studies Programme in South Africa had to say about that country's system:

---

7 Hansard, House of Lords, 14 December 2006, col. 1688-90 et seq. <http://www.publications.parliament.uk, Sarah Rapson Interim Director UK Visas and Immigration Section told the Commons Home Affairs Select Committee on 11 June 2013 'Is it ever going to be fixed? I don't think so' http://www.publications.parliament.uk/pa/cm201314/cmselect/cmhaff/uc232-i/uc23201.htm (accessed on 9 July 2013)

8 See Care, G. (2012), 'Disowned in their Own Land: The Courts and Protection of the Internally Displaced Person', *Ashgate Research Companion to Migration Law, Theory and Policy*, Chapter 12, esp p. 258 n 4

> A system that fails to protect those most in need of refuge cannot adequately be characterized as a refugee protection framework … Yet, significant resources continue to be devoted to the status determination process, without any real recognition of its administrative failures. As a result, South Africa is devoting scarce resources to maintaining a refugee system that is, at best, functioning as a perfunctory immigration control mechanism – without fulfilling any of its protective purposes, and without adhering to the administrative procedures required by law.[9]

How governments think about controlling the influx of asylum-seekers should depend more heavily on whether to conceptualize the problem as primarily one of preventing abuse (by economic migrants, for example) or of restricting the number of successful claimants (whether among people with potentially strong claims or not). The legislation and its frequency, looked at in earlier pages would suggest each government, in shooting terms, is 'browning the covey', that is, firing wild in the hope of hitting something – a practice calculated to wound and not to kill.

Some examples of mechanisms, which have been tried and do not attempt to distinguish between genuine refugees and those with no legitimate (moral) claim are:

- 'streamlined determinations which will quickly identify those who do not qualify as refugees so they can be sent home',
- 'a quick and accurate disposition of cases which will reduce the incentives for those with weak claims to apply' yet again,
- 'when procedures are tightened, it will limit the number of people who successfully claim asylum'.

Whilst governments may desire a more restrictive interpretation of the Convention's definition and use procedural mechanisms to achieve this desire, such mechanisms clearly conflict with the principle that each case should be judged solely on its own merits. The first mechanism is simply the expression of a wish, a laudable aim which in itself judges aspire to, but then having done so, they see that their efforts are wasted when the government does not act on the decision to remove the appellant, who has exhausted all available efforts to stay. The second also few would quarrel with as a wishful expression. Unfortunately, accuracy is elusive and speed depends to a large extent on how well and how quickly the government handles the claims.

Attempts to preempt the arrival of asylum-seekers by interception on the high seas has not figured among the UK remedies, but it has used airlines as unpaid early border guards and it does resort to bilateral agreements with countries through which a claimant has passed to receive them back. Concepts such as

9 Forced Migration Studies Programme, University of the Witwatersrand, South Africa, April 2010 <www.migration.org.za>.

'buffer states' (which in a way is how the North African countries are perceived) and 'safe havens', such as Kurdish Iraq, have been considered. The question of whether or not that country is safe is not addressed, which is one of the main reasons for including the systems in North Africa in Chapter 6.

The intention behind the removal of the asylum-seekers' welfare rights[10] would seem to be a fairly clear discouragement to anyone coming to the UK in order to seek asylum – genuine or not. In *R v SSSS ex p JCWI*, Lord Justice Simon Brown said, 'This Regulation … must now be regarded as rendering these rights nugatory. Either that, or the[y] … contemplate for some a life so destitute that … no civilized nation can tolerate it', and he reminded us of what Lord Ellenborough CJ had said 200 years earlier: 'As to there being no obligation for maintaining poor foreigners before the statutes ascertaining the different methods of acquiring settlements, the law of humanity, which is anterior to all positive laws, obliges us to afford them relief, to save them from starving.'[11]

The House of Lords upheld the Court of Appeal's decision[12] which found that the section where those who do not apply for asylum at the earliest opportunity must not be provided with the limited support normally made available to asylum-seekers would be in breach of human rights and thus unlawful, thus undermining the entire policy of enforced destitution.

Recall the times when no right to appeal from a decision to refuse admission to the country existed because the boundaries, the sovereignty of the nation state was a matter solely for the exercise of the Royal Prerogative which was at the time considered unchallengeable in the courts. Over time, those boundaries drawn on a map have become a boundaries entrenched in the mind and this influences our thinking and consequently our instinctive reactions.

Since the terrorist attacks of 9/11, countries have imposed more, and tighter, security measures, aimed at combating terrorism. There has also been a marked increase in reliance on the exclusion clauses of the 1951 Refugee Convention,[13] and other methods – some not always moral or legal, such as 'Rendition' – to control immigrants.

---

10 S. 55 of the Nationality, Immigration and Asylum Act 2002, provides that the Home Secretary 'may not provide or arrange for the provision of support [under provisions in the 1999 and 2002 Acts which legislate for support for asylum-seekers] if he is not satisfied that the claim was made as soon as reasonably practicable after the person's arrival in theUnited Kingdom'.

11 *R v Inhabitants of Eastbourne* (1803) 4 East 103.

12 *R (Limbuela, Tesema and Adam) v SSHD* [2005] UKHL 66: CA [2004] EWCA Civ 540.

13 Article IF –the RC excludes a claimant from protection where there are serious reasons to believe s/he has committed a crime against humanity or a serious non political crime outside the country on which protection is sought. Also see Chapter 5.

The change from set-piece wars of nation against nation to more fliud forms of conflict has added to the challenge[14] to formulate effective security policies without going overboard, but in the process, nation states have put the refugee in the terrorist frame, even though there appears to be little evidence to that refugees, as a group, are an especially effective spawning ground for terrorists. Such demonization of the refugee not only adds to their predicament; it also adds to the pressures under which the judge in an immigration appeal works.

The refugee is not the only victim of anti-terror and security legislation: every would-be traveller, tourist, student, or businessperson is caught up its net, usually in a visa regime. These all form some part of the immigration judges' daily work. The all-pervasive aspect of heightened security measures has conditioned the public's attitude toward the immigrant, and has made the public less welcoming, more suspicious. The EU, as a whole, now has an expanded outer perimeter, which has both land and sea boundaries,[15] which it tries to protect. Africa has seen the largest mass movements of people, whether refugees or not, though it is the region that can least afford it; as a result, despite its culture of hospitality, Africa too has become 'refugee resistant'.

The thousands of miles of porous borders drawn on maps in the 'Scramble for Africa' at the Berlin Conference of 1885[16] may be further afield than Europe, but their significance lies in the fact that they are unpoliceable. The numbers of IDPs (internally displaced persons) have, as we've noted, increased mostly in those very areas where they can, if so minded cross a border (now or five years' hence) with little difficulty. Considering whether it is safe to return a refugee who has passed through another country on the way to the UK involves knowing how that country's security system works. For example, security in Mali, Somalia, or even Nigeria, is bound up with control over its borders, and the internal flight alternative becomes far more complex and problematic.

It has been pointed out that the numbers of asylum-seekers in the industrialized world has dropped significantly (59 per cent in the United Kingdom). However, as has been mentioned, the numbers of IDPs in the world has increased and is expected to reach 250 million – that is, a number equal to almost double the population of Nigeria – over the next 30–40 years. It seems self-evident, therefore,

14 The game of Go or Wei-chi, which has influenced the strategies of war in China and elsewhere (perhaps even as much as the nineteenth-century military strategist Carl von Clausewitz has in the West) may have a lesson here. Mao-Tse Tung used Go game strategy, which eschews set positions and is fluid, being directed at the mind as well as at the forces on the ground. It is said to favour the sort of battles, which are fought indirectly over vast, loosely connected areas, in contrast to western strategy, which has concentrated on single areas.

15 A process which bypasses due process; see, for example, *Nasr & Ghali v Italy* 22 November 2011, pending.

16 'Sometimes just straight lines in the desert': <http://africanhistory.about.com/od/eracolonialism/l/bl-BerlinAct1885.htm>.

that those who may have either now or in the future, some claim to asylum under one or more of the Conventions has not decreased. They are simply somewhere else. The apprehension regarding asylum-seekers lies in the fear that at some time these numbers will reach a figure equal to what it is forecast. It seems that a massive dam is a better analogy than a warehouse for what holds back the number of asylum-seekers: if the dam bursts, it really will be a flood.

In regard to the public image, it should surely be unnecessary to go so far as to remove asylum-seekers welfare rights, as was attempted by legislation in 1999 and again in 2006.

Turning now to analyse the issues or threads, which of these are outside of judges' control?

The Policies and Legislation

The Home Office, and some senior ministers in more recent times, have taken to attacking judges for decisions which they do not like and to arguing that the judges are thwarting the wishes of Parliament. This seems in keeping with other attempts to circumvent judicial intervention. Whether this is done in ignorance of what democracy is all about or is due to a growing design to arrogate all power to the executive (not Parliament) is for others to debate; however, tyranny does not arrive with a sudden fanfare of trumpets, but by stealth

One example of this was an attack by then Home Secretary David Blunkett, upon the President of the AIT Sir Andrew Collins [17]for making a decision the effect of which, like Lord Justice Simon Brown's above, gave protection to a sick and destitute asylum-seeker. However, perhaps Mr Blunkett and others of like mind should ponder over Sir Stephen Sedley's comments on a speech by Lord Sumption, entitled 'Judicial and Political Decision-Making: The Uncertain Boundary',[18] in which he reproved the judiciary for 'failing to keep out of the political arena'. Sir Stephen, referring to the US, remarked:

> Sumption gives no serious instances to the contrary. It is the executive – the departments of state over which ministers preside, along with quangos and local government – which is subject to public law controls. This is how originalists have sought to present the issue, purporting to restrict lawful interpretation to the framers' original intent and denouncing liberals who treat the Constitution

17 *The Times* 4 March 2003, The Law Frances Gibb Blunkett v the Bench: the battle has begun. She noted Justice Albie Sachs remark that such behaviour was dispiriting. And see Lord Woolf Judicial Independence 'Controversies' Politics.co.UK http://www.politics.co.uk/reference/judicial-independence (accessed on 3 July 2013) and also in Sir Stephen Sedley's article in the London Review n 19 below

18 The F.A. Mann Lecture 2001 <www.pem.cam.ac.uk/wp-content/uploads/.../1C-Sumption-article.pdf>.

> as a living instrument for using interpretation to make new law. We have not conflated government and legislature, as Sumption does in order to suggest that both ought to be equally immunized by their democratic credentials from judicial oversight. The courts go to considerable lengths to respect the constitutional supremacy of Parliament.[19]

But the Home Office should have heeded the trenchant criticism meted out to it in 2007 by Mr Justice Munby, who said that what it had not done was inimical to justice and with an unacceptable disdain for the rule of law.[20] If it had done so, maybe one of the Home Office's own ministers, John Reid (who replaced Charles Clarke as Home Secretary), may not have needed to accuse it of not being 'fit for purpose' in 2006. The quotation in the heading to this chapter – 'New institutional architecture is needed at international level for enlightened policies' – could have been an apt observation on the debate in the EU in Brussels concerning suggestions for a single, EU-wide determining body.[21]

In the House of Lords, Lord Simon Brown said, '... when it eventually came to be exercised ... it may be changed at any moment',[22] and proceeded to draw an analogy with planning law, which required applications to be determined in accordance with whatever policies were in force at the time the decisions were made. These instructions take effect whenever they say they take place and (unless otherwise provided) affect both new and pending applications. Fairness does not come into it, nor does any principle of requiring that the rule should not operate retrospectively.

The then Lord Chief Justice Lord Maltravers of Worth, speaking to a Commonwealth Law Conference in Nairobi, called for dialogue, between administration and judiciary; he said there should be a partnership,[23] but that partnership must avoid either side encroaching on the function of the other; this is a balance that is easy to speak about but difficult to achieve, as was demonstrated in the events leading up to and following the transfer of the IAA to the LCD.[24]

---

19 Sedley, S. (23 February 2012), 'Judicial Politics', *London Review of Books* 34.4: 15. The attempts by government to remove judicial review will be recalled; see a well-referenced account of this attempt to oust judicial review in Rawlings, R. (2005), 'Review, Revenge and Retreat', *Modern Law Review* 68.3: 378–410.

20 Per Munby J, in *Reg (G) v SSHD*, reported in *The Times*, 12 May 2007.

21 The Commission is drifting towards a common processing of all asylum applications, 'to introduce a common administrative approach to the examination procedures, such as the introduction of a single authority for the examination of applications for both refugee status and subsidiary protection', COM (2007) 301, final Green Paper on the future Common European Asylum System <http://eur lex.europa.eu/LexUriServ/LexUriServ.do?uri=CELEX:52007DC0301:EN:NOT#_blank>.l.

22 *Odelola v SSHD*, *The Times*, 22 May 2009.

23 Lord Phillips of Maltravers (2007), 'Judicial Independence', *The Commonwealth Lawyer* 16.3, a speech given in Nairobi, September 2007, especially at p. 19.

24 See Chapter 2.

Lord Prosser's facilitative interpretation of the immigration rules and the House of Lords in *Musisi*[25] may reduce the sense of grievance amongst even those whose appeals fail.

Ministerial Management

'Ministerial' in this context includes the two main departments, which exert control over the tribunal: the Home Office and the Ministry of Justice.

The tribunal, in order to give its best, needs to receive from the Ministry of Justice (or the LCD, as it was) the right sort of support in the way of resources, as well as some protection from excessive interference by the Home Office in its demands for productivity over justice. The Home Office has now been freed from an obligation to be 'whiter than white', by virtue of its detachment from the judiciary; currently, much of the legislation has the effect of emasculating the judicial role of the tribunal, in part by procedural rules and in part by removing cases from its jurisdiction.

The aspect of support in relation to judicial appointments is a matter in which the judges themselves have a limited say. In the 1970s, there were potential recruits with overseas experience at least. They did have some exposure to different cultures and, especially when obtained by living amongst people in other countries, there was often a familiarity with 'how the other half of the world lives'. These potential recruits also had the experience of handling evidence through interpreters, intervention without compromise of their role and a knack of introducing personal knowledge without offence. If they brought too much of a colonial attitude to their work, how serious a problem was this, and would not any new judges bring their own, perhaps less obvious, inclinations?

Today the tribunal must rely on the Ministry of Justice establishing and following the right criteria for recruitment of judges from different walks of life, as compared to those of the 1970s. They are not, as one judge observed, recruited from the 'Clapham omnibus'. The American writer Posner talks of the needs in recruitment, but he is of course looking at judges and judging very much in the context of his own country, where the system of selection is different. He makes the point that the US system is more democratic than that in the UK. We may disagree, but his analysis of how a judge approaches decision making, the relevance of background and experience, and especially the approach to decisions of fact and belief in, or rejection of, a witness's testimony give a useful insight into the issues involved.

---

25 *R v Home Secretary ex parte Bugdaycay (Musisi)* [1987] AC 514, at p. 531. Andrew Collins was one of the Counsel at this appeal.

If the Home Office devoted more time, effort and money to the first decisions[26] that would greatly reduce cost, time and distress to everyone, including most of the appellants. The trouble therefore is that if the first examination of the claim and the decision based on it are inadequate, the tribunal may be unable to put it right.

Any shortcomings in adversarial approach to hearings in this jurisdiction would at least be minimized, if the Home Office supplied adequate representation at appeals or, even better, still gave up attending at all except in selected cases – in a manner similar to the intervention by the UNHCR. The continental European systems (Belgium, for example) allow the file of papers, which is created when the claim is first lodged, to travel with the progress of the case. This creates transparency, encourages the initial decision maker to give their best and makes the attendance of a Presenting Officer, at the first hearing at least, much less important.

The Media

Enough has been said about the media; the damage, which their often loose and uninformed comments have caused, could be greatly limited if politicians, especially ministers, refrained from lending support to the media. Naïvety does not stretch to any expectations that the media's comments will cease, but if Ted Heath's advice to treat immigration as a cross-party issue were adopted, then the need for the confrontational approach to immigration should evaporate.

Where the Judges do have an Input

The independence of, and the respect for, the judiciary is not automatic, it has to be earned. It is a commodity to be held by the judiciary in trust for the public. It took our forebears many years and much grief to achieve both and it has to be fought for – and won anew every day.

There are three threads in which immigration judges are able make an input and have a real influence in achieving a 'good', that is to say, a defensible decision, as opposed to a 'correct' one, that is to say one where procedures are followed. They are, first, the judges' own attitudes – how they approach the exercise of a discretion; secondly, their approach to credibility, including the reception and evaluation of evidence – written, oral and expert – and as well as their approach to the hearing process itself (that is, whether it is adversarial or interventionist). Third, there is the manner in which the judiciary handles its own internal administration, which can make or mar a good outcome.

26 See UK Border Independent Monitor Report (2010), p. 6 <www.official-documents.gov.uk> and <www.independent.gov.ukIndependent.gov.uk>.

Attitudes and Prejudices of the Judges

The use of the word 'good' in any definition of what standard a decision should reach immediately founders on the impossibility of agreeing what 'good' means; it is therefore better to avoid its use in this context. There is no *perfect* procedure for determining who qualifies as a refugee under the Convention (or, for making most other decisions regarding immigration cases), but one must aim to adopt some way of reaching transparently acceptable decisions quickly and at a reasonable cost. Robert Thomas[27] considers that there are four core qualities by which to measure a decision: accuracy, fairness, resource demand and, last, timeliness. The third is clearly linked to the trade-offs (between timeliness and perfection) which are probably unavoidable, but can work against other important qualities The problem with the first is that there is no real means of measuring accuracy in this context except accuracy in law. This is relatively unimportant, except to minimize appeals to a higher level. Fairness and timeliness are important. Under the first are subsumed obvious ones, such as impartiality and transparency; the judges in this jurisdiction, and perhaps in most tribunal systems, can, as has been seen, have their hands tied by the ease with which government can undermine their judicial role.

Justice and fairness recalls what John Rawls was essentially addressing in saying how procedures can manipulate an outcome.[28] He drew a distinction between perfect and imperfect procedures; he describes a perfect procedure as one whose outcome is correct, or just, simply because it is the outcome of the procedure. But there is no independent standard of what the outcome ought to be: a lottery is a good example. An imperfect procedure is one in which there is an independent standard for the appropriate outcome.

Professor Carens puts it this way:[29]

> Like a trial (in the criminal justice system), a refugee determination process is an imperfect procedure in which there are claims that too many are getting away with something. We want to sort out those who fit the definition from those who do not, but the process may or may not succeed in achieving that outcome in any given case. Just as there are two types of error that we risk making in a criminal trial (acquitting the guilty and convicting the innocent), so there are two types of error we risk making in a determination process (admitting the unqualified, rejecting the qualified). In both trials and refugee determination processes, we have to establish procedures for gathering and evaluating information. We need

---

27 Thomas, R. (2011), *Administrative Justice and Asylum Appeals* (Oxford: Hart).

28 Rawls, J. (1971), *A Theory of Justice (*Cambridge, MA: Belknap Press).

29 Carens, J.H., 'Open Borders and the Claims of the Community'; see<http://www.law.nyu.edu/ecm_dlv2/groups/public/@nyu_law_website__academics__colloquia__legal_political_and_social_philosophy/documents/documents/ecm_pro_069496.pdf>. The analogy with the criminal trial risks reinforcing the already existing associate of asylum-seekers with spongers, beggars and other threats to society.

> systems of adjudication, rules of evidence, burdens of proof, and so on. The fundamental challenge is to construct these procedures to balance appropriately the two types of risks.

Hopefully, if recruitment is well-conducted, training, exposure and experience will do the rest and the variety of approaches by judges from different backgrounds should ensure the judges are good 'road-builders', as Stephen Sedley put it, and are better able to reach an overall satisfactory outcome. But as immigration judges, they still sit as judge and jury and with the removal of any effective review of most of their decisions which are based on fact, the element of chance remain very high indeed. The removal of the lay member and the absence of one at least sitting with an immigration judge is as unfortunate as it is incomprehensible. Posner's concern about using other countries' decisions does not apply to the UK scene in which the immigration judge operates.[30]

The IARLJ and similar international judges' institutions, such as the Commonwealth Magistrates and Judges Association, the International Bar Association, the Commonwealth Lawyers Association, to name the main English speaking ones, probably help to bring the diversity of the judges into focus, reducing that element of 'lottery' for the asylum-seeker, in the sense that there is often no choice where an application for recognition as a refugee will be decided.

The attitude of a judge is most evident when dealing with issues of 'soft' law, the reception of evidence and interpretation, and can change a relatively benign law into a weapon of oppression. One example is the dismissal of the evidence of an expert for no better reason than that the judge feels their role as the decision maker is threatened;[31] another example is where there is a choice between being facilitative (that is, the rules are made to say who may enter) or restrictive (the rules are made to say who cannot enter).[32] The decisions on the exclusion clauses of the Refugee Convention, particularly in regard to 'forgiveness' dealt with below are restrictive.

In the case of *KK*,[33] the appellant had engaged in activities which fell within the exclusion clauses, but the judge who heard the evidence was satisfied that the person had totally changed his views and that he presented no current threat; yet the tribunal held he still had to be excluded. The judge in *KK* (and in *AA*

30 Not a matter for discussion here, but Posner seems to doubt the value of referring to decisions of courts in other countries – he calls it 'Judicial Cosmopolitanism' (Posner, *How Judges Think*, Chapter 12).

31 The Guidelines in Appendix 5, n. 2 to para 1.2.5, as addressed the subsequent criticism of Ibrahim in HE (DRC) [2004] UKIAT 00321, that there is no necessary obligation to give them weight merely because they are medical or psychiatric reports.

32 *Mohd Saffer v SSHD* [1992] Imm AR 513.

33 *KK (Turkey)* [2004] UKIAT 00101.

Palestine)[34] rejected the notion that expiation, that is, punishment, pardon, or amnesty could apply, affirming the decision in *KK*, cited below, and concluding 'that we should reject all the arguments put before us for applying glosses to Article 1F, and should instead apply its words exactly as they are'. He rejected the UNHCR guidelines contained in the Handbook,[35] which urge 'Where expiation of the crime is considered to have taken place, application of the exclusion;clauses may no longer be justified',[36] since they were not binding. One asks why it was not binding and why the acknowledged authority of the Handbook was not recognized as such?[37] The judge appears to have reached this conclusion by viewing the provisions of Article 1F as being unambiguous and mandatory. No interpretation therefore came into it. It seems a little odd that he did not explain why the Vienna Convention[38] was not material and it was even more difficult to understand the judges' approach (in both cases) which appears to conflate *interpretation* and *application*. Nevertheless, the decision of the German Federal Administrative Court, although reached in the context of the country's Basic Law, went into the question of expiation at great length, with more closely reasoned and persuasive arguments than did either of the UKIAT decisions.[39] The approach in *KK* and *AA* brings to mind the long-running theatre production *Les Miserables*, in which Jean Valjean,[40] as the reader will recall, has been convicted as a thief for stealing a loaf of bread and spends the rest of his life pursued by the police, even though he had totally abandoned his earlier criminal tendencies.

Richard Posner in his book *How Judges Think* considers matters which affect how the judge interprets a provision consciously or, sometimes, unconsciously. In this jurisdiction, as in the US, the judges are drawn from different occupations and he thinks that the judge with an academic background is, for example, less forgiving in their approach, at least in relation to deadlines and procedural rules. Why this should necessarily be so is difficult to understand except that practice at the bar does expose one to the frailties of human nature and may render one less critical, in a censorious sense, of people's actions and to have more regard to their attitudes.

Before 2000, it was rare in the UK for the state to raise exclusion in an appeal. Perhaps this only meant that the Home Office did not then make any investigations

34 [2005] UKIAT 00104.

35 'On Procedures and Criteria for Determining Refugee Status 1992' <http://www.unhcr.org/>.

36 Paras 149 and 157 of the UNHCR Handbook.

37 Lord Steyn, in *R v SSHD ex parte Adan HL* [2000], said 'although not binding on states it [the Handbook] has high persuasive authority.'

38 Art. 31 deals with the interpretation of treaties which are to be given their broad meaning in the light of their purpose: 1969 UNTS 1155, p. 331; *Horvath v SSHD* [2001] AC HL 489 at 495B.

39 BVerwG10c 48 07.

40 Hugo, V. *Les Miserables* <http://www.gutenberg.org/ebooks/135>.

on this subject before reaching a decision. It is now being raised much more frequently, though there are occasions when it is not raised at the first hearing of the appeal before the immigration judge; this may be due to a positive decision or accidental omission, or simply because the Home Office does appear.

Gurung, which was discussed in Chapter 3, held that even if the state does not raise the point, and evidence appears which suggests it should be, the judge is required to do so at least at first sight; this seems in conflict with a judge's role especially in an adversarial hearing. It also seems at variance with what Mr Justice Ouseley himself said in *XS*.[41] This issue could prove fatal both to the appeal and the appellant and therefore a decision that a court must raise it of its own accord has an importance beyond the interpretation put upon Article 1Fof the Convention.

A closer look at the decision[42] does, however, seem to limit any obligation to infill the state's case to those where it should be obvious that the question of exclusion does arise whether specifically relied on or not, but to draw a general principle from this decision would seem something of a minefield. The judges surely need to go out of their way to ensure that they are not made to look like an instrument of the executive. Robert Thomas's fears on this score, whether one agrees with them or not, are worth bearing in mind.

Reception of Evidence

Credibility

The sort of 'good' decision aimed at rests more upon the understanding of the role credibility should play in decision making and how the tribunal conducts its hearings .Once again Professor Posner has an opinion – it is controversial, but has a ring of truth about it:

> A judge in a non jury proceeding who has to decide whether to believe a witness's testimony will often have formed before the witness begins to testify an estimate of the likelihood that the testimony will be truthful. His estimate may be based on previous experience with witnesses in similar cases (perhaps experience acquired as a practicing lawyer)[43] on a general sense of the honesty of the class of persons to which the witness belongs or even on the manner of striding to the witness box.

He calls this *a priori*, and considers that it may be unconscious. The detailed circumstances from which he draws his conclusions may differ from those in the

41 2005 UKIAT 00093. See also Chapter 3, p. 101.

42 Examined in Arokiyanathan Appeal no. AA 09777-06, before the AIT.

43 And probably even more so as an immigration judge, if he has been a trial judge in the courts before.

UK, but the theory is the same,[44] and it is material at two levels; the first being the sort of people who are selected as judges, and the second, the nature of the training given to them. The judge of fact in any jurisdiction is faced with the dilemma of how to make a judgment on the plausibility of a story and the reliability or credibility of the witness. In immigration appeals, the witness may not be present, or may be difficult to understand and from an unfamiliar culture, usually speaking through an interpreter and with a story which can sound very far-fetched. The judge in a civil or criminal case does not face such a multifaceted conundrum.

In general terms, various authors have proposed some guidelines to help the judge with the issue of credibility. These have included cultural and language filters; contamination of memory theories; vulnerability; consistency; verifiable country backgrounds and – somewhat questionably – demeanour (especially the demeanour of a witness giving evidence through one or more interpreters).Telling the judges how to interpret the actions of an appellant is no different in principle from telling them what decision they should reach. At another level, those with a macabre sense of humour may think that the direction of what conclusion to draw from a lack of, or forged, documents has a 'Catch 22' logic to it.[45].

Experienced judges (at least in the UK) are unanimous in their opinion that picking out the liar is difficult 'he has little or no check on the accuracy of his own impressions' .[46] Whether or not it is a skill, which can be learned, must be open to doubt, but what is clear is that it is a quicksand of which to be wary.This may be a good reason for adopting the Canadian approach; that is, 'if the story hangs together the appellant should not readily be branded a liar.' In this respect, the presumptive legitimacy of an applicant's refugee claim as a way of allocating the burden of proof, may or may not be strictly required by liberal democratic principles. A shift in the burden of proof, resisting calls to tighten procedures for their own sake, adopting a restrictive as opposed to a broad and facilitative approach to areas where there is some discretion, all have the potential for turning the judge's role into yet another government 'gatekeeper'.[47]

Returning to the issue of credibility, it may seem illogical, even nonsensensical, to relegate it to second place but, if having heard the story and been given no contradictory evidence the judge gives the appellant the benefit of any doubt, it makes it less likely that a decision maker will be likely to allow their own

---

44 For those interested it has a name and an algebraic formula! Bayes's Theorem $\Omega(H|x)=p(x|H)/p(x|{\sim}H)\ x\Omega(H)$. Anyone who wants an explanation can look it up or see it at p. 66 of Posner, *How Judges Think.*

45 S. 8, Asylum and Immigration (Treatment of Claimants) Act 2004. If the claimant has proper documents, they cannot be a refugee; if they have false ones or none, their story is untrustworthy.

46 *The Judge as Juror: The Judicial Determination of factual issues* Bingham, Sir, esp at p 9T. vol. 35, 1985 Current Legal Problems Stevens London.

47 For her own view of this debate, see Bhaba, J. (2002), 'The Tension between Asylum Advocacy and Human Rights', *Harvard Human Rights Journal* 15 (Spring).

preconceptions, wittingly or unwittingly, to skew the decision. This is particularly important when there can be no rigorous review of fact on appeal and the superior courts give a deference to the fact-finder which may be put in place in this jurisdiction.

Looked at this way, it is less likely that a decision is justified on the 'I just don't believe his story' approach. As Professor Jackson said in *Chiver*,[48] a finding of exaggeration or even untruth in one area does not mean the whole story is untrue. A test of 'apparent reasonableness' or even common sense takes one no further, since the question remains of 'apparent to whom?' and 'common to whose sense?'.

Evidence, Training and the Nature of the Hearing

Fact-finding by a single judge occurs in no other jurisdiction where the consequences of getting it wrong can be so serious and far-reaching, not even in the criminal courts or the civil ones either. The need for experienced help from a representative of one or preferably both parties becomes a necessity, not a luxury, and therefore action or legislation, which makes this facility less available, must be detrimental to a good decision. The 'one-stop' approach to a new system, which is examined later, could render otiose most intervention by the Home Office.

With regard to medical evidence, a great deal of progress has already been made toward ensuring a judge no longer rejects a medical report without giving some meaningful reason for doing so, and failure to do so in this case would be likely to be considered a 'reviewable error'.[49]

Referring once again to reliance on one's own knowledge of facts, if a judge may not use what has been learned in an earlier case by another judge, how can he or she build up a fund of specialized (implying reliable and up-to-date) information on third countries? In retrospect, perhaps the adjudicators did rely on each other's decisions on fact, when there was a consensus that it was unsafe for any asylum-seeker to be returned to any Channel port, because the procedures adopted at each port put the asylum-seeker at risk of onward refoulement.

The view that the tribunal is an 'expert' therefore needs further investigation. Hardly any judge hears what happens to the appellant after they leave the hearing room. They do not know if a decision had the expected result or not. They take into account often repeated facts about a country or about which more senior judges have decided shall be the accepted position; yet they often have no real idea of how those facts impact on people – even if they may be correct as general statements.

Then there is the extent to which judges may safely 'descend into the arena' (by asking questions) in order to test for themselves to their own satisfaction the relevance of the facts in issue? Questioning by the judge is often thought to

48 IAT 10758, which was an (unsuccessful) appeal from a decision of Professor Ken Counter in 1993, which was only belatedly reported in 1997 sub nom *SSHD v Chiver* [1997] INLR p. 212.

49 X.E.B. (Re), [2002] R.P.D.D. No. 230, at para. 17.

be a pitfall in adversarial hearings, but it is suggested that it is not so confined and can arise in any type of judicial inquiry. The superior courts could consider laying down the extent to which it is proper for immigration judges to use their own knowledge in deciding cases – knowledge acquired before appointment or knowledge acquired during service – and giving some guidance on when a judge may and indeed should intervene. This presupposes that the tribunal retains at least a nominal adversarial approach.

Those who find fault with the investigative approach seem to do so because they consider that it suffers from the greater opportunity to give an appearance of bias and is much more prone to variations in approach by individual decision makers. This may be so and needs to be weighed against any disadvantages to the parties in the present system. Any change to an investigative mode may require retraining judges, and possibly support staff as well, because very few of present judges, with the exception of a few coroners or judges from other jurisdictions, have had experience of non-adversarial systems.

One shortcoming in a system which is non-investigative lies in the area of language. Language is not necessarily coincident with nationality. There are examples to be found in Africa where borders disregard local cultural and family links. To the knowledgeable, it is nearly always possible to tell where someone comes from with amazing accuracy. Anthropologists, however well-qualified and experienced but who are not themselves from the area will, despite great learning and even experience, be very unlikely to be able to do this. The use of the anthropologist, however, in relation to informing a judge about cultural practices can often be as valuable as that of any expert or background evidence – probably more so. Ignorance of how a culture influences beliefs and actions can seriously interfere with both plausibility and credibility.[50]

The UNHCR Handbook[51] calls for three major steps in a refugee status determination; first, a shared search for the evidence; secondly, a search for the 'truth', and third, the application of a standard of proof which is not as high as that required in an ordinary civil or a criminal case. This is where there are substantial grounds for believing the appellant. The overall process of decision making, starting with the Home Office and ending in the tribunal, requires the facts to be examined (in asylum cases) afresh at each stage. If there are material facts or other information missing, it is difficult if not impossible to include them. The gradual erosion of good representation as the case proceeds breaks down the aim of the enquiry and denies help to the judge, who has limited power to call for evidence.

The question which seems to hang over any modification, which would change an adversarial model of hearing into an interventionist one, is whether

50 Kälin, W. (1986), 'Troubled Communication: Cross Cultural Misunderstandings in the Asylum Hearing', *International Migration Review* 20.2 (Summer): 230–41.

51 'Handbook on Procedures and Criteria for Determination of Refugee Status under the 1951 Convention and the 1967 Protocol relative to the status of Refugees', Part 2, paras 190 and 195–2002.

any modification needs a change in the law or merely a change in attitude, with some backing from the courts. A recent exchange of views in the correspondence columns of *The Times*[52] actually arose out of a criminal case, but some of the views expressed in the letters apply to England (there appears to be a less straitjacketed view in Scotland).[53] To take three of those views:

- The first was that 'our justice system is in fact adversarial rather than inquisitorial.'
- The second was 'A contrary view … would be that our system is concerned with proof rather than truth … a quest for truth would be … as Graham Greene noted … "a symbol for mathematicians and philosophers to pursue".'
- The third was 'by acting effectively as a contest between lawyers, the adversarial system creates incentives for withholding (or loss) of evidence … There is of course a much better alternative, where a more humane approach to witnesses is taken and where establishing the truth becomes the overriding imperative … It is used in the majority of Europe and … in Coroners Courts.'

It is worth repeating a passage on the *Surendran Guidelines* at the end of Chapter 3 – it captures both the situation and the answer:

> By the end of the decade, [2010] immigration judges were under a positive duty to probe evidence which was in issue before them, even where the opposite party had chosen not to be represented (*TR*) They were encouraged, not only to use their judicial common sense in deciding which points needed to be put … but also to use their expertise as a specialist tribunal, not only in the relevant law, but in the 'fund of information about different third countries' which they had acquired. Naturally, they needed to put such information to the parties.
>
> Thus as has been seen that, whilst asylum (and other immigration) appeals are still adversarial in form in England and Wales and Scotland, the immigration judge intervenes more than it was, formerly, thought to be proper. If a judge feels it, necessary to intervene it must not seem hostile or partial and clearly requires skill and experience; but that is part of the craft for judges.

The best advice would seem to be 'No modern system of criminal (and immigration?) justice is either truly inquisitorial (investigative or interventionist)

52 *The Times*, 28 June 2011, p .23.

53 A history of the adversarial system in so far as the criminal trial in concerned has been considered in Langbein, J. (2003), *The Origins of Adversary Criminal Trial* (Oxford: Oxford University Press), and see Sedley, *Ashes and Sparks*, especially Chapter 3, which draws extensively on Langbein.

or truly accusatorial (non interventionist or adversarial); in the initial phase of the inquiry … all have elements of open contest.'[54]

The benefits to be gained from training are undisputed and, as we have seen, much has been achieved over the last 15 years and hopefully its content will continue to be reviewed. This would appear to be the case when a hearing is interventionist rather than adversarial. The approach to all testimony can make the difference between a good and a flawed decision, especially expert evidence in asylum appeals.[55] In the approach to expert oral evidence, reliability may well depend on how good an observer the expert is. The extent of cross-cultural misunderstandings can be a minefield without understanding of the contribution the anthropologist can make as an expert, which may mean educating judges to become conscious of possible misunderstandings caused by their own cultural perceptions.

Difficult though it may be to find people who are able to give instruction in matters such as the evaluation of expert and other country evidence, language usage or perhaps in the assessment of the plausibility of a story,[56] the need for such instruction grows exponentially with the numbers of judges recruited, and their age and backgrounds. There is little doubt, drawn from experience when judges were involved with both the selection and training of interpreters, that this does need to be revisited to ensure that interpreters are qualified and security vetted.

It is encouraging to see that the present President of the Immigration and Asylum Chamber of the Upper Tribunal, Mr Justice Blake, is determined to correct any lack of respect there may in the minds of all interested parties. It would be the most effective way toward creating that proper partnership Lord Phillips saw to be in the interests of society as a whole. The lack of trust of the tribunal, hitherto demonstrated by successive governments, to allow it to get on with its job,[57] might be the single most inhibiting factor toward the tribunal's smooth running.

Management of the Hearing by the Judges

Previously, judges did not receive the files of their cases in sufficient time to look through them before going into a hearing. One hopes that this has now been rectified. Failure to obtain access to the files in time to read them and know

54 Sedley, *Ashes and Sparks*, p. 32.

55 One judges' attitude is illustrated by the paper by John Barnes, Expert Evidence – The Judicial Perception in Asylum and Human Rights Appeals: *Int J Refugee Law (2004)* 16(3): 349–57, doi:10.1093/ijrl/16.3.349. Views which are not without their critics

56 Kagan, M., 'Refugee credibility assessment and the "religious imposter" problem', *A case study of Eritrean Pentecostal claims in Egypt* Working Paper No. 9. December 2009. Center for Migration and Refugee Studies www.aucegypt.edu/GAPP/cmrs/Documents/KaganReligiousImposters.pdf (accessed on 4 July 2013), which is instructive, for deciding whether a claim to religious persecution is true or false.

57 Franks Report on Administrative Tribunals and Inquiries, Cmnd 218 1957.

what the cases are about, coupled with the strict time limit for cases is a serious impediment to reaching a 'good' decision. This is particularly so when the judge is under pressure to avoid adjournment and to make an immediate decision.

As remarked earlier, to allow the Home Office file to follow the case and to have some pre-assessment made by a suitably trained person before it reaches the judge would go a long way to overcoming the need for a Home Office representative to attend every hearing; it may avoid the argument on appeal that a point was not taken. The adverse impact of a bad first decision would be reduced and decision making might be improved and expedited, thus reducing the need for further appeals.

The Country Guidance Case (CGC) has removed the need to wade through masses of background material for countries where a CGC has been promulgated, but that leaves those appeals where there is no CGC. In Belgium, every appeal has been made the subject of a brief prepared for the judge dealing with fact and law. However, a model closer to home is the precis writer for the Court of Criminal Appeal; there too, the Court is presented with, often, a single page, which encapsulates the issues, the law and facts, and the arguments: in the case of the most experienced and trusted writer, the precis will end up forming the judgment! Whatever variation is used, the principle is 'optimum resource use'.

The judges need not do much of the spadework, both in law and background fact. Admittedly, one may not want to follow the Canadian system, where all the judge gets is a precis of background material seen through the resource person's eyes, but that does not prevent the material being collated and indexed in a way which makes access for the judge faster – again, optimum resource use.

What Alternative Approaches are There?

It may be an oversimplification to expect non partisan approaches such as that put forward by Edward Heath's as a general panacea of all the ills of the system, butthere have still been a number of suggested alternatives if it is decided to scrap the present one and replace it with something new. Some of these are mentioned below[58].

The decision to make the Upper Tribunal (as it is called now) a Court of Record is merely the removal by stealth of as much as government could get away with of judicial review, under the guise of simplifying and shortening the entire appeal process. If there were evidence that it improved the quality of protection and at the same time reduced an unnecessary step, it may more defensible. What would be a major improvement would be to restore to the Upper Tribunal the power to overturn an asylum tribunal decision on fact.

58 See also Spencer, S., s. 16 Immigration written from the standpoint of the advocate and the academic – albeit a well informed one. http://www.compas.ox.ac.uk/fileadmin/files/People/staff_publications/Spencer/Seldon%20ch%2016%20Spencer%20Immigration.pdf.

The somewhat tentative move toward a European Asylum System, as indicated by the Green Paper,[59] is one possible alternative system, thus creating one single EU body to make first-line decisions. This would not preclude such a body having devolved offices and would work from common rules and guidelines.

A single European Tribunal as an Independent Refugee Board – an all-in-one body to deal with determination of claims to refugee status from beginning to end – is one possibility modeled on the Canadian system, but sitting divisionally in each member country, with a right of appeal to a centralized body. This perhaps could resemble the International Federation Motor Sports appeals bodies, which sit in Geneva.[60]

Decisions could even be made in the country of origin in some instances. But there are shortcomings to that proposal, for example, the decision makers would have to stay in a country with which they may be unfamiliar and where they will be dependent on the host country for everything, including interpretation, day-to-day communication (usually in a closed community) secretarial services, and so on. That dependency will usually come from the Mission of their own country, whose own perceptions may be transferred to the decision maker, like an image onto a photographic plate.

The approach which seems implicit in both *Ravichandran* and *Karanakaran* is that decision making in immigration matters is throughout essentially administrative. This could lead to the conclusion that perhaps there should be no pretence to any absolute independence in the review until the case reaches the Court of Appeal. Looking at the progress of a claim in such a way, whether as a domestic or a regional system, it should progressively take less and less time as the influence of the first decisions recedes. The 'judicial' part of the review will not be inhibited in how they handle the cases, provided there is transparent fairness. The picture conjured up is that of a pyramid with the Court of Appeal at the apex.[61] This logically leads to a closer examination of the choices: interventionist, confrontational, or adversarial?

Professor Guy Goodwin-Gill saw another way forward as an answer to most, if not all, the shortcomings of the present system and one that would also conform to the EC Directives on minimum standards and harmonization. He envisaged, in his system, a better chance of an impartial assessment of the merits; greater consistency in the background material used and a more effective opportunity for all parties to be heard. It would also make a reasoned and timely decision easier to achieve.[62]

---

59 Common European Asylum System, COM 301, final.

60 FIA International Court of Appeal and International Tribunal <www.fia.com>.

61 And not that of the picture of the experiences of one asylum-seeker which he drew as a game of Snakes and Ladders!

62 Refugee Legal Centre (2001–02), *Annual Review*, at p. 12, quoted with permission, if it were needed, from Guy Goodwin-Gill.

He suggests his idea has the following attributes:

1. a single fact database updated regularly and openly,
2. an improved-quality first decision,
3. totally interventionist,
4. open to judicial review and appeal on points of law (I would add even more importantly on fact as well), with
5. less of any attempt to make immigration into a political football.

An oral hearing may not always be required; additional factual evidence may be less frequent. Switzerland manages without oral hearings, just as Belgium conducts its hearings without the need for any representative from the Ministry of the Interior. What has lengthened the time from the start to the finish of any immigration appeal in the UK have been the delays within the Home Office itself, bad decision making and a system which gives a multiplicity of appeals (by both parties) at each stage of which the facts and the law are re-examined.

Another suggested system would allow the Home Office to make affirmative decisions only and send the rest to an independent, quasi-judicial, review from which an appeal would lie on an error of law to a judicial body. Whether any loss of control by government would be too high a price to pay, when it would not be compensated by savings in other directions, only government could decide. A variation on the same theme, but less drastic, would be the suggestion made earlier, for the file which is opened at the initial stages in the Home Office to travel throughout the entire process including every appeal that follows and allow no documents to be withheld except those in which State Privilege is claimed.

Some of the critics of the UK system have decried a lack of any independent monitoring of the decision-making process as, for example, are to be found in management systems or environmental control.[63] The International Organization for Standardization (ISO) has produced 15,000 standard measurements since 1947.[64] A certification body could seek to develop detailed, universal sets of criteria based upon which the professional standards of a national immigration asylum authority would be assessed and audited, with criteria relating to everything from good practice to detention and removal.

63 Round Table on Migration and Governance, 16 November 2006, which addressed 'ways and means to improve the governance of international migration namely through its better coordination with European development policies', which was followed by an EU African Union Ministerial Conference on Migration and Development in Sirte on 22 November 2006.

64 2004 UN ISSN 1020-1688: See especially para. 104/5, Appendix 3 to the Synopsis – see 2007/0167 CNS, building on the Laeken European Council in 1901 and databases such as CIREFI, ICOnet, Roxen, Eurostat, etc. It would involve academics and be available to the public.

A universally acceptable set of guiding principles could follow the precedent of the Istanbul Protocol,[65] which sets out international guidelines for the assessment of medical expert reports on persons alleging torture – for the medical expert as well as the decision maker. The guidelines set out what to look for and they establish a consistency of phraseology on expert evidence. The IARLJ has ongoing working parties on the reception of medical and other expert evidence and country-background material for the guidance of decision makers globally.[66]

Judge Jack Chlebny, a member of the Polish Supreme Administrative Tribunal, in a paper written for the European Commission, dwelt upon some of the issues, which he sees to be essential, if there is to be real protection. In condensed form, they are:

- To strike a balance between the public interest and the individual rights,
- To ensure access to the court and the right to an effective remedy,
- To promote the principle that all administrative acts must be subject to judicial review.

In Poland, as in Belgium, the administrative authority is obliged to make available the entire document upon which the decision by the executive bases its decision. This should surely be a first step toward improving the transparency, efficiency and speed of all decision making.

It may be that the European Court of Human Rights does keep an overarching watch on the application of the European Convention on Human Rights in EU countries, but in that case, why draw a distinction between criminal proceedings, which Article 6 does cover, and regulatory decisions, which it does not, except where Article 3 is involved?[67] As Stephen Sedley points out, many of the latter carry powers far more draconian than the former and the result is to 'throw the substantive baby out with the procedural bathwater'.[68] For those unfamiliar with the point, the Court had held that an immigration appeal is not a '(criminal) proceeding' covered by Article 6 which guarantees the right to a fair hearing. However, Article 3 forbids return to a country where the claimant may be subjected to *inhuman* treatment; therefore, even if the proceedings do not otherwise fall within Article 6, they will do so if the case involves a risk under Article 3.

65 Istanbul Protocol Manual on the Effective Investigation and Documentation of Torture and Other Cruel, Inhuman or Degrading Treatment or Punishment 1999, HR/P/PT/8/Rev.1 <www.ohchr.org>.

66 IARLJ Guidelines on the Judicial Approach to Expert Medical Evidence <www.iarlj.nl> see Appendix 5.

67 *Maaouia v France*, decided by a majority; 26 90 9CJQ, p. 27; *Moro v SSHD* [2001] EWCA Civ 1680; Jastram, K., 'Economic Harm as a Basis for Refugee Status', paper delivered a symposium, York University, 2008.

68 Sedley, *Ashe s*and *Sparks* p. 117.

In the absence of any form of any international tribunal (the establishment of which has been the subject of debate but little action in recent years) to oversee refugee and refugee-related cases globally, the only way forward will be that the dissenting opinion of Judges Loucaides and Traja in *Maaouia v France*[69] become the preferred opinion of the court.[70] Perhaps this is yet another example of the 'law spend[ing] its life stretched on the rack between certainty and adaptability', as Stephen Sedley observed when he was a High Court Judge. The immigration judge will recognize the analogy and doubtless will have learned to be adaptable.[71] The comments of another experienced judge, Lord Justice Laws, reflects the importance of the role of the immigration judges:

> That the appeal system has survived and works at all, is, even though an imperfect system, something of a miracle and is due greatly to the foundations laid in the early days, for which little credit has been given and even less regard paid to the reasons why the system was constructed as it was.[72]

It was in the same case that Lord Justice Laws noted that the Asylum and Immigration Tribunal was specialist and should be able to identify current trends and problems and give general guidance on in-country conditions. He added that, after section 101 of the Nationality, Immigration and Asylum Act 2002 came into force in June 2003 (which ever more strictly confined appeals to points of law alone), it would no longer be possible for the AIT to overturn a decision of the first-tier tribunal, even if it did disagree with the first-tier tribunal's finding on fact. Much of the criticism of the existing system revolves around such a restriction and when most cases depend on fact, and the decisions on fact are made by one person – not always experienced and in 60 per cent of the cases a part-time employee – this is a damning criticism.

After surveying a century of public and parliamentary protection of our borders and remembering Margaret's Mar's none too complimentary remarks upon our system, perhaps Lewis Carroll's *The Hunting of the Snark* is germane::

> The Bellman, who was almost morbidly sensitive about appearances, used to have the bowsprit unshipped once or twice a week to be re-varnished, and it

69 [2000] 33 EHRR 42, p. 1037, paras I–VI et seq.

70 What is interesting is that it seems that the ECtHR considers that the right to a fair hearing must be before an adversarial tribunal, see InterRights Manual for Lawyers (Article 6), para 3.3.1. There may be little hope for any change in approach as long as the distinction remains between regulatory and criminal proceedings. See also Sedley, *Ashes and Sparks*, especially in the chapter 'Wringing out the Fault', p. 117.

71 With the EU Directive of 29 April 2005, the (much to be desired) achievement of some uniformity in interpretation will, so it is thought, no longer be the role of the courts but of the bureaucrats.

72 *Subesh and others v SSHD* [2004] Imm AR 112.

more than once happened, when the time came for replacing it, that no one on board could remember which end of the ship it belonged to. They knew it was not of the slightest use to appeal to the Bellman about it – he would only refer to his Naval Code, and read out in pathetic tones Admiralty Instructions which none of them had ever been able to understand – so it generally ended in its being fastened on, anyhow, across the rudder. The helmsman used to stand by with tears in his eyes; he knew it was all wrong, but alas! Rule 42 of the Code, 'No one shall speak to the Man at the Helm,' had been completed by the Bellman himself with the words 'and the Man at the Helm shall speak to no one.' So remonstrance was impossible, and no steering could be done till the next varnishing day. During these bewildering intervals the ship usually sailed backwards.[73]

73 Carroll, L. (1874), 'The Hunting of the Snark' <www.gutenberg.org/ebooks/13

APPENDICES

Appendix 1
Diagram of the Immigration Appeals System (as at 1995)

IMMIGRATION APPEALS

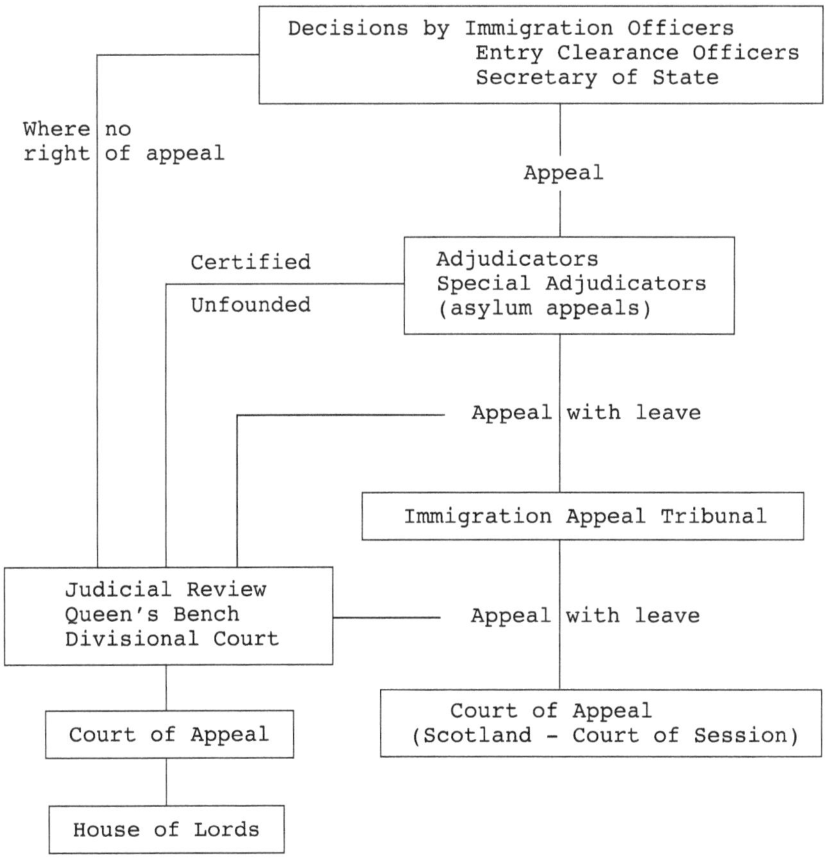

Appendix 2
Statistics of Adjudicator Appeals

Year	Receipts	Disposals	Outstanding
70	740	350	390
71	3,581	2,443	1,465
72	4,458	4,114	1,809
73	6,262	5,292	2,779
74	8,766	7,666	3,879
75	15,242	10,937	8,184
76	10,750	12,412	6,522
77	12,118	11,671	6,969
78	16,219	11,455	11,733
79	17,782	13,176	16,339
80	16,142	16,599	15,884
81	14,154	18,010	12,026
82	13,791	16,875	8,942
83	14,057	15,100	7,924
84	13,993	12,073	9,843
85	11,178	12,098	8,927
86	13,343	12,273	10,147
87	11,605	11,120	10,532
88	17,131	11,484	16,179
89	22,136	16,550	21,765
90	24,124	16,524	24,830
91	27,340	25,071	27,080
92*	27,105	32,619	21,040
93/94	25,250	27,580	18,710
94/95	20,800	26,770	12,810
95/96	32,426	21,282	24,564
96/97	37,660	29,182	33,020

Source: Glover et al., 'Migration: An Economic and Social Analysis', Home Office (25 October 1990), Immigration and Nationality and Passports Annual Report.

Appendix 3
Report on Trip to West Africa 2006

Catriona Jarvis SIJ

West Africa Highway – February 2006

With our time in West Africa fast running out, I want to take just a few moments to reflect a little and to tell you of some of the ideas and thoughts that have been voiced during the course of the trip. We have travelled, although not all by land; almost the full length of the West Africa Highway, from Dakar to Cotonou, not far from Lagos, where, I am told, the road terminates.

We have been afforded a glimpse into the lives of those who people the highway and of the land on which they live and work. We have been able to visit the doors of no return at the L'Isle de Gorée at the one end and Ouidah at the other, giving opportunity to contemplate the enormity of historic events that should not have happened and to recall the acknowledgement of past wrongs, and of the consequences of slavery, by the international community as well as by individual states.

Freetown, lying between those two doors of no return, and created in order to provide a haven for former slaves, has unhappily proved to be anything but a place of safety, certainly in recent years. It would be invidious to single out any one place as more important than others that we have visited. But for me, and I know for numbers of you, our brief encounter with post-war Sierra Leone and in particular Freetown, was amongst the most compelling. One felt drawn to the people and engaged with their struggle to re-build their shattered lives and country.

Sierra Leone has stumbled. But the broom has been firmly grasped. With help, the stones are being swept from the path and the country has begun its post-war reconstruction. A highly significant aspect of this slow process is the essential exercise of bringing to justice, through the Special Court, those guilty of war crimes. It was a real privilege to have been able to spend time at the court, listening to the judges and others who work there, and to have observed the court in action. Our respect and thanks must go to all who are doing this difficult work on our behalf.

Interspersed with these profound experiences of both past and present pain, have been many of sheer pleasure, surprise and delight. Youssou N'Dour playing at home in Dakar. A rainstorm releasing the smell of the deep red earth in the botanic gardens at Aburi. Fluttering, multi-coloured sails easing the passage of a fish-laden pirogue into the home straight to Ganvie. Communal early Sunday morning exercise on the beachfront at Lome. Dolphins at 6.35 on the river Gambia.

Each of you will hold myriad such memories of your own and we shall continue to learn and to benefit from everything that we have experienced, including the good company and support of all our colleagues and their family members.

Was there ever really anyone taking photos at the Aflao/Lome border as we waited, interminably, to cross from Ghana to Togo? Would the Togolese break off diplomatic relations after the rendezvous with ministers at the 2 Fevrier Hotel? Would we make it to the next airport before the flight left? (Should the password for the website be 'slok'?).

Appendix 4
Address to Annual Residential Conference of Immigration Judges of the Asylum and Immigration Tribunal

Birmingham, Wednesday, 14 June 2006

Keith Best, Chief Executive, Immigration Advisory Service

Introduction

I regard it as both a pleasure and a privilege to be invited to deliver this speech to the immigration judiciary. For me, it is one way of keeping in touch with many former members of staff whom I see in the audience. I hope that you agree that there is little point in my delivering platitudes during the time I have so I intend to be frank and, therefore, possibly provocative but, I trust, always disinterested and objective. It may mean, of course, that I shall not be invited to attend again so I had better say all that I should on this occasion! I do genuinely wish to pay tribute to the dedication of the immigration judiciary through a period of turmoil and change. You will forgive me if I do not emulate the PM at the notorious reception for some immigration judiciary last year at No. 10 Downing Street when I understand that he congratulated you on your part in immigration control. Surprisingly, for a barrister, such an alleged comment and others more recently by the Prime Minister display a disconcerting inability to appreciate the role and independence of the judiciary.

I realize that many of you know about IAS (indeed many have worked for the organization in the past) but perhaps you will forgive me if I let you have a potted sketch of where we are today. We are a charity now having 20 offices throughout the UK, one in Bangladesh and one in Pakistan with plans to open more. Our more than 350 staff handle some 7,000 appeals cases every year. In England and Wales we are funded by the Legal Services Commission but, as we have to apply a financial eligibility as well as a merits test, we also offer a not-for-profit fee-paying service for those ineligible. In Scotland we are funded by the Scottish Executive and income from the Scottish Legal Aid Board. We undertake legal training courses, seminars and, of course, research and production of the leading publications all of which are available to others.

In my presentation this morning I should like to share some thoughts about the nature of the immigration judiciary, the attacks on it by politicians and press, the important role it fulfils in providing an independent check on executive authority, access to justice by our clients and then my observations about you and the Asylum and Immigration Tribunal and what the future might hold.

What are the hallmarks of an effective judiciary? Independence, access to high-quality information and research, the ability to arbitrate fairly between opposing interests are essentials. Moreover, in our Tribunal system, an immigration judge must be able to reach into the well of the court in a quasi-inquisitorial way and not just as an arbiter in an accusatorial system. I would add that there is an especial responsibility of the immigration judiciary to ensure that there is justice and an equality of arms when on one side there is the full panoply of the state and administrative law ranged against the vulnerable and often inarticulate individual.

The System

Independence of Individual Judges

Each judge must be responsible for their own decisions. Of course, there is a place for collective training in the law, practice and procedure and for coaching but when it is suggested that a failure to follow directions issued by the president could constitute a disciplinary matter or when supervision by another judge involves criticism of allowing a specific appeal then it becomes easy for the individual integrity of the judge to be impugned. Excessive time taken over cases or excessive grants of adjournments may give rise to legitimate questions but this is all about degree.

Attacks on the Judiciary, Lawyers and Civil Rights

Of greater concern are attacks on the judiciary and the legal profession by politicians and the press which undermine their authority and independence. It cannot be right that the Prime Minister should recently describe a High Court ruling as 'an abuse of common sense'. It is worse when it comes from the Home Secretary such as John Reid's description of the judgement as 'inexplicable'. Home Secretaries need to understand that they have to make decisions on cases themselves in a judicial manner. We can all remember the embarrassment of Jack Straw when, as Home Secretary, he assured the House of Commons that the Afghan hijackers would all be removed but it was pointed out to him that he would be responsible for adjudicating on their asylum claim. The then Home Secretary David Blunkett's intemperate outburst at Third Reading in the Commons of the 2004 Bill made it clear that this was his punishment of the legal profession. He said of the infamous ouster clause:

> Clause 11 (as it then was) has caused controversy and will cause it in another place. It is a classic example, which shows that had people been more modest in their operation of the law and their approach to their job, they would not have cooked the goose that laid the golden egg. I am talking about lawyers who simply abused the judicial review system by dragging out cases for months and, in some instances, years. That is what happens when those who preach liberalism lead us down the wrong path so that those who try to protect human rights and individual interests find that the system has been so abused that we have to remove the golden thread.

Yet in most cases the government has created a rod for its own back. The string of judicial decisions on removal of access of asylum-seekers to facilities being contrary to their human rights should have been anticipated and not put into the legislation in the first place.

We now see legislative intrusion into judicial affairs and the way in which judges can make their decisions which goes far beyond setting out the law which must be applied and this must compromise independence. Why is it that immigration judges must now be told legislatively as to how to judge credibility? As the Parliamentary Joint Committee on Human Rights suggested, 'Requiring a deciding authority to make an irrational inference might appear to compromise the fairness of the decision-making process.'

Alongside these issues, we have seen a constant erosion of civil liberties on the Benthamite principle of the needs of the greatest number. This is in the belief that the tabloid press and general public are content with the proposition that in order to protect the many the few must see their rights removed. They do not realize that human rights are indivisible and that if you take them away from the alleged terrorist then you take them away from all. For a government determined to have greater control over people's lives, however philanthropically motivated, individual civil liberties are an impediment. As Lord Hoffman 'remarked in the Belmarsh case 'The real threat to the life of the nation, in the sense of people living in accordance with its traditional laws and political values, comes not from terrorism but from laws like these.' The public must wake up to the reality: they may now ring the bells but they will soon wring their hands. They should be reminded of the words of Martin Niemoller:

> When Hitler attacked the Jews I was not a Jew, therefore, I was not concerned. And when Hitler attacked the Catholics, I was not a Catholic, and, therefore, I was not concerned. And when Hitler attacked the unions and the industrialists, I was not a member of the unions and I was not concerned. Then Hitler attacked me and the Protestant church – and there was nobody left to be concerned.

Asylum-seekers have been the subject of legislative discrimination and inflammatory language of politicians and press with chilling reminiscences of the last century. Whether it is the public labelling through separate queues in supermarket check-outs for voucher holders which were rightly scrapped but should never have been introduced, or the removal of in-country rights of appeal denying the judiciary the right to see and hear the most important person in the case, the appellant, the government have legitimized discrimination against asylum-seekers and must bear their share of responsibility when this is translated by thugs into physical attacks on members of the ethnic communities. It is an alarming proposition that inferior rights and poorer access to justice are reserved for a section of those who are nevertheless within the jurisdiction. Yet this seems to be the underlying principle: that, despite having access to legal advice and representation like anyone else, those subject to immigration control or claiming asylum do not enjoy the same rights of justice. The role of the judiciary is crucial in being vigilant about the reducing rights of those who, arguably, have greatest need of them in matters of life or death and their future.

Access to Justice – Justice for All?

There is a perversity sometimes in that the titles of Acts often signify that they create the opposite of what is intended. The Access to Justice Act was well-intentioned but the route to hell is paved with good intentions. The degree of intrusion by the body responsible for publicly funded legal representation into the way in which practitioners can conduct themselves with their clients, such as time limits for particular parts, has caused disillusion among lawyers. Clearly, there was a need for improvement by some publicly funded lawyers and the old green form scheme had been abused, but was the dramatic change in funding the way to deal with that?

The main problem about granting extensions under the previous system was that the decisions were taken by Legal Aid Board staff who were not qualified to argue with an articulate lawyer familiar about their own case. That has been resolved under the new system by having lawyers make decisions about whether extensions of time or grants of Controlled Legal Representation should be made in particular cases for those without devolved powers.

Controversially, in the face of universal opposition from practitioners, the Legal Services Commission will now make it part of contract compliance to be successful in at least 40 per cent of appeals. What is the inevitable consequence of this? It is that, notwithstanding the safeguard in the merits test of representation being available where there is a 50 per cent chance of success, lawyers fearful of losing their contracts if they do not achieve the arbitrary 40 per cent success rate will refuse representation to borderline cases. We oppose this measure as being inimical to access to justice for those who, under the current merits rules, should be given legal representation but will be refused it. No doubt the Legal Services Commission would say that all clients refused legal representation can appeal to themselves against that refusal but while the clock is ticking on their appeal hearing. Moreover, unless there is automatic appeal against refusal of legal representation (which, probably, is administratively and financially impractical) then there is no guarantee that my fears will not be realized.

This may well lead to more unrepresented appellants in which the immigration judiciary have a direct interest and it would be encouraging to hear you also being critical of this measure.

Another bar to access to justice is the complexity of the law and administrative hurdles placed in front of applicants and appellants. Time limits seem designed to trip the unwary rather than being an effective way to accelerate justice: the old adage of 'more haste, less speed' applies. It is of concern that the constant changes in the law has now made this field the most volatile and complicated of any. An individual now needs the advice of a competent lawyer in order to make what should be a simple application, which, of course, makes access to competent legal advice even more important. The former president of the Immigration Appeal Tribunal Sir Duncan Ouseley in response to the Department for Constitutional Affairs' proposals to limit the hours which can be spent on any individual case, stated:

> As a last comment which has a bearing on all the points which you raise, the parties before the IAA and their advisers, the judiciary at all levels and indeed administrators are significantly hampered in their work and the cost to public funds is increased by the chaotic way in which Parliament legislates and approves the commencement of legislation. In an area in which accessibility to the law ought to be straightforward, there are now in force a scattering of bits of every major Act in this area since 1971. These Acts are brought into force piecemeal, parts of the existing Acts are repealed piecemeal, and other parts are subject to piecemeal amendment of varying length and importance, all of varying commencement and transitional provisions. Indeed, we had the 12th Commencement Order for the 1999 Act shortly before the 4th Order for the 2002 Act.

We have seen legislative attempts to remove access to judicial review, despite this being an ancient remedy against maladministration rather than just another tier of appeal as so many Ministers seem to have thought. It would be good if reality reflected the assertion of the Minister Baroness Scotland: 'It is essential that we have a properly functioning system of immigration and asylum appeals and the opportunity for High Court judicial scrutiny of decisions' (on 29 July 2002). How can we have such a system when so much is done to impede access to justice? You will be more intimate than I with the evidence which indicates that the retrospective funding regime for those who seek reconsideration has had the desired effect of limiting lawyers willing to risk having to do the work pro bono and so denying access to justice to some of their clients.

Importance of Appeals

There is a sustained attack on the right of appeal. The government has now legislated to remove it in all categories of case except those in which it is specifically preserved. The first casualties will be those seeking to come as for work or study under the new points based system which will be phased in between July next year and the end of 2008. Taking away rights of appeal from students when initial decisions are so flawed (IAS won 59 per cent of all its student appeals in 2004) will give no guarantee of competent initial decisions. We argued that the government should not remove any rights of appeal until there has been a demonstrable improvement in decision making by entry clearance officers. Rights of appeal protect overseas applicants where decisions can often be based on cultural insensitivity or ignorance and prejudice. The highest rates of refusal are from Africa and Asia. This legislation is as racially discriminatory in its effect as the legislation of the 1960s leading to the 1971 Immigration Act which favoured the (largely white) Old Commonwealth against the (largely black and Asian) New Commonwealth. It risks further damaging Britain's unique relationship with Commonwealth countries.

During the extensive parliamentary debates over the Immigration, Asylum and Nationality Bill there was great criticism. Perhaps the most coruscating attack on the removal of rights of appeal, however, came not from these debates but from those around what became the 1993 legislation which removed rights of appeal for visitors. The then Shadow Home Secretary said

> No justification has been advanced [for the withdrawal of rights of appeal from visitors and students by the Asylum and Immigration Appeals Act 1993] other than this, which we heard again from the Secretary of State: the system is overloaded. It is a novel, bizarre and misguided principle of the legal system that if the exercise of legal rights is causing administrative inconvenience, the solution is to remove the right. No doubt that might satisfy the bureaucrats and Government administrators in many areas, but it can hardly be a justification for removing rights … When a right of appeal is removed, what is removed is a valuable and necessary constraint on those who exercise original jurisdiction. That is true not merely of immigration officers but of anybody. The immigration officer who knows that his decision may be subject to appeal is likely to be a good deal more circumspect, careful and even handed than the officer who knows that his power of decision is absolute. That is simply, I fear, a matter of human nature, quite apart from anything else.

That, of course, was Tony Blair (House of Commons, 2 November 1992). On 11 January 1993 [Col. 641], Mr Blair stated: 'We oppose the Bill not just because the removal of the right of appeal in immigration cases is wholly wrong and unfair, but because the Bill will not apply in the way that it should the rules of natural justice, which must be applied to such cases.'

In the Lords the Minister Baroness Ashton put great store on the administrative review of decisions as though this were an adequate safeguard but we all know what happens when the body responsible for the decision becomes judge and jury in its own cause. Despite assurances from Baroness Ashton that she would come forward with a model of what administrative review would look like, we are no further forward with the details. Current thinking in the Home Office is that this will be only on matters of fact and there will be 14 days in which to make representations which will be considered by a separate panel. If the administrative review of disputed decisions shows that entry clearance managers consider the majority of the original decision to be correct, then the efficacy of review becomes self-fulfilling as more effective than appeal to an independent body. Will other categories of case such as family settlement become casualties and lose the right of appeal?

We must be vigilant. No doubt the judges and practitioners who defend the rights of appeal will be accused of special pleading, but the disappearance of those functions is not the issue: it is whether in a system of administrative law, in which the applicant has few rights against the panoply of the state, in which there has been the sustained legislative erosion of those rights for more than a decade, in which so much power is vested in the Secretary of State and where the Immigration Rules themselves are not even a statutory instrument, there needs to be an independent arbiter to determine whether the rules of natural justice and other hallmarks of a civilized society based on the constitutional pillars of the executive, the legislature and the judiciary.

The Wilson Committee [Cmnd 3387 August 1967] which gave birth to the immigration tribunal system recognized the importance of independent appeals. It stated [page 21 §66] 'On the question which is central to our terms of reference – the question of rights of appeal – opinion among our witnesses was virtually unanimous in favour of establishing some kind of system of appeals.' It was responsible also for suggesting the creation of a voluntary organisation to help with those rights of appeal which, of course, became UKIAS and now IAS. One must wonder if the system were being devised afresh there would be such enthusiasm for appeals to be heard in the tribunal system designed for matters of fact rather than in the regular courts where matters of law are argued regularly, such has this field of administrative law become so legally complex. It is now some twenty years since, in practice and now in law, immigration judges are chosen from the ranks of lawyers and not lay persons.

We need to remind succeeding generations of the attempted outrage which became known as the ouster clause' which appeared on the face of the Bill when it first appeared in November 2003. It should be pinned on every lawyer's wall as it sought to exclude from any judicial oversight decisions reached through lack of jurisdiction, irregularity, error of law, breach of natural justice, or any other matter, other than when alleging that a member of the Tribunal had acted in bad faith. It would have excluded habeas corpus applications in immigration cases. The Parliamentary Joint Committee on Human Rights was especially critical (Joint

Committee on Human Rights, Third Report of Session 2003–04, *Scrutiny of Bills: Progress Report*, HL: Paper 23, HC 252) stating:

> These provisions cause us serious concern in relation to the attempt in the Bill to limit the remedies for violations of Convention rights provided by section 7 of the Human Rights Act 1998. These provisions also raise issues relating to the right to an effective remedy for a violation of Convention rights under ECHR Article 13, as well as serious issues relating to the maintenance of the rule of law … It would allow the immigration and asylum process to operate outside normal arrangements for protecting Convention rights. Any step which immunizes an area of public administration in this way sets a dangerous precedent.

The measure flew in the face of Magna Carta and hundreds of years of hard won establishment of the supremacy of the law over all, including the executive. The famous jurist Sir Edward Coke to whom is attributed the immortal phrase in reference to the King 'However high ye may be the law is above ye' turned in his grave. We fought a civil war over whether the monarch who then embodied the executive could act outside the law. The jurisprudence leading to the concept of Wednesbury unreasonableness and the need for Ministers to act in a judicial way was under threat. It took the combined opposition of members of the House of Lords and of the then Lord Chief Justice to persuade the government to withdraw this infamy. The Lord Chief Justice Lord Woolf described it as 'fundamentally in conflict with the rule of law' and a 'blot on the reputation of ministers'. What continues to worry me is that someone not only conceived of such a removal of the supremacy of the rule of law but also thought that it could be bulldozed through Parliament. Truly, for evil to triumph it needs only for good people to do nothing.

Equality of Arms

I lay no charge against the judiciary for the unfair nature of the procedure rules and I know that, over the years and behind the scenes, there has been much discussion with government officials about inherent unfairness and impracticality of many of the rules that have been effected. I realize that the failure to appreciate these points has been a source of great frustration to those who proffered them. The fact remains that it is a feature of what I have described above in terms of unfairness that the tight rules that apply to appellants do not apply equally to the Home Office. Time limits are often not only inimical to the proper consideration and preparation of a case by practitioners but are often the cause of wasted expenditure when appeals are lodged protectively because the time frame is too tight for a full assessment to be made. We argued for ten days in which to submit an application for reconsideration. By the time one of our Tribunal Counsellors has considered the merits of an application and advised against an application it is too late for the appellant to lodge in person without asking for an extension and alleging that IAS is responsible for it being out of time!

The Actors

Immigration Judges

I am mindful that immigration judges have had to operate against the same legislative and other changes over the last few years as practitioners but with the added burden of a new tribunal so I have every sympathy and admiration for the work that has been done. Seven major pieces of primary legislation on immigration, asylum and nationality in thirteen years, on top of the Human Rights Act and secondary legislation and changes to the immigration rules so numerous that I have lost count do not bring confidence that the government has either a strategic plan in this field of law or that it can resist the temptation to legislate as an alternative to administrative amelioration and increased competence. We have argued that many of the shortcomings of the system could have been overcome through better administration rather than new legislation. Some parts of legislation have never seen the light of day, such as Part III of the 1999 Act (the right to automatic bail hearings) which was never implemented and then repealed only three years later! Now that the government has established a biennial as against a triennial cycle of new legislation let me predict that the 2008 Act, besides setting up the sponsorship register for the points-based system, will be the great consolidating one – long overdue if only thereafter the government can withhold its legislative hand and not itch to interfere with matters which it does not understand – to quote Lord Mountararat in *Iolanthe*. It is time for Parliament to do nothing in particular and to do it very well!

I realize that immigration judges undergo a great deal of training and have access to the best materials on the current law – the most prominent of which, as you would expect me to acknowledge, are the IAS quarterly *Immigration Law Digest*, the fortnightly *Immigration Law Update* and the *Index*! I remain chair of Trustees of the Electronic Immigration Network which won the selection by the DCA to be the immigration part of the judicial portal. I am disturbed, therefore, that not just my own staff but many other practitioners who talk to me express the view that they know what will happen to their case as soon as they see before whom they have been listed for hearing. This has been an ongoing criticism for many years but it is not one I heard, for example, when I practised as a member of the Bar in the civil courts so I have to wonder if it is a particular feature of immigration hearings. I have no means of quantifying the extent of this concern or to whom it applies but I hope that it is to a very few. Libby Arfon-Jones heard this criticism directly from the participants at our public conference in Leicester last year. Henry Hodge and I have discussed this in the past and I accept entirely that it would be wrong in principle to have a publicly available register of how many appeals have been allowed and dismissed by an individual immigration judge. So much depends on the nature of the cases that come before you and the evidence that is presented. Yet this concern has reached such proportions that I believe that the Asylum and Immigration Tribunal needs to show that it is addressing the issue. The issues are complicated enough without it being a lottery.

Quality of Forensic Advocacy

We supported the introduction of accreditation, although not the manner and haste with which it were done, as there were serious question marks over the competence of publicly funded lawyers, just as we supported the regulation of immigration advisers in the 1999 legislation. We are subject to the requirements of both the Legal Services Commission and the Office of the Immigration Services Commissioner. The problem with regulation, however, is that it tends to be cumulative so that when the Legal Services Commission introduced accreditation the old 2004 changes on how to conduct a case remained in force. We are in grave danger of over-regulation. That said, I do not believe that sufficient emphasis has been placed on forensic advocacy at Level 2 (Office of the Immigration Services Commissioner Level 3). If a video recording is good enough for the interview part of the tripartite test, then why is there not a video assessment made of the ability of an advocate to present a case? I hope that you might exempt IAS from this sort of criticism as we do give training specifically on this but whenever I observe other advocates in immigration appeal hearings I am none too impressed at either the preparation or the advocacy of the material points in the case. I include in this the Home Office Presenting Officers. You may share that view.

The Future and Review of the Asylum and Immigration Tribunal

There is a bright spot on access to legal advice, however, in the New Asylum Model now being rolled out. We and others have argued for a long time that there needs to be front loading in the system so that if more initial decisions are correct then there will be fewer appeals. It cannot be right that often the first time all the evidence in a case is properly assembled is at the hearing of an appeal. We welcomed the Home Office inviting the UNHCR to examine its initial decision making in what became the Quality Initiative and we welcome the New Asylum Model which has been developed in full consultation with practitioners and in which we are seeing at long last legal representation at the substantive interview and a possible pilot this autumn of pre-screening legal advice.

As to the Review of the Asylum and Immigration Tribunal, we regret greatly that the scope of this was so limited and feel that an opportunity to articulate concerns was missed. In our own commentary we noted that, with the emphasis on speed and discouragement of appeals going higher, the interests of justice are only indirectly mentioned in the objectives. This cannot be dismissed as an unfortunate oversight. It is highly revealing in the view of IAS and it accurately reflects the actual priorities of the Asylum and Immigration Tribunal, the Department for Constitutional Affairs and the Home Office.

The *asylum* appeals process has been speeded up but arguably not in a way that is compatible with fairness. The *immigration* appeals process has, if anything, slowed down and has certainly not speeded up. This is in line with the priority the government, now institutionalized as the respondent before the Asylum and Immigration Tribunal, attaches to speeding up asylum cases. It highlights the danger that the Asylum and Immigration Tribunal becomes in perception or reality no longer in a position of neutrality.

The effectiveness of Case Management Review hearings depends on the immigration judge being properly prepared as well as the representative and the Home Office Presenting Officer. This does not always prove to be the case in practice, leading to ineffective Case Management Reviews that add no value or efficiency and do not in any meaningful sense manage or review the management of the case. Case Management Reviews are now routinely equivalent to one unit of time for IAS staff, that is, less than six minutes. The Home Office Presenting Officer is unable or unwilling to limit issues or make concessions and the immigration judge is unwilling to give non-standard directions. The travel and waiting time for such hearings is nevertheless considerable. We had three cases where the full hearing had been listed to take place on the fourth working day or less after the Case Management Review. Complying with any directions in that time clearly is impossible. It is indicative of the sacrifice of fairness, efficiency and case management on the altar of speed. We listed lack of case ownership at the Home Office and at the Asylum and Immigration Tribunal, ineffectual administration and organization at the Home Office, lack of sanction against the Home Office or individual Home Office Presenting Officers, lack of consistency and passive approach by immigration judges and lack of proper preparation by the parties as reasons for the ineffectiveness of Case Management Reviews. I shall not give the detail of our submission but I urge you to read it if you have not already done so.

The two-stage approach to reconsideration hearings adopted in Practice Direction 14 is a sensible and useful one, particularly given the retrospective funding regime and the strong incentive thus given to representatives to do the minimum possible preparation work at the reconsideration stage of proceedings. Representatives need as much clarity as possible in order not to jeopardize costs but the two-stage process is not as clear as it could or should be. Representatives (and the Asylum and Immigration Tribunal in fact) at the stage two reconsideration hearing are often unaware of the basis of reconsideration. This is partly because the reasons are not disclosed, although IAS hopes that this practice will change in the light of Collins J's recent decision in *R (Wani) v SSHD and AIT* [2005] EWHC 2815 (Admin).

The Asylum and Immigration Tribunal, appellant's representative and Home Office Presenting Officer sometimes all come away from the hearing with a different view on what has just taken place, so even if there was to be unusual continuity of personnel through to the stage two hearing this would not help. IAS has experience of cases where directions that were understood by IAS (and, we contend, when properly read and understood) to limit the issues at stage two have been ignored by the Asylum and Immigration Tribunal stage two panel. One very serious problem is the extreme reluctance of many panels at first stage reconsideration hearings to make a final decision on a case. IAS has requested appellants and witnesses to attend first stage reconsideration hearings from outside London in the hope that final resolution might be achieved only to find that the Senior Immigration Judges hearing the case refuse to do so, despite having full bundles and witnesses available. This is a particular problem in entry clearance cases that have already been much delayed by the ECO and the IAA/AIT, with serious prejudice being caused to the applicant and sponsor as a result.

We note that the Home Office regularly abandons its own appeals and often concedes appellants' appeals on the day of the hearing (and the Asylum and Immigration Tribunal often plays a useful role by putting appropriate pressure on representatives), but this should be done far sooner and without a hearing. It is particularly galling in entry clearance cases where the appellant has already been kept waiting for years by the time of reconsideration. We feel that Case Management Review of reconsideration hearings could be helpful.

We strongly condemned the way in which the Civil Procedure Rules were introduced into the Asylum and Immigration Tribunal process. In our submission we list a series of problems which were all avoidable and have led to serious injustice in individual cases. These involve the 4 p.m. cut-off time, the unnecessary faxing of large bundles to the Asylum and Immigration Tribunal.

On the other hand, the opt-in review process appears to be working relatively smoothly and we welcome the clarity regarding the interpretation of the funding test provided by the case of *RS (Iran)* [2005] UKAIT 00138.

I referred earlier to the appearance that the system is designed to discourage *all* appeals, not just those with little merit, when the retrospective funding regime is considered alongside the five-day time limit for lodging reconsideration applications. There has never been any attempt to show how these procedures and systems differentiate between a strong case and a weak one, for example, by enabling the potential appellant to take good-quality legal advice on the true prospects of success. If anything, the system encourages poor applications for reconsideration as there is insufficient time and funding to do the applications well or make an informed judgment on the ultimate prospects of success.

On listing, we note that asylum cases are listed too soon and entry clearance cases are listed too far ahead. The pressure on immigration judges not to adjourn cases is not conducive to the interests of justice in all cases: the timescale can make the commissioning of medical or country-expert evidence almost impossible. The standard practice of allowing the respondent in entry clearance appeals around 18 weeks to produce documents is considered by IAS to be totally unacceptable. It is far too long and can cause considerable hardship to applicants in family immigration cases, for example, where a child is applying to join a parent on the grounds of inadequate care in the country of origin. There appears to be no attempt to prioritize cases nor to examine the individual circumstances. We were informed at a stakeholder meeting that this period was agreed with UK Visas yet they are one of the parties to the appeals in question and this arrangement was clearly reached with that party's administrative convenience in mind. An unfavourable comparison can be drawn with the attention that is given to the administrative convenience of appellants and their representatives and to the short time limits that are given to appellants for them to comply with directions. Again, Case Management Reviews in immigration cases would be a far more appropriate way forward and would also serve to reduce the number of late adjournments when documents are not produced at all by the respondent or are produced on the day of the hearing.

We like to congratulate ourselves on the research and published work on the nature and scope of Country Guideline cases and our recommendations on how they should be approached if they are to fulfil their stated aims and objectives. The original report, published in February 2005, can be downloaded from www.iasuk.org under 'IAS Publications'. Many of the recommendations effectively were adopted by the president of the Immigration Appeal Tribunal in the case of *NM and Others (Lone Women – Ashraf) Somalia CG* [2005] UKIAT 00076 and the quality and transparency of many Country Guideline cases has noticeably improved since then. Many subsequent decisions have been characterized by thorough referencing of sources, well-structured reasons that consider the range of available evidence and a clear demonstration of how the evidence has contributed to the ultimate conclusions.

The original IAS report was followed by an article in the quarterly *IAS Digest* which I hope that many of you had a chance to read. One of the remaining problems, however, is the use of reported determinations to supplement Country Guideline cases. The principle behind Country Guideline cases is that they are unambiguous, authoritative and current. They cease to become so when supplemented in an ad hoc way and it is confusing for representatives and immigration judges alike. In two cases referred to in our submission the more recent cases add considerably to the designated Country Guideline cases, arguably replacing them, yet are only designated as 'reported'. IAS has advocated for many years a wholly independent source of country information as in the Canadian system. We like to think that we were largely responsible for the former Immigration Minister Des Browne distancing the information section of the Country Information Policy Unit from policy but we must remember that this was a unit which prided itself on not having anyone with an analytical research background.

I fear that the government has gone as far as it will on this and that we must hope that there will be created a truly independent country information source at the European level – it makes sense that in a common European asylum system applying the qualification Directive all EU countries should make decisions on the same information about countries of origin which should be available to all. Although the Home Office country information has improved a great deal since our original report, it is still produced by one of the sides in an adversarial arena and we have concerns that immigration judges often do not subject it to the same level of scrutiny as evidence submitted by appellants.

Often this is true of expert evidence whether on country-of -origin or medical matters. Expert witnesses come from different academic disciplines and do not use the same language as the courtroom and may not know about the presentation of evidence, but that does not mean that they do not know what they are talking about or have something important to say. We see the evidence of highly regarded professionals in their own area of expertise sometimes treated with disdain by some immigration judges. A general practitioner may be dismissed by as having insufficient expertise to diagnose a physical or mental condition, yet have received extensive and ongoing training and have seen countless other similar cases, and is certainly considered able to diagnose and treat by the NHS. An anthropologist may seem evasive by refusing to state definitely that something is or is not a practice in a given country but that is because there are variations or there is disagreement among anthropologists or she or he is uncomfortable with the idea of certainty. Not all expert reports are favourable to the appellant but it is unlikely that the negative ones will be seen by the judiciary.

I have referred to the legislative intrusion into the way in which decisions are reached but I fear that this is compounded when immigration judges themselves regard an occurrence as implausible based on their own environment rather than within the context of the habits and realities in the appellant's country.

Sadly, we note a culture in the Asylum and Immigration Tribunal of reluctance to work with appellants' representatives or stakeholder groups to improve the management of the appeals process. This contrasts with the close working relationship the Asylum and Immigration Tribunal has with the Department for Constitutional Affairs and the Home Office. By way of example, although regular stakeholder meetings are held, they are invariably used by the Asylum and Immigration Tribunal to inform stakeholders of what has already happened. There is no opportunity for constructive engagement and there is little or no attempt to elicit stakeholder views or contributions prior to implementing change. The poor management of the reconsideration process since its introduction in April 2005 could perhaps have been avoided with meaningful and well-managed consultation. This is in stark contrast with a new desire by the IND to engage in a meaningful way with stakeholders which has coincided with the advent of Lin Homer as director-general.

Our staff has identified many of these cultural problems as attributable to senior immigration judges who are in danger of becoming an obstruction to fairness and efficiency. Senior immigration judges are extremely reluctant to hear oral evidence or undertake the judicial work necessary finally to determine an appeal, even where the representative and appellant are prepared to do so. They are unwilling to perform case-management functions. They regard representatives as superfluous to the giving of legal or country guidance. They fail to respond until the day of the hearing to applications by representatives, for example, for the amendment of grounds, the calling of oral evidence, the amendment of directions given and the lodging of a cross appeal.

I did warn you that I would not mince my words so if there was any earlier scintilla of doubt that I might be invited on a subsequent occasion I suspect that it has now been put beyond peradventure!

Will there be further changes to the Asylum and Immigration Tribunal after only such a short time of its existence? We warned that it would not work and, moreover, we could not see how it sat comfortably within the Leggatt proposals. In our briefing on the Second Reading debate in the Commons on 17 December 2003 we said:

> If the Government cannot be persuaded to retain a two-tier system in line with the Leggatt proposals then it is essential that there is judicial review of decisions which are not in accordance with the law. If this is not to be by way of judicial review to the Administrative Court (hearing oral argument) then we urge that this should be by way of statutory review, as introduced by the Government in the 2002 Act. As Baroness Scotland claimed 'statutory review is an important part of our policy to provide a fair but swift and efficient system … Statutory review provides a quick process to correct errors that may have been made by the tribunal, so that cases can be sent back to the tribunal, where oral evidence can be given.

Rights of appeal in student cases (Tier 4 of the new points based system) are likely to go in February 2008 when Tier 4 is introduced.

What should be the response of the judiciary to the threats and dangers I have identified if, indeed, you feel they have substance and are not the paranoia of one who has been involved in this field for perhaps too long? The attitude of the senior judiciary is admirable: seeking to maintain the integrity of the law and the rights of citizens while respectful that in a democracy the judges interpret the law and do not make it. I urge the Asylum and Immigration Tribunal also to be proactive and, if I may distort the words of the poet, not to go gentle into the removal of right but rage, rage against the dying of the light.

Appendix 5
The International Association of Refugee Law Judges' Guidelines on the Judicial Approach to Expert Medical Evidence

1. Introduction

1.1. The International Association of Refugee Law Judges (IARLJ) is committed to ensuring the provision of fair hearings and decisions to all claimants.
1.2. For the purposes of these Guidelines all references to judges include judicial and quasi-judicial decision makers.
1.2.1. These Guidelines are a tool designed to assist judges in the fulfilment of their task of ensuring that proper and adequate account is taken of all evidence, including any expert medical evidence,[1] within the refugee status determination process or other similar determination processes, for example immigration/migration appeals, humanitarian protection and human rights appeals, which are all matters that affect the lives of individuals directly and profoundly.
1.2.2. For the purposes of these Guidelines 'expert medical evidence' encompasses all matters relating to the physical and/or mental/psychological health/well-being of the claimant.
1.2.3. For the purposes of these Guidelines 'expert medical evidence' includes both written and oral evidence.
1.2.4. In some jurisdictions there may be no procedural provisions for expert medical evidence in place or little use is made of them. Judges should be receptive to expert medical evidence whenever it is thought helpful.
1.2.5. Any medical report or psychiatric report deserves careful and specific consideration, bearing in mind, particularly, that there may be psychological consequences from ill-treatment which may affect the evidence which is given by the applicant. Attention should be given to each and every aspect of medical reports.[2] The consideration given to a report depends on the quality of the report

1 See below para 1.2.5, Section 4, and 6.(c) & (d) for elaboration of 'expert'.
2 As noted for example in Ibrahim [1998] INLR 511. These Guidelines address the subsequent criticism of Ibrahim in HE (DRC) [2004] UKIAT 00321, namely that it 'was not a sound approach, of relevance to each and every medical or psychiatric report on issues of credibility, or indeed more generally. The experience of the Tribunal ... since then is that the quality of reports is so variable and sadly often so poor and unhelpful, that there is no

and the standing and qualifications of the medical or health care professional/expert. If the judge decides to reject any medical report there is a positive obligation to do more than merely state that it had been 'considered'. The decision maker must provide some meaningful discussion as to how he or she had taken account of the applicant's serious medical condition before making a negative credibility finding. The failure to do so in this case would be likely to be considered to be a 'reviewable error.'[3]

2. Use of Guidelines

2.1. These Guidelines should be used and considered in conjunction with any relevant guidelines on vulnerable persons. It is necessary to ensure equal treatment, with differentiation where appropriate, before the mandated asylum determination body.[4]
2.1.2. The United Nations' *Istanbul Protocol: Manual on the Effective Investigation and Documentation of Torture and Other Cruel, Inhuman or Degrading Treatment or Punishment* (1999) represents an attempt to establish international guidelines for the assessment of persons who allege torture and ill-treatment, for investigating cases of alleged torture and for reporting findings to the judiciary or any other investigative body. The manual includes principles for the effective investigation and documentation of torture and other cruel, inhuman or degrading treatment or punishment.[5] For the current edition of the *Istanbul Protocol* see Office of the United Nations High Commissioner for Human Rights Geneva Professional Training Series No. 8/Rev. 1 United Nations New York and Geneva, 2004 *Istanbul Protocol: Manual on the Effective Investigation and Documentation of Torture and Other Cruel, Inhuman or Degrading Treatment or Punishment.*

3. The Role of Expert Medical Evidence

3.1. Expert medical evidence is obtained for one or more of the following purposes:

- to substantiate claims of ill-treatment;

---

necessary obligation to give them weight merely because they are medical or psychiatric reports. The consideration given to a report depends on the quality of the report and the standing and qualifications of the doctor.' (para. 16).

3 See also note 8.

4 See, for example, Guideline 8 – Guideline on Procedures with Respect to Vulnerable Persons appearing before the Immigration and Refugee Board of Canada, December 2006, which aims to provide procedures for dealing with claimants who may encounter additional difficulties due to, for example, physical or mental health problems, age, or gender issues.

5 The guidelines contained within the Istanbul Protocol represent minimum standards.

- to establish a correlation between physical or psychological injuries and the alleged torture or ill-treatment;
- to explain a claimant's difficulties in giving evidence or recounting events by
  - (a) providing possible explanation(s) for inconsistencies and/or contradictions within a claimant's narrative of events;[6]
  - (b) providing possible explanation(s) for reticence or reluctance in divulging a full account of events, for example delay in divulging allegations of sexual assault and/or other forms of violence directed against an individual[7],
- to address the possible effect of removal and return to the country of origin upon a person's physical or mental well-being or that of a family member;
- to assess treatment needs.
- to reduce the need for the claimant to give testimony about traumatic events.[8]

3.2. Expert medical evidence may not prove conclusively whether or not someone was tortured or had suffered serious physical or psychological injury. Rather, the medical report provides expert opinion on the degree to which the injuries or behaviour presented correlate with the allegations of torture/ill-treatment.[9]

6 See, for example, Feleke, 2007 FC 539 in which it was stated that 'The medical assessment, which the Refugee Protection Division (RPD) accepted, stated that the Applicant suffered from "cognitive difficulties, avoidance behaviours, generalized anxiety symptoms", all of which could have provided an explanation for the Applicant's behaviour. The RPD, in finding a decision either way, with regards to credibility, had an obligation to explain how the diagnosis impacts the RPD's assessment of any discrepancies.' (para. 18).

7 Supra note 2. See also *Atay v Canada (Minister of Citizenship and Immigration)*, 2008 FC 201 at para. 16, stating 'Simply referring in its reasons to a psychological report addressing posttraumatic stress disorder is not sufficient; the Board must consider whether the psychological circumstance might help explain an omission, lack of detail, or confusion regarding the events if these are the exact cognitive errors referred to in the psychologist's report.'

8 *X.E.B. (Re)*, [2002] R.P.D.D. No. 230 at para. 17.

9 See, for example, *CASE OF R.C. v SWEDEN* (Application no. 41827/07), European Court of Human Rights, 9 March 2010, in which the 'Court notes that the forensic medical report submitted at its request has documented numerous scars on the applicant's body. Although some of them may have been caused by means other than by torture, the Court accepts the report's general conclusion that the injuries, to a large extent, are consistent with having been inflicted on the applicant by other persons and in the manner in which he described, thereby strongly indicating that he has been a victim of torture. The medical evidence thus corroborates the applicant's story' (para. 53).

3.3. Expert medical evidence should form an integral part of any findings of credibility and should not be separated from other evidence.[10]
3.4. The judge may, in the context of the evidence as a whole, have to consider the possibility that the claimant is feigning the symptoms he or she puts forward.

4. Standards to Ensure Uniformity and Consistency of Expert Medical Evidence

4.1. Expert medical evidence should include the credentials of the author of the expert medical report, including:

- medical education and clinical training;
- psychological/psychiatric training;
- medical qualification;
- membership of any professional bodies;
- experience in documenting evidence of torture/ill-treatment;
- experience of treating asylum seekers, refugees or victims of torture/ill-treatment;
- whether the expert is familiar with the *Istanbul Protocol* (see below);
- whether the *Istanbul Protocol* informs the medical opinion;
- current Curriculum Vitae including relevant publications, presentations and Continuing Professional Development.

4.1.2. In situations where no formal medical training/qualification has been gained by the examiner, any relevant practical experience working with refugees/victims of torture which has culminated in the author of the report gaining expertise should be stated. However, this expertise must be recognised as having weight by a relevant authority, e.g., the Minister of Health. As in all instances, circumstances peculiar to a particular country, e.g., having relatively few trained medical practitioners, should be considered.

10 *C.A. v Canada (Minister of Citizenship and Immigration)* [1997] F.C.J. No. 1082 at para. 12 ('In this case, credibility was also the "linchpin" to the Board's decision. Nonetheless, the Board failed to indicate, how, if at all, the psychological report was considered when making its credibility finding. The Board was obliged to do more than merely state that it had "considered" the report. It was obliged to provide some meaningful discussion as to how it had taken account of the applicant's serious medical condition before it made its negative credibility finding. The failure to do so in this case constitutes a reviewable error and justified the matter being returned to a newly appointed Board'); *Hassan v Canada (Minister of Citizenship and Immigration)* (1999), 174 F.T.R. 288 (F.C.) (finding that the medical evidence at issue (a psychological report), formed a part of the basis for evaluating the claimant's credibility).

4.2. Expert medical evidence should deal with the individual claimant's particular case so as to:

- advise on the duration, frequency and regularity of interviews and/or consultations the author of the report had with the claimant;
- advise on the examination (including the nature and the extent of) and diagnosis of the claimant, and make clear the diagnostic tests used and methodology employed;
- advise as to any suggested prescribed treatment;
- advise on the long term prognosis including;
  (i) the likely impact return to country of origin could have on the claimant's physical and/or mental health including likelihood of re-traumatization;
  (ii) availability of medical and psychiatric services in the country of origin;
  (iii) drug availability and rehabilitation services in the country of origin;[11]

4.3. Expert medical evidence should be restricted to the author's area(s) of competence and expertise.
4.4. Expert medical evidence should demonstrate a critical and objective analysis of the injuries and/or symptoms displayed, rather than an unquestioning acceptance of the claimant's account of how any injuries were sustained.[12] As a norm the evaluation should involve:

- An objective description of the injury;
- A description of how the injury was incurred according to the claimant;
- An opinion on the consistency between the nature of the injury and the manner in which it was incurred, preferably with precise reasons;

4.5. Expert medical evidence should address the relative likelihood of any other possible cause for the injury in question.
4.6. Expert medical evidence should provide an overall evaluation of all lesions and note the consistency of each lesion with a particular form of torture. However, the overall conclusion should not go further than what is commensurate with findings as detailed by the expert. That is, if all that a doctor does is say that

---

11 4.1. (b)(ii) & (iii) should only be addressed when such knowledge lies within the recognized expertise of the report's author. However a report should not be considered to be deficient if it does not include such information.

12 *Mendez v Canada (Minister of Citizenship and Immigration)* 2005 FC 75 at para. 41, stating 'The general rule is that while a diagnosis drawn from a claimant's account of facts already found not to be credible can be disregarded, a diagnosis drawn from independent observation of symptoms is not so easily set aside.'

the scarring/injury is 'highly consistent' with the claimed history, without also addressing the relative likelihood of the few other possible causes, the report will clearly be of less potential value than if it does and an immigration judge may hold that a finding of 'highly consistent' has very limited value.[13]
4.7. Expert medical evidence should remain impartial and refrain from giving any opinion as to the overall credibility of the claimant or of the merits of the claimant's case.
4.8. A holistic approach should be adopted to the evaluation of expert medical evidence. A report which does not contain all of the above should not be disregarded as deficient.

5. Assessment of Injuries Pursuant to the *Istanbul Protocol* Criteria

The following has been extracted from the *Istanbul Protocol* and is offered as what may be regarded as aspirational best practice. The *Istanbul Protocol* sets out in some detail the terms which should be generally used in describing/establishing the correlation between the alleged ill treatment and the injury sustained.
5.1. Visible Injuries
It is advocated that in cases of visible scarring each lesion and the overall pattern of lesions the physician should indicate the degree of consistency between the lesion(s) and the alleged injurious conduct. The following terms, referred to as the five-fold hierarchy of degrees of consistency between the injury and 'the attribution', are generally used:

a. (*a*) *Not consistent*: the lesion could not have been caused by the trauma described;
b. (*b*) *Consistent with*: the lesion could have been caused by the trauma described, but it is non-specific and there are many other possible causes;
c. (*c*) *Highly consistent*: the lesion could have been caused by the trauma described, and there are few other possible causes;
d. (*d*) *Typical of*: this is an appearance that is usually found with this type of trauma, but there are other possible causes;
e. (*e*) *Diagnostic of*: this appearance could not have been caused in any way other than that described.[14]

---

13 Reservations have been expressed that this could demand speculation and enumeration about a range of other possible causes. It is enough for the expert to state that there are other possible causes for the injury, and how likely they are considering what is known about the claimant's life history and experiences. The problem of this not being addressed can be seen in *RT (medical reports – causation of scarring) Sri Lanka* [2008] UKAIT 00009 (paras 28–35).

14 This hierarchy is taken from the Istanbul Protocol, para. 187 and has received judicial endorsement in the UK in *RT (medical reports - causation of scarring) Sri Lanka*

5.2. Non-visible Scarring

The *Istanbul Protocol* at para. 287, whilst referring to cases of torture, suggests in assessing persecution/abuse/ill-treatment that the following should likewise be considered:

(a) The extent to which the psychological findings are consistent with the alleged report of torture, abuse/ill-treatment;
(b) Given the individual's circumstances the extent to which the psychological findings are expected or may be typical reactions to extreme stress;
(c) The stage at which the individual is in the course of recovery given the time frame in relation to the torture events and the fluctuating nature of some psychological symptoms;
(d) The impact of external factors on the individual, such as ongoing persecution, forced migration, exile, loss of family and social role;
(e) Special physical conditions, such as head injury sustained during torture or detention.

5.3. Clinicians should comment on the consistency of psychological findings and the extent to which these findings correlate with the alleged abuse. The emotional state and expression of the person during the interview, his or her symptoms, the history of detention and torture and the personal history prior to torture should be described. Factors such as the onset of specific symptoms related to the trauma, the specificity of any particular psychological findings and patterns of psychological functioning should be noted.

6. The Application of Expert Medical Evidence

6.1.

(a) Expert medical evidence should be treated as an integral element of all the evidence considered in establishing the facts;[15]
(b) If expert medical evidence is dismissed by a decision-maker as being of little evidential value, this should be stated accompanied by appropriate reasoning.[16] This is particularly the case if the expert medical evidence

---

[2008] UKAIT 00009; *SA (Somalia)* [2006] EWCA Civ 1302; *R (on the application of PB) v Secretary of State for the Home Department* [2008] EWHC 364; and in the Republic of Ireland in *S v MJELR & Anor* [2007] IEHC 305.

15 See *Mibanga vs SSHD* [2005] EWCA Civ 36. See also Paragraph 42 of the UNHCR Handbook further advocating such a holistic approach to evidence.

16 *Bains v Canada (Minister of Employment and Immigration)* (1993), 63 F.T.R. 312 at para. 9 (F.C.).

has been submitted by an organisation which has established itself as an objective and reliable provider of medico-legal reports in asylum or asylum-related cases;

(c) A decision-maker, as a layperson, should not attempt to substitute his or her own opinion in preference to that of a reliable expert.[17]

17 Lozano Pulido, 2007 FC 209 in which in response to a decision not to give weight to a psychiatric report it was reiterated that 'while members of the Refugee Protection Division have expertise in the adjudication of refugee claims, they are not qualified psychiatrists, and bring no specialized expertise to the question of the mental condition of refugee claimants' (para. 28), June 2010.

Appendix 6
Resignation of Lady Mar, House of Lords[1]

The Countess of Mar: My Lords, it was with deep regret that I tendered my resignation to the Asylum and Immigration Tribunal a fortnight ago. I did that because I could no longer bear the incompetence of the whole business. I was giving cases my most careful and anxious scrutiny day after day knowing full well that the whole system that that was built on was flawed.

The noble Viscount, Lord Bridgeman, gave a list of faults under this Government. I attribute quite a lot of the problems to the Tory Party's removal of work permits in 1992, which led to an increase in the number of asylum cases. Before that, asylum claimants used to be the intelligentsia from other countries but after that we got the people who came over mainly from the Asian subcontinent to work here for two or three years, to build their brick house in Pakistan, Bangladesh or India, and then to go back; then someone else would come over. A whole industry built up with agents taking thousands of pounds from families in order to get one person into this country to work. The agents used to say, 'You will have to go through the system but at the end don't worry – you will not be removed; you will stay'. Those people would have gone back in the past but they now stay.

Does the Minister agree that it is necessary to pay much more attention to people at entry points in airports? I know that in some cases – Heathrow Airport, for example – the immigration and customs posts are not manned in the early hours of the morning. Don't kid me – the agents know this and that is when they bring people in. We do not know who goes out. I think it was this Government who stopped counting the people who leave. We need to know who comes in and who goes out. We also need much more co-operation between the Home Office and the Department for Constitutional Affairs. The Department for Constitutional Affairs is now cutting back on immigration judges and wondering why the cases are piling up, causing another backlog. Perhaps the noble Baroness could pay attention to those factors.

1 <http://www.publications.parliament.uk> 19 July 2006: Column 1306.

Appendix 7
States Parties Dates of Ratification, Accession and Succession to the 1951 Convention and 1967 Protocol[1]

1950s (22)

Australia	22 Jan 1954 a	13 Dec 1973 a
Austria	01 Nov 1954 r	05 Sep 1973 a
Belgium	22 Jul 1953 r	08 Apr 1969 a
Denmark	04 Dec 1952 r	29 Jan 1968 a
Ecuador	17 Aug 1955 a	06 Mar 1969 a
France	23 Jun 1954 r	03 Feb 1971 a
Germany	01 Dec 1953 r	05 Nov 1969 a
Holy See	15 Mar 1956 r	08 Jun 1967 a
Iceland	30 Nov 1955 a	26 Apr 1968 a
Ireland	29 Nov 1956 a	06 Nov 1968
Israel	01 Oct 1954 r	14 Jun 1968 a
Italy	15 Nov 1954 r	26 Jan 1972 a
Liechtenstein	08 Mar 1957 r	20 May 1968 a
Luxembourg	23 Jul 1953 r	22 Apr 1971 a
Monaco (C)	18 May 1954 a	16 June 2010
Morocco	07 Nov 1956 d	20 Apr 1971 a
Netherlands	03 May 1956 r	29 Nov 1968 a
Norway	23 Mar 1953 r	28 Nov 1967 a
Sweden	26 Oct 1954 r	04 Oct 1967 a
Switzerland	21 Jan 1955 r	20 May 1968 a
Tunisia	24 Oct 1957 d	16 Oct 1968 a
United Kingdom of Great Britain and Northern Ireland	11 Mar 1954 r	04 Sep 1968 a

1 United Nations High Commissioner for Refugees, *Handbook and Guidelines on Procedures and Criteria for Determining Refugee Status, Under the 1951 Convention and the 1967 Protocol Relating to the Status of Refugees*, Reissued Geneva, December 2011, pp. 66–9, Annex IV, List of States Parties to the 1951 Convention Relating to the Status of Refugees and the 1967 Protocol.

1960s (35)

Algeria 21 Feb 1963 d	08 Nov 1967 a
Argentina 15 Nov 1961 a	06 Dec 1967 a
Benin 04 Apr 1962 d	06 Jul 1970 a
Botswana 06 Jan 1969 a	06 Jan 1969 a
Brazil 16 Nov 1960 r	07 Apr 1972 a
Burundi 19 Jul 1963 a	15 Mar 1971 a
Cameroon 23 Oct 1961 d	9 Sep 1967 a
Canada 04 Jun 1969 a	04 Jun 1969 a
Central African Republic 04 Sep 1962 d	30 Aug 1967 a
Colombia 10 Oct 1961 r	04 Mar 1980 a
Congo 15 Oct 1962 d	0 Jul 1970 a
Congo, Democratic Republic of 19 July 1965 a	13 Jan 1975 a
Côte d'Ivoire 08 Dec 1961 d	16 Feb 1970 a
Cyprus 16 May 1963 d	09 Jul 1968 a
Ethiopia 10 Nov 1969 a	10.Nov 1969 a
Finland 10 Oct 1968 a	0 Oct 1968 a
Gabon 27 Apr 1964 a	8 Aug 1973 a
Gambia 07 Sep 1966 d	29 Sep 1967 a
Ghana 18 Mar 1963 a	30 Aug 1968 a
Greece 05 Apr 1960 r	07 Aug 1968 a
Guinea 28 Dec 1965 d	16 May 1968 a
Jamaica 30 Jul 1964 d	30 Oct 1980 a
Kenya 16 May 1966 a	13 Nov 1981 a
Liberia 15 Oct 1964 a	27 Feb 1980 a
Madagascar (C) 18 Dec 1967 a	
New Zealand 30 Jun 1960 a	06 Aug 1973 a
Niger 25 Aug 1961 d	02 Feb 1970 a
Nigeria 23 Oct 1967 a	02 May 1968 a
Peru 21 Dec 1964 a	15 Sep 1983 a
Portugal 22 Dec 1960 a	13 Jul 1976 a
Senegal 02 May 1963 d	03 Oct 1967 a
Tanzania, United Republic of	12 May 1964 a 04 Sep 1968 a
Togo 27 Feb 1962 d	01 Dec 1969 a
Turkey 30 Mar 1962 r	31 Jul 1968 a
United States of America	01 Nov 1968
Zambia 24 Sep 1969 d	24 Sep 1969 a

1970s (18)

Chile 28 Jan 1972 a	27 Apr 1972 a
Costa Rica 28 Mar 1978 a	28 Mar 1978 a

Djibouti 09 Aug 1977 d	09 Aug 1977 d
Dominican Republic 04 Jan 1978 a	04 Jan 1978 a
Fiji 12 Jun 1972 d	12 Jun 1972 d
Guinea-Bissau 11 Feb 1976 a	11 Feb 1976 a
Iran, Islamic Republic of 28 Jul 1976 a	28 Jul 1976 a
Mali 02 Feb 1973 d	02 Feb 1973 a
Malta 17 Jun 1971 a	15 Sep 1971 a
Panama 02 Aug 1978 a	02 Aug 1978 a
Paraguay 01 Apr 1970 a	01 Apr 1970 a
Sao Tome and Principe 01 Feb 1978 a	01 Feb 1978 a
Somalia 10 Oct 1978 a	10 Oct 1978 a
Spain 14 Aug 1978 a	14 Aug 1978 a
Sudan 22 Feb 1974 a	23 May 1974 a
Suriname 29 Nov 1978 d	29 Nov 1978 d
Uganda 27 Sep 1976 a	27 Sep 1976 a
Uruguay 22 Sep 1970 a	22 Sep 1970 a

1980s (26)

Angola 23 Jun 1981 a	23 Jun 1981 a
Bolivia 09 Feb 1982 a	09 Feb 1982 a
Burkina Faso 18 Jun 1980 a	18 Jun 1980 a
Chad 19 Aug 1981 a	19 Aug 1981 a
China 24 Sep 1982 a	24 Sep 1982 a
Egypt 22 May 1981 a	22 May 1981 a
El Salvador 28 Apr 1983 a	28 Apr 1983 a
Equatorial Guinea 07 Feb 1986 a	07 Feb 1986 a
Guatemala 22 Sep 1983 a	22 Sep 1983 a
Haiti 25 Sep 1984 a	25 Sep 1984 a
Hungary 14 Mar 1989 a	14 Mar 1989 a
Japan 03 Oct 1981 a	01 Jan 1982 a
Lesotho 14 May 1981 a	14 May 1981 a
Malawi 10 Dec 1987 a	10 Dec 1987 a
Mauritania 05 May 1987 a	05 May 1987 a
Mozambique 16 Dec 1983 a	01 May 1989 a
Nicaragua 28 Mar 1980 a	28 Mar 1980 a
Papua New Guinea 17 Jul 1986 a	17 Jul 1986 a
Philippines 22 Jul 1981 a	22 Jul 1981 a
Rwanda 03 Jan 1980 a	03 Jan 1980 a
Samoa 21 Sep 1988 a	29 Nov 1994 a
Seychelles 23 Apr 1980 a	23 Apr 1980 a
Sierra Leone 22 May 1981 a	22 May 1981 a
Tuvalu 07 Mar 1986 d	07 Mar 1986 d

Yemen 18 Jan 1980 a	18 Jan 1980 a
Zimbabwe 25 Aug 1981 a	25 Aug 1981 a

1990s (32)

Albania 18 Aug 1992 a	18 Aug 1992 a
Antigua and Barbuda 07 Sep 1995 a	07 Sep 1995 a
Armenia 06 Jul 1993 a	06 Jul 1993 a
Azerbaijan 12 Feb 1993 a	12 Feb 1993 a
Bahamas 15 Sep 1993 a	15 Sep 1993 a
Belize 27 Jun 1990 a	27 Jun 1990 a
Bosnia and Herzegovina 01 Sep 1993 d	01 Sep 1993 d
Bulgaria 12 May 1993 a	12 May 1993 a
Cambodia 15 Oct 1992 a	15 Oct 1992 a
Croatia 12 Oct 1992 d	12 Oct 1992 d
Czech Republic 11 May 1993 d	11 May 1993 d
Dominica 17 Feb 1994 a	17 Feb 1994 a
Estonia 10 Apr 1997 a	10 Apr 1997 a
Georgia 09 Aug 1999 a	09 Aug 1999 a
Honduras 23 Mar 1992 a	23 Mar 1992 a
Kazakhstan 15 Jan 1999 a	15 Jan 1999 a
Kyrgyzstan 08 Oct 1996 a	08 Oct 1996 a
Korea, Republic of 03 Dec 1992 a	03 Dec 1992 a
Latvia 31 Jul 1997 a	31 Jul 1997 a
Lithuania 28 Apr 1997 a	28 Apr 1997 a
Macedonia, The Former Yugoslav Republic of	18 Jan 1994 d 18 Jan 1994 d
Namibia 17 Feb 1995 a	17 Feb 1995 a
Poland 27 Sep 1991 a	27 Sep 1991 a
Romania 07 Aug 1991 a	07 Aug 1991 a
Russian Federation 02 Feb 1993 a	02 Feb 1993 a
Saint Vincent and the Grenadines 03 Nov 1993 a	03 Nov 2003 a
Slovakia 04 Feb 1993 d	04 Feb 1993 d
Slovenia 06 Jul 1992 d	06 Jul 1992 d
Solomon Islands 28 Feb 1995 a	12 Apr 1995 a
South Africa 12 Jan 1996 a	12 Jan 1996 a
Tajikistan 07 Dec 1993 a	07 Dec 1993 a
Turkmenistan 02 Mar 1998 a	02 Mar 1998 a

2000s (12)

Afghanistan 30 Aug 2005 a	30 Aug 2005 a

Belarus 23 Aug 2001 a	23 Aug 2001 a
Mexico 07 June 2000 a	07 June 2000 a
Moldova, Republic of 31 Jan 2002 a	31 Jan 2002 a
Montenegro 10 Oct 2006 d	10 Oct 2006 d
Nauru 28 June 2011 a	28 June 2011 a
Saint Kitts and Nevis (C)	01 Feb 2002 a
Serbia 12 Mar 2001 d	12 Mar 2001 d
Swaziland 14 Feb 2000 a	28 Jan 1969 a
Timor-Leste 07 May 2003 a	07 May 2003 a
Trinidad and Tobago 10 Nov 2000 a	10 Nov 2000 a
Ukraine 10 Jun 2002 a	04 Apr 2002 a

Bibliography

Abella, I. and Troper, H. (1982), *None is too Many: Canada and the Jews of Europe, 1933–1948* (Toronto: Lester & Orpen Dennys).

Amnesty International (June 2010), '"Libya of tomorrow" What hope for human rights?' (London: AI).

Amor Boubakri, A. (2007), 'L'adhésion de la Tunisie aux instruments internationaux relatifs aux réfugiés', *Etudes Internationales (Tunis)* 105 (December): 93–118.

Angell, N. and Buxton, M. (1939), *You and the Refugee* (Harmondsworth: Penguin).

Archer, L. (2010), *Ricin! The inside story of the plot that never was* (London: Pluto).

Awuku, E.O., (1995), 'Refugee Movements in Africa and the OAU Convention on Refugees', *Journal of African Law* 39.1: 79–86.

Barcott, R. (2011), *It Happened on the Way to War* (USA: Bloomsbury).

Barnes, J. (2004), 'Expert Evidence: The Judicial Perception in Asylum and Human Rights Appeals', *International Journal of Refugee Law* 16.3: 349–57.

Beauthier, G.H. (1984), *Le droit des Etrangers et le Code de la Nationalité*, Bruxelles, Vie Ouvrière, p. 458.

Bhaba, J. (2002), 'The Tension between Asylum Advocacy and Human Rights', *Harvard Human Rights Journal* 15 (Spring).

Bhagwati, J. (2004), *In Defense of Globalisation* (Oxford: Oxford University Press).

Bingham, T. (2003), 'The Judge as Juror: The judicial determination of factual issues', in P. Rideout and J. Jowell (eds), *Current Legal Problems* (London: Steven and Sons).

Bobbitt, P. (2008), *Terror and Consent* (London: Allen Lane).

—— (2002), *The Shield of Achilles* (London: Allen Lane).

Boubakri, A. (2005), 'Protection of Refugees and Asylum Seekers in the Migration Flows', *International Studies (Tunis)*, 94 (March): 81–9 (in Arabic).

Bronkhorst, D. (1990), *Een tijd van komen*, Federatie VON, Buber, M. (1947), *Between Man and Man* (London: Collins Fontana).

Caestecker, F. (2000), *Alien policy in Belgium, 1840–1940: The creation of guest workers, refugees and illegal aliens* (New York, Oxford: Berghann Books), p. 330.

Caestecker, F. (2005) *Het reëel bestaande socialisme in West-Europa en de vlucht uit Nazi-Duitsland, 1933–1934*, Cahiers d'Histoire du Temps présent/Bijdragen tot de Eigentijdse Geschiedenis, Vol.15, Brussel, p. 107–22

Caestecker, F. and Roobrouck, T. (2010), *De jacht of Duitsers in het bevrijde België, 1918–1925*, Universiteit Gent, p. 225–54.

Caestecker, F. and Morelli, A. (2010), *Het bewogen ontstaan van een vluchtelingenbeleid (1918–1940), Belgisch Tijdschrift voor Nieuwste Geschiedenis – Revue belge d'histoire contemporaine,* XL, 2010, pp. 383–413

Caestecker, F. and Luyckx, L. (2009), *Het individuele vreemdelingendossier: een unieke bron over migratie en migranten*, In Tallier A. (red.), 'Grensgevallen. *biblio.ugent.be/input/download?func=downloadFile&fileOId=1088613*

Care, G. (1991), 'Representation in Immigration appeals: an adjudicator's view', *Immigration and Nationality Law and Practice* 5.2.

—— (2005), 'The Judiciary, The State and the Refugee. Evolution of Judicial Protection – A UK Perspective', *Fordham International Law Journal* 28.5 (May): 1421.

—— (2008), 'Life after Refusal to Enter: Reflections of an Immigration Judge', *Refuge* 25.2 <https://pi.library.yorku.ca/ojs/index.php/refuge/article/view/26040>.

Carens, J.H. (1998), 'The Ethics of Refugee Policy: The Problem of Asylum in Western States' Refugee Studies Council, pp. 16–17.

—— (n.d.), 'Open Borders and the Claims of the Community'; see <http://www.law.nyu.edu/ecm_dlv2/groups/public/@nyu_law_website__academics__colloquia__legal_political_and_social_philosophy/documents/documents/ecm_pro_069496.pdf>.

CGRS, Commissariaat-generaal voor de vluchtelingen en de staatlozen, Asielstatistieken (2010), Overzicht 2010, http://www.cgvs.be/

Chowdhury, Z. (1982), *Split Families An Examination of the British Immigration Control System Relating to Dependants in Bangladesh* (London: UKIAS).

Citizenship and Immigration Canada, 'Frequently Asked Questions: The refugee system, Balanced Refugee Reform, "Why are these changes necessary?"' <http://www.cic.gc.ca/english/information/faq/refugees/ref-reform-faq.asp#changes>.

Coluccello, S. and Massey, S. (2007), 'Out of Africa: The human trade between Libya and Lampedusa', *Trends in Organized Crime* 10.4 (December): 77–90.

Cuvelier, F. (1939), *Technique de l'arbitraire ou le 'statut' des étrangers en Belgique* (Bruxelles), pp. 26–7.

Davidson, R. (1996), *Desert Places* (London: Viking).

Department of Constitutional Affairs (2004), *Delivering Justice, Rights and Democracy DCA Strategy 2004–09* <www.dca.gov.uk>.

de Diesbach, E. (1972), *L'étranger devant la loi belge*. Brussel, Centre de documentation du Barreau de Bruxelles.

Dirks, G.E. (1995), *Controversy and Complexity: Canadian Immigration Policy during the 1980s* (Montreal and Kingston: McGill-Queen's University Press).

Durieux, J.F. and McAdam, J. (2004), 'Non-refoulement through time: The case for a derogation clause to the refugee convention in mass influx emergencies', *International Journal of Refugee Law* 16.1: 4–24.

Elmadmad, K. (2002), *Asile et réfugiés dans les pays afro-arabes* (Rabat: éd. Eliff).

Flory, M. (1966) 'La succession aux Traités lors de la décolonisation de l'Afrique du Nord', *Annuaire de l'Afrique du Nord*: 11–24.

Fombeno, H.J.T. (2004), 'Réflexions sur la question des réfugiés en Afrique', *Revue Trimestrielle des Droits de l'Homme* 57 (January): 245–74.

Fransman, L. (2011), *British Nationality Law* (London: Bloomsbury).

Geertz, C. (1983), *Local Knowledge* (New York: Basic Books).

Glover, S. et al. (2001) 'Migration: An Economic and Social Analysis' Home Office Research Development and Statistics Directorate Paper 67 (ISBN 1 84082 599 5).

—— et al., 'Migration: An Economic and Social Analysis'; Home Office (25 October 1990), *Immigration and Nationality and Passports Annual Report*.

Good, A. (2007), *Anthropology and Expertise in the Asylum Courts* (London: Routledge-Cavendish).

Goodwin-Gill, G. and Lambert, H. (eds) (2010), *The Limits of Transnational Law* (Cambridge: Cambridge University Press).

Gousseff, C. (2008), *L'Exil russe (1920–1939). La fabrique du réfugié apatride*, Paris, CNRS-Editions, coll. "mondes russes"

Grahl-Madsen, A. (1980), *Territorial Asylum*, Almqvist & Wiksell International, Stockholm).

Graycar, R. 'The Gender of Judgments: An Introduction', in Thornton, M. (ed.), *Public and Private: Feminist Legal Debates* (Oxford: Oxford University Press).

Grayling, C.G. (2007), *Towards the Light* (London: Bloomsbury).

Griffith, J.A.G. (1997), *The Politics of the Judiciary*, 5th edn (London: Fontana).

Guild, E. (1996), *European Community Law from a Migrant's Perspective* (The Hague, Boston, MA and London: Kluwer International Law).

Hansen, R. (2000), *Citizenship and Immigration in Post-war Britain* (Oxford: Oxford University Press).

Harvey, C. (2000), *Seeking Asylum in the UK: Problems and Prospects* (London: Butterworths.

Hathaway, J. (1991), *The Law of Refugee Status* (Toronto: Butterworths).

Hayter, T. (2004), *Open Borders – The Case Against Immigration Control*, 2nd edn (London: Pluto Press).

Herlihy, J. (2006), 'Should Discrepant Accounts given by an Asylum Seeker be Taken as Proof of Deceit?', *Torture* 16.

Human Rights Watch (2006), 'Stemming the flow: Abuses against migrants, asylum seekers and refugees' (New York: HRW), September.

—— (2008), 'Sinai perils: Risks to migrants, refugees and asylum seekers in Egypt and Israel' (New York: HRW), November.

Huysmans, J. (2006) *Politics of Insecurity Migration and Asylum in the EU* (London: Routledge).

IARLJ Conference Papers 1995, 1997, 1998, 2000, 2002 and 2005 <www.iarlj.nl>.

Ihenacho, J. (1991), 'The Effect of DNA Testing on Immigration Control Procedures: Case Studies of Bangladeshi Studies', Research Paper No. 16, Warwick University.

Jarvis, C. (2000), 'For these or any other reasons: an examination of judicial assessment of the credibility of asylum seekers in the United Kingdomwith particular reference to the role of the immigration adjudicator' (unpublished LLM Dissertation, London: University of East London, 2000).

—— (2003), 'The Judge as Juror revisited', *Immigration Law Digest* 7 (Winter).

Juss, S.S. (1997), *Discretion and Deviation in the Administration of Immigration Control* (London: Sweet and Maxwell).

—— (2007), 'The Slow Death of Citizenship Rights', *King's Law Journal* 18.1: 95–118.

Justice, Immigration Law Practitioners' Association (ILPA) and Asylum Rights Campaign (ARC) (July 1997), 'Providing Protection: The Joint Report'.

Kagan, M. (2009), 'Refugee Credibility Assessment and the "religious impostor" Problem', CMRS Working Paper 9 12/2009 <http://www.aucegypt.edu/GAPP/cmrs/Documents/KaganReligiousImposters.pdf>.

Kälin, W. (1986), 'Troubled Communication: Cross-Cultural Misunderstandings in the Asylum-Hearing' *International Migration Review* 20.2: 230–41.

Kelley, N. and Trebilcock, M. (1998), *The Making of the Mosaic: A History of Canadian Immigration Policy* (Toronto: University of Toronto Press).

Keyserlingk, R.H. (1993), *Breaking Ground: The 1956 Hungarian Refugee Movement to Canada* (Toronto: York Lanes Press).

Knowles, V. (2000), *Forging Our Legacy: Canadian Citizenship and Immigration, 1900–1977* (Ottawa: Public Works and Government Services).

Kushner, T. and Knox, K. (1999), *Refugees in an Age of Genocide* (London: Frank Cass).

Lam, L. (1996), *From Being Uprooted to Surviving: Resettlement of Vietnamese-Chinese 'Boat People' in Montreal, 1980–1990* (Toronto: York Lanes Press).

Landa, M.J. (1911), The Alien Problem and its Remedy (PS King) <http://archive.org/details/alien problemitsr00landrich>.

Langbein, J. (2003), *The Origins of Adversary Criminal Trial* (Oxford: Oxford University Press).

Lawyers Committee for Human Rights (1991), *Uncertain Haven* (New York: LCHR).

Leggatt, A. (2001), *The Report of the Review of Tribunals* <www.tribunal-review.org.uk>.

Loescher, G. (1993), *Beyond Charity: International Cooperation and the Global Refugee Crisis* (Oxford: Oxford University Press).

London, L. (1992), 'British Immigration Control Procedures and Jewish Refugees 1933–1942', unpublished thesis, University of London.

—— (2001), *Whitehall and the Jews 1933–48: British Immigration Policy, Jewish Refugees and the Holocaust* (Cambridge: Cambridge University Press).

Lukashuk, I.I. (1989), 'The Principle Pacta Sunt Servanda and the nature of obligation under international law', *American Journal of International Law* 83.3 (July): 513–18.

Luykx, T. (1962) *Napoleon III and the Belgian Press*, International Communication Gazette *1962, 8,* p. 133–44

—— (1964) *Politieke geschiedenis van België*, Brussel, Elsevier, p. 95–112.

Macdonald, I. and Blake, N., *Immigration Law and Practice* (London: Butterworths).

Morelli, A (1984), *Fascisme et antifascisme dans l'immigration italienne en Belgique (1922–1945)*, ULB.

Munroe, S. (2006) 'Canada Gives Formal Apology for the Chinese Head Tax', *Canada Online*, 25 June <http://canadaonline.about.com/b/2006/06/25/canada-gives-formal-apology-for-chinese-head-tax.htm>.

Nivet, P. (2004), Les réfugiés de guerre dans la société française (1914–1946), Histoire, économie et société, Vol. 23, 2, p. 247–59

Okoth-Obbo, G. (2001), 'Thirty Years on: A Legal Review of the 1969 OAU Refugee Convention Governing the Specific Aspects of Refugee Problems in Africa', *Refugee Survey Quarterly* 20.1 (January): 79–138.

Oppenheim, L. (2005), *International law: a treatise,* Volume 1, Clark, New Jersey, p. 335–7.

Peirce, G. (2010), *Dispatches from the Dark Side: On Torture and the Death of Justice* (London: Verso).

Pettit, J. et al. (2007), 'The Problem with Country of Origin Information (COI) in Refugee Status Determinations', *Immigration Law Digest* 13.

—— (2008), 'The use of COI in the Refugee Status Determination Process in the UK: Looking Back, Reaching Forward', *Refuge* 25/2 (Fall).

Phelan, M. and Gillespie, J. (2013), *Immigration Law Handbook* (Oxford: Oxford University Press).

Phillips of Maltravers, Lord (2007), 'Judicial Independence', *The Commonwealth Lawyer* 16.3.

Pirouet, L. (2001), *Whatever Happened to Asylum in Britain? A Tale of Two Walls* (Oxford: Berghahn).

Popper, K. (1979), *Objective Knowledge: An Evolutionary Approach* (Oxford: Oxford University Press).

Posner, R.A. (2008), *How Judges Think* (Cambridge, MA: Harvard University Press).

Rawlings, R. (2005), 'Review, Revenge and Retreat', *Modern Law Review* 68.3: 378–410.

Refugee Legal Centre (RLC) (1997), 'Reviewing the Asylum Determination Procedure A Casework Study'.

Refugee Women's Legal Group (1998), 'Gender Guidelines for Determinations in Asylum Claims' (London: RWLG).

RIC Foyer vzw, 2009, http://www.foyer.be/article.php3?id_article=7773

Richmond, A. (2002), 'Globalization; Implications for Immigrants and Refugees', *Ethnic and Racial Studies* 25.5: 707–27.

Rikhof, J. (2012), 'The Criminal Refugee: the Treatment of Asylum Seekers with a Criminal Background in International and Domestic Law (PB)', *Human Rights Series*, 3 (Library of Human Rights).

Sedley, S. (2005),'Asylum: Can the Judiciary Maintain Its Independence?' (Working Paper, IARLJ World Conference, 21 April.

—— (2011), *Ashes and Sparks: Essays on Law and Justice* (Cambridge: Cambridge University Press).

—— (2012), 'Judicial Politics', *London Review of Books* 34.4 (23 February).

Showler, P. (2006), *Refugee Sandwich* (Montreal and Kingston:McGill-Queens University Press).

Simeon, J.C. (1998), 'Organizational and Administrative Renewal at the Immigration and Refugee Board', in R. Hoffman. et al. (eds), *Public Administration: Canadian Materials*, 3rd edn (North York, Ontario: Captus Press, Inc.).

Smith, M. (2004), 'Development without Refugee Rights? A Civil Society Response', *Fordham International Law Journal* 28.5.

Spencer, I.R.G. (1997), *British Immigration Policy since 1939* (London: Routledge).

Stevens, D. (1998), 'The Case of UK Asylum Law and Policy: Lessons from History?', in F. Nicholson and P. Twomey (eds), *Current Issues of UK Asylum Law and Policy* (Aldershot: Ashgate).

—— (2004), *UK Asylum Law and Policy* (London: Sweet and Maxwell).

Sûreté de l'Etat (2011), http://suretedeletat.belgium.be/fr/historique/

Talbot, T. (2004), 'Credibility and Risk: One Adjudicator's View', *Immigration Law Digest*: 29.

Thomas, R. (2003), 'Impact of Judicial Review on Asylum', *Public Law*: 479–510.

—— (2005), 'Evaluating tribunal adjudication: administrative justice and asylum appeals', *Legal Studies* 25 (September): 462–98.

—— (2011) *Administrative Justice and Asylum Appeals* (Oxford: Hart).

Travers, M. (1999), *British Immigration Courts: A Case Study in Law and Politics* (Bristol: The Policy Press), <http/www.bristol.ac.uk/Publication/TPP>.

UNHCR (1992), *Handbook on Procedures and Criteria for Determining Refugee Status under the 1951 Convention and the 1967 Protocol relating to the Status of Refugees* (Geneva: UNHCR), January.

—— (2008), *States Parties to the 1951 Convention Relating to the Status of Refugees and its 1967 Protocol, As of the 1 October 2008* <http://www.unhcr.org/3b73b0d63.pdf>.

Van den Wijngaert, C. (1994), *Strafrecht en Strafprocesrecht in hoofdlijnen, Maklu*, Antwerpen, pp. 145–6.

Van Doorslaer, R. and Verhoeyen, E. (1986), *L'allemagne Nazie, La Police Belge et L'anticommunisme en Belgique (1936–1944), Un aspect des relations Belgo-Allemandes,BTNG-RBHC* , 17, 1–2, p. *61–126.* http://www.flw.ugent.be/btng-

rbhc/pdf/BTNG-RBHC,%2017,%201986,%201-2,%20pp%20061-125.pdf
terrescontees.com 2011,http://www.terrescontees.com/gouvernement/france/quatrieme_republique.htm
van Selm, J., et al. (eds) (2003), *The Refugee Convention at Fifty: A View from Forced Migration Studies* (Lanham, MD: Lexington).
Wallace, R.M.M. and Brown, A. (1999), *Asylum Practice and Procedure – Country by Country Handbook* (London: Trenton).
Wagner, J., *A Changing Immigration System; Immigration Policies under Tony Blair and George Brown* <http://pages.wustl.edu> 'Wagner J'.
Winder, R. (2004), *Bloody Foreigners* (London: Abacus).
Zemanek, K. (1965), 'State Succession after Decolonization', *Collected Courses of the Hague Academy of International Law* 116.3: 213–15.

Index

Bold page numbers indicate figures, *italic* numbers indicate tables.

For Product Safety Concerns and Information please contact our EU representative GPSR@taylorandfrancis.com
Taylor & Francis Verlag GmbH, Kaufingerstraße 24, 80331 München, Germany

www.ingramcontent.com/pod-product-compliance
Ingram Content Group UK Ltd.
Pitfield, Milton Keynes, MK11 3LW, UK
UKHW020021200926
475702UK00014B/1997

* 9 7 8 1 0 3 2 6 5 2 4 0 5 *